THE CHURCH AND THE MINISTRY
IN THE EARLY CENTURIES

THE CHURCH AND THE MINISTRY IN THE EARLY CENTURIES

by

Thomas Martin Lindsay, D.D.

Principal of the Glasgow College of
the United Free Church of Scotland

WIPF & STOCK · Eugene, Oregon

Wipf and Stock Publishers
199 W 8th Ave, Suite 3
Eugene, OR 97401

The Church and the Ministry in the Early Centuries
By Thomas Martin Lindsay
ISBN 13: 978-1-55635-847-0
Publication date 2/8/2008
Previously published by Hodder and Stoughton, 1903

PREFACE

THE aim of these Lectures is to pourtray the organized life of the Christian Society as that was lived in the thousands of little communities formed by the proclamation of the Gospel of our Lord during the first three centuries.

The method of description has been to select writings which seemed to reveal that life most clearly, and to group round the central sources of information illustrative evidence, contemporary or other. The principle of selection has been to take, as the central authorities, those writings which, when carefully examined, reveal the greatest number of details. Thus, the Epistles of St. Paul, especially the First Epistle to the Corinthians, have been chosen as furnishing the greatest number of facts going to form a picture of the life of the Christian Society during the first century, and the material derived from the other canonical writings such as the Acts of the Apostles, the Apocalypse and the Pastoral Epistles, have been arranged around them. Similarly the *Didache*, the *Sources of the Apostolic Canons* and the *Epistles of Ignatius* have been selected for the light they throw on the life and work of the Church during the second century. The *Canons of Hippolytus*, supplemented by the writings of Irenaeus and of Tertullian, have furnished the basis for the description of the organization during the first, and the *Epistles of Cyprian* of Carthage for that of the second half of the third century.

The method used has the disadvantage of making necessary some repetitions, which the form of Lectures rendered the more inevitable; but it puts the reader in possession of the contemporary evidence in the simplest way.

Quotations from the original authorities have been given in English for the most part, and, as a rule, the translations have been taken from well known versions—from the Ante-Nicene Library, from the late Bishop Lightfoot's translations of Clement of Rome and of Ignatius, and from Messrs. Hitchcock and Brown's version of the *Didache*. This has been done after consultation with friends whose advice seemed to be too valuable to be neglected.

Dr. Moberly, in his eminently suggestive book, *Ministerial Priesthood*, has warned all students of early Church History to beware of mental presuppositions, unchallenged assumptions, hypotheses or postulates. The warning has been taken with all seriousness, even when the perusal of his book has suggested the thought that mental presuppositions, like sins, are more readily recognized in our neighbours than in ourselves. I feel bound to admit that three assumptions or postulates may be found underlying these lectures. Whether they are right or wrong the reader must judge.

My first postulate is this. I devoutly believe that there is a Visible Catholic Church of Christ consisting of all those throughout the world who visibly worship the same God and Father, profess their faith in the same Saviour, and are taught by the same Holy Spirit; but I do not see any Scriptural or even primitive warrant for insisting that catholicity *must* find visible expression in a uniformity of organization, of ritual of worship, or even of formulated creed. This visible Church Catholic of Christ has had a life in the world historically continuous; but the ground of this historical continuity does not necessarily exist in any one method of selecting and setting apart office-bearers who rule in the Church; its basis is the real succession of the generations of faithful followers of their Lord and Master, Jesus Christ. It is with devout thankfulness that I can make this assumption with perfect honesty of heart and of head, because it relieves me from the necessity—sad, stern and even hateful it must seem to many pious souls who feel themselves under its power—of unchurching and of excluding from the "covenanted" mercies of God, all who do not accept that form of Church government which, to my mind, is truest to scriptural principles and most akin to the ecclesiastical organization of the early centuries.

My second postulate concerns the ministry. There is and must be a valid ministry of some sort in the churches which are branches of this one Visible Catholic Church of Christ; but I do not think that the fact that the Church possesses an authority which is a direct gift from God necessarily means that the authority must exist in a class or caste of superior office-bearers endowed with a grace and therefore with a power "specific, exclusive and efficient," and that it *cannot* be delegated to the ministry by the Christian people. I do not see why the thought that the authority comes from "above," a dogmatic truth, need in any way interfere with the conception that all official ecclesiastical power is representative and delegated to the officials by the membership and that it has its divine source in the presence of Christ promised and bestowed upon His people and diffused through the membership of the Churches. Therefore when the question is put: "Must ministerial character be in all cases conferred from above, or may it sometimes, and with equal validity, be evolved from below?" it appears to me that a fallacy lurks in the antithesis. "From below" is used in the sense "from the membership of the Church," and the inference suggested by the contrast is that what comes "from below," i.e. from the membership of the Church, cannot come "from above," i.e. cannot be of divine origin, warrant and authority. Why not? May the Holy Spirit not use the membership of the Church as His instrument? Is there no real abiding presence of Christ among His people? Is not this promised Presence something which belongs to the sphere of God and may it not be the source of an authority which is "from above"? The fallacious antithesis has apparently given birth to a formula,—that no valid ministry can be evolved from the membership of the Christian congregation; and this formula has been treated as expressing a dogmatic truth which has been compared with the truth of the dogma of the Incarnation, and which has been used as a guiding principle in the interpretation of the references in the New Testament writings and in other early Christian literature to the origin and growth of the Christian ministry. Fortified by this supposed dogmatic truth one Anglican divine can contentedly rest the Scriptural warrant for the theory of "Apostolic Succession" and all the sad and stern practical consequences he deduces from it, on an hypothesis and on a detail in a parable, and another can find evidence for the same "gigantic figment" in a statement of Clement of Rome which describes the earliest missionaries of the Christian Church doing what missionaries of all kinds, from those of the Church of England to those of the Society of Friends, have done in all generations to secure the well-being and continuance of the communities of believers who have been converted to the faith of Jesus.

My third postulate belongs to an entirely different sphere from the two already mentioned, but it has been so much in my mind that it ought to be mentioned. It is that analogies in organization illustrative of the life of the primitive Christian communities can be more easily and more safely found on the mission fields of our common Christianity than among the details of the organized life of the long established Churches of Christian Europe. In the early centuries and on the Mission field we are studying origins. It was my good fortune some years ago to spend twelve months in India, examining there the methods, work and results of the Missions of the various branches of the Church of Christ. One seemed at times to be transported back to the early centuries, to hear and to see what the earliest writers had recounted and described. Portions of the *Didache*, of the *Sources of the Apostolic Canons*, of the *Canons of Hippolytus* were living practices there. One lived among scenes described by Tertullian and by Clement of Alexandria. The *Arabian Nights* tell us of the fortunate possessor of a magic carpet who, when seated on his treasure, had only to wish it to be carried anywhere in space he desired. Historians might long to be owners of a similar mat to carry them anywhen backwards and forwards throughout the past centuries. A visit to the Mission field, especially to one among a people of ancient civilization who have inherited those original speculations which were the fertile soil out of which sprang the earliest Christian Gnosticism, is the magic carpet which transports one back to the times of primitive Christianity. The visitor sees the simple meaning of many a statement which seemed so hard to understand with nothing but the ancient literary record to guide him. He learns to distrust some of the hard and fast canons of modern historical criticism, and to grow somewhat sceptical about the worth of many of those "subjective pictures" which some modern critics first construct and then use to estimate the date, authorship and intention of ancient documents. He learns that the modern western mind cannot so easily gauge the oriental ways of thought as it persistently imagines. Modern missionary work appears to me to be full of helpful illustrations of the life and organization of the early centuries.

These Lectures are the fruit of long, careful, and, I trust, reverent study of the literary remains of the early Christian centuries. The last quarter of a century has brought many ancient documents to light which were formerly unknown, and these have not been passed over. The extent of my obligations to others may be seen in the notes; but the debt owed to such writers as Bishop Lightfoot, Professor Harnack and Dr. Hort far exceeds what can be acknowledged in such a way.

I have to express my sense of the great assistance given to me by my old friend, the Rev. A. O. Johnston, D.D., who read the lectures in MS., and who has also gone over the proofs with great care. The book owes much to his labour and to his criticisms.

THOMAS M. LINDSAY.

EXTRACT DECLARATION OF TRUST.

March 1, 1862.

I, WILLIAM BINNY WEBSTER, late Surgeon in the H.E.I.C.S., presently residing in Edinburgh,—Considering that I feel deeply interested in the success of the Free Church College, Edinburgh, and am desirous of advancing the Theological Literature of Scotland, and for this end to establish a Lectureship similar to those of a like kind connected with the Church of England and the Congregational body in England, and that I have made over to the General Trustees of the Free Church of Scotland the sum of £2,000 sterling, in trust, for the purpose of founding a Lectureship in memory of the late Reverend William Cunningham, D.D., Principal of the Free Church College, Edinburgh, and Professor of Divinity and Church History therein, and under the following conditions, namely,—*First*, The Lectureship shall bear the name, and be called, ' The Cunningham Lectureship.' *Second*, The Lecturer shall be a Minister or Professor of the Free Church of Scotland, and shall hold the appointment for not less than two years, nor more than three years, and be entitled for the period of his holding the appointment to the income of the endowment as declared by the General Trustees, it being understood that the Council after referred to may occasionally appoint a Minister or Professor from other denominations, provided this be approved of by not fewer than Eight Members of the Council, and it being further understood that the Council are to regulate the terms of payment of the Lecturer. *Third*, The Lecturer shall be at liberty to choose his own subject within the range of Apologetical, Doctrinal, Controversial, Exegetical, Pastoral, or Historical Theology, including what bears on Missions, Home and Foreign, subject to the consent of the Council. *Fourth*, The Lecturer shall be bound to deliver publicly at Edinburgh a Course of Lectures on the subjects thus chosen at some time immediately preceding the expiry of his appointment, and during the Session of the New College, Edinburgh ; the Lectures to be not fewer than six in number, and to be delivered in presence of the Professors and Students under such arrangements as the Council may appoint ; the Lecturer shall be bound also to print and publish, at his own risk, not fewer than

750 copies of the Lectures within a year after their delivery, and to deposit three copies of the same in the Library of the New College; the form of the publication shall be regulated by the Council. *Fifth*, A Council shall be constituted, consisting of (first) Two Members of their own body, to be chosen annually in the month of March, by the Senatus of the New College, other than the Principal; (second) Five Members to be chosen annually by the General Assembly, in addition to the Moderator of the said Free Church of Scotland; together with (third) the Principal of the said New College for the time being, the Moderator of the said General Assembly for the time being, the Procurator or Law Adviser of the Church, and myself the said William Binny Webster, or such person as I may nominate to be my successor: the Principal of the said College to be Convener of the Council, and any Five Members duly convened to be entitled to act notwithstanding the non-election of others. *Sixth*, The duties of the Council shall be the following:—(first), To appoint the Lecturer and determine the period of his holding the appointment, the appointment to be made before the close of the Session of College immediately preceding the termination of the previous Lecturer's engagement; (second), To arrange details as to the delivery of the Lectures, and to take charge of any additional income and expenditure of an incidental kind that may be connected therewith, it being understood that the obligation upon the Lecturer is simply to deliver the Course of Lectures free of expense to himself. *Seventh*, The Council shall be at liberty, on the expiry of five years, to make any alteration that experience may suggest as desirable in the details of this plan, provided such alterations shall be approved of by not fewer than Eight Members of the Council.

CONTENTS

LECTURE I

THE NEW TESTAMENT CONCEPTION OF THE CHURCH OF CHRIST

	PAGE
The Promise of the Church (Ecclesia)	3
Jewish and Greek Meanings of Ecclesia	4
The Word has its Home in the Pauline Literature	5
It includes five great Thoughts	5
i. *Fellowship* with Christ and with the Brethren	6–9
St. Paul rings the changes on this Thought	7
Fellowship with Christ manifested in " gifts " to the Church	8
Fellowship among Believers implied in the early Names for Christians	9
ii. *Unity*	10–15
Church and Churches	10
The Unity of the Church a primary Verity of the Christian Faith	13
iii. The Church is a visible Community	16–24
It can be seen in every Christian Community large or small for it is an ideal Reality	16
This Ideal ought to be made manifest	18
St. Paul's way of manifesting the Unity of the Church of Christ	20
His leading thought was " fellowship " (κοινωνία)	20
How he grouped his Churches	21
The great " Collection "	22
The Methods of the Twelve	23

CONTENTS

	PAGE
iv. The Church has *Authority*	24–33
The Promise of Authority made to St. Peter, to the Twelve and to the whole Company of the Believers	25
How these Promises were interpreted by the primitive Church	32
The Self-government and Independence of the Apostolic Churches	32
v. The Church is a *Sacerdotal* Society	33–37
The ideal Israel	33
The sacerdotal Character belongs to the whole Membership	34
Luther on the sacerdotal Character of the Church	35
No Idea of a maimed Sacerdotalism in primitive Times	36

LECTURE II

A CHRISTIAN CHURCH IN APOSTOLIC TIMES

The local Churches in primitive Times met in private Houses	41
The Brethren had three Kinds of Meetings	43
i. The Meeting for Edification	44
The Service and the Arrangement of the Parts	44
Almost unlimited Freedom in Worship	49
ii. The Meeting for Thanksgiving (Eucharistia)	50
The Details indistinctly given	50
May be reconstructed	52
iii. The Congregational Business Meeting	54
It was the Centre of the Unity and the Seat of the Independence of the local Church	55
It settled even the civil Disputes among the Brethren	55
Every local Church was a little self-governing Republic	57
Leadership within the Christian Communities had a Distinctive Character, and implied Service and the possession of "Gifts"	62
Traces of a double Ministry, the prophetic and the local	64
These Ministries quite separate, but the Men composing them might belong to both	66

LECTURE III

THE PROPHETIC MINISTRY OF THE PRIMITIVE CHURCH

	PAGE
The Christian Community is a Body of which the Spirit of Christ is the Soul	69
The " Gift " to " speak the Word of God " the most prized	70
Its Complement was the " Gift " to " discern " or test those who " spoke the Word of God "	70
The prophetic Ministry was three-fold, Apostles, Prophets and Teachers	73
This three-fold Ministry is to be traced throughout the Church of the first and second Centuries	74
i. Apostles were the Missionaries who founded the Churches.	75
Various Classes of Apostles.	76
Their Number increased during the earlier Decades	82
The wider and narrower uses of the Word " Apostle "	85
The special Character of Apostolic Work and Authority	87
St. Paul as the Type of an Apostle	88
ii. Prophets were found in every Christian Community, and sometimes wandered from one to another.	90
What Prophecy was	93
Prophecy and Ecstasy	94
Prophecy and visions	94
Prophets were not Office-bearers	95
They exercised a great deal of influence in matters of discipline, and had a unique place in the restoration of the lapsed	96
Wandering Prophets and the Firstfruits	97
Their Claims were to be tested by the " Gift " of Discernment	99
False Prophets	100
iii. Teachers, their special Work	103
The Prophets of the Old and of the New Testaments compared.	106

LECTURE IV

THE CHURCH OF THE FIRST CENTURY—CREATING ITS MINISTRY

	PAGE
Traces of several Types of Organization in the New Testament Churches	113
The Seven of Acts vi. and the Jewish Village Community.	115
Elders in Churches outside Palestine.	118
The Supremacy of James in Jerusalem, and a Series of Rulers who were of the Kindred of Jesus	119
Office-bearers in the Pauline Gentile Churches	121
The *Prohistamenoi* and the Relation of Patron and Client.	123
The heathen Confraternities and their Organization	125
The Jewish Synagogues outside Palestine and their Organization.	129
The Christian Churches did not copy either the Synagogue or the Confraternities	131
They had an *external* Resemblance to both Synagogue and Confraternity	132
The Organization in the Pastoral Epistles.	137
The Information given in the Pastoral Epistles is complementary to what is to be found in the earlier Epistles of St. Paul	148
Names for Office-bearers in early Christian Literature	152
Episcopus designates the Kind of Work done and is not the Name of an Office	153
The Meaning and Origin of the Christian "Elders"	153
The Churches in the first Century were ruled by a College of Presbyter-bishops who were assisted by a Body of Deacons	154
The Unity of the Church never forgotten in the Independence of the local Churches	155
Note on "Presbyter" and "Bishop"	
Harnack's Theory that Bishops were distinct from Presbyters from the first.	157
The Witness of Clement	159
The Identity of the New Testament "Presbyters" and "Bishops"	163

CONTENTS

LECTURE V

THE CHURCHES OF THE SECOND AND THIRD CENTURIES— CHANGING THEIR MINISTRY

	PAGE
The Ministry of the first Century was changed during the second	169
The Ministry in the *Didaché*	171
The Congregational Meeting	173
The Prophetic Ministry	174
Elected Office-bearers	175
The Ministry in the *Sources of the Apostolic Canons*	177
The smallest Christian Communities to be organized under Bishop or Pastor, Elders and Deacons	178
A Ministry of Women	181
The Reader and uneducated Bishops	182
The Document shows a three-fold Ministry in a transitional Stage	183
The *Letters of Ignatius*	186
Their Characters and Contents	187
They plead for *Unity* through Obedience to the Office-bearers	190
The Organization they bear Witness to: a Bishop, a Session of Elders and a Body of Deacons, which form one whole	196
They reveal a three-fold Ministry but not Episcopacy	198
The Authority of the Bishop or Pastor limited	198
The Powers of the Congregational Meeting	200
An unpaid Ministry explains how the smallest Body of Christians could have a complete Organization	200
The Organization of Bishop, Session of Elders and body of Deacons became almost universal within the Empire	204
The Reasons for the Change from a two-fold collegiate Ministry to a three-fold Ministry and the Paths by which the Change advanced can only be guessed	205
The Church has always the Power to change its Ministry	210

CONTENTS

LECTURE VI

THE FALL OF THE PROPHETIC MINISTRY AND THE CONSERVATIVE REVOLT

	PAGE
The Work of Edification began to pass from the prophetic Ministry to the ordinary Office-bearers	213
The Causes which led to the Fall of the prophetic Ministry are not specifically known but may be guessed.	217
The Need to make a combined Stand against Heresies	217
The Gnostic Treatment of Christianity	218
Marcion's Canon, Creed, and Churches	219
Irenaeus voiced the Need which his Time felt	221
The Guarantee for Christian Truth is to be found in the Succession of Office-bearers in the Churches from the Times of the Apostles	223
Office-bearers were supposed to have a *charisma veritatis*.	227
Effect of this on the prophetic Ministry	228
The Growth of a Desire to come to some Accommodation with the Empire	229
The Apologists	230
The Deterioration of Prophecy	233
Protests against the silent Movement in the Church	235
The Phrygian Movement the Centre and Exaggeration of what was affecting the whole of the Churches	236
Montanism properly speaking was conservative	238
Proof from Montanist Prophecy	239
The Break with the "great" Church	243
The Fate of the later Montanists	243
The Organization of the Churches after the Montanists were outside	244
What the Canons of Hippolytus tell us	245
A three-fold Ministry of Bishop, Elders, and Deacons	245
Qualifications, Choice and Ordination (which might be done by an Elder) of Bishops	246
Elders and Bishops were theoretically equal but practically very distinct	247
The two Meetings for public Worship	250
The Meeting for Exhortation	251
The Eucharistic Service	252
The Distribution of the Offerings	255
Comparison between the Organization of the Churches in the Beginning of the third Century and those of modern Times.	259

CONTENTS

LECTURE VII

MINISTRY CHANGING TO PRIESTHOOD

	PAGE
In the Course of the third Century the Conceptions of the local and of the universal Church began to change	265
The Changes led in the End to the Idea that a local Church was a Body of Christians obedient to their Bishop and that the universal Church was the Federation of these obedient Communities	266
The Phases in this Change	266
The novel Position and Autocracy of the Bishop needed a Sanction which was found in the legal Fiction of an Apostolic Succession	278
The Idea first emerged in the Quarrels between Hippolytus and Calixtus	280
The Work and Influence of Cyprian	283
The Decian Persecution	287
The Lapsed	290
The "Authority" of the Martyr confronts the "Authority" of the Bishop	295
Cyprian's Theory of the Position and Power of the Bishop	299
The Bishop is the Representative of Christ and has the Right to forgive Sins	305
Cyprian's maimed Sacerdotalism: the Bishop a unique Priest and the Eucharist a unique Sacrifice	307
Cyprian's Method of exhibiting the universality of the visible Church by Means of Councils	313
His Theory confronted by a Roman one which was in the End triumphant in the West	317

LECTURE VIII

THE ROMAN STATE RELIGION AND ITS EFFECTS ON THE ORGANIZATION OF THE CHURCH

The Instrument for effecting the Grouping of federated Churches round the definite Centres was the Council or Synod	323
Sohm's Theory of the Origin and Meaning of Synods	327

CONTENTS

	PAGE
The Synod was really the Application of the Congregational Meeting to a wider ecclesiastical Sphere	334
This democratic Principle of Organization confronted with an imperialist one; the two subsisted for long side by side	335
Councils became a regular part of the Organization of the Churches before the End of the third Century	336
The same Period saw other Changes	337
In the more compact Organization of the federated Churches the Roman Organization for the State pagan Religion was largely copied	340
The religious Reforms of Augustus	341
The Worship of the Emperors	342
The Organization of the Priesthood of the imperial Cult	348
This Organization copied within the Christian Churches	350
The Churches also copied the State Temple Service	353
The Church thus organized was still a Federation of Churches	358
Numerous and flourishing Christian Churches existed which did not belong to the Federation	359
After the Conversion of Constantine these outside Christians were vehemently persecuted by the State, which only acknowledged the federated Churches	359

APPENDIX

Sketch of the History of modern Controversy about the Office-bearers in the primitive Christian Churches 364

INDEXES

Index of References to Contemporary Authorities, Canonical and Non-canonical 379
Index of Names and Subjects 386

CHAPTER I

THE NEW TESTAMENT CONCEPTION OF THE CHURCH

AND I say also unto thee, that thou art *Petros*, and on this *petra* I will build My Church (Ecclesia); and the gates of Hades shall not prevail against it."[1] Our Lord was far from Galilee and farther from Jerusalem when He uttered these words. He was sojourning in an almost wholly pagan land. The rocks overhanging the path were covered with the mementos of a licentious cult; and in the neighbouring city of Caesarea Philippi Herod Philip had built and consecrated a temple to the Emperor Augustus, who was there worshipped as a god.[2] It was among

[1] Matt. xvi. 18. Some modern critics (cf. Schmiedel in the *Encyc. Bibl.* p. 3105) declare that this passage could not have come from the lips of our Lord in the form in which it has been recorded, and in particular that He could not have used the word "ecclesia"; the main reason given being that our Lord sought to reform hearts and not external conditions. To argue from that statement, however true it may be, that Jesus had no intention of founding a religious community and could not have used the word "church," seems to me to be purely subjective and therefore untrustworthy reasoning. Besides, the use of the word by St. Paul in Gal. i. 13, shows that St. Paul found the word existing within Christian circles when he embraced the new faith; and to find it in common use at so early a period entitles us, in my judgment, to trace it back to Jesus Himself. The trend of modern criticism has been to place St. Paul's conversion much closer to the crucifixion than it was formerly held to be. St. Paul implies that the words of the eucharistic formula (Mk. xiv. 22-24, Matt. xxvi. 26-28) came from Jesus; he takes it for granted that every one who becomes a Christian (himself included) must be baptized. We have thus, quite independently of the Gospels or of the Acts, "church," "baptism," "the eucharist"—all implying a religious community, all in common use at a time scarcely two years after the death of our Lord. That entitles us to attribute them to Jesus Himself.

[2] Compare Josephus, *Antiq.* XV. x. 3; *Bell. Jud.* I. xxi. 3. See also

scenes which showed the lustful passions of man's corrupt heart and the statecraft of Imperial Rome seating themselves on the throne of God, that Jesus made to His followers the promise which He has so marvellously fulfilled.

The word translated Church is *Ecclesia*—a word that had a history both theocratic and democratic, and that came trailing behind it memories both to the Jews who were then listening to Him, and to the Greeks, who, at a later period, received His Gospel. To the Jew, the *Ecclesia* had been the assembly of the congregation of Israel,[1] summoned to meet at the door of the Tabernacle of Jehovah by men blowing silver trumpets. To the Greek the *Ecclesia* was the sovereign assembly of the free Greek city-state,[2] summoned by the herald blowing his horn through the streets of the town. To the followers of Jesus it was to be the congregation of the redeemed and therefore of the free, summoned by His heralds to continually appear in the presence of their Lord, who was always to be in the midst of them. It was to be a theocratic democracy.

Schürer, *Geschichte des Jüdischen Volkes* (1898, 3rd ed.), ii. 158 f. ; G. A. Smith, *Historical Geography of Palestine*, p. 473 ff. ; Wissowa, *Religion und Kultus der Römer* (1902), p. 284, n. 3.

[1] Numbers x. 2, 3. In the Old Testament two words are used to denote the assembling of Israel, qāhāl and 'edāh ; the former is translated "assembly" and the latter "congregation" in the Revised Version. In the Septuagint ἐκκλησία is almost always always used to translate qāhāl, and συναγωγή to translate 'edāh. Both Greek words appear continually in the later Hellenistic Judaism, and it is difficult to distinguish their meanings ; but Schürer is inclined to think that συναγωγή means the assembly of Israel as a matter of fact ; while ἐκκλησία has always an ideal reference attached to it. Compare Schürer, *Geschichte des Jüdischen Volkes* (3rd ed. 1898), ii. 432, n. 10 ; Hort, *The Christian Ecclesia*, pp. 5-7.

[2] This is the common use of the word in classical Greek ; in the later Greek the word denotes any popular assembly, even a disorderly one ; it is this use that is found in Acts xix. 41. Dio Cassius uses the word to denote the Roman comitia or ruling popular assembly of the sovereign Roman people. The ruling idea in the word, whether in classical or in Hellenistic Greek, is that it denotes an assembly of the *people*, not of a committee or council. Against this view compare Hatch, *The Organization of the Early Christian Churches* (1881), p. 30, n. 11 ; and for a criticism of Hatch, see Sohm, *Kirchenrecht* (1892), i. 17, n. 4.

The New, if it is to be lasting, must always have its roots in the Old; and the phrase "My Ecclesia" recalled the past and foretold the future. The roots were the memories the word brought both to Jew and to Greek; and the promise and the potency of the future lay in the word "My." The *Ecclesia* had been the congregation of Jehovah; it was in the future, without losing anything of what it had possessed, to become the congregation of Jesus the Christ. Its heralds, like James, the brother of our Lord, could apply to it the Old Testament promises, and see in its construction the fulfilment of the saying of Amos about the rebuilding of the Tabernacle of David;[1] or, like St. Paul, could call it the "Israel of God," and repeat concerning it the prayer of the Psalm, "Remember thine *ecclesia*, which Thou hast purchased of old, which Thou hast redeemed to be the tribe of Thine inheritance."[2] It had been the self-governing Greek republic, ruled by elected office-bearers; hereafter the communities of Christians, which were to be the *ecclesiae*, were to be little self-governing societies where the individual rights and responsibilities of the members would blend harmoniously with the common good of all.

The word with its memories and promises appealed to none of our Lord's "Sent Ones" more strongly than to St. Paul, who was at once an "Hebrew of the Hebrews," and the apostle to the Gentiles. The term "ecclesia" has its home in the Pauline literature.[3] It is met with 110 times within the New Testament, and of these 86 occur in the Epistles of St. Paul and in the Acts of the Apostles. We naturally turn to the writings of St. Paul to aid us in expounding the thought which is contained in the term. When we do so we are entitled to say that the conception contains at least five different ideas which embody the essential features of the "Church of Christ."

The New Testament Church is fellowship with Jesus and with

[1] Acts xv. 16; cf. Amos ix. 11.
[2] Gal. vi. 16; Acts xx. 28; cf. Ps. lxxiv. 2.
[3] Weizsäcker, *Jahrbücher für deutsche Theologie*, xviii. 481.

the brethren through Him; this fellowship is permeated with a sense of unity; this united fellowship is to manifest itself in a visible society; this visible society has bestowed upon it by our Lord a divine authority; and it is to be a sacerdotal society. These appear to be the five outstanding elements in the New Testament conception of the Church of Christ.

1. The Church of Christ is a *fellowship*. It is a fellowship with Jesus Christ; that is the divine element in it. It is a fellowship with the brethren; that is the human element in it. The Rock on which the Church was to be built was a *man confessing*—not the man apart from his confession, as Romanists insist, nor the confession apart from the man, as many Protestants argue. It was a man in whom long companionship with Jesus and the revelation from the Father had created a personal trust in His Messianic mission;[1] and the faith which had grown out of the fellowship had the mysterious power of making the fellowship which had created it more vivid and real; for faith, in its primitive sense of personal trust, is fellowship become self-conscious. Faith is what makes fellowship know itself to be fellowship, and not haphazard social intercourse.

The faith of Peter, *seer* as he was into divine mysteries, and *prophet* as he was, able to utter what he had seen, did not involve a very adequate apprehension of the fellowship he had confessed. He knew so little about its real meaning that shortly after his confession he made a suggestion which would have destroyed it;[2] a thought prompted by the Evil One succeeded the revela-

---

[1] The rock on which the Church is founded is "a human character acknowledging our Lord's divine Sonship." Gore, *The Church and the Ministry*, 3rd ed. p. 38. "In virtue of this personal faith vivifying their discipleship, the Apostles became themselves the first little Ecclesia, constituting a living rock upon which a far larger and ever enlarging Ecclesia should very shortly be built slowly up, living stone by living stone, as each new faithful convert was added to the society." Hort, *The Christian Ecclesia*, p. 17.

[2] Matt. xvi. 22, 23. The suggestion of the Evil One to Peter, and presented to our Lord by Peter—the possibility of Messiahship without suf-

tion from the Father—so strangely and swiftly do inspirations of God and temptations of the Devil succeed each other in the minds of men. The sad experience of Peter has been shared by the Church in all generations. He did not cease to be the Rock-Man in consequence; nor has the promise failed the Church which was founded on him and on his confession, although it has shared his weakness and sin.

St. Paul rings the changes on this thought of fellowship with Jesus which makes the Church. The churches addressed in his epistles are described as *in* Christ Jesus. He is careful to impress on believers the personal relation in which they stand to their Lord, even when he is addressing the whole Church to which they belong. If he writes to the Church of God which is in Corinth,[1] he is careful to add " to them that are sanctified in Christ Jesus, called to be saints"; and in his other epistles he addresses the brethren individually as "saints," "saints and faithful brethren," "all that are in Rome, beloved of God, called to be saints."[2] The individual believer is never lost in the society, and he is never alone and separate. The bond of union is not an external framework impressed from without, but a sense of fellowship springing from within. The believer's union to Christ, which is the deepest of all personal things, always involves something social. The call comes to him singly, but seldom solitarily.

fering—met the Saviour at the great moments of His earthly ministry; at the beginning, in the Temptation scene; here, when he had the vision and gave the promise of the Church; at the end, in the Garden of Gethsemane. There are indications in the Gospels that it was the temptation never absent from his mind. In the form in which it presents itself to His followers—the possibility of saving fellowship with Jesus apart from trust on a suffering Saviour—it has perhaps also been the crowning temptation of His Church and followers. If our Lord alluded to this special temptation when He said to St. Peter, near the end, "Simon, Simon, behold Satan asked to have you that he might sift you as wheat," as is most likely from His references to His own temptations and to St. Peter's relation to his brethren, there is a delicate suggestion of fellowship softening rebuke and vivifying the promise; Luke xxii. 31.

[1] 1 Cor. i. 2.   [2] Phil. i. 1; Eph. i. 1; Col. i. 2; Rom. i. 7.

Perhaps, however, St. Paul's conception of the fellowship with Christ which is the basis of the Church, comes out most clearly in the way he speaks of the "gifts" of grace, the *charismata*, which manifest the abiding presence of our Lord in His Church and His continuing fellowship with His people.[1] He enumerates them over and over again. He points to "apostles," the missionary heralds of the Gospel; to "prophets," to whom the Spirit had given special powers for the edification of the brethren; to "teachers," who are wise with the wisdom of God, and have those divine intuitions which the apostle calls "knowledge"; to "pastors," who feed the flock in one community. He speaks of "helps" ($\dot{a}\nu\tau\iota\lambda\acute{\eta}\psi\epsilon\iota\varsigma$) or powers to assist the sick, the tempted and the tried; of "insight" to give wise counsels; of gifts of rule ($\kappa\upsilon\beta\epsilon\rho\nu\acute{\eta}\sigma\epsilon\iota\varsigma$); of gifts of healing, and in general of all kinds of service. They are all gifts of the Spirit, and are all so many different manifestations of the presence of Jesus and of the living fellowship which His people have with Him.[2]

These various gifts are bestowed on different members of the Christian society for the edification of all, and they serve to show that it is one organism, where the whole exists for the parts, and each part for the whole and for all the other parts. They also show that the Christian society is not a merely natural organism; there is divine life and power within it, because it has the abiding presence of Christ; and the proof of His presence is the possession and use of these various "gifts," all of which come from the one Spirit of Christ in fulfilment of the promise that He will never leave nor forsake His Church. Their presence is a testimony to the presence of the Master which each Christian community can supply. It is a Church of Christ if His presence is manifested by these fruits of the Spirit which come

---

[1] 1 Cor. xii.; Eph. iv. 4–13; Rom. xii. 3-16. It is important to notice that St. Paul, in Rom. xii. 7, makes $\delta\iota\alpha\kappa o\nu\acute{\iota}\alpha$ a "gift" which manifests the presence of Christ, and that this word is used to mean any kind of "ministry" within the Church. See below p. 62. [2] See p. 63 n.

from the exercise of the "gifts" which the Spirit has bestowed upon it; for the Church as well as the individual Christian is to be known by its fruits.[1]

This sense of hidden fellowship with its Lord was the secret of the Church. It was a bond uniting its members and separating them from outsiders more completely than were the initiated into the pagan mysteries sundered from those who had not passed through the same introductory rites. While Jesus lived their fellowship with Him was the external thing which distinguished them from others. They were His disciples ($\mu\alpha\theta\eta\tau\alpha\iota$) gathered round a centre, a Person whom they called Rabbi, Master, Teacher—names they were taught not to give to another. They shared a common teaching and drank in the same words of wisdom from the same lips; but even then they could not be called a "school," for they were united by the bond of a common hope and a common future. They were to share in the coming kingdom of God in and through their relation to their Master. After His departure the other side of the fellowship became the prominent external thing—their relation to each other because of their relation to their common Lord. New names arose to express the change, names suggesting the relation in which they stood to each other. They were the "brethren," the "saints," and they had a fellowship ($\kappa o \iota \nu \omega \nu \iota \alpha$) with each other.[2] This thought of fellowship, as we shall see, was the ruling idea in all Christian organization. All Christians within one community were to live in fellowship with each other; different Christian communities were to have a common fellowship. Visible fellowship with each other, the outcome of the hidden fellowship with Jesus, was to be at once the leading characteristic of all Christians and the bond which united them to each other and separated them from the world lying outside.

[1] For St. Paul's statement about the "gifts" compare Hort, *The Christian Ecclesia*, pp. 153-70; Heinrici, *Das Erste Sendschreiben des Apostel Paulus an die Korinther* (1880), pp. 347-463; Kühl, *Die Gemeindeordnung in den Pastoralbriefen* (1885), pp. 42-49.

[2] Weizsäcker, *The Apostolic Age* (English translation), I. p. 44 ff.

10 THE CONCEPTION OF THE CHURCH

2. The second characteristic of the Church of Christ is that it is a *Unity*. There was one assembly of the congregation of Israel; one sovereign assembly of the Greek city-state. There is *one* Church of Christ.

It must be admitted that the *word* Church is seldom used in the New Testament to designate one universal and comprehensive society. On the contrary, out of the 110 times in which the word occurs, no less than 100 do not contain this note of a wide-spreading unity. In the overwhelming majority of cases the word "church" denotes a local Christian society, varying in extent from all the Christian congregations within a province of the Empire to a small assembly of Christians meeting together in the house of one of the brethren. St. Paul alone,[1] if we except the one instance in Matt. xvi., uses the word in its universal application; and he does it in two epistles only—those to the Ephesians and to the Colossians—both of them dating from his Roman captivity.[2] But there are numberless indications that the thought of the unity of the Church of Christ was never

---

[1] It ought to be noted, however, that although we do not find the word "ecclesia" in 1 Peter, we do find the thought of the unity of all believers strongly expressed in a variety of ways: "Ye are an elect race, a royal priesthood, a holy nation, a people for God's own possession" (1 Peter ii. 9); and in v. 17 we have the word "brotherhood" used to bring out the same idea. This word in the early centuries was technically used as synonymous with *ecclesia*. See below p. 21. The double meaning of ecclesia is found in Matt. xvi. 18 compared with Matt. xviii. 17. In the Apocalypse the unity is expressed in the phrase " the Bride, the Lamb's wife," and the plurality in the " Seven Churches " (Rev. xxi. 9 ; ii. 1, etc).

[2] The various passages in which the word "ecclesia" occurs in the sense of the Christian society have often been collected and grouped. The following classification is based on that of Dr. Hort.

  i. The word "ecclesia," in the singular and with the article, is used to denote:—
  1. The original Church of Jerusalem and Judea, when there was no other; Acts v. 11; viii. 1, 3; Gal. i. 13; 1 Cor. xv. 9; Phil. iii. 6.
  2. The sum total of the churches in Judea, Samaria and Galilee; Acts ix. 31.
  3. The local church:—*Jerusalem*, Acts xi. 22; xii. 1, 5; xv. 4; *Thessalonica*, 1 Thess. i. 1; 2 Thess. i. 1. *Corinth*, 1 Cor. i. 2;

absent from the mind of the Apostle. The Christians he addresses are all brethren, all saints, whether they be in Jerusalem, Damascus, Ephesus or Rome. The believers in Thessalonica are praised because they had been "imitators of the churches of God which are in Judea," who "are in Jesus Christ" as the Thessalonians "are in Jesus Christ."[1] The Epistles to the Corinthians are full of exhortations to unity within the local

    vi. 4 ; xiv. 12, 23 ; 2 Cor. i. 1 ; Rom. xvi. 23. *Cenchrea*, Rom. xvi. 1. *Laodicea*, Col. iv. 16. *Antioch*, Acts xiii. 1 ; xv. 2. Each of the *Seven Churches of Asia*, Rev. ii. iii. *Ephesus*, Acts xi. 26 ; xiv. 27 ; xx. 17 ; 1 Tim. v. 16. *Caesarea*, Acts xviii. 22. Also in Jas. v. 14 ; 3 John 9, 10.

  4. The *assembly* of a local church :—Acts xv. 22 ; 1 Cor. xiv. 23.

  5. The *House Church* :—at *Ephesus*, 1 Cor. xvi. 19 ; at *Rome*, xvi. 5 ; at *Colossae*, Col. iv. 15 ; Philem. 2.

 ii. The word "ecclesia," in the singular and without the article, is used to denote :—

  1. Every local church within a definite district :—Acts xiv. 23.

  2. Any or every local Church :—1 Cor. xiv. 4 ; iv. 17 ; Phil. iv. 15 ; and probably 1 Tim. iii. 5, 15.

  3. The *assembly* of the local church :—1 Cor. xiv. 19, 35 ; xi. 18 ; 3 John 6.

 iii. The word "ecclesia" in the plural is used to denote :—

  1. The sum of the local churches within a definite district, the name being given or implied :—*Judea*, 1 Thess. ii. 14 ; Gal. i. 22. *Galatia*, 1 Cor. xvi. 1 ; Gal. i. 2. *Syria and Cilicia*, Acts xv. 41. *Derbe and Lystra*, Acts xvi. 5. *Macedonia*, 2 Cor. viii. 1, 19; *Asia*, 1 Cor. xvi. 19 ; Rev. i. 4, 11, 20 ; ii. 7, 11, 17, 29 ; iii. 6, 13, 22 ; xxii. 16.

  2. An indefinite number of local churches :—2 Cor. xi. 8, 28 ; viii. 23, 24 ; Rom. xvi. 4, 16.

  3. The sum total of all the local churches :—2 Thess. i. 4 ; 1 Cor. vii. 17 ; xi. 16 ; xiv. 33 ; 2 Cor. xii. 13.

  4. The *assemblies* of all the local churches :—1 Cor. xiv. 34.

 iv. The word "ecclesia" is used in the singular to denote :—

  1. The one universal Church as represented in the individual local Church :—1Cor. x. 32 ; xi. 22 ; (and probably) xii. 28 ; Acts xx. 28 ; (and perhaps) 1 Tim. iii. 5, 15.

  2. The one universal Church absolutely :—Col. i. 18, 24 ; Eph. i. 22 ; iii. 10, 21 ; v. 23, 24, 25, 27, 29, 32.

Compare also Bannerman, *The Scripture Doctrine of the Church*, p. 571 ff. ; Hort, *The Christian Ecclesia*, pp. 116-118.

[1] 1 Thess. ii. 14 ; cf. i. 1.

church, and the warnings are always based on principles which suggest the unity of the whole wide fellowship of believers. The divisions in the church at Corinth had arisen from a misguided apostolic partizanship which implied a lack of belief in Christian unity at the centre; the apostle repudiates this by holding forth the unity of Christ, and by pointing to the one Kingdom of God to be inherited.[1] He has the same message for all the local churches. However varied in environment they may be, these local churches have common usages, and ought to unite in showing a common sympathy with each other.[2]

Besides these minor indications of the thought, we have, in various of his epistles what may be called its poetic expression. The Church of Christ is such a unity that it has thrown down all the walls of race, sex, and social usages which have kept men separate.[3] It has reconciled Jew and Gentile. It has bridged the gulf between the past of Israel and the present of apostolic Christianity.[4]

These thoughts and phrases, which run through all the epistles of St. Paul, lead directly to the description of the glorious unity of the one Church of Christ which fills the great Epistle to the Ephesians. Thus, though it is true that we cannot point to a single use of the word "church" in the earlier epistles which can undoubtedly be said to mean a universal Christian society, the thought of this unity of all believers runs through them all. The conception of the unity of the Church of Christ is one of the abiding possessions of St. Paul in the earliest as in the latest of his writings; but it is only in the writings of his Roman captivity that it attains to its fullest expression.[5]

---

[1] 1 Cor. i. 12, 13; vi. 9.
[2] 1 Cor. iv. 17; vii. 17; xi. 2, 23; xvi. 1.
[3] Gal. iii. 28.   [4] Rom. xi. 17.
[5] Professor Ramsay traces a growth of definiteness in St. Paul's use of the word "Church" from its application to a single congregation to its use to denote what he calls the "Unified Church," and ingeniously connects the use in each case with political parallels. Thus the phrase "the Church of the Thessalonians" corresponds in civil usage to the *ecclesia*

This unity of the Church of Christ which filled the mind of St. Paul was something essentially spiritual. It is a reality, but a reality which is more ideal than material. It can never be adequately represented in a merely historical way. It is true that we can trace the beginnings of the formation of Christian communities, and the gradual federation of these Christian societies into a wide-spreading union of confederate churches; but that only faintly expresses the thought of the unity of the Church of Christ. It is true that we can see in the fellowship of Christians the illustration of the pregnant philosophical thought that it is not good for man to be alone, and that personality itself can only be rightly conceived when taken along with the thought of fellowship.[1] Apart, however, from all surface facts and philosophical ideas, there is something deeper in the unity of the Christian Church, something which lies implicitly in the unformed faith of every believer, that in personal union with Christ there is union with the whole body of the redeemed, and that man is never alone either in sin or in salva-

---

of the Greek city-state, while the phrase "the Church in Corinth," suggesting as it does, "the Church" in other places as well as in Corinth, corresponds in civil usage to a universal and all-embracing political organization like the Roman Empire. Ramsay, *St. Paul the Traveller*, pp. 124-7. Whether this be true or not, few will fail to find a connexion betwen the wide meaning the apostle puts into the word "Church" in the Epistles to the Ephesians and to the Colossians, and the imperial associations of the city from which he wrote. "Writing now from Rome, he (St. Paul) could not have divested himself, if he would, of a sense of writing from the centre of all earthly human affairs; all the more since we know from the narrative in Acts xxii. that he himself was a Roman citizen, and apparently proud to hold this place in the Empire. Here then he must have been vividly reminded of the already existing unity which comprehended both Jew and Gentile under the bond of subjection to the emperor at Rome, and similarity and contrast would alike suggest that a truer unity bound together in one society all believers in the crucified Lord." Hort, *The Christian Ecclesia*, p. 143.

[1] "Not in abstraction or isolation, but in communion lies the very meaning of personality itself," Moberly, *Ministerial Priesthood*, p. 5. "Fellowship is to the higher life what food is to the natural life—without it every power flags and at last perishes," Hort, *Hulsean Lectures*, p. 194.

tion. The unity of the Church of Christ is a primary verity of the Christian faith: "There is One Body, and One Spirit, even as ye are called in one hope of your calling; One Lord, One Faith, One Baptism, One God and Father of all, Who is over all and through all and in all."[1] And because the Unity of the Church of Christ is a primary verity of the Christian faith, it can never be adequately represented in any outward polity, but must always be, in the first instance at least, a religious experience. Its source and centre can never be an earthly throne, but must always be that heavenly place where Jesus sits at the Right Hand of God.[2]

This enables us to see how the word "church" can be used, as it is in the New Testament, to denote communities of varying size, from the sum total of all the Christian communities on earth down to the tiny congregation which met in the house of Philemon. For the unity of the Christian Church is, in the first instance, the oneness of an ideal reality, and is not confined within the bounds of space and time as merely material entities are. It can be present in many places at the same time, and in such a way that, as Ignatius says, "Where Jesus Christ is, there is the *whole* Church."[3] The congregation at Corinth was, in the eyes of St. Paul, the Body of Christ or the whole Church in its all-embracing unity—not *a* Body of Christ, for there is but one Body of Christ; not part of the Body of Christ, for Christ is not divided; but *the Body of Christ* in its unity and filled with the fulness of His powers.[4] It is in this One Body, present in *every* Christian society, that our Lord has placed His

---

[1] Eph. iv. 4-6.

[2] This thought has been beautifully expressed by Dr. Sanday, *The Conception of Priesthood* (1898), pp. 11-14.   [3] *To the Smyrnaeans*, 8.

[4] Exegetes differ about the exact translation of 1 Cor. xii. 27: ὑμεῖς δέ ἐστε σῶμα Χριστοῦ. A few (such as Godet) translate it: "a body of Christ"; by far the largest number translate: "the Body of Christ"; many "Christ's Body," leaving the exact thought indeterminate. It seems to me that the exact rendering, *a* or *the*, cannot be reached from purely grammatical reasoning. St. Paul is completing his metaphor or interpreting his parable. He has been emphasizing the fact that the

"gifts" or *charismata*, which enable the Church to perform its divine functions; and all the spiritual actions of the tiniest community, such as the Church in the house of Nymphas—Prayer, Praise, Preaching, Baptism, the Holy Supper—are actions of the whole Church of Christ.

The Christians of the early centuries clung to this thought, and we have a long series of writers, from Victor of Rome,[1] in the second century, down to Clement of Alexandria and Origen,[2] who tell us that the whole Church of the redeemed, with Christ and the angels, is present in the public worship of the individual congregation. The promise of the Master, that where two or three were gathered together in His Name there would He be in the midst of them, was placed side by side with the thought in the Epistle to the Hebrews that believers are surrounded with a great cloud of witnesses; and the combination suggested that in the simplest action of the smallest Christian fellowship there was the presence and the power of the whole Church of Christ. Tertullian pushes the thought to its furthest limits when he says in a well-known passage: "Accordingly, where there is no joint session of the ecclesiastical order, you Offer, Baptize, and are Priest alone for yourself; for where three are there the Church is, although they be laity."[3]

Christian community at Corinth is an organism with a variety of parts differing in structure and function. It is a perfect organism in the sense that there is no necessary part lacking that is required for the purpose the organism is intended, to serve for its suport or increase or for work. The life which pervades the organism in its totality and in every minutest part is Christ (Col. iii. 14). The organism is *the* Body of Christ.

[1] "Esto potius ... Christianus, pecuniam tuam adsidente Christo spectantibus angelis et martyris praesentibus super mensam dominicam sparge." *De Aleatoribus*, 11; Harnack und v. Gebhardt, *Texte u. Untersuchungen*, V. i. 29.

[2] Origen, *De Or.* 31:— "Καὶ ἀγγελικῶν δυνάμεων ἐφισταμένων τοῖς ἀθροίσμασι τῶν πιστευόντων καὶ αὐτοῦ τοῦ κυρίου καὶ σωτῆρος ἡμῶν δυνάμεως ἤδη δὲ καὶ πνευμάτων ἁγίων, οἶμαι δὲ, ὅτι καὶ προκεκοιμημένων σαφὲς δὲ, ὅτι καὶ ἐν τῷ βίῳ περιόντων, εἰ καὶ τὸ πῶς οὐκ εὐχερὲς εἰπεῖν."

[3] Tertullian, *De exhortatione castitatis*, 7; compare *De poenitentia*, 10; *De pudicitia*, 21; *De fuga in persecutione*, 14.

3. The Church of our Lord's promise was to be a *visible community*. This note of visibility is suggested by the word *ecclesia* itself, and by the whole environment of its earliest Christian use.

The "congregation of Israel" and the "sovereign assembly" of the Greek city-state had been visible things. The time of the promise suggested a visible community. It came when the visible people of Israel had manifestly refused to accept Jesus as the Messiah. His Church was set over against the Israel which had denied Him—one visible community against another. The earliest uses of the word *ecclesia* refer unmistakably to visible communities. When St. Paul persecuted the "Church of God," he made havoc of something more than an abstraction. He haled men and women to prison and confined real bodies within real stone walls. The churches spoken of in the Acts and in the Epistles were societies of men and women, living in families, coming together for public worship, and striving in spite of many infirmities to live the life of new obedience to which they had been called. They were little societies in the world, connected with it on all sides and yet not of it—lamps set on lamp-stands to enlighten the darkness of surrounding paganism. The "gifts" of the Spirit, which manifested the presence of Christ, were seen at work in the public assembly of the congregation, and were given to edify a visible society.

The two universal rites of the new society—Baptism and the Lord's Supper—show that it was a visible thing. St. Paul makes it clear that entrance into the Church was by the visible rite of Baptism, and that he himself had come into the Church by this door.[1] The Lord's Supper was a visible social institution, and could only occupy the place it did in a visible society.[2]

Even the Church Universal, which is described in the Epistle to the Ephesians, is a *visible* Church. It is an ideal reality; but an ideal Church is not invisible because it is ideal. It can be seen in any Christian community, great or small; seen in a

[1] Rom. vi. 3-8.; Gal. iii. 27.   [2] 2 Cor. xi. 23-27.

measure by the eye of sense, but more truly by the eye of faith. For it is one of the privileges of faith, when strengthened by hope and by love, to see the glorious ideal in the somewhat poor material reality. It was thus that St. Paul saw the universal Church of Christ made visible in the Christian community of Corinth.

St. Paul has described the Church in that great trading and manufacturing city of Corinth, where the rich were very rich and the poor were very poor; where the thoroughness of character, inherited from the early Roman colonists, had pushed the sensuous side of Greek civilization into all manner of excesses, until the city had become a by-word for foul living, and religion itself had become an incentive to lust.[1] This environment had tainted the Christian society. St. Paul saw it all and has described it. He has made us see the very Lovefeasts, which introduced the Holy Supper, changed into banquets of display on the part of the rich, while the poor were swept into corners or compelled to wait till their wealthier brethren were served. He has shown us petty rivalries disguising themselves under the mask of faithfulness to eminent apostolic teachers. He has depicted the tainted morals of the city appearing unchecked within the Christian society. What a picture the heathen satirist Lucian, with his keen eye and his outspoken tongue, would have drawn of such a community! St. Paul saw all the frailty, the feebleness to resist the evil communications and the fickleness; and yet he saw in that community *the Body of Christ*. He needed the love that "beareth all things, that believeth all things, and that hopeth all things," to make his vision clear—and that is perhaps the reason why the wonderful chapter on Christian love comes in the middle of this epistle; but his vision was clear, and he saw the life there with its potency and promise. He could say to that Church *Ye are the Body of Christ*. He could see it, as he saw the Ephesian Church,

[1] Compare Dobschütz, *Die Urchristlichen Gemeinden, Sittensgeschichtliche Bilder* (1902), pp. 18 ff.

becoming gradually rooted and grounded in love, gradually strengthened to apprehend with all saints the height, the depth, the length and the breadth of that love of Christ which passeth knowledge, and at last filled with all the fulness of God.

All things earthly have a double element, whether they be of good or evil report. They are in the present and they are making for the future. They are what they are to be. It is the same with all things belonging to Christianity on the human side. We *are* " sons of God," and yet we " *wait* for the adoption " ; we *are* redeemed, and yet our redemption " *draweth nigh.*" Those who " have been saved " are enjoined to " work out their own salvation." So it is with the Church of God. It is what it is to be.[1] And we are definitely taught by the very ways in which St. Paul uses the word " Church " to see the Church Universal in the individual Christian community.[2]

It will be admitted, however, that ideals are given us to be made manifest to the eye of sense as well as to the vision of faith, and that a duty is laid upon every Christian and upon every Christian society to make the universality of the Church of Christ which is manifest to faith plainly apparent to the eyes of sense. If the duty has been but scantily performed since the beginning of the third century, we may find that the neglect has come from abandoning apostolic methods in favour of others suggested by the great pagan empire of Rome. The duty of trying to make visible to the senses the inherent unity of the Church of Christ was always distinctly present to the mind of the great apostle to the Gentiles, and it may be useful to see how he set himself to the task.

One thing meets us at the outset. He would not for the sake

---

[1] Compare Robertson, *Regnum Dei*, p. 54 :—" It (the kingdom of Christ) is the Kingdom of God in its idea—in potency and in promise : but visibly and openly not yet. This is St. Paul's well-known paradox of the Christian life. Our whole task as Christians is to become what we are."

[2] As in 1 Cor. x. 32 ; xi. 22 ; and xii. 28 ; compare above p. 11, note 2, § iv, 1.

of an external universality agree to anything which would set limits on the *real* universality of the Church of Christ. The preservation of the liberty with which Jesus had made His people free was of more importance in His eyes than the manifestation of the visibility of the universal fellowship of Christians with each other. Jewish believers were inclined to think that the practice of circumcision "embodied the principle of the historical continuity of the Church," [1] and that no one who was outside the circle of the "circumcised," no matter how strong his faith nor how the fruits of the Spirit were manifest in his life and deeds, could plead the "security of the Divine Covenant." For this they could give reasons stronger than are brought forward by many who, in our own day, insist on different external "successions" as marks of catholicity. The Scripture had said: "My covenant shall be *in your flesh*, an *everlasting* covenant." [2] The Saviour Himself had been circumcised on the eighth day. He had never, in so many words, either publicly to the people or privately to His disciples, declared that circumcision was no longer to be the sign of the covenant of God.

St. Paul recognized that to limit "the security of the covenant" to something defined by what the Jews believed to be the "principle of the historical continuity of the Church," would be to destroy the real for a limited, though more sensibly visible, universality. He bent his whole energies to break down this false principle of continuity which placed the "succession" in something external, and not in the possession and transmission from generation to generation of the "gifts" of the Spirit within the community. This done, he used his administrative powers, and they were those of a statesman, to create

---

[1] The principle which underlies the claim generally associated with the ambiguous phrase "apostolic succession" is so curiously like the demand made by "those of the sect of the Pharisees who believed" in the days of St. Paul, that it can be most naturally expressed in the same language if only a "succession of bishops" takes the place of "circumcision."

[2] Gen. xvii, 13.

channels for the flow of the manifestation of the visible unity of the Church of Christ.

His ruling thought was to provide that all the various Christian communities should manifest their real brotherhood in the cultivation of the " fruits of the Spirit." The method of carving out a visibly universal Church by means of regulations affecting organization and external form is not without its attractions, which are irresistible to minds of the lawyer type and training, such as we see afterwards in Cyprian of Carthage. It seems a short and easy method of showing that the whole Church is visibly one. But it was not Paul's method. He seems to have thought as little about the special "construction of sheep-folds" as his Master. What concerned him was that the sheep should be gathered into one flock around the One Shepherd. He nowhere prescribed a universal ecclesiastical polity, still less did he teach that the universality of the Christian brotherhood must be made visible in this way. He regarded all the separate churches of Christ as independent self-governing societies. He strove to implant in all of them the principle of brotherly dealing with one another, and he dug channels in which the streams of the Spirit might flow in the practical manifestation of Christian fellowship.

Fellowship (κοινωνία), word and thought, is what filled his mind. All the brethren within one Church were to have fellowship with each other. The local churches within a definite region were to be in close fellowship. The churches among the Gentiles were to maintain brotherly relations with the Mother-Church in Jerusalem. What this fellowship primarily meant can be learnt from what the apostle says in Gal. ii. 9.[1] He tells us that the apostles to the Jews, and he the apostle to the Gentiles, gave each other the right hand of *fellowship*,

[1] Gal. ii. 9: "And when they perceived the grace that was given unto me, James and Cephas and John, they who were reputed to be pillars, gave to me and Barnabas the right hands of fellowship, that we should go unto the Gentiles, and they unto the circumcision."

because they recognized that they had a common faith in the same Christ. It was the recognition of a common belief in the One Christ, the knowledge that they all had within them a new faith which had revolutionised their lives, and was to express itself in their whole character and conduct, that made them feel the kinship with each other which was expressed in the common name "brethren." All down through the early centuries this idea that Christians form one brotherhood finds abundant expression. *Brotherhood* alternates with *Ecclesia* in the oldest sets of ecclesiastical canons,[1] while *omnis fraternitas* and πᾶσα ἡ ἀδελφότης are used to denote the whole of Christendom.[2]

The graceful deference which St. Paul always showed to the leaders in Jerusalem, who had been in Christ before himself; his anxieties about the welfare of the poor "saints" at Jerusalem, and his care to provide for their needs;[3] the letters he asks to be read to all the members of the churches to which they are addressed, and sometimes to other churches also;[4] the eagerness with which he communicates the fact that the church he is writing to enjoys a reputation for hospitality towards wayfaring brethren;[5] the salutations his letters contain from one church to another,[6] and from individual Christians to the churches;[7] the messages sent by his assistants; his and their frequent journeyings from church to church—are all evidences of his unwearied efforts to make the universality of the Christian brotherhood widely manifest.

He did more. He grouped his churches in a statesmanlike

---

[1] See *Sources of the Apostolic Canons*, where ἐκκλησία appears in § 1 and ἀδελφότης in § 2; *Texte u. Untersuchungen*, II. v. 7. 12.

[2] For *universa fraternitas*, see the tract *De Aleatoribus*, 1; *Texte u. Untersuchungen*, V. i. 11; *omnis fraternitas*, V. i. 14; compare Tertullian, *Apologia*, 39; *De praescriptione*, 20; *De pudicitia*, 13. For πᾶσα ἡ ἀδελφότης, see 1 Clem. ii. 4; and Harnack's note on the passage; also 1 Peter ii. 17.   [3] Acts xi. 30; cf. xii. 25.

[4] Col. iv. 16; where St. Paul asks that his letter be read to the Church of Laodicea.

[5] 1 Thess. iv. 9–11.   [6] Rom. xvi. 16; 1 Cor. xvi. 19.

[7] Rom. xvi. 21–23; 1 Cor. xvi. 19; Gal. i. 2; Phil. iv. 21, 22; Col. i. 1, 2.

way so that each could support the others. His statesmanship discerned the advantages which the imperial system, with its trade routes, its postal arrangements and its provincial capitals, gave not merely for the propagation of the Gospel, but for the fellowship of the churches. Corinth was the centre for the churches of Achaia, and the second Epistle to the Corinthians is addressed to all the Christians within that important Roman province.[1] Round Ephesus[2] were grouped the churches of Asia—Smyrna, Pergamos, Thyatira, Sardis, Philadelphia, Laodicea, with Troas and others on the coast, and Colossae and Hierapolis in the Lycus valley.[3] The churches of Macedonia were, in all probability, grouped round Thessalonica,[4] and those of Galatia formed another group, although we are not told what the centre was.[5]

While engaged in giving visibility to the unity of the churches he had planted St. Paul was never unmindful that he wished also to see them united visibly with the churches of Jerusalem and Judea. He had started with the thought of a visible fellowship between Jew and Gentile, and the union which was symbolised when Barnabas and he gave and received the right hand of fellowship with Peter, James and John, was never far from his thoughts. He thought of One Church of Christ which embraced Jew and Gentile all the world over.[6]

But perhaps the evidence of the apostle's method of implanting a sense of a visible unity within the Church of Christ is best seen in the methods, plan and motive of the great collection for the saints at Jerusalem, which fills so large a place in his epistles.

This great collection was no mere spontaneous outburst of Christian charity like the previous succours sent to the poor of Jerusalem. It was a carefully-planned attempt to unite a host of independent churches, which represented wide areas,

[1] 2 Cor. i. 1.   [2] 1 Cor. xvi. 19; Acts xix. 10.
[3] Ramsay, *St. Paul the Traveller*, p. 274.   [4] 1 Thess. iv. 10.
[5] 1 Cor. xvi. 1.   [6] 1 Cor. x. 32; xii. 13; Rom. iii. 29.

in co-operative brotherly action. The preparations occupied more than a year's time. The principle of representation was introduced. Each group of contributing churches sent deputies, all of whom joined the apostle at different places and at different dates, and accompanied him to Jerusalem, bearing with them the money collected. The anxiety which the apostle displayed in the careful arrangement of all the details; the patience with which he awaited the complete mustering of the delegates on the road; the determination that nothing should prevent him from accompanying the delegates to Jerusalem—not even prophetic warnings of danger nor the hindrance of cherished plans to visit Rome—all combine to show that he regarded it as the fulfilment of long cherished plans for making visible the fellowship of all believers in the way that best commended itself to his mind.[1]

It may be that the success of this mustering of his mission churches, this triumphant experiment of co-operation and representation, combined with the assurance that Jew and Gentile were at last dwelling harmoniously within the One Household of God, kindled the thoughts which find expression in the epistles of his Roman captivity. The unity of the wide-spreading Church of Christ was at last made visible to the eyes of sense, not by uniformity of external polity, but by the manifestation of brotherly love. The actual unity of all believers was conspicuous in this great fruit of the Spirit of Christ.

If we follow the accounts given us in the *Acts*, the tests of what was required for visible fellowship by the leaders of the church in Jerusalem did not differ greatly from those demanded by St. Paul. It seemed to be their custom when they heard of some new and unexpected appearance of faith in Jesus to send down

---

[1] Rendall, *The Pauline Collection for the Saints*, *Expositor*, Nov. 1893. For St. Paul's conception of what was meant by "fellowship" and the methods he took to make it visible, see Weizsäcker, *The Apostolic Age of the Christian Church* (Eng. Trans.) I. p. 46 ff.; II. pp. 307-9; and Ramsay, *St. Paul the Traveller*, pp. 54, 130 ff.

some one to inquire about it. Peter and John were sent to Samaria to inquire into the conversions among the Samaritans made by the preaching of Philip.[1] Barnabas was sent down to Antioch on a similar errand.[2] The tests applied in both cases seem to have been: Are there any manifestations of the fruits of the Spirit in the lives of the new converts? The case of Antioch is most instructive. The Gospel had been proclaimed there, we know not how or by whom. The apostles at Jerusalem seem to have had nothing to do with the proclamation. An infant church had come into being without their guidance or assistance. Its birth is unrecorded; its earliest history unknown; the congregation is in being before the apostles seem to have heard of it. When the delegate from Jerusalem appeared and made his inquiries, what satisfied him was that the grace of God was manifestly with the brethren there. The believers in Antioch and the delegate from Jerusalem had the same faith in the same Saviour, and their faith found its proper outcome in a renewed life. That was enough for fellowship or visible and fraternal union. We see no attempt to impose any external ecclesiastical ordinances, no suggestions about the need for showing themselves to be in the line of the "historic continuity of the church" by accepting circumcision or otherwise. Whether we take the reception of Cornelius, the welcome accorded to the Samaritan converts, or the joy of Barnabas when he perceived that the grace of God was manifest in Antioch, the unity of the Christian Church was made visible to the eyes of sense, not by uniformity of organization, but by the manifestation of the fruits of the Spirit; that was the one feature that was regarded as proof that it was worthy of being received into the common fellowship.

IV. To this *visible society* belongs *Authority*. The very thought of a Christian Church visible suggests the idea of a separate community with a distinct sphere of religious life; and this in turn implies that the society must have, like every form of cor-

[1] Acts viii. 14-27.   [2] Acts xi. 22, 23.

ITS AUTHORITY

porate social existence, powers of oversight and discipline to be exercised upon its members. But the authority which the Church possesses is altogether different from what a voluntary association of men may exercise upon its members, and of another kind from what is possessed by lawful civil government. The authority comes from Christ Himself. The Christian Democracy is also a Theocracy; it combines the two ideas of rule associated with the Greek and the Hebrew uses of the word "ecclesia." While the authority belongs to the whole membership, and is therefore democratic; it nevertheless comes from *above*, and is therefore theocratic.[1] It comes from Jesus Christ, who is the Head of the Church.[2]

Our Lord has intimated that He has imparted this authority to His Church in many recorded sayings, and in particular in three well-known passages: in Matt. xvi. 13–19; Matt. xviii. 15–20, and in John xx. 21–23.

The first promise was made to St. Peter in very special circumstances. Our Lord had asked a question of all His disciples. St. Peter, answering impetuously in their name, made himself their representative. His answer was an adoring confession of his faith in the Person of Christ[3]—a confession which contained in germ all the future confessions of the Church of Christ, and which made him the spokesman for the mighty multitude which

---

[1] Some Anglican divines make strange deductions from the truth that the authority which belongs to the Church comes from *above*. They at once infer that inasmuch as the authority comes from above it cannot come directly to the whole Christian society; but must come through an official class of ministers who act as a species of *plastic medium* between our Lord and His people. Strange how Gnostic and Arian ideas banished from the creeds of the Church linger in thoughts about Orders! Then by a confusion of ideas they transfer the phrase "from above" to the human sphere, and make it an essential idea of legitimate ecclesiastical rule that it must be invariably communicated from a higher to a lower order of ministry! Why should authority imparted through the Christian Society be regarded as "from beneath," as of the earth earthy?

[2] Ephes. v. 23; Col. i. 18.

[3] "There is a tone of loving reverence and worship in the words 'Thou art the Christ, the Son of the Living God.' They answer to our Lord's

no man can number, who were to make the same confession of adoring trust in their Saviour. The confession was an inspired one; it had been revealed to St. Peter by the Father; there was divinity in it, for God gave the revelation which prompted the confession; and there was humanity in it, for the man appropriated and made his own what the Father had revealed to him. It was the first of what was to become a multitudinous sea of voices of men inspired by the Father to know and to confess that Jesus was the Christ, the Son of the Living God. It was to the Peter who answered as representing the Twelve, to Peter who was the spokesman for countless thousands of the faithful who down through the march of Time would make the same glad confession, that the promise was given.

The promise was of authority to bear the key of the household of the faithful, to have the power to let in and keep out from the household. The words and metaphor used were the familiar Jewish terms to denote a delegated authority. The thought conveyed is commonly and correctly explained by a reference to the substitution of Shebna for Eliakim in the stewardship of the House of David;[1] and it is implied that our Lord, in the word He used, made St. Peter, and those he represented, stewards of the Household of the faithful with the authority to "bind" and to "loose," to "prohibit" and to "permit," to "admit" and "exclude." Other passages in the New Testament, making use of the same simile of the major-domo with his key and his power of letting in or locking out, assist us to see the fuller meaning of the promise recorded. The one is a warning and the other

picture of the spiritual experience of His disciples in His great intercessory prayer; [1] I manifested Thy name unto the men whom Thou gavest Me out of the world; Thine they were, and Thou gavest them to Me; and they have kept Thy word. Now they know that all things, whatsoever Thou hast given Me, are from Thee; for the words which Thou gavest Me, I have given unto them; and they received them, and knew of a truth that I came forth from Thee, and they believed that Thou didst send Me." Bannerman, *The Scripture Doctrine of the Church*, p. 169.

[1] Isaiah xxii. 20, 22. Compare Gore, *The Church and the Ministry*, p. 223.

an encouragement. Our Lord called the attention of his followers to the scribes and Pharisees, who "sat in Moses' seat," and had to be obeyed. They had the keys and they used them to shut the door of the kingdom of heaven against men.[1] Jesus pronounces woe on them for using the keys in this way. Their shutting out, although they have the keys officially, was evidently not ratified in heaven. Hence we must infer that the mere official position of being the bearer of the "keys" does not always ensure that what is done on earth by the bearer will be ratified in heaven. Then in the message to the Church in Philadelphia, the brethren there were told that the real bearer of the "keys" is the Lord Himself.[2] It is only when He lets in that there can be no exclusion; it is only when He shuts out that there is any real exclusion. A real authority is bestowed, and real powers are given; but just as Peter's confession depended on the inspiration of the Father, so the ratification of the exercise of power depends on its Christ-like use.

It is doubtful whether the second saying was addressed to the Twelve, or to a larger group of disciples, but the advice which precedes the promise is to be applied and can only be applied to all the followers of Jesus within a community. It gives directions for dealing with offences and offenders within the Christian society, and has been commonly regarded as the Scriptural warrant for the exercise of discipline within the Church. It proceeds on the idea that offences may arise from thoughtlessness as well as from wilful sin, and that the offender, in spite of his offence, is a brother to be won back to brotherliness. It prescribes a threefold attempt to win back the erring brother to a state of brotherly feeling. If everything fails, if the offender has refused to hear the offended person pleading with him in his own person, if he has rejected the remonstrances of two or

---

[1] Matt. xxiii. 2, 3, 13 :—ὅτι κλείετε τὴν βασιλείαν τῶν οὐρανῶν ἔμπροσθεν τῶν ἀνθρώπων.
[2] Rev. iii. 7 :—τάδε λέγει ὁ ἅγιος, ὁ ἀληθινός, ὁ ἔχων τὴν κλεῖν Δαβίδ, ὁ ἀνοίγων καὶ οὐδεὶς κλείσει, καὶ κλείων καὶ οὐδεὶς ἀνοίγει.

three fellow-Christians pleading with him, if he finally spurns the warnings of the Church or whole Christian society, then, and not till then, does the thought of punishment enter. The punishment, if punishment it can be called, is expulsion of a certain kind from the Christian communion. The offender is to be treated as the Jewish Synagogue acted towards a Gentile or a publican. He was to be looked on as if he had never belonged to the society, or as if he had voluntarily excluded himself by the course of life he had chosen to persist in.

We are told that the decisions of the Church on earth in such cases as those described will be ratified in Heaven. This is a confirmation of the promise given to St. Peter, and like it is strictly conditional. The condition attached is that there must be a real and living communion between the Church and its Head the Lord Jesus Christ, so that the Church decides in a Christ-like spirit. It is impossible to separate the promise from the verses which immediately follow. Our Lord Himself joins them together by very solemn words. This condition does not render the promise of ratification deceptive. The fellowship with Christ, which is the condition, is to be had provided it is sought for earnestly, honestly and trustingly in prayer (v. 19).

The authority is given to the society of believers, whether two or three meeting together in a place far from any others, or a great and organised community. It is not entrusted by our Lord directly to any official class; it is not given to any human power not rising out of the company of the faithful. It is given to the visible fellowship, and it belongs to them in reality, as well as in name, in the measure in which they have living communion with Him Who is their Head.

The third promise seems to have been made to the nucleus of the infant Church in Jerusalem, if we are to accept Luke xxiv. 33 ff. as the parallel passage—to " the disciples and those who were with them." It is commonly held to include all that is bestowed in the other two, and perhaps something even more solemn—the power to pronounce the divine sentence of pardon involved in the proclamation of the Gospel of Christ. Whatever be the powers granted, they are given to the whole company of believers and not to any class among them. They are also, as in the earlier passages, given under conditions. The power can only manifest itself in those who are filled with the Spirit of Christ.[1] In virtue of this promise with its gift of power the visible Church of Christ can with absolute confidence declare the gospel of pardon through the work of Christ, and can assert that the divine conditions are those which it proclaims. In virtue of the same promise every individual Christian is entitled to affirm with absolute certainty to every penitent sinner that God pardons his sins if he accepts Jesus as his All-sufficient Saviour.[2]

The authority was given in the first passage to one man; in the second probably to the Twelve; in the third to the whole Christian community. In each case the more particular is absorbed in the more general. The power given to St. Peter

---

[1] John xx. 22, 23 :—καὶ τοῦτο εἰπὼν ἐνεφύσησεν καὶ λέγει αὐτοῖς, Λάβετε Πνεῦμα Ἅγιον ἄν τινων ἀφῆτε τὰς ἁμαρτίας, ἀφίενται (ἀφέωνται Ti., W. H.) αὐτοῖς· ἄν τινων κρατῆτε, κεκράτηνται.

[2] "The main thought which the words convey is that of the reality of the power of absolution from sin granted to the Church and not of the particular organization through which the power is administered. There is nothing in the context to show that the gift was confined to any particular group (as the apostles) among the whole company present. The commission must therefore be regarded as properly the commission of the Christian society, and not as that of the Christian ministry (cf. Matt. v. 13, 14). The great mystery of the world, absolutely insoluble by thought, is that of sin; the mission of Christ was to bring salvation from sin; and the work of the Church is to apply to all that which He has gained. Christ risen was Himself the sign of the completed overthrow of death, the end of sin, and the impartment of His life necessarily carried with it the fruit of His conquest. Thus the promise is in one sense an interpretation of the gift. The gift of the Holy Spirit finds its application in the communication or withholding of the powers of the new life. ... The promise, as being made not to one but to the Society, carries with it of necessity ... the character of perpetuity: the society never dies. ... The exercise of the power must be placed in the closest connexion with the faculty of spiritual discernment, consequent on the gift of the Holy Spirit." Westcott, *Gospel of St. John*, p. 295.

in the first passage is merged in the authority given to the Twelve in the second; and the authority given to the Twelve is in turn merged in the authority given to the whole congregation. St. Peter received the power because he represented the Twelve directly, and the whole Church founded on him and on his confession indirectly. The Twelve received it because they represented the Church which was to come into existence through their ministry. After the Resurrection the whole infant Church received the same, if not greater, authority. St. Peter was to die; the Twelve also were to go the way of all flesh; but the society was to remain, and with it the authority bestowed upon it by its Lord.

It is needless to say that very varying interpretations of these three passages have been given by different schools of theologians; that Romanists found on the promise given to St. Peter, and that some Anglicans insist that the third promise was made to the Eleven only, even if the company included other disciples, and build up the edifice of Apostolic Succession on this narrow foundation; and that both affirm that the authority which our Lord gave to His Church was placed directly in the hands of office-bearers, and not in those of the whole membership.

To examine at length the various exegetical arguments brought forward in support of these positions would lead far beyond the space at our disposal; but two general considerations may be adduced. Such an interpretation seems to be against the analogy of our Lord's teaching; and He was not so understood by His New Testament Church.

While our Lord chose Twelve to form an inner circle of disciples, while He trained them by close companionship with Himself for special service, while He weaned them in half-conscious ways from their old life, it nowhere appears that He bestowed upon them a special rank or instituted a peculiar or exceptional office of stewardship of divine mysteries in their persons.[1] It

---

[1] Cf. 1 Peter iv. 10: "According as *each* hath received a gift, ministering it among yourselves, as good stewards of the manifold grace of God."

is improbable that He bestowed on them the name *apostles* to be a general and distinguishing title, and one unshared in by other disciples besides the Twelve. Our Lord called them *apostles* when He sent them on a special mission among the villages; they were apostles while this mission lasted; when it came to an end they were the Twelve or inner circle of intimates of the Master.[1] After the Death and Resurrection of the Lord the task to which they had been trained by companionship with the Saviour and in the apprentice mission among the villages, became their life work, but it was shared in from the very beginning by others who bore with them the common name apostle.[2] Nor does our Lord make any promises to the Twelve which imply that He had bestowed upon them a special rank in the Church which was to come. He told them that whoever received them received Him; but this was a privilege shared in by the least of His followers, for whoever received a little child in His name received Him.[3] It is impossible to avoid noticing how the ancient manuals of church organization have caught the spirit of Christ's teaching, that there are to be no lordships in His Church. The qualifications set forth for office

---

[1] The relations of the Twelve to the Church of Christ are strikingly brought out by Dr. Hort in his *Christian Ecclesia*, pp. 23-41. On the title *apostle* he says: "Taking these facts together respecting the usage of the Gospels, we are led, I think, to the conclusion that in its original sense the term Apostle was not intended to describe the habitual relation of the Twelve to our Lord during the days of His ministry, but strictly speaking only that mission among the villages, of which the beginning and the end are recorded for us." . . . "If they (the Twelve) represented an apostolic order within the Ecclesia then the Holy Communion must have been intended only for members of that order, and the rest of the Ecclesia had no part in it. But if, as the men of the apostolic age and subsequent ages believed without hesitation, the Holy Communion was meant for the Ecclesia at large, then the Twelve sat down that evening as representatives of the Ecclesia at large; they were disciples more than they were apostles."

[2] St. Paul in his account of the appearances of our Lord after His Resurrection distinguishes between the Twelve and apostles; 1 Cor. xv. 5-8; cf. below, pp. 74-85.

[3] Matt. x. 40; cf. Luke x. 16; Matt. xviii. 5; Mark ix. 37; Luke ix. 48.

are those which every Christian ought to possess; and the duties said to belong to office are those which for the most part all Christians ought to perform. We do not see *orders* in the sense of ecclesiastical rank whose authority does not come from the people; we see ecclesiastical *order* and arrangement of service. Whatever power and authority the Church of Christ possesses in gift from the Lord resides in the membership of the Church and not in any superior rank of officials who have received an authority over the Church directly from Christ Himself.

The Church of the New Testament evidently interpreted the words of our Lord to mean that He placed the authority which He had bestowed upon His Church in the hands of the membership, of the community which formed the local church.

Even in the Primitive Church in Jerusalem, where the presence of an apostle was seldom lacking, the community was self-governing, and acted on the conviction that the authority bestowed by Christ on His Church belonged to the whole congregation of the faithful and not to an apostolic hierarchy. The assembly of the local church appointed delegates and elected office-bearers. The vice-apostle Matthias and the Seven were elected by the assembly,[1] and a similar assembly appointed Barnabas to be its delegate to Antioch.[2] The assembly of the local church summoned even apostles before it, and passed judgment upon their conduct.[3] The apostles might suggest, but the congregation ruled.

When we pass from the Church at Jerusalem to the churches planted by the ministry of St. Paul, the proofs of democratic self-government are still more abundant. When the apostle urges the duty of stricter discipline, or when he recommends

---

[1] Acts i. 23; vi. 5.   [2] Acts xi. 22.

[3] On the conduct of St. Peter at Caesarea, Acts xi. 1-4; on the opinions and practices of St. Paul, xv. 12, 22-29, and whatever differences may be found in the account of the proceedings in this chapter and in St. Paul's statement in the Epistle to the Galatians (Gal. ii. 1 ff.) there is no question that both recognize the supremacy of the assembly of the Church.

a merciful treatment of one who had lapsed, he writes to the whole community in whose hands the authority resides. He pictures himself in their midst while they are engaged in this painful duty. He assures them that they have the authority of the Lord for the exercise of discipline. For however thoroughly democratic the government of the New Testament Church was, it was still as thoroughly theocratic. The presence of the Lord Himself was with them in the exercise of the authority He had entrusted to their charge.[1] The evidence of the presence of Christ was of the same kind as witnessed His presence in the actions of public worship. The local churches recognised His presence in the manifestation of the "gifts" of His Spirit bestowed upon them. These "gifts" included not only the bestowal of grace needed for exhortation to edification, but also the wisdom to "govern" and to "guide." The theocratic element was not given in a hierarchy imposed upon the Church from without; it manifested itself within the community. It appeared in the presence, recognition and use made of gifts of government bestowed upon its membership which were none the less spiritual, divine and "from above," because they concerned the ordinary duties of oversight and manifested themselves in the natural endowments of members of the community. The presence of Christ among His people may be as easily manifested in the decision which the assembly of the local church arrives at by a majority[2] of votes as in the fiat launched from an episcopal chair. The latter is not necessarily from above, and the former is not of necessity from beneath.

V. Lastly, the Church of Christ is a *sacerdotal* society.

The Church of Christ is continually represented as the "ideal Israel." This is a favourite thought of St. Paul's, and it implies that the special function of the Church of Christ is to do in a

[1] 1 Cor. v. 3–5; Gal. vi. 1.
[2] The censure inflicted on the member of the Corinthian Church who had disobeyed the Apostle Paul was carried by a majority: 2 Cor. ii. 6, ἡ ἐπιτιμία αὕτη ἡ ὑπὸ τῶν πλειόνων.

better manner what the ancient Israel did imperfectly. When we ask what the special function of the ancient Israel was, we find it given in a great variety of ways, all of which include one central thought, best expressed perhaps by the phrase, "To approach God." This central idea was connected with the thoughts of special times of approach, or Holy Seasons; with a special place of approach, which was the Temple of God's Presence; and with a special set of men who made the approach on behalf of their fellows, and who were called Priests. When we turn to the Church of Christ we find the same central thought and the same dependent ideas. The main function of the New Testament Church is also to approach God. Just as in the Old Testament economy the priests when approaching God presented sacrifices to Him, so in the New Testament Church gifts are to be presented to God, and these gifts or offerings bear the Old Testament name of sacrifices. We are enjoined to present *our bodies*;[1] our *praise*, "that is the fruit of our lips which make confession to His name";[2] our *faith*;[3] our *almsgiving*;[4] our "doing good and communicating."[5] These are all called "sacrifices," or "sacrifices well-pleasing to God," and, to distinguish them from the offerings of the Old Testament economy, "spiritual or living sacrifices."[6] The exertions made by St. Paul to bring the heathen to a knowledge of the Saviour is also called a sacrifice or offering.[7] The New Testament Church is the ideal Israel, and does the work which the ancient

---

[1] Rom. xii. 1: "I beseech you therefore, brethren, by the mercies of God, to present your bodies a living sacrifice, holy, well-pleasing to God, which is your reasonable service ($\tau\grave{\eta}\nu$ $\lambda o\gamma\iota\kappa\grave{\eta}\nu$ $\lambda\alpha\tau\rho\epsilon\iota\alpha\nu$ $\dot{\upsilon}\mu\hat{\omega}\nu$)." The thought expressed is that the Christian should consecrate the whole personality, body, soul and spirit to God; and thus all service whether of work or worship became a sacrifice. Compare Ps. li. 15-17.

[2] Heb. xiii. 15.   [3] Phil. ii. 17.

[4] Paul's great collection for the poor saints in Jerusalem is an offering: Acts xxiv. 17; so is the contributions which the members of the Church at Philippi sent to the apostle: Phil. iv. 18.   [5] Heb. xiii. 16.

[6] $\Theta \upsilon\sigma\iota\alpha\iota$ $\pi\nu\epsilon\upsilon\mu\alpha\tau\iota\kappa\alpha\iota$: 1 Pet. ii. 5; $\theta\upsilon\sigma\iota\alpha$ $\zeta\hat{\omega}\sigma\alpha$: Rom. xii. 1; of. Phil. ii. 17.   [7] Rom. xv. 16.

Israel was appointed to do. The limitations only have disappeared. There is no trace in the New Testament Church of any specially holy places or times or persons. The Christian ideal is, to quote the late Dr. Lightfoot, a Holy Season extending all the year round, a Temple confined only by the limits of the habitable globe, and a Priesthood including every believer in the Lord Jesus Christ.[1]

This does not mean that the New Testament Church may not select special days for the public worship of God; that it may not dedicate buildings where the faithful can meet together to unite in offering the sacrifices of prayer and praise; that it may not set apart men from among its membership and appoint them to lead its devotions. But it does mean that God can be approached at all times, and in every place, and by every one among His people. His fellow believers may select one from among themselves to be their *minister*. There may be a *ministering priesthood*, but there cannot be a *mediating priesthood* within the Christian society. There is one Mediator only, and all, men, women and children, have the promise of immediate entrance into the presence of God, and are priests.

Luther has expressed the thought of the sacerdotal character of the Church of Christ when he says, in a description of the Eucharistic service: " There our priest or minister stands before the altar, having been publicly called to his priestly function; he repeats publicly and distinctly Christ's words of the Institution; he takes the Bread and the Wine, and distributes it according to Christ's words; and we all kneel beside him and around him, men and women, young and old, master and servant, mistress and maid, all holy priests together, sanctified by the blood of Christ. We are there in our priestly dignity. . . . We do not let the priest proclaim for himself the ordinance of Christ; but he is the mouthpiece of us all, and we all say it with him in our hearts with true faith in the Lamb of God Who feeds us with His Body and Blood."

[1] *Commentary on the Epistle to the Philippians* (1881), 6th ed. p. 183.

This sacerdotal character of the whole Church of Christ was maintained in the primitive Christian Church down to at least the middle of the third century. Whatever evinced a wholehearted dedication of one's self to God was a sacrifice which required no mediating priesthood in the offering. For the Christian sacrifice always means a sacrifice of self. When Polycarp gave his body to be burnt for the faith of Jesus, he gave it in sacrifice, and every martyr's death or suffering was a sacrifice well-pleasing to God.[1] When poor and humble believers fasted that they might have food to give to the hungry, they were sacrificing a spiritual sacrifice.[2] When Christians, either at home and in private or in the assembly for public worship, poured forth prayers and thanksgivings, they were offering sacrifice to God.[3] Justin Martyr does not hesitate to call such devotions "the only perfect and well-pleasing sacrifices to God."[4]

And the Holy Supper, the very apex and crown of all Christian

---

[1] Compare *Letter of the Smyrnaeans on the Martyrdom of Polycarp*, 14: "Then he, placing his arms behind him and being bound to the stake, like a goodly ram out of a great flock for an offering, a burnt sacrifice made ready and acceptable to God, looking up to heaven, said: O Lord God Almighty. . . ."

[2] Aristides, *Apology*, 15: "And if any among the Christians is poor and in want, and they have not overmuch of the means of life, they fast two or three days, in order that they may provide those in need with the food they require."

A favourite phrase to describe widows and orphans was "the altar of God" on which the sacrifices of almsgiving were offered up. It is used by Polycarp, *To the Philippians*, 4; also in the *Apostolic Constitutions*, ii. 26 and iv. 3, of the orphans, the old and all who were supported by the benevolence of the faithful. Tertullian says of the widow: "aram enim Dei mundam proponi oportet," *Ad Uxor.* i. 7.

[3] Clement of Alexandria spiritualizes the Old Testament sacrifices to make them the forerunners of Christian prayers. "And that compounded incense which is mentioned in the Law, is that which consists of many tongues and voices in prayer . . . brought together in praises with a pure mind, and just and right conduct, from holy works and righteous prayer," *Strom.* vii. 6. In the same chapter he says: "For the sacrifice of the Church is the word breathing as incense from holy souls, the sacrifice and the whole mind being at the same time unveiled to God."

[4] *Dialogue*, 117.

public worship, where Christ gives Himself to His people, and where His people dedicate themselves to Him in body, soul and spirit, was always a sacrifice as prayers, praises and almsgiving were. The Church of Christ was a sacerdotal society, its members were all priests, and its services were all sacrifices.[1]

Such is the New Testament thought of the Church of Christ —a Fellowship, a United Fellowship, a Visible Fellowship, a Fellowship with an Authority bestowed upon it by its Lord, and a sacerdotal Fellowship whose every member has the right of direct access to the throne of God, bringing with him the sacrifices of himself, of his praise and of his confession.

[1] The conception of a mutilated sacerdotalism, where one part of the Christian worship is alone thought of as the true sacrifice, and a small portion of the fellowship—the ministry—is declared to be the priesthood, did not appear until the time of Cyprian, and was his invention.

CHAPTER II

A CHRISTIAN CHURCH IN APOSTOLIC TIMES

CAN we, piercing the mists of two thousand years, see a Christian Church as it was in Apostolic times—a tiny island in a sea of surrounding heathenism? Our vision gets most assistance from the Epistles of St. Paul, which not only are the oldest records of the literature of the New Testament, but give us much clearer pictures of the earliest Christian assemblies for edification and thanksgiving than are to be found in the Acts of the Apostles. The more we study these epistles the more clearly we discern that we must not project into these primitive times a picture taken from any of the long organized churches of our days. On the other hand, we can see many an analogy in the usages of the growing churches of the mission field. This is not to be wondered at. The primitive church and churches growing among heathen surroundings have both to do with the origins of organization.

For one thing, we must remember that the meetings of the congregation were held in private houses;[1] and as the number of believers grew, more than one house must have been placed at the service of the brethren for their meetings for public worship and for the transaction of the necessary business of the congregation. We are told that in the primitive church at Jerusalem the Lord's Supper was dispensed in the houses,[2] and that the brethren met in the house of Mary the mother of John Mark,[3]

---

[1] It is true that we read in Acts xix. 9, 10 that St. Paul held meetings in the *Schola* of Tyrannus: but this is a unique instance.

[2] Acts ii. 46: κλῶτές τε κατ' οἶκον ἄρτον.

[3] Acts xii. 12: "The house of Mary, the mother of John whose surname was Mark; where many were gathered together and were praying."

42 A CHRISTIAN CHURCH IN APOSTOLIC TIMES

in the house of James the brother of our Lord,[1] and probably elsewhere. At the close of the Epistle to the Romans, St. Paul sends greetings to three, perhaps five, groups of brethren gathered round clusters of distinguished Christians whom he names. One of these groups he calls a "church," and the others were presumably so also.[2] The account of Saul, the persecutor, making havoc of the Church, entering every house and haling men and women to prison, reads like a record of the persecution of the Huguenots among the house-churches of Reformation times in France, or like raids on house-conventicles in the Covenanting times in Scotland. It becomes evident too as we study these early records that when it was possible, that is, when any member had a sufficiently large abode and was willing to open his house to the brethren, comparatively large assemblies, including all the Christians of the town or neighbourhood, met together at stated times and especially on the Lord's Day, for the service of thanksgiving. Gaius was able to accommodate all his fellow Christians, and was the "host of the whole Church."[3]

Traces of these earliest house-churches survived in happier days. The ground plan of the earliest Roman church, discovered in 1900 in the Forum at Rome, is modelled not on the basilica or public hall, but on the audience hall of the wealthy Roman burgher, and the recollections of the familiar surroundings at the meetings in the house-churches probably guided

---

[1] Acts xxi. 18; xii. 17.

[2] Rom. xvi. 3-5: "Salute Prisca and Aquila . . . and the church that is in their house"; xvi. 14: "Salute Asyncritus, Phlegon, Hermes, Patrobas, Hermas, and the brethren that are with them"; 15: "Salute Philologus and Julia, Nereus and his sister, and Olympas, and all the saints that are with them"; 10: "Salute them which are of the household of Aristobulus"; 11: "Salute them of the household of Narcissus." The groups saluted in verses 10 and 11 may have been a number of freedmen or slaves belonging to the households of the two wealthy men mentioned; but the other three groups are evidently house-churches.

St. Paul sends salutations to other house-churches; to that meeting in the house of Philemon at Colossae (Philem. 2), to that meeting in the house of Nymphas in Laodicea (Col. iv. 15), and to that meeting in the house of Stephanas (1 Cor. xvi. 15).   [3] Rom. xvi. 23.

the pencil of the architect who first planned the earliest public buildings dedicated to Christian worship.[1] Old liturgies which enjoin the deacon, at the period of the service when the Lord's Supper is about to be celebrated, to command the mothers to take their babies on their knees, bring [2] with them memories of these homely gatherings in private houses, which lasted down to the close of the second century and probably much later, except in the larger towns.[3]

It is St. Paul, in his *First Epistle to the Corinthians*, who gives us the most distinct picture of the meetings of the earliest Christian communities. The brethren appear to have had three distinct meetings—one for the purposes of edification by prayer and exhortation, another for thanksgiving which began with a

---

[1] Compare C. Dehio, *Die Genesis der christlichen Basilika* in the *Sitzensber. d. München. Akad. d. Wiss.* 1882, ii. 301 ff.

[2] In the so-called *Liturgy of St. Clement* there is the following rubric:—
"The order of James, the brother of John, the son of Zebedee.
"And I James, the brother of John, the son of Zebedee, command that forthwith the deacon say,
"Let none of the hearers, none of the unbelievers, none of the heterodox stay. Ye who have prayed the former prayer, depart. *Mothers, take up your children.* Let us stand upright to present unto the Lord our offerings with fear and trembling.": Neale and Littledale, *Translations of Primitive Liturgies*, p. 75.

The writer had the privilege of worshipping in a house-church in the Lebanon under the shoulder of Sunim in the autumn of 1888. The long low vaulted kitchen had been swept and garnished for the occasion, though some of the pots still stood in a corner. The congregation sat on the floor—the men together in rows on the right and the women in rows on the left. During the services which preceded the Holy Communion, babies crawled about the floor making excursions from mother to father and back again. When the non-communicants had left, and the "elements," as we say in Scotland, were being uncovered, the mothers secured the straggling babies and kept them on their laps during the whole of the communion service, as was enjoined in the ancient rubric quoted above.

[3] The earliest trace we find of buildings set apart exclusively for Christian worship dates from the beginning of the third century (202-210): Clement of Alexandria, *Stromata*, vii. 5. Clement speaks of a building erected in honour of God, while he insists that it is the assembly of the people and not the place where they assemble that ought to be called the church.

common meal and ended with the Holy Supper,[1] and a third for the business of the little society.

1. In his description of the first the apostle introduces us to an earnest company of men and women full of restrained enthusiasm, which might soon become unrestrained. We hear of no officials appointed to conduct the services. The brethren fill the body of the hall, the women sitting together, in all probability on the one side, and the men on the other; behind them are the inquirers; and behind them, clustering round the door, unbelievers, whom curiosity or some other motive has attracted, and who are welcomed to this meeting " for the Word."

The service, and probably each part of the service, began with the benediction: " Grace be to you and peace from God our Father and the Lord Jesus Christ," which was followed by an invocation of Jesus and the confession that He is Lord.[2] One of the brethren began to pray; then another and another; one began the Lord's Prayer,[3] and all joined; each prayer was followed by a hearty and fervent " Amen."[4] Then a hymn was sung; then another and another, for several of the brethren

---

[1] The best account of the *Agape* is in Keating's *The Agape and the Eucharist* (1901).

[2] St. Paul does not mention the benediction as forming part of the Christian worship, but the way in which it occurs regularly at the beginning of his epistles, preserving always the same form, warrants us in supposing its liturgical use in the manner above indicated. The invocation of Jesus as the Lord is made the test of all Christian public utterance for edification, and must have preceded the prophetic addresses if not the whole service: 1 Cor. xii. 3.

[3] The use of the Lord's prayer is not mentioned but it may be inferred. " Paul nowhere mentions the Lord's prayer. But we may assume that we have a trace of it in Rom. viii. 15, and in Gal. iv. 6. In speaking of the right to call God Father, he gives the Aramaic form for father, in each instance adding a translation; and this is only to be explained by supposing that he had in mind a formula which was known wherever the Gospel had penetrated, and which, by preserving the original language, invested the name with peculiar solemnity, in order to maintain its significance unimpaired in the believer's consciousness." Weizsäcker, *The Apostolic Age*, ii. p. 258 (Eng. Trans.). According to the *Didache* the Lord's Prayer was to be said three times every day (*Did.* viii.).

[4] 1 Cor. xiv. 16.

THE MEETING FOR EDIFICATION

have composed or selected hymns at home which they wish to be sung by the congregation.[1] Several of these hymns are preserved in the New Testament, and one is embodied in one of our Scotch paraphrases:[2]—

> To Him be power divine ascribed,
> And endless blessings paid;
> Salvation, glory, joy, remain
> For ever on His Head.
>
> Thou hast redeemed us with Thy Blood,
> And set the prisoners free;

---

[1] 1 Cor. xiv. 26.

[2] If it be permitted, as I think it is, to believe that the author of the Apocalypse used the outline of the Christian worship of the earliest age as the canvas on which he painted his glorious prophetic visions, then we can disentangle many a short hymn used in the services of the apostolic Church and also get many a detail about that service. The paraphrase quoted above combines two of the songs given in Revelation (v. 9–13). We have another in xv. 3 f.:—

> Great and marvellous are Thy works,
> O Lord God the Almighty;
> Righteous and true are Thy ways,
> Thou King of the Ages.
> Who shall not fear Thee, O Lord, and glorify Thy Name?
> For Thou only art Holy;
> All the Nations shall come and worship before Thee;
> For Thy righteous acts have been made manifest;

and yet another in xi. 17:—

> We give Thee thanks, O Lord God, the Almighty,
> Which art and which wast;
> Because Thou hast taken Thy great power and didst reign;
> And the Nations were wroth,
> And Thy wrath came,
> And the time of the dead to be judged,
> And the time to give their reward to Thy servants,
> To the prophets and to the saints,
> And to them that fear Thy Name,
> The small and the great;
> And to them who destroy the earth.

It is likely that the singing was antiphonal; there are alternate strophes in the hymns in the heavenly worship, and Pliny says that the Christians " carmen Christo quasi Deo dicere secum invicem " (Ep. 96 [97]).

> Thou mad'st us kings and priests to God,
> And we shall reign with Thee.
> * * * * *
> To Him that sits upon the throne
> The God whom we adore,
> And to the Lamb that once was slain;
> Be glory evermore.[1]

After the hymns came reading from the Old Testament Scriptures, and readings or recitations concerning the life and death, the sayings and deeds of Jesus.[2] Then came the "instruction"—sober words for edification, based on what had been read, and coming either from the gift of "wisdom," or from that intuitive power of seeing into the heart of spiritual things which the apostle calls "knowledge."[3] Then came the moment of greatest expectancy. It was the time for the prophets, men who believed themselves and were believed by their brethren to be specially taught by the Holy Spirit, to take part. They started forward, the gifted men, so eager to impart what had been given them, that sometimes two or more rose at once and spoke together;[4] and sometimes when one was speaking the message came to another, and he leapt to his feet,[5] increasing the emotion

---

[1] *Scotch Paraphrases*, lxv, 7-11.

[2] St. Paul does not mention the reading of Scripture in his order of worship; but it must have been there. In his epistles to the Corinthians, to confine ourselves to them, he implies such a knowledge of the Old Testament and of deeds and sayings of Jesus as could only be got from the continuous public reading of the Scriptures, and the reciting sentences about Jesus. He takes it for granted that the Old Testament Scriptures are known and known to be the law for life and conduct, in 1 Cor. vi. 16; ix. 8-13; xiv. 21; 2 Cor. vi. 16, 18; viii. 15; ix. 9. In the beginning of 1 Cor. xv. he clearly refers to formal statements, not yet perhaps committed to writing, which he himself had handed over as he had received them, and which recited the facts about the sayings and deeds of Jesus. The opening and reading from the book comes after the singing in the heavenly worship (Rev. v. vi.).

[3] Instruction ($\delta\iota\delta\alpha\chi\acute{\eta}$), teaching or doctrine includes the "wisdom" and "knowledge" of 1 Cor. xii. 8; "wisdom," ($\lambda\acute{o}\gamma o\varsigma\ \sigma o\phi\acute{\iota}\alpha\varsigma$) is described in 1 Cor. ii. 7; vi. 5; and "knowledge" ($\lambda\acute{o}\gamma o\varsigma\ \gamma\nu\acute{\omega}\sigma\epsilon\omega\varsigma$) in 2 Cor. x. 5; xi. 6; and perhaps the $\pi\acute{\iota}\sigma\tau\iota\varsigma$ of 1 Cor. xii, 9, which may mean depth of loyal spiritual experience.

[4] 1 Cor. xiv. 31.   [5] 1 Cor. xiv. 30.

THE MEETING FOR EDIFICATION

and taking from the edification. When the prophets were silent, first one, then another, and sometimes two at once, began strange ejaculatory prayers,[1] in sentences so rugged and disjointed that the audience for the most part could not understand, and had to wait till some of their number, who could follow the strange utterances, were ready to translate them into intelligible language.[2] Then followed the benediction: "The Grace of the Lord Jesus be with you all"; the "kiss of peace"; and the congregation dispersed. Sometimes during the meeting, at some part of the services, but oftenest when the prophets were speaking, there was a stir at the back of the room, and a heathen, who had been listening in careless curiosity or in barely concealed scorn, suddenly felt the sinful secrets of his own heart revealed to him, and pushing forward fell down at the feet of the speaker and made his confession,[3] while the assembly raised the doxology: "Blessed be God, the Father of the Lord Jesus, for evermore.[4] Amen."

[1] I have followed Weizsäcker's conception of what was meant by speaking "in a tongue." These things have to be noted about the phenomenon. It occurred in prayer only (1 Cor. xiv. 2, 14); it appeared like a soliloquy (1 Cor. xiv. 2); the speaker edified himself (xiv. 4), but seems to have lost conscious control over himself (xiv. 14); what was said was not intelligible to others (xiv. 2); it could be compared to the sound of a trumpet which gave no clear call (xiv. 7, 8); or to the use of a foreign and barbarous language (xiv. 10, 11); the speaker in a tongue ought to interpret what he has said, and that he may be able to do this he ought to pray for divine assistance (xiv. 13); that such speaking was not all of one sort —there were "kinds of tongues" (xii. 10). Upon the whole then we may conceive it to have been rapt ejaculatory prayer uttered during unrestrained emotion, where words often took the place of sentences. This enables us to see how brethren, who were sympathetic enough, could follow the obscure windings of thought and expression, and interpret. Our knowledge is exclusively derived from 1 Cor. xiv.; the two passages in Acts x. 46; xix. 6, and the references in the post-apostolic period do not enlighten us. Compare Heinrici, *Das Erste Sendschreiben an die Korinther*, pp. 376-393; Bleek, *Studien u. Kritiken* (1829), pp. 3-79; Hilgenfeld, *Die Glossolalie in der alten Kirche*, Leipzig, 1850. This "gift" of tongues is referred to by Irenaeus, v. 6, and Tertullian, *Adv. Marcion*, v. 8.   [2] 1 Cor. xiv. 27, 28.   [3] 1 Cor. xiv. 25.

[4] The other form of doxology common to St. Paul's epistles is "Unto

Such was a Christian meeting for public worship in Corinth in apostolic times; and foreign as it may seem to us, the like can be still seen in mission fields among the hot-blooded people of the East. I have witnessed everything but the speaking "with tongues" in meetings of native Christians in the Deccan in India, when European influence was not present to restrain Eastern enthusiasm and condense it in Western moulds.

The meeting described by the apostle is not to be taken as something which might be seen in Corinth but was peculiar to that city; it may be taken as a type of the Christian meeting throughout the Gentile Christian Churches; for the Apostle, in his suggestions and criticisms, continually speaks of what took place throughout all the churches.[1]

It is to be observed that if the apostle finds fault with some things, he gives the order of the service and expressly approves of every part of it, even of the strange ejaculatory prayers.[2] He gives his Corinthian converts one broad principle, which he expects them to apply for themselves in order to better their service. Everything is to be done for the edification of the brethren, and the first qualification for edification is that all things be done "decently and in order," for God is not a God of confusion but of peace.[3] He gives examples of his principle. The prophets were to restrain themselves; they were to speak one at a time, and not more than two or three at one meeting;[4] and those who prayed "in tongues" were to keep silence altogether unless some one who could interpret was present, for it is better to speak five words with understanding than ten thousand in a tongue. The women too who had the gift of prophecy were to

---

God our Father, be glory for ever, Amen." These doxologies are found running through St. Paul's and other epistles in the New Testament. They are used to end a prophetic utterance, or an exposition of divine wisdom, and they occur in the description of the heavenly worship in the Apocalypse.   [1] 1 Cor. xiv. 33; xi. 16.

[2] 1 Cor. xiv. 39. The order of service is given by St. Paul in 1 Cor. xiv. 26; where the "psalm" includes the supplication and thanksgiving of xiv. 15.   [3] 1 Cor. xiv. 33, 40,   [4] 1 Cor. xiv. 29-33.

use it in private, and not start forward at the public meeting and deliver their message there. So far from finding fault with the kind of meeting described, St. Paul seems to look on the manifestation of these gifts of praise, prayer, teaching, and prophecy, within the congregation at Corinth, as an evidence that the Christian community there was completely furnished within its own membership with all the gifts needed for the building up in faith and works.[1]

What cannot fail to strike us in this picture is the untrammelled liberty of the worship, the possibility of every male member of the congregation taking part in the prayers and the exhortations, and the consequent responsibility laid on the whole community to see that the service was for the edification of all. When we consider the rebukes that the apostle considered it necessary to administer, it is also somewhat surprising to find so few injunctions which take the form of definite rules for public worship, and to observe the confidence which the apostle had that if certain broad principles were laid down and observed, the community was of itself able to conduct all things with that attention to decency and order which ensured edification.

Our wonder is apt to be increased when we remember the social surroundings and conditions of these Corinthian Christians. They were a number of burghers, freedmen and slaves, who, as their names show, were mostly of Roman origin, gathered from the wealthiest and most profligate city on the Mediterranean. The population of Corinth was as mixed as that of Alexandria. At Cenchrea, on the eastern shore of the isthmus, the wealth of Asia and Egypt poured in, and was sent off to Rome and Italy from Lechaeum, the western harbour. The flow of commerce brought with it the peoples, religions and habits of all lands. The religion of the city was a strange medley of cults Eastern and Western. Aphrodite and Astarte, Isis and Cybele, were among her deities; Romans, Jews, Egyptians and Phoenicians among her people. The familiar illustrations

[1] 1 Cor. xii. 4 ff.: cf. Eph. iv. 16.

which the apostle uses in his epistles indicate the habits of the population. He speaks of the arena and the wild-beast fights,[1] of the theatre,[2] of the boxing match and the stadium race,[3] of the great idol-feasts and processions.[4] The city, we know, was honeycombed with "gilds"—religious corporations for the practices of the Eastern religions, and trades unions for the artizans and the seamen. The Christian society was gathered from all classes; from the poor and the slaves,[5] from the well-to-do like the city treasurer,[6] and an elder from the Jewish Synagogue;[7] it included ladies of rank like Chloe,[8] and men of abounding wealth like Gaius.[9] It was this heterogenous society, including so many jarring elements, that the apostle expected to develop into an orderly Church of Christ in virtue of the "gifts" of the Spirit implanted *within* it.

2. It is by no means so easy to get a clear picture of the second meeting of the Christian community—the meeting for thanksgiving—as it is to see what the meeting for edification was like.[10] With the latter we have only to remove the blemishes which the apostle found, and the vision of the meeting as he approved of it stands clearly before us. But the abuses which had corrupted

---

[1] 1 Cor. xv. 32.   [2] 1 Cor. iv. 9; vii. 31.   [3] 1 Cor. ix. 24-27.
[4] 1 Cor. viii. 10.   [5] 1 Cor. i. 26.   [6] Erastus, Rom. xvi. 23.
[7] Crispus, Acts xviii. 8; 1 Cor. i. 14.   [8] 1 Cor. i. 11.
[9] Rom. xvi. 23; 1 Cor. i. 14.

[10] It is strange that, apart from the descriptions of the Last Supper in the Synoptic Gospels (and for obvious reasons they cannot be taken as descriptions of the way in which the Eucharistic service was celebrated in the Apostolic and post-Apostolic Church), we have no very clear account of how the Service of Thanksgiving was observed among the primitive Christians till the middle of the second century, when we have the statement of Justin Martyr in his *Apology*, i. 67. The earliest account, so far as I know, which gives as full a description of the Holy Communion as we have of the meeting for exhortation in the First Epistle to the Corinthians, is to be found in the *Canons of Hippolytus* (Gebhardt and Harnack, *Texte u. Untersuchungen*, VI. iv. pp. 118–22). Yet the whole line of the history of worship, of the organization of the local churches, and of the administration of ecclesiastical property follows the development of this part of the public worship of the Church. We can learn many details, but we have no complete account. In the account of the Last

the meeting for thanksgiving had so changed it, from what it ought to have been, that it could not serve what it was meant to do. The framework of the degenerate meeting and of the same gathering re-organized according to the apostle's directions can easily be traced. The members of the Christian community in Corinth assembled together in one place, where they ate together a meal which they themselves provided; and this meeting ended with the celebration of the Lord's Supper. The Holy Supper was the essential part. The common meal and what belonged to it were accessories, the casket to contain the one precious jewel, the body to be vivified by this soul. It was the Holy Supper that really brought them together; but their conduct had made it impossible for them to be the Lord's guests at His Table.[1] The apostle tells the Corinthians that their meeting could not be a Lord's Supper nor even a love-feast if each ate his own meal and one was hungry, while another drank his fill.[2] The common meal showed that all the brethren belonged to one living organism which was the Church in Corinth, of which the Lord was the Head. Nothing could so wound this thought as making the distinctions between rich and poor, which had been done. It banished the whole idea of fellowship, and sensuality was introduced where, above all places, it ought to have been absent.[3] God had manifested His displeasure by sending sickness and death into the congregation.[4] The apostle lays down a general principle, and gives instances of its application, which if followed out will make the common meal a fitting introduction to the Holy Supper, and then shows how the Lord's Supper itself is to be solemnly and fitly cele-

Supper, here in the Epistle to the Corinthians, in the *Didache* (x. 1), in the description of Pliny, in Clement of Alex. (*Paidagogos*, ii. 1), in Ignatius (*Ad Smyrnæos*, viii.), the celebration follows a common meal; in Justin it takes place during the meeting for exhortation; in the *Canons of Hippolytus*, the meeting for exhortation, the Holy Communion, and the Lord's day common meal are all separate from each other.

[1] 1 Cor. xi. 20.   [2] 1 Cor. xi. 21.
[3] 1 Cor. xi. 22.   [4] 1 Cor. xi. 30-32.

brated according to the commands of Jesus. If we take the principles which the apostle lays down and suggestions from other portions of the New Testament, with those which come from the earliest post-apostolic descriptions of similar meetings, we may perhaps venture to reconstruct the scene.

The apostle shows that this meeting for thanksgiving is to be a *social* meal representing the fellowship which subsists between all the members of the brotherhood, because they have each a personal fellowship with their Lord. They are therefore to eat all together, and if anyone is too hungry to wait for his neighbours he ought to eat at home. It is also to be a fitting introduction for the Lord's Supper, which both symbolises and imparts that personal fellowship with Christ which is the permanent basis of their fellowship with each other. This thought that the Holy Supper is to come at the end of it must dominate the meeting during its entire duration. From beginning to end the brethren are at the Lord's Table and are His guests.

The whole membership of the Church at Corinth met together at one place on a fixed day, the Lord's day,[1] for their Thanksgiving Meeting. The meeting was confined to the membership; even catechumens, as well as inquirers and unbelievers, were excluded. The partakers brought provisions, according to their ability. Some of the brethren, who belonged to that honoured number who were recognized to have the prophetic gift, presided.[2] The food brought was handed over to them, and they distributed so that the superfluity of the rich made up for the lack of the poor. They also conducted the devotional services at the feast and at the Holy Supper which followed. The presidents began with prayers of thanksgiving for the food prepared for them and before them;[3] it was an

---

[1] The Lord's day: Acts xx. 7; *Didache*, xiv. 1; *Canons of Hippolytus* (*Texte u. Untersuchungen*, VI. iv. p. 105, cf. p. 183 n.).

[2] *Didache*, x.

[3] The beautiful prayer given in the *Didache* is (x.): "We thank Thee, Holy Father, for Thy holy name, which Thou hast caused to dwell in our

evidence of the bounty of God the Creator; a pledge of His fellowship with them His creatures; a warrant for their continuous trust in His Fatherly care and providence; and a suggestion of the bounties of His redemption which were more fully symbolised in the Holy Supper which followed.[1] During the feast the brethren were taught to regard themselves as in God's presence and His guests; but this did not hinder a prevailing sense of gladness, nor prevent them satisfying their hunger and their thirst; God the creator had placed the food and drink before them for that purpose.[2] It did prevent all

hearts, and for the knowledge and faith and immortality which Thou hast made known to us through Jesus Thy Servant; to Thee be the glory for ever. Thou, Lord Almighty, didst create all things for Thy Name's sake, both food and drink Thou didst give to men for enjoyment, in order that they might give thanks to Thee; but to us Thou hast graciously given spiritual food and drink and eternal life through Thy Servant. Before all things we thank Thee that Thou art Mighty; to Thee be the glory for ever. Remember Thy Church, Lord, to deliver it from every evil and to make it perfect in Thy Love, and gather it from the four winds, the sanctified, into Thy Kingdom. Let Grace come and let this world pass away. Hosanna to the Son of David. Whoever is holy, let him come; whoever is not let him depart. Maranatha. Amen." This prayer was to be said at the *close* of the feast. "Now after ye are filled thus do ye give thanks" is the introductory sentence. It is also to be remembered that when prophets conducted the love-feast they were not confined to prescribed prayers. "Permit the prophets to give thanks as much as they will."

[1] The common meals which our Lord shared with His disciples were always looked upon as showing His intimate fellowship with them, and spiritual associations clustering round the thought were enhanced by His frequent comparison of the Kingdom of God to a common meal (Matt. xxii. 4; Luke xiv. 15 f.; Luke xxii. 30; cf. Rev. iii. 20). Those who had sat at meat with Him supposed that they had a claim upon Him (Luke xiii. 26); while the miraculous feeding was a picture of the providence of God which ought to awaken our continuous trust in Him. There are evidences of all these thoughts.

[2] The note of gladness is always marked. The brethren in the primitive Church at Jerusalem "breaking bread at home, did eat with gladness and singleness of heart." Acts ii. 46; cf. Acts xxvii. 33-35. "Both food and drink Thou didst give to man for enjoyment, in order that they might give thanks to Thee," *Didache*, x. "Edant bibantque ad satietatem, neque vero ad ebrietatem; sed in divina praesentia cum laude Dei," *Canons of Hippolytus* (*Texte u. Untersuchungen*, VI. iv. p. 107).

unseemly behaviour, all unbrotherly conduct in speech or action, and it insisted on the absence of all who were at variance with their neighbours until the quarrel had been put an end to.[1] During the feast hymns were sung at intervals, and probably short exhortations were given by the prophets.[2] Then when all was decently finished the Holy Communion was solemnly celebrated as commanded by the apostle.

3. It is to be remembered that the apostle regarded the community of Christians at Corinth as something more than a society for performing together acts of public worship, whether eucharistic or for prayer, praise and exhortation. It was a little self-governing republic. This made the third kind of meeting necessary. The common worship of the society, especially the eucharistic service, united it with the whole brotherhood of believers throughout the world, and showed it to be in the

---

[1] "But every one that hath controversy with his friend let him not come together with you until they be reconciled," *Didache*, xiv. In the special "Lord's day" love-feast which may be given to the poor, as set forth in the *Canons of Hippolytus*, it is said: "Ne quis multum loquatur neve clamet, ne forte vos irrideant, neve sint scandalo hominibus, ita ut in contumeliam vertatur qui vos invitavit, cum appareat, vos a bono ordine aberrare" (*Texte*, etc. VI. iv. p. 108). These love-feasts naturally became the means of helping the poor attached to the Christian congregations, as we can see in the primitive Church at Jerusalem (Acts vi. 1, 2), and from such ancient ecclesiastical manuals as the *Canons of Hippolytus*. Gentile Christians had been accustomed to pagan banquets and the more modest common meals of the "gilds," and could the more readily accommodate themselves to the Christian observance, but this familiarity with the heathen usages would the more readily lead to such corruptions as St. Paul censures in the Corinthian Church. Cf. W. Liebenam, *Zur Geschichte u. Organisation des Römischen Vereinswesens*, pp. 260-264. Liebenam thinks that the evidence goes to prove that the eating at these common meals of the confraternities was for the most part frugal and that the excess arose from over-drinking. He and Foucart (*Des associations religieuses chez les Grecs*, p. 153 ff.) have collected the evidence. The excesses at Corinth arose from the pagan associations connected either with these common meals of the contraternities or more probably with the temple banquets (1 Cor. x. 14-22).

[2] "Psalmos recitent, antequam recedant," *Can. Hipp.* (*Texte*, VI. iv. 106).

succession from the ancient people of God;[1] but it had a corporate unity of its own which manifested itself in actions for which the whole body of the Corinthian believers were responsible. This local unity took shape in the meeting of the congregation which is expressly called the "Church"[2] by the apostle, at which all the members apparently had the right of appearing and taking part in the discussion and voting—women at first as well as men.

This meeting had charge of the discipline of the congregation and of the fraternal relations between the community and other Christian communities. Letters seeking apostolic advice were prepared and dispatched in its name;[3] it appointed delegates to represent the church and gave them letters of commendation,[4] and in all probability it took charge of the money gathered in the great collection for the poor saints at Jerusalem.[5] The whole administration of the external affairs of the congregation was under its control; and this was a work of very great importance, because it was this fraternal intercourse that made visible the essential unity of the whole Church of Christ.

It exercised the same complete control over the internal administration of the affairs of the congregation. It expelled unworthy members;[6] it deliberated upon and came to conclusions about the restoration of brethren who had fallen away and showed signs of repentance.[7] It arrived at its decisions when necessary by voting, and the vote of the majority decided the case.[8] We hear nothing in the epistles of a common congregational fund for purposes common to the brethren; if such existed it was probably under the care of this meeting also.

All these things implied independent self-government; and the apostle asks the brethren to undertake another task which shows even more clearly how independent and autonomous he

---

[1] 1 Cor. x. 1-4.   [2] 1 Cor. xiv. 19, 34, 35; xi. 18.
[3] 1 Cor. vii. 1. The epistle known as the *First Epistle of Clement* begins: "The Church of Rome to the Church of Corinth, elect and consecrate, greeting.".   [4] 2 Cor. iii. 1, 2; viii. 19.   [5] 1 Cor. xvi. 1-2.
[6] 1 Cor. v. 1-8.   [7] 2 Cor. ii. 6-9.   [8] 2 Cor. ii. 6.

expected the congregation to be. He censured Christians for bringing their fellow-believers before the ordinary law-courts should disputes arise between brethren; he urged that such matters should be settled within the congregation. He used stronger language about this than about any other side of the practical expression of their religious life. "Dare any of you," he says, "having a matter against his neighbour, go to law before the unrighteous, and not before the saints?"[1] To grasp the full significance of his meaning we must remember that the apostle is speaking to men living in the busiest commercial city of the age, and to a little community within it which included city officials, merchants, and artizans, as well as slaves. He is not addressing men belonging to a small rural village where life is simple and the occasions of dispute few and mainly personal. The Christians of Corinth lived in the grasp of a highly artificial and complicated commercial life, where the complexity of affairs offered any number of points at which differences of opinion might honestly arise between brethren

---

[1] 1 Cor. vi. 1. This advice of St. Paul passed into the ecclesiastical legislation of the primitive Church. We read in the *Apostolic Constitutions* (II. xlvi. xlvii. xlviii. xlix.): "Let not therefore the heathen know of your differences among one another, nor do you receive unbelievers as witnesses against yourselves, nor be judged by them . . . but render unto Caesar the things that are Caesar's . . . as tribute, taxes or poll-money. . . . Let your judicatures be held on the second day of the week, that if any controversy arise about your sentence, having an interval till the Sabbath, you may be able to set the controversy right and to reduce those to peace who have the contests one with another before the Lord's day. Let the deacons and the elders be present at your judicatures, to judge without acceptance of persons, as men of God with clear conscience. . . . Do not pass the same sentence for every sin, but one suitable to each crime, distinguishing all the several sorts of offences with much prudence, the great from the little. Treat a wicked action after one manner, and a wicked word after another; a bare intention still otherwise . . . Some thou shalt curb with threatenings only; some thou shalt punish with fines to the poor; some thou shalt mortify with fastings; others shalt thou separate according to the greatness of their several crimes. . . . When the parties are both present (for we will not call them brethren until they receive each other in peace) examine diligently concerning those who appear before you. . . ."

related as masters and servants, buyers and sellers, traders and carriers. It was men living in these surroundings whom the apostle ordered to abstain from going before the ordinary law courts for the purpose of settling disputes which might arise between them, and whom he commanded to create tribunals within the community before which they were to bring all differences. Have they not one single "wise man," he asks, among them who could act as judge?[1] We are apt to forget that Christianity came to establish a new social living as well as a religion, and that from the first it demanded that all the relations between man and man ought to be regulated on Christian principles. That means now that our national laws ought to conform to the principles of the Gospel; it meant then that all disputes were to be settled within the Christian community, and that nothing was to be taken before the heathen tribunals.

Such is the picture of a Christian church in the Apostolic age, as it appears in the pages of the Epistles of St. Paul to the Corinthians, and, although no such clear outline is given us of any other Christian community, still we are warranted, as we shall see, in assuming that the Church in Corinth did not differ much from the other churches which came into being through the mission work of the great apostle to the Gentiles.[2] We see a little self-governing republic—a tiny island in a sea of surrounding paganism—with an active, eager, enthusiastic life of its own. It has its meetings for edification, open to all who care to attend, where the conversions are made which multiply the little community; its quieter meetings for thanksgiving, where none but the believing brethren assemble, and where the common meal enshrines the Holy Supper as the common fellowship among the brethren embodies the personal but not solitary fellowship which each believer has with the Redeemer; its business meetings where it rules its members

---

[1] 1 Cor. vi. 5.

[2] Compare Weizsäcker's *The Apostolic Age*, ii. 246-290. Heinrici, *Das Erste Sendschreiben des Apostels Paulus an die Korinther*, *passim*.

in the true democratic fashion of a little village republic, and attaches itself to other brotherhoods who share the same faith and hope, trust in and live for the same Saviour, and have things in common in this world as well as beyond it. The meeting for thanksgiving represents the centre of spiritual repose, the quiet source of active life and service; the meeting for edification, the enthusiastic, eager, aggressive side of the life and work; and the business meeting, the deliberative and practical action of men who recognize that they are in the world though not of it.

We can see our brethren in the faith living, loving, working together, quarrelling and making it up again, across these long centuries, and all very human as we are.

The evidence for the independence and self-government of the churches to which St. Paul addressed his epistles is so overwhelming that it is impossible even to imagine the presence within them of any ecclesiastical authority with an origin and power independent of the assembly of the congregation, and the apostle does not make the slightest allusion to any such governing or controlling authority, whether vested in one man or in a group of men. The apostle was so filled with the sense of high rank to which all Christians are raised in being called to be "sons of God" through Jesus Christ, that in his view this sublime position makes all believers of equal standing no matter with what spiritual gifts and natural abilities particular individuals may be endowed.[1] It was a natural and practical consequence of this thought that all believers should share the responsibilities of control in the community to which they belonged. So we find it as a matter of fact in the churches to which St. Paul addressed his epistles. He did not write to ecclesiastical persons to whom the brethren owed obedience as to an authority different from, and superior to, the assembly of the congregation. He addressed his letters to the whole community, who, in his eyes, are responsible for the progress

[1] Gal. iii. 26-28; cf. 1 Cor. xii. xiii.

and good behaviour as for the misdeeds and decline of the society and of individual Christians within it. His letters are quite consistent with the existence of ministering officials who owe their position to the assembly and are responsible in the last resort to it; but they are not consistent with the existence within the community of any authority whose power comes directly from a source outside the brotherhood.

In his letters to the Church at Corinth, the apostle makes scant allusion to office-bearers of any kind. The meeting of the congregation is the one thing which gathers up the unity of administration within the community. The apostle appears to acquiesce in this state of matters, unless we consider the query as to whether there are no wise men within the society who can settle disputes within the brotherhood to be a suggestion that some kind of recognized officials are needed for the furtherance of the orderly life of the local church. In verses 3-15 of the last chapter of the Epistle to the Romans, whether these be a short letter addressed to the Church at Ephesus, as some think, or whether they be an integral part of the letter to "all that be in Rome, beloved of God, called to be saints," the apostle addresses Christians who appear to be living in an even less organized condition of Christian fellowship. They form a unity because of their common faith and love; but that unity does not appear to find expression even in one common congregational meeting. Little companies, to whom the apostle unhesitatingly gives the name of "churches," have gathered round prominent persons who appear to have been the first converts, or those who had placed their houses at the disposal of the brethren for holding meetings for worship, or those who had voluntarily done special services to their fellow believers. The same condition of things is to be found at Colossae and at Laodicea. The apostle sends greetings to persons of different sexes and positions in life, but never to office-bearers as such. Nor among his many exhortations does he allude to the need of organization under hierarchical authority, still less does he prescribe a form of organization which was to be uniform throughout the whole Church of Christ.

We do, however, find traces of an organization within the Christian communities, if we use the word in the most general way, in the Epistles of St. Paul. The meeting of the congregation is almost as prominent in the Church of the Thessalonians as it is at Corinth; it exercises discipline;[1] it selects faithful men to accompany the apostle to Jerusalem with the money brought together in the great collection;[2] it evidently has all administrative powers in its hands. But besides this, we hear of men who are called "those who are over you in the Lord," and the brethren of Thessalonica are told to value them highly for their works' sake.[3] In the Corinthian Church we hear of "gifts," of "helps" (ἀντιλήψεις), anything that could be done for the poor or outcast brethren, either by rich and influential brethren, or by the devotion of those who stood on no such eminence; and guidances or "governments" (κυβερνήσεις), men who by wise councils did for the community what the steersman or pilot does for the ship.[4] These "gifts" were bestowed on members of the community for the service of all; and men who were recognized to be able to guide wisely as well as others from whom all kinds of subordinate service could be expected, were present within the Christian community at Corinth.[5] Again the Corinthian Christians are told "to be in subjection" to Stephanas, the first convert, and others like him who have ministered to the saints and who have laboured among them, putting heart into their work.[6] In the Epistle

---

[1] 1 Thess. v. 14.   [2] 2 Cor. viii. 19.   [3] 1 Thess. v. 13.
[4] Hort, *The Christian Ecclesia*, p. 159.   [5] 1 Cor. xii. 28.
[6] 1 Cor. xvi. 15, 16. The phrase "to minister unto the saints" (εἰς διακονίαν τοῖς ἁγίοις) corresponds with the διακονεῖν τραπέζαις of Acts vi. 2. This ministry to the saints, which is connected with leadership of some kind, is expanded in the Epistle to the Romans to include liberality, showing mercy and leadership (Rom. xii. 6-8); and these three heads read like a brief summary of the qualifications of the elder or episcopus enumerated in the First Epistle to Timothy (1 Tim. iii. 1-9). In the First Epistle to the Thessalonians the thought of ministry to the

to the Romans there is express mention of men who are over their brethren, and they are told to do their work diligently.[1] These references and others show us that there were men in these Christian societies who were recognized as leaders and who rendered continuous and valued services to their brethren by so doing. They may not have been office-bearers by election and appointment, but they were engaged in doing the work that office-bearers do in a Christian church.

Altogether apart, however, from the organization of the local churches, whether developed or undeveloped, we find a ministry which existed in all the churches of the Epistles of St. Paul, and indeed in all the churches of the New Testament. We meet everywhere with men who are called prophets, and who occupy a distinguished place in the primitive churches. St. Paul esteemed them highly. He placed them second to apostles in his enumeration of the "gifts" bestowed by God on the churches.[2] He exhorts the Corinthian Christians to cultivate the "gift" of prophecy, and the Thessalonian Christians are told to cherish "prophesyings." It becomes evident the more these epistles of St. Paul are studied, that teaching and exhortation, associated afterwards in a very special manner with the functions of rule and leadership, were in the hands of the prophets to a very large extent in the apostolic Church, and that no inquiry into the "ministry" of the primitive Church can omit the functions and position of prophets and prophecy.

This brings us to consider the "ministry" and organization of the churches in the apostolic age, a thing necessary to complete our conception of what a Christian society was like in these early times. The subject is interesting, but confessedly difficult. Yet we have light enough, from the writings of the New Testament and the earliest extra-canonic literature, to

---

saints includes the three heads of caring for the spiritual and bodily wants of the brethren, having oversight of moral behaviour, and leadership or presidency—κοπιῶντες, νουθετοῦντες, and προϊστάμενοι (1 Thess. v. 12).

[1] Rom. xii. 8.   [2] 1 Cor. xii. 28.

show us that it was entirely unlike anything which has existed in any part of the Christian Church from the beginning of the third century downwards.

Before we begin to inquire what this ministry and organization were, it may be useful to note two things: first, it must be remembered that our Lord has clearly intimated that leadership within His Church was to have a distinctive character of its own; and secondly, there is from the very first beginnings of organization a clearly marked separation between two different kinds of ministry.[1]

[1] If we examine the various uses of the words " minister " or " servant " or " deacon " (διάκονος), " he who ministers or serves " (ὁ διακονῶν) " ministry or service " (διακονία), and " to minister or to serve " (διακονεῖν) we have the following extensive application :—

1. The ordinary service which a hired servant renders to his master, such as waiting at table, etc., as in Luke xii. 37 and elsewhere.
2. Kindly personal attentions rendered to our Lord, as by St. Peter's mother-in law (Matt. viii. 15; Mk. i. 31; Luke iv. 39), by Martha (Lu. x. 40; John xii. 2), or by the women from Galilee (Matt. xxvii. 55; Mk. xv. 41; Luke viii. 3); or rendered to our Lord's followers and looked on as done to Himself (Matt. xxv. 44; Heb. vi. 10); or rendered to St. Paul by Timothy, Erastus and Onesimus (Acts xix. 22; Philem. 13; 2 Tim. i. 18).
3. The service of angels rendered to our Lord and to men (Matt. iv. 11; Mark i. 13; Heb. i. 14).
4. The service rendered by the O. T. economy (1 Peter i. 12; 2 Cor. iii. 7).
5. The work of our Lord Himself (Matt. xx. 28; Mark x. 45; Luke xxii. 26, 27; 2 Cor. iii. 8; v. 18; Rom. xv. 8).
6. WITHIN THE CHRISTIAN CHURCH we find the following widely extended application :—
    a. Discipleship in general (John xii. 26).
    b. Service rendered to the Church because of " gifts " bestowed and specially connected with the bestowal and posesssion of these " gifts " (Rom. xii. 7; 1 Cor. xii. 5; 1 Peter iv. 10, 11).
    c. Hence all kinds of service, whether the " ministry of the Word " or ministry not distinctly of the Word (Acts vi. 2; Matt. xx. 26; xxiii. 11; Mark ix. 35; x. 43).
    d. Specifically the " ministry of the Word " (Acts vi. 4; Eph. iv. 12; 2 Tim. iv. 5); and most frequently the " Apostleship " (Acts i. 17; xx. 24; xxi. 19; Rom. xi. 13; 2 Cor. iii. 3, 6; iv. 1; vi. 3 f.; 1 Tim. i. 12; 1 Cor. iii. 5; Eph. iii. 7; Col. i. 23, 25).
    e. Service which was not a " ministry of the Word " :—Feeding the

RULE, SERVICE, AND GIFTS

The distinctive character of leadership in the Christian Church is given in the saying of our Lord contained in Luke xxii. 26: "He that is greater among you let him become as the younger, and he that is chief as he that doth serve"; and this junction of service and leadership is maintained throughout the Epistles of St. Paul. The Corinthian Christians were to place themselves under the guidance of Stephanas and those like him who had served them and laboured among them. Those that are "over the Thessalonian brethren in the Lord" are the men who spend most labour upon them. Everywhere service and leadership go together. These two thoughts are continually associated with a third, that of "gifts"; for the qualifications which fit a man for service and therefore for rule within the Church of Christ are always looked upon as special "gifts" of the Spirit of God, or *charismata*.[1] Thus we have three thoughts:

> poor (Acts vi. 1); providing, bringing and dispensing resources in the time of famine (Acts xi. 29; xii. 25); organizing, gathering and conveying the great collection for the poor saints at Jerusalem (Rom. xv. 25, 31; 2 Cor. viii. 4, 19, 20; ix. 1, 12, 13); to which we may probably add the service of the whole Church of Thyatira (Rev. ii. 19).
>
> *f.* Services rendered by specially named men, and which probably included both the "ministry of the Word" and other kinds of service:—The ministry of Stephanas (1 Cor. xvi. 15), of Archippus (Col. iv. 17), of Tychicus (Eph. vi. 21; Col. iv. 7), of Epaphras (Col. i. 7), and of Timothy (1 Thess. iii. 2; 1 Tim. iv. 6).
>
> *g.* Men who are office-bearers in a local church and are called "deacons" as a title of office (1 Tim. iii. 8-13); men who *may* be office-bearers but who *may* get the name applied to them not because of office but because of the work they do—a work which has not yet ripened into a permanent office as in Phil. i. 1, and as in Rom. xvi. 1 ("Phoebe, our sister, who is a deacon of the Church which is at Cenchrea," and who is also called "patroness").
>
> 7. The idea of "rule" is conveyed in Rom. xiii. 4, where kings are called the "deacons" of God; and in John xii. 26; Matt. xxv. 44; Heb. vi. 10, where it is said that those who serve are honoured of the Father, and where all service done to the Church or its members is said to be done to our Lord Himself.

[1] The "gifts" (χαρίσματα) are individual capacities or excellencies laid hold on, strengthened, vivified and applied by the Spirit to service

of qualification, which is the "gift" of God; the service to the Church of Christ which these "gifts" enable those who possess them to perform; and lastly the promise that such service is honoured by the Father,[1] and is the basis of leadership or rule within the Church of Christ.

The earliest evidence we have for the beginnings of the organization of a local church is given in Acts vi., where we are

within the community. They are the natural capacities which men possess apart from their own power of acquiring them and which come from the free bounty of God the Creator. Men are not all alike; their capacities and natural powers differ; and thus when the Spirit works through these powers there is nothing mechanical in the activities set in motion. These natural endowments are laid hold on by the Spirit, strengthened by His agency, and used, each of them, for a special service (διακονία) within the Christian society. They may be the natural capacities for teaching, for evangelization, for the vision, and utterances of spiritual truths, for ecstatic praise, for leadership of men, for organization, for duties to the poor and sick, for the performance of all the practical and social duties needed for the welfare of the community. These natural endowments are seized by the Spirit and so influenced that they become the specialized "gifts" of the Spirit, and fit the possessors for all kinds of service, so that as Chrysostom says, " ἐνεργήματα καὶ χαρίσματα καὶ διακονίαι ὀνομάτων διαφοραὶ μόναι, ἐπεὶ πράγματα τὰ αὐτά" (*Cat.* 233). Lists of these "gifts" are given, none of them being meant to be exhaustive. In 1 Cor. xii. 4-11 appear: the word of wisdom (λόγος σοφίας), the word of knowledge (λόγος γνώσεως), faith (πίστις) gifts of healing (χαρίσματα ἰαμάτων), prophecy (προφητεία), workings of powers (ἐνεργήματα δυνάμεων), testing of spirits (διακρίσεις πνευμάτων), kinds of tongues (γένη γλωσσῶν), and interpretation of tongues (ἑρμηνεία γλωσσῶν). In 1 Cor. xii. 28-31 appear: apostles (ἀπόστολοι), prophets (προφῆται), teachers (διδάσκαλοι), powers (δυνάμεις), gifts of healing (χαρίσματα ἰαμάτων), helps (ἀντιλήψεις), governments (κυβερνήσεις), kinds of tongues (γένη γλωσσῶν). In Rom. xii. 6-8 appear:—prophecy (προφητεία), service (διακονία), teaching (διδασκαλία), the liberal man (ὁ μεταδιδούς), the ruler (ὁ προϊστάμενος), and the merciful man (ὁ ἐλεῶν). And in Eph. iv. 11 we have: Apostles (ἀπόστολοι), prophets (προφῆται), evangelists (εὐαγγελισταί), pastors and teachers (ποιμένες καὶ διδάσκαλοι). To these we may add "a man's capacity for the married or celibate life" (1 Cor. vii. 7). The conception of "gifts" in their relation to the Christian society is given in its widest extent in 1 Peter iv. 9-11: "Using hospitality one to another without murmuring: each, as he hath received a 'gift,' ministering it to one another, as good stewards of the manifold bounty of God."

[1] John xii. 26.

told about "seven" men being set apart for what is called the "ministry of tables," and which is contrasted with the "ministry of the Word."[1] We have thus at the very beginnings of organization a division of ministry, or rather two different kinds of ministry, within the Church of Christ in the apostolic age. Harnack calls this division the "earliest datum in the history of organization."[2] The distinction which comes into sight at the very beginning runs all through the apostolic Church, and goes far down into the sub-apostolic period. It can be traced through the Pauline epistles and other New Testament writings, and down through such sub-apostolic writings as the *Didache*, the *Pastor* of Hermas, the *Epistle of Barnabas*, the *Apology* of Justin Martyr, and the writings of Irenaeus. It is also found in the Christian literature which does not belong to the main stream of the Church's history, among the Gnostics, the Marcionites and the Montanists.[3] The distinction ceases to be an essential one or one inherent in the very idea of the ministry when we get down as far as Tertullian, but it does not cease entirely. Prophets are found long after Tertullian's time, but they no longer occupy the position which once was theirs.

The common name for those who belong to the first kind of ministry is "those speaking the Word of God," and this name is given to them not only in the New Testament, but also in the *Didache*, by Hermas, and by Clement of Rome. To the second class belonged the ministry of a local church by whatever names they came to be called, pastors, elders, bishops, deacons. We may call the first kind the prophetic, and the second kind the local ministry. The great practical distinction between the two was that the prophetic ministry did not mean office-bearers in a local church; while the local ministry consisted of these office-bearers. The one was a ministry to the whole Church of God, and by its activity bound all the scattered parts of the Church

---

[1] Acts vi. 2. [2] *Expositor*, Jan.–June, 1887, p. 324.
[3] The evidence has been collected by Harnack in *Texte u. Untersuchungen*, II. ii, pp. 111 f.

visible together; the other was a ministry within a local church, and, with the assembly of the congregation, manifested and preserved the unity and the independence of the local community. In the apostolic and early sub-apostolic church the prophetic ministry was manifestly the higher and the local ministry the lower; the latter had to give place to the former even within the congregation over which they were office-bearers.

But while this higher ministry can be clearly separated from the lower ministry of the local churches, it does not follow that these office-bearers did not from the first count among their number men who possessed the prophetic gift. Prophecy or the gift of magnetic utterance might come to any Christian, and St. Paul desired that it might belong to all.[1] The two ministries can be clearly distinguished, but no hard and fast line can be drawn between the men who compose the ministries. The "prophetic" gift of magnetic speech was so highly esteemed that it is only natural to suppose that when congregations chose their office-bearers they selected men so gifted, if any such were within their membership. This, we can see, was the case in later times. Polycarp was an office-bearer in the Church at Smyrna, but he was also a "prophet."[2] Ignatius of Antioch was a prophet.[3] Cyprian and other pastors in North Africa had the same gift, which was a personal and not an official source of enlightenment.[4] We have by no means obscure indications that what took place later happened in the earliest period. The "Seven," who were selected for the lower ministry in Jerusalem, did not confine themselves to the "service of tables," but were found among those who "spoke the Word of God" with power.[5]

[1] 1 Cor. xiv. 5.
[2] "The glorious martyr Polycarp, who was found an apostolic and prophetic teacher in our own time." *Epistle of the Smyrnaeans*, 16.
[3] *Epistle to the Philadelphians*, 7.
[4] *Epistles*, lvii. 5 (liii.): lxvi. 10 (lxviii.). [5] Acts viii. 5, 40.

CHAPTER III

THE PROPHETIC MINISTRY

ST. PAUL'S conception of a Christian community[1] is a body of which the Spirit of Christ is the soul. The individual members are all full of the Spirit, and their individual powers and capacities are laid hold of, vivified, and strengthened by the indwelling Spirit in such a way that each is "gifted" and enabled to do some special service for Christ and for His Church in the society in which he is placed. Every true Christian is "gifted" in this way. In this respect all are equal and of the same spiritual rank. The equality, however, is neither monotonous nor mechanical. Men have different natural endowments, and these lead to a diversity of "gifts," all of which are serviceable in their places, and enable the separate members to perform different services, useful and necessary, for the spiritual life of the whole community and for the growth in sanctification of every member. Some have special "gifts" bestowed on them which enable them to do corresponding services, and some are "gifted" in a pre-eminent degree. Thus, although every Christian is the dwelling place of the Spirit, and is therefore to be called "spiritual"[2] ($\pi\nu\epsilon\upsilon\mu\alpha\tau\iota\kappa\grave{o}\varsigma$), some are more fitted to take leading parts than others, and are called the "spiritual" in a narrower and stricter sense of the word.

---

[1] This is equally true of the whole Church of Christ throughout the whole world: for each local church is the Church in miniature. The relation of the prophetic ministry to the whole Church on the one hand and to the local church on the other is an instructive illustration of the visibility of the Church Universal in every Christian community

[2] 1 Cor. iii. 1; cf. Gal. vi. 1, and 1 Cor. ii. 15

THE PROPHETIC MINISTRY

These specialized gifts of the Spirit included all kinds of service, and were all, in their own place, valuable and equally the "gifts" of the one Spirit. Some of them, however, were sure to be more appreciated than others. To men and women, quivering with a new fresh spiritual life, nothing could be more thirsted after than to hear again and again renewed utterances of that "word of the Spirit," which had first awakened in them the new life they were living. Hence among the specially "gifted" persons, those who had the "gift" to speak the "Word of God," for edification and in exhortation, took a foremost place, and were specially honoured.[1] It would be a mistake, however, to call this ministry of the "Word" *the* "Charismatic Ministry," as if it alone depended on and came from the "gifts" of the Spirit; for every kind of service comes [2] from a "gift," and the ministry of attending to the poor and the sick, or advising and leading the community with wise counsels, are equally charismatic.[3]

St. Paul always assumes that this "gift" of speaking the "Word of God" required a "gift" in the hearers which corresponded to the "gift" in the speakers, and that it would have small effect apart from the general "gift" of discernment of spirits. The spiritual voice needs the spiritual ear. The ministry of the Word depends for its effectiveness upon the ministry

---

[1] Compare the τετιμημένοι of the *Didache* (iv. 1; xv. 2) and 1 Tim. v. 17: "οἱ καλῶς προεστῶτες πρεσβύτεροι διπλῆς τιμῆς ἀξιούσθωσαν, μάλιστα οἱ κοπιῶντες ἐν λόγῳ καὶ διδασκαλίᾳ."

[2] Rom. xii. 7: "εἴτε διακονίαν, ἐν τῇ διακονίᾳ," and διακονία is any kind of service in the Christian community.

[3] "Helps" (ἀντιλήψεις) and "wise counsels" (κυβερνήσεις) are placed in the same list of "gifts" with apostles, prophets, teachers and those who have powers of healing. The ministry of the local church, which is the foundation whence has come the present ministry in the Church in all its branches, was as much founded on the "gifts" of the Spirit as was the ministry of the Word. Sohm appears to ignore this in his otherwise admirable discussion of the "*Lehrgabe*" (*Kirchenrecht*, i. 28 ff.); and Harnack does not have it always before him, as it ought to be, in the dissertations appended to his epoch-making edition of the *Didache* (*Texte u. Untersuchungen*, II. ii.).

THE PROPHETIC MINISTRY

of discernment: for the "natural man receiveth not the things of the Spirit of God; for they are foolishness unto him; and he cannot know them because they are spiritually examined."[1] There was therefore in this ministry of the "Word" the exercise of a two-fold "gift" or *charisma*; on the one hand the *charisma* which enabled the speaker to declare what was the message of God, and on the other hand the *charisma* in the hearers which enabled them to recognize whether the message was really what it professed to be, a declaration of the Spirit, to receive it if it was and to reject it if it was not. The duty laid upon the speakers was to speak forth the Word of God in the proportion of the faith that was in them, or to the full measure of the Christ that was in them; and the duty laid upon the hearers was to test whether what was said to them was really an utterance of the Spirit.[2]

This "ministry of the Word" was the creative agency in the primitive Church, and it may almost be said to have had the same function throughout the centuries since. It was overthrown or thrust aside and placed under subjection to an official ministry springing out of the congregation, and it has never regained the *recognized* position it had in the first century and a half. But whenever the Church of Christ has to be awakened out of a state of lethargy, this unofficial ministry of the Word regains its old power though official sanction be withheld. From

---

[1] 1 Cor. ii. 14.

[2] The prophets who speak the "Word of God" are told to prophesy according to the measure of the faith that is in them: κατὰ τὴν ἀναλογίαν τῆς πίστεως (Rom. xii. 6); and the hearers are told to test the speakers (1 Cor. xii. 10, compare vv. 1, 4; 1 Thess. v. 21; cf. 1 Cor. x. 15; xi. 13); and in 1 John iv. 1–3 it is said, "Beloved, believe not every spirit, but test the spirits whether they be of God," etc. This *charisma* of discernment lay at the basis of the "call" given by the congregation to men to be their office-bearers: compare *Canons of Hippolytus*, ii. 7–9 (*Texte und Untersuchungen*, VI. iv. pp. 39, 40); and its use showed that the spiritual "gift" which belonged to the whole community was higher than the "gift" possessed by an individual prophet inasmuch as it was the judge of that gift." Compare Sohm, *Kirchenrecht* (1892), i. 56 ff., whose remarks, however valuable, seem too doctrinaire.

one point of view, and that not the least important, the history of the Church flows on from one time of revival to another, and whether we take the awakenings in the old Catholic, the mediaeval, or the modern Church, these have always been the work of men specially gifted with the power of seeing and declaring the secrets of the deepest Christian life, and the effect of their work has always been proportionate to the spiritual receptivity of the generation they have spoken to. The Reformation movement, which may be simply described as the translation into articulate thought of the heart religion of the mediaeval Church, and which revived in so many ways the ideas and usages of the primitive times, has expressed the two cardinal ideas of this primitive ministry of the Word, in its declaration that the essential duty of the ministry of the Church is the proclamation of the Gospel, and in its statement that the principle of authority in the last resort is always the witness of the Spirit in the hearts of believers.[1]

The divine "gift," whose possession placed men among the class of those who spoke the Word of God (λαλοῦντες τὸν λόγον τοῦ Θεοῦ)[2] gave the primitive Church its preaching ministry.[3] Those so endowed were in no sense office-bearers in any one Christian community; they were not elected to an office; they were not set apart by any ecclesiastical ceremony; the

---

[1] "Ut hanc fidem consequamur, institutum est ministerium *docendi Evangelii* et porrigendi Sacramenta" (*Augsburg Confession*, Pt. I. art. v.). "Nam sicuti Deus solus de se idoneus est testis in suo sermone; ita etiam non ante fidem reperiet sermo in hominum cordibus, quam interiore Spiritus testimonio obsignetur" (Calvin, *Instit.* I. vii. 4). "Our full persuasion and assurance of the infallible truth and divine authority thereof is from the inward work of the Holy Spirit bearing witness by and with the Word in our hearts" (*West. Conf.* i. 5).

[2] Heb. xiii. 7: *Didache* iv. 1: "My child, him that *speaketh to thee the Word of God* thou shalt have in remembrance day and night, and honour him as the Lord: for, where that which pertaineth to the Lord is spoken, there the Lord is."

[3] This statement ought to be qualified: the local presidents or προϊστάμενοι of 1 Thess. v. 12 seem to have had other duties besides merely to exercise oversight; they had also to warn and instruct,

Word of God came to them, and they spoke the message that had been sent them. They all had the divine call manifested in the "gift" they possessed and could use. They were sent for the extension and edification of the whole Church of God, and although they used their gifts in the meetings of the local communities yet they were always to be conceived as the ministers of the Church universal. Some of them were wanderers by the very nature of the work they were called to; many of them, perhaps most, did not confine themselves to one community. They came and went as they pleased. They were not responsible to any society of Christians. The local church could only test them when they appeared, and could receive or reject their ministrations. The picture of these wandering preachers, men burdened by no cares of office, with no pastoral duties, coming suddenly into a Christian community, doing their work there and as suddenly departing, is a very vivid one in sub-apostolic literature. Their presence—men who were the servants of all the churches and of no one church—was a great bond which linked together all the scattered independent local churches and made them one corporate whole.

We find in this "prophetic ministry" a threefold division. They are *apostles, prophets* and *teachers*. It does not seem possible to make a very strict or mechanical division between the kinds of "Word of God" spoken by each class of men, but it may be said that what was needed for zealous missionary endeavour was the distinguishing characteristic of the first class, exhortation and admonition of the second, and instruction of the third. In virtue of their personal "gifts" they were the venerated but not official leaders[1] (ἡγούμενοι) of every community where they were for the time being to be found, and were worthy, not only of honour, but of honorarium.[2] We can

[1] Heb. xiii. 7: "Μνημονεύετε τῶν ἡγουμένων ὑμῶν, οἵτινες ἐλάλησαν ὑμῖν τὸν λόγον τοῦ Θεοῦ."

[2] 1 Cor. ix. 13, 14; Gal. vi. 6; cf. 2 Cor. xi. 8, 9, and Phil. iv. 10 ff, "But every true *prophet* who will settle among you is worthy of his support. Likewise a true *teacher*, he also is worthy, like the workman, of

trace this threefold ministry of the Word from the most primitive times down till the end of the second century, if not later. It existed in the oldest Gentile Christian community, that of Antioch, where a number of prophets and teachers sent forth two apostles from among their own number.[1] Apostles, prophets and teachers are mentioned in the First Epistle to the Corinthians and in the Epistle to the Ephesians.[2] The same threefold ministry is given in the *Pastor* of Hermas, which dates about[3] 140 A.D., and in the *Pseudo-Clementine Homilies*, which can scarcely be earlier than 200 A.D.[4] In all these authorities we have the three classes mentioned together, and in all save one we have them in the same order. The three classes are also placed in pairs: apostles and prophets in the Epistle to the Ephesians and in the Apocalypse;[5] prophets and teachers in the *Didache* and in the *Pseudo-Clementine Letters*;[6] apostles and teachers in *Hermas* and in the Epistles to Timothy.[7]

1. Apostles. The distinguishing characteristic of an apostle[8]

his support. Every first-fruit then, of the products of the wine-press and threshing-floor, of oxen and of sheep, thou shalt take and give to the prophets." *Didache*, xiii, 1–3. Τιμή has the two meanings of "honour" and "honorarium," and it is difficult to know sometimes how to translate it; a case in point is 1 Tim. v. 17.

[1] Acts xiii. 1–3.   [2] 1 Cor. xii. 28; Eph. iv. 11.

[3] Hermas, *Simil.* ix. 15: "The thirty-five are the *prophets* of God and His ministers; and the forty are the *apostles* and *teachers* of the preaching of the Son of God."

[4] *Homilies*, xi. 35: "Wherefore, above all, remember to shun *apostle* or *prophet* or *teacher* who does not first accurately compare his preaching with that of James, who was called the brother of my Lord."

[5] Rev. xviii. 20: "Rejoice over her, thou heaven, and ye saints and ye *apostles* and ye *prophets*." Eph. ii. 20: "Being built on the foundation of the *apostles* and the *prophets*." *Didache*, xi.

[6] *Didache*, xiii. 1, 2; xvi. 2. *Pseudo-Clementines, De Virginitate*, i. 11, "Ne multi inter vos sint *doctores*, fratres, neque omnes sitis *prophetae*"; but this is a quotation, said to be from Scripture. For fuller list of authorities compare Harnack, *Texte u. Untersuchungen*, II. ii. 93–110, and tabular summary in note pp. 110–112.

[7] Hermas, *Pastor, Vis.* iii. 5: 1 Tim. ii. 7; 2 Tim. i. 11.

[8] For the meaning and work of an apostle: compare Lightfoot, *St. Paul's Epistle to the Galatians*, 7th ed. pp. 92–101; note on *The name and*

was that he had given himself, and that for life,[1] to be a missionary, preaching the gospel of the Kingdom of Christ to those who did not know it. He had received the "gift" of speaking the "Word of God," and he was distinguished from others who had the same "gift" in this, that he had been called either inwardly or outwardly to make this special use of it. The prophet and the teacher had the same "gift" in the same or in less measure than the apostle, but they found their sphere of its use within the Christian community, while the apostle's sphere was for the most part outside, among those who were not yet within the Church of Christ. They built on the foundation laid by the apostle; he laid the foundation for others to build upon.[2] The apostles were men who in virtue of the implanted "gift" of "speaking the Word of God" and of the "call" impelling them, were *sent forth* to be the heralds of the kingdom of Christ. This was their life-work. They were not appointed to an office, in the ecclesiastical sense of the word, but to a *work* in the prosecution of which they had to do all that is the inevitable accompaniment of missionary activity in all ages of the Church's history.

Our Lord has Himself shown us where to look for the origin and meaning of the term "apostle." He declared Himself to be the Apostle or *Sent One* of the Father; as the Father had sent Him, so He sent others in His name to be His apostles or *sent ones*, to deliver His message of salvation.[3] The apostles

office of an apostle; Harnack, *Texte u. Untersuchungen*, II. ii. 111-118; Weizsäcker, *The Apostolic Age* (Eng. Transl.), ii. 291-299; Sohm, *Kirchenrecht*, i. 42-45; Loening, *Die Gemeindeverfassung des Urchristenthums*, pp. 33-37; Armitage Robinson, *Encyc. Bibl.*, art. *Apostle*, pp. 264-6; Schmiedel, *Encyc. Biblic.*, art. *Ministry*, pp. 3114-3117; Hort, *The Christian Ecclesia*, pp. 22-41; Seufert, *Ursprung und Bedeutung des Apostolats*; Gwatkin, art. *Apostle*, *Hastings' Bible Dictionary*, i. 126.

[1] 1 Cor. xv. 10; Gal. ii. 7, 8.   [2] Rom. xv. 20.

[3] This appears to be the line of thought in our Lord's address in the synagogue at Nazareth. He quoted from Isaiah lxi. 1, about the one *sent* from God, and declared that He was the "Sent One" (Luke iv. 18, 21); He had come to deliver a message from the Father which was to be proclaimed in the cities of Palestine (Luke iv. 41; cf. Matt. xv. 24). He

were the representatives and "envoys" of Christ, the pioneers of Christianity. The word, therefore, lends itself to a very wide application, for in a sense every Christian ought to be an "envoy" or herald of the Master. Our Lord sanctioned the widest use of the word when He declared that whoever received a little child in His name received Himself;[1] the little ones can be and are His "envoys."

But there were concentric rings in this wide circle of application; and the men belonging to each were distinguished from the others by the kind of preparation they had received, and by the nature of the call which had come to them.

Our Lord, personally and by living human voice, selected twelve men and called them "apostles,"[2] that by personal com-

made His followers His representatives in Matt. x. 40-42 (cf. the parallel passages in Mark ix. 37, and Luke ix. 48). The two thoughts are combined in John xx. 21: "Jesus therefore said unto them again, Peace be unto you; as the Father hath sent Me, even so I send you"; cf. Clement, *Ep.* I. xlii. 1, 2; Tertullian, *De Praescriptione*, 37.

In earlier classical Greek "apostolos" meant a messenger who is also a representative of the man who sent him; in later Greek, the Attic use of the word to mean "a naval expedition, a fleet dispatched on foreign service," seems to have superseded every other. The word however was used in later Judaism to mean the messengers sent from Jerusalem to collect the Temple tribute from the Jews of the Dispersion and who were at the same time charged with the business of carrying letters and advice from the Jewish leaders in the capital of Judaism, and of promoting religious fellowship throughout all the Jews scattered over the civilized world. Hence Dr. Lightfoot says, "In designating His immediate and most favoured disciples 'Apostles' our Lord was not introducing a new term, but adopting one which from its current usage would suggest to His hearers the idea of a highly responsible mission." *Commentary on the Epistle to the Galatians* (7th ed.); *The name and office of an Apostle*, pp. 93, 94; cf. also Seufert, *Ursprung und Bedeutung des Apostolats*, pp. 8-14. But is is very doubtful if the word was in use in Judaism until after the time of our Lord, and it seems in every way simpler to believe that the Christian origin and use of the word were what are given above.

[1] Matt. xviii. 5.

[2] In Mark iii. 13-16 we are told that Jesus appointed Twelve, " whom He also called Apostles" (that is the reading adopted by Westcott and Hort) for a double purpose (the two parts of the purpose being made emphatic by the repetition of ἵνα), of being in close companionship with Him, and of sending them forth to preach and to cast out demons. This,

panionship with Him in the inner circle of His disciples, and by experience gained in a limited mission of apprenticeship among the villages of Galilee, where following their Master's example closely they preached and cast out demons, they might have the training to be witnesses for Him in the universal mission which was to be theirs after His death. Their preparation was their intimate personal companionship with their Lord and their apprentice work under His eyes. Their call was the living voice of the Master while He was with them in the flesh. These two things separated the "Eleven" from all others; they were both of them incommunicable and rested on a unique experience.

One, Matthias, who had enjoyed the personal companionship with Jesus, though in a lesser degree, and who had been an eyewitness during the Lord's ministry on earth and could testify to the Resurrection, was called by the voice of his fellow-believers and by the decision of the lot to the same "service and sending forth" (διακονία καὶ ἀποστολή).[1] His preparation was the same as that of the "Eleven," though less complete; but his call was quite different.

Another, Paul, was "called" and prepared by Jesus Himself, but in visions and inward inspirations. We have no evidence that St. Paul ever saw Jesus in the flesh, still less that he had any opportunity of converse with Him. His "call" came to him on the road to Damascus in the vision of the Risen Christ Whom he had been persecuting; it was repeated from the lips of Ananias, also instructed in vision;[2] it came to him over and over again in his lonely musings, where he was obliged to think out for himself the principles which were to guide him in

---

that they had to do, was what Jesus Himself had been doing (Mark i. 39; cf. Mark i. 14-34). Thus their training was both intimate companionship and close imitation in service. The acount is confirmed by Luke vi. 13, where He called the Twelve; by Luke ix. 2, where He sent them forth to *do* and to *teach*; and by Luke ix. 10, where we are told that they did what they had been commanded. Hort, *The Christian Ecclesia*, pp. 22-41. [1] Acts i. 25. [2] Acts ix. 10 ff.

his new life. His preparation was altogether different both from that of the "Eleven" and of Matthias. They had been gradually prepared; they had been led step by step, and had been weaned from their old life in half-conscious ways. He had been torn out of his by a sudden wrench; and his preparation had been given him in inward moral struggle and spiritual experience, in musings and visions and raptures, "whether in the body or out of the body" he could not tell.[1] It was this difference in "call" and preparation—the difference between personal intercourse with Jesus in the flesh and intercourse with Him in visions—that separated St. Paul from the "Eleven." And it was this difference that St. Paul's opponents of the "sect of the Pharisees who believed" seized upon when they refused to acknowledge his claims to apostolic authority. If we take the Pseudo-Clementine literature to represent the opinions of these men and their successors, and discern in the attacks made on Simon Magus an example of their arguments against the apostle to the Gentiles, there is abundant proof of this. The whole argument in the last chapter of the 17th Homily turns on the impossibility of trusting to information received in visions, or of verifying and authenticating them. The argument comes to a climax in the question: "Can any one be rendered fit for instruction through visions? And if you say, 'It is possible,' then I ask, Why did our teacher abide and discourse a whole year to those who were awake? And how are we to believe your word, when you tell us that He appeared to you?"[2]

In others who were called "apostles" the Spirit had implanted the inward "call" to consecrate themselves to a life of missionary endeavour, and had given them that gift of speaking the Word of God which made the "call" fruitful. Yet another class had been selected by Christian communities and sent forth to be *their* apostles, the "apostles of the churches," who were

[1] 2 Cor. xii. 1-4; Gal. i. 15-17.
[2] *Clementine Homilies*, xvii. 13-20; the quotation is from sect. 19.

also the apostles of the Master, and who were called by St. Paul "the glory of Christ."[1]

Men belonging to all these classes, and to others besides, are called "apostles" in the writings of the New Testament, where the name is by no means confined to the "Eleven," Matthias, and St. Paul. Barnabas[2] was an "apostle." He had been selected at the bidding of the Spirit by the circle of prophets and teachers at Antioch, and had been sent, with prayer and laying on of hands, to be the companion missionary of St. Paul; he is called an apostle to the Gentiles in the Epistle to the Galatians, and St. Paul associates him with himself when he claims the privileges everywhere accorded to acknowledged apostles. Andronicus and Junias were "apostles," who had been in Christ before St. Paul.[3] Silas or Silvanus and Timothy are, on the most natural interpretation, classed as apostles in the First Epistle to the Thessalonians. St. Paul and

---

[1] 2 Cor. viii. 23: "Our brethren, the apostles of the churches, the glory of Christ."

[2] Acts xiii. 2, 3: "The Holy Ghost said, Separate me Barnabas and Saul for the work whereunto I have called them. Then when they had fasted and prayed and laid their hands on them, they sent them away"; xiv. 4: "But the multitude of the city was divided; and part held with the Jews and part with the apostles (Barnabas and Paul)"; xiv. 14: "But when the *apostles*, Barnabas and Saul heard it . . ."; Gal. ii. 9: "They who were reputed to be pillars gave to me and to Barnabas the right hands of fellowship that we should go unto the Gentiles and they to the circumcision." Compare 1 Cor. ix. 5, 6.

[3] Rom. xvi. 7: "Salute Andronicus and Junias, my kinsmen and my fellow prisoners, who are of note among the apostles, who also have been in Christ before me." The phrase "of note among the apostles" has often been translated "highly esteemed among the apostles." Upon this Dr. Lightfoot remarks: "Except to escape the difficulty involved in such an extension of the apostolate, I do not think the words οἵτινές εἰσιν ἐπίσημοι ἐν τοῖς ἀποστόλοις would have been generally rendered 'who are highly esteemed by the apostles'"; and he goes on to say that the Greek fathers took the more natural interpretation and included Andronicus and Junias among the apostles. He quotes Origen and Chrysostom. The latter thought that Junias or Junia was a woman's name, and yet he numbered her among the apostles. Lightfoot, *Commentary on the Epistle to the Galatians* (7th ed.), p. 96 n.

his companions in his missionary work among the Thessalonians had received no material support for their labours, " though *we* might have been burdensome to you, being *apostles* of Christ "; and the *we* most probably includes Silas and Timothy, whose names appear with that of St. Paul in the superscription of the letter.[1] In 1 Cor. iv. 9, when St. Paul says : "I think that God hath set forth us the apostles last of all as men doomed to death ; for we are a spectacle unto the world, both to angels and to men," Apollos, on the most natural interpretation of the passage, is classed with St. Paul among the apostles who are thus set forth.[2] Epaphroditus is mentioned as one of the

---

[1] 1 Thess. i. 1, 6. Dr. Lightfoot includes Silas among those who are called apostles by St. Paul, but refuses to include Timothy: (1) because Timothy had not seen the Lord, and (2) because when the apostle mentions Timothy elsewhere he carefully excludes him from the apostolate. He writes in Col. i. 1 and in 2 Cor. i. 1, " Paul an *apostle* and Timothy the *brother* "; and in Phil. i. 1 : " Paul and Timothy *servants* of Jesus Christ." In the Pastoral Epistles Timothy is described as an *evangelist*: " Do the work of an evangelist ; fulfil thy ministry " (2 Tim. iv. 5). It is held by many, among others by Lightfoot and Sohm, that the *evangelists* of 2 Tim. iv. 5, of Eph. iv. 11, and of Acts xxi. 8 (Philip the evangelist), were men who did the work of wandering missionaries but lacked the indispensable characteristic (as they think) of an *apostle*, viz. having seen the Lord and received a commission from Him (Luke xxiv. 48 ; Acts i. 22 ; 1 Cor. ix. 1). This distinction *may* prove good for the apostolic period, though it seems doubtful that it does, but it entirely falls to the ground in the immediately succeeding times. I am inclined to conclude that there is really no distinction between a wider use of the term *apostle* and the *evangelist*. The word " evangelist " occurs very seldom. The three references exhaust the New Testament uses ; it disappears entirely in the immediately post-apostolic literature, it is not to be found in the Apostolic fathers nor in the *Didache*. When it reappears, as in Tertullian, *De Praescriptione* 4 (Qui pseudopostoli nisi adulteri evangelizatores) and in Eusebius (*Hist. Eccl.* III. xxxvii. 2, 4) it is used to describe such men as were called " apostles " in the *Didache*. On the other hand the apostles are described as " entrusted with the evangel " (Gal. i. 7, 8) ; as those who " preach the evangel " (1 *Clement*, 42) ; as the twelve evangelizers (*Barnabas*, viii. 3). Light., *Com. on the Epistle to the Galatians* (7th ed.), p. 96 n., 97. Sohm, *Kirchenrecht*, i. 42 n. ; Harnack, *Texte und Unters.* II. ii. 113 n., 114 ; *Sources of the Apostolic Canons* (Eng. Trans.), p. 16, n. 8.

[2] Lightfoot excludes Apollos on the double ground that it is extremely unlikely that he had seen the Lord, and because Clement of Rome, speaking

"apostles of the churches," (the church of Philippi), and is called by St. Paul " my brother, and fellow-worker and fellow-soldier." [1] Many scholars include James the brother of our Lord among those called *apostles* by St. Paul; but the evidence is very doubtful, and James had not the missionary work which belongs to an apostle.[2] Besides these St. Paul speaks of men whom he calls ironically " pre-eminent apostles," [3] and more gravely " false apostles," who had come among the Corinthian believers to seduce them from their allegiance to the apostle, probably from Jerusalem, furnished with letters of commendation [4] from St. Paul's enemies there, and who had insinuated that St. Paul was no true apostle. There is no reason to believe that St. Paul denied that these men were apostles so far as outward marks went. They were missionaries and had given themselves to the work; they had come furnished with credentials. In all outward respects they were apostles like many

of Peter, Paul and Apollos, calls the two former ἀπόστολοι μεμαρτυρημένοι and the latter ἀνὴρ δεδοκιμασμένος (1 *Clem.* 48).

[1] Phil. ii. 25.

[2] The evidence for including James, the brother of our Lord among those called *apostles* by St. Paul is contained in 1 Cor. xv. 7: " Then He appeared to James; then to all the apostles; and, last of all, as unto one born out of due time, He appeared to me also "; in 1 Cor. ix. 5: " Even as the rest of the apostles, and the brethren of our Lord, and Cephas "; and Gal. i. 19, which may read: " But other of the apostles saw I none, save James the Lord's brother," and would then include James among the apostles, or: " But I saw no other apostle, but only James the Lord's brother." which would exclude James. James is included by Lightfoot, Sohm, Weizsäcker (*Apostolic Age* (Eng. Trans.), ii. 294) and many others.

[3] The phrase, τῶν ὑπερλίαν ἀποστόλων, is translated in the R. V. " the chiefest apostles," which would imply that the " Twelve " were meant. But this is impossible. St. Paul would never have called the " Twelve " " false apostles, deceitful workers, fashioning themselves into apostles of Christ " (2 Cor. xi. 13), as he does the men mentioned in xi. 5 and xii. 11. The marginal reading. " those pre-eminent apostles," is in every way to be preferred. Cf. Heinrici's masterly exposition, *Das Zweite Sendschreiben des Apostel Paulus an die Korinther*, pp. 401–412; also Schmiedel, *Encyc. Bibl.* art. *Ministry*, p. 3114.

[4] 2 Cor. iii. 1.

others; but their message was false; they preached another Christ; they were among the false prophets who the Master had said would come.[1]

As the earlier decades passed the number of men who were called *apostles* increased rather than diminished. They were wandering missionaries whose special duties were to the heathen and to the unconverted. In writings like the *Didache* they are brought vividly before us. They were highly honoured,[2] but had to be severely tested. They were not expected to remain long within a Christian community nor to fare softly when they were there. They were the special envoys of One Whose kingdom is not of this world, and Who had sent forth His earliest apostles with the words: "Go, provide neither gold nor silver nor brass in your girdle nor wallet for your journey, neither two coats, neither shoes nor staff."[3] Primitive Christians insisted on as rigorous an imitation as did St. Francis, and accordingly formulated the saying into the rule that if the apostle spent more than three days among his fellow Christians, if he asked for money, if he were not content with bread and water, he was no true apostle, and was not to be received.[4]

All these men, called *apostles*, have one distinguishing characteristic: they have given themselves for life to be missionary preachers of the Gospel of the Kingdom of Christ. Hence it seems superfluous to accumulate from the epistles of St. Paul a great variety of marks of the apostolic character and work.[5]

---

[1] Matt. xxiv. 11; Mark xiii. 22.

[2] *Didache*, xi. 4: "Every apostle who cometh to you let him be received as the Lord."

[3] Matt. x. 10; cf. Luke ix. 3; Mark vi. 8.

[4] *Didache*, xi. 5, 6: "He shall not remain except for one day; if however, there be need, then the next day; but if he remain three days, he is a false prophet. But when the apostle departeth, let him take nothing except bread enough till he lodge again; but if he ask for money, he is a false prophet."

[5] Dr. Lightfoot has made a list of what he conceives St. Paul thought were the indispensable qualifications for the apostolic office:—the apostle must have been a witness of the Resurrection (Acts i. 21-23); and this was

The one distinctive feature about all of them was not so much what they were, but what they did. They were all engaged in a life work of a peculiar kind, aggressive pioneering missionary labour. The crowning vindication of their career was what they put into it and what they were able to accomplish; their courage,[1] their self-sacrificing endurance,[2] the "signs, wonders and mighty deeds" which accompanied their labours,[3] and, above all, the results of their work. It was to this last that St. Paul appealed over and over again. His Corinthian converts were *the* seal of his apostleship; he did not need written certificates from coterie or council, from Jerusalem or Antioch, for the Corinthians were his living "letter" of commendation known and read of all men.[4] He appealed to what every great missionary would point to if he were asked to justify his work, to what our Lord Himself appealed to when He was put to the question.[5]

supplied to St. Paul by a miraculous revelation; a commission received either directly from our Lord or through the medium of the Church as was the case with Matthias (Acts i. 23-26), and with St. Paul himself, who was not actually invested with the rank of apostle till he received it along with Barnabas at Antioch (Acts xiii. 2); the conversions which resulted from his work (1 Cor. ix. 2); possessing the *signs* of an apostle, which were partly moral and spiritual gifts such as patience, self-denial, effective preaching, and partly supernatural "signs, wonders and mighty deeds.": *Com. on the Epistle to the Galatians* (7th ed), pp. 98, 99.

Weizsäcker has also made a collection of the qualifications of an apostle, but he, rightly enough, considers that they were the qualifications demanded from St. Paul by his enemies, and are therefore what *they* declared a true apostle ought to possess. "According to them the candidate for the apostolate required above all to be a Jew by birth (2 Cor. xi. 22). He must have seen Jesus (1 Cor. ix. 1; cf. 2 Cor. v. 16) and been an acknowledged promoter of His cause (2 Cor. xi. 23; cf. Acts i. 21). Personal qualities, like courage (2 Cor. x. 1 ff.) and eloquence seem also to have been required. On the other hand the apostle was then expected to attest himself by certain signs (2 Cor. xii. 12), above all by miraculous powers and achievements; again by visions and revelations (2 Cor. xii. 1), and further, by attacks which could not fail to be made upon him, and by his bearing under them (2 Cor. xi. 13 ff.)." He adds, "All this would have been meaningless, if only a given number of definite individuals had been recognized as apostles.": *The Apostolic Age*, ii. 295 (Eng. Trans.).

[1] 2 Cor. iii. 12; x. 1 ff.; xi. 21.   [2] 2 Cor. vii. 5; xii. 10.
[3] 2 Cor. xii. 12;   [4] 1 Cor. ix. 2; 2 Cor. iii. 1-3.   [5] Matt. xi. 2-5.

There could not but be gradations in this wide company of apostles, and these depended on things personal and incommunicable. Nothing could take from the "Eleven" the fact that they had been personally selected and trained for their missionary work by Jesus while He was still with them in the flesh. This gave them a unique position not only within the Jewish Christian Church, but also throughout all Christendom. This also was the basis of the apostolate in the narrower sense of the term. Others might be, and were, " separated unto the Gospel of God," might devote themselves, in obedience to the " call " that came, to a life of active missionary work, and have their " call " vindicated in the abundant fruit of their labours. The Risen Christ had appeared to many others besides themselves. What separated the " Eleven " from other apostles was that the Lord, *while in the flesh*, had selected them and had spent long months in training them for their work. They were missionaries like the others, and made missionary tours like them, but this special and unique preparation which no others possessed gave them a position apart. St. Paul claimed that he too belonged to this inner circle; his claims were admitted when Peter, James and John " saw that he had been entrusted with the Gospel of the uncircumcision, even as Peter with the Gospel of the circumcision," in that memorable interview, when the older apostles gave Barnabas and Paul the right hand of fellowship. St. Paul proved to them that *his* call and preparation had been as intimate as theirs. Christ, Who " had *wrought for* Peter unto the apostleship of the circumcision," had " *wrought for* Paul unto the Gentiles," [1] and they had seen that it was so. And as his preparation had been the same, so the " call " had come to him directly, as distinctively, and as immediately from God, as it had come to the Twelve,[2] and his vision of the Risen Saviour had been as evident.[3]

[1] Gal. ii. 7-9.
[2] 1 Cor. i. 1: " Paul called to be an apostle of Jesus Christ, by the will of God." 2 Cor. i. 1. Gal. i. 1: " Paul, an apostle not from men nor through man, but through Jesus Christ, and God the Father."
[3] 1 Cor. ix. 1; xv. 8.

These two uses of the term apostle, the wider and the narrower, continued beyond the apostolic age. We can see this in the *Didache*, which carries the reference to the narrower circle in its title,¹ while in its description of the wandering " apostles " it paints the itinerant missionaries to whom the term belonged in its widest extent. We can also see it in the difficulties which the early fathers had to determine what was the number of the apostles, and who were to be included within it.²

The unique position occupied by the " Eleven " and by St. Paul was personal to themselves; it was based on a unique and immediate experience; no succession could come from it. But apostles, in the wider sense of the term, have always existed in the Church of Christ, and are with us still in the missioners and missionaries of the various branches of the Christian Church. In lands where the language of the New Testament is still spoken, the name as well as the thing survives; the missionaries and missioners of the modern Greek Church are still called " holy apostles." ³

It was the apostolate in its widest extent that was a part of the " prophetic ministry " of the primitive Church. When we think of apostles as part of the triad of " apostles, prophets and teachers," we must have in mind, not twelve or thirteen, but large numbers who were missionaries in the Church, and took the first rank in the prophetic ministry because their duty was to extend the boundaries of the Church of Christ. They all belonged to the class of those " gifted " to " speak the Word of God," men who were to be tested by the discriminating " gift,"

---

¹ The full title is Διδαχὴ τῶν δώδεκα Ἀποστόλων, " The Teaching of the Twelve Apostles."

² Compare Lightfoot, *Commentary on the Epistle to the Galatians*, 99, 100.

³ Missionaries and missioners in the Greek Church are called ἱεραπόστολοι. " The delegates of the Archbishop of Canterbury's mission to the Nestorians are regularly called apostles by the Syrians of Urmi " (Armitage Robinson, *Encyc. Bibl.*, art. *Apostle*, p. 265). So are the priests who itinerate in the Peloponnesus preaching to great open air gatherings on the market-days at such towns as Tripolitza.

but who, when received, were to be honoured and their word obeyed. The spiritual "gift" which they possessed was a personal and not an official thing; and in one sense they were all on the same level, for they had all the same "gift." But they differed in natural endowments, and the spiritual gift had been bestowed in larger measure on some than on others. Some could, and did, fill a large sphere and wield an enormous influence; others had to content themselves with a much inferior position; but whether their sphere was large or small they had the same work to do. They were the pioneers of primitive Christianity. They cannot be compared with the officials of a long established church. The only safe comparison is with the missionary of modern times, and their work has the curious double action which must characterize pioneer Christian work in all places and at all times.

They had to teach Christian morality to converts ignorant of its first principles, and this could only be done when stern command mingled with sweet persuasiveness. They had to deal with people who could but awkwardly apply the moral principles they had been taught, and had to select typical cases, and to point out how they must be decided. On the one side their action must appear to be highly autocratic; on the other their influence was entirely personal, and their only means of enforcing their decisions was by persuasion.

They had to show their converts not merely how to live lives worthy of their new profession; they required to train them in the art of living together in Christian society, and they had to do it in such a way as to foster social as well as individual responsibility. So on the one hand they can be represented as shaping constitutions, selecting and appointing office-bearers, and generally controlling in autocratic fashion the communities their teaching had gathered together; and on the other hand this very work can be truly described as the almost independent effort of the communities themselves.[1] For it is the missionary's

[1] Many of the differences, which make the Pastoral Epistles so different

business, and often the hardest part of it, to create the feelings of corporate responsibility and independent action. His work is that of a parent training his children, and dependent on natural relationship and personal character for the obedience he demanded, not that of an ecclesiastical superior with official rights to support his injunctions.

If this double characteristic inherent in all missionary work be forgotten, it is possible to take the most opposite views of apostolic methods and of the rights which an apostle claimed to have and to exercise.[1] Men, like Sohm, who dwells upon the power to command inherent in the possession of the "gift" of speaking the Word of God, search for, find and point to St. Paul's interference in the details of the life of his communities.

from the earlier epistles of St. Paul, disappear when the *missionary* character of the apostle's work is kept steadily in view.

[1] Sohm (*Kirchenrecht*, i. pp. 42-5) declares that with the "gift" of "speaking the Word of God" there went as its accompaniment the "gift" of spiritual rule, and that all "apostles, prophets and teachers" who had the one were also entrusted with the other. He shows how the apostles in the primitive church of Jerusalem led in all things: in the ministry of the "Word," in prayer, in the appointment of office-bearers (the community elected but the apostles appointed — καταστήσομεν, Acts vi. 3—and presided in the laying on of hands); and when they were absent at their missionary work James took their place. St. Paul decided for his communities questions of arrangement, sometimes by quoting a "word of the Lord," sometimes by giving his own opinion (1 Cor. xiv. 37); decided upon questions of marriage (1 Cor. vii. 10, 12), of virgin daughters (1 Cor. vii. 25, 40), and generally declared "how ye ought to walk" (1 Thess. iv. 1). Timothy and Titus, not because they were the apostle's delegates, but because they had the "gift" of the "Word," appointed to office (Titus i. 5; 1 Tim. iii. 1 ff. 8 ff.), and directed ecclesiastical discipline (1 Tim. v. 19, 20; Titus iii. 10).

Loening (*Die Gemeindeverfassung des Urchristenthums*, pp. 34, 35), on the other hand, thinks that the duties of an apostle were purely ethical: to teach believers how they should behave as Christians, and in particular what changes they had to make in their conduct (1 Cor. iv. 16, 17); when the apostle has a "word of the Lord" then he commands, but otherwise the apostle is not master of the faith of his converts (2 Cor. i. 24), and his directions are only counsels founded on his own experience; and it is with entreaties and persuasion that he asks the exclusion of a grievous sinner and the reception again of a repentant one (1 Cor. v. 3 ff.; 2 Cor. ii. 5 ff.; vii. 11 ff.).

While others, like Loening, who see the plain evidences of the independence and self-government in these same communities, insist that the apostle's whole relation to his converts was purely ethical, and had nothing to do with organization and its working. Six months spent in watching a missionary at work would have taught them how to combine their views.

No apostle stands forth so clearly before later generations as does St. Paul. His letters reveal the man, his modes of work, the authority he possessed and the way in which he used it. We may take him as the highest type of the first order of the prophetic ministry. His duties and the authority which lay behind them were what belonged to the *planting* of Christianity.

His claims to authority rested upon a double basis. He had received words, sayings and commandments of Jesus which he could hand on to his converts and which were the "traditions" which he asked them to hold fast;[1] and being filled with "the Spirit of God," i.e., one of those who were "gifted," to "speak the Word of God," he could give the authoritative interpretation of these commands, and could show the true application of the principles of Christian morality.[2] He might have demanded to be honoured for these possessions and "gifts,"[3] but he preferred to rest his claims to the obedience, reverence, and affection of his converts on the personal relation which had grown up between them and himself.[4]

He was the first who had made the Gospel known to them, and their faith in the Lord was of itself witness to his power over them and to his claims upon them; and this intimate personal relation between teacher and pupil, between preacher

---

[1] 1 Cor. xi. 2: "Hold fast the *traditions*, even as I delivered them to you."

[2] The direct command of Jesus St. Paul calls ἐπιταγή, while his own suggestions receive the name of συγγνώμη or γνώμη; cf. 1 Cor. vii. 6, 10, 25; these suggestions have a measured authority for the giver has the Spirit of God: 1 Cor. vii. 40; xiv. 37.

[3] 1 Thess. ii. 6: "When we might have claimed honour from you, as apostles of Christ."   [4] 1 Cor. ix. 2; 2 Cor. iii. 1-3.

and convert, between guide and follower on the pathway heavenward, ought to beget on their part gratitude, affection, trust and imitation.[1] He was their spiritual father, and he could claim the affectionate obedience due to a parent, while as a father he had the right both to praise and to blame, and that with severity.[2]

St. Paul never forgot that he was doing the work of a pioneer, and that his work was but half done if his communities of converts remained in a state of pupilage. He was therefore careful to cultivate their sense of personal and corporate responsibility. While he was ready to answer any questions about difficulties[3] which had arisen in the communities, he was very careful to make suggestions only, and to leave the full responsibility for the decisions to come on the shoulders of the society. Even in the case of the gross sin of incest "the condemnation he pronounces is not from a distance or in his own name only; he twice represents himself as present, present in spirit, in an assembly where the Corinthians and his spirit are gathered together with the power of our Lord Jesus. That is, while he is peremptory that the incestuous person shall be excluded from the community, he is equally determined that the act shall be their own act, and not a mere compliance with a command of his."[4]

It is not to be supposed that all the numerous apostles of the primitive Church were men like St. Paul; his natural

---

[1] Gal. iv. 13 ff.; 1 Cor. iv. 16; xi. 1; Phil. iii. 17.
[2] Gal. iv. 19; 1 Cor. iv. 14; 18–21; 2 Cor. ii. 9; xiii. 2, 3.
[3] 1 Cor. vii.–x.
[4] Hort, *The Christian Ecclesia*, p. 130; cf. pp. 84–5. For the case mentioned above, cf. 1 Cor. v. 1–13, with the conclusion: "Do ye not judge them that are within, whereas them that are without God judgeth? Put away the wicked man from among yourselves." For the authority exercised by the apostles, besides Hort as above, compare Weizsäcker, *The Apostolic Age*, ii. 297–299; (Eng. Trans.); Schmiedel, *Encyc. Bibl.*, art. *Ministry*, pp. 3116, 3117. Gore, *The Church and the Ministry* (3rd ed.), pp. 233–238, an account in which history suffers from being looked at through the coloured glass of apostolic succession. Gwatkin, art. *Apostle* in *Hastings' Bible Dictionary*, i. 126.

endowments and the large "gift" of the Spirit he possessed give him a place by himself. Yet, the due deductions made, we can see in him the type of these unknown men who were the pioneers of Christianity in the first century; men who carried the Gospel to Antioch, who sowed its seeds in imperial Rome, who made hundreds of little barren spots the gardens of the Lord. They went first; the prophets and the teachers followed in their steps.

2. While the apostle was the missionary of the primitive Church, the prophet[1] found his work within the Christian communities which had been created by the energy of the apostles. Prophecy was the universal and inseparable accompaniment of primitive Christianity and one of its most distinctive features. Wherever the Spirit of Jesus had laid hold on men, and believers were gathered into societies, there appeared among them some who believed themselves to be specially filled with the Spirit of the Master, and able to speak His Word as He wished it to be spoken. When such an one addressed them, his fellow Christians seemed to hear the Lord Himself speaking: "for," they said, "where that which pertaineth to the Lord is spoken, there the Lord is."[2]

Prophecy had its home in Palestine; the ancient prophets, with the "Word of Jehovah" on their lips, were the spiritual guides in Israel of old. It had been silent for generations, but its reappearance was expected and longed for by pious Israelites as a sign of the nearness of the Messianic time. They looked

[1] For the Prophetic Ministry compare: Mosheim, *Dissertationes ad historiam ecclesiasticam pertinentes* (1743), ii. pp. 132-308: *De prophetis ecclesiae apostolicae dissertatio*; Harnack, *Encyclopædia Britan.* art. *Prophet (New Testament)*; *Texte und Untersuchungen*, II. ii. 119 ff.; Heinrici, *Das erste Sendschreiben des Apostel Paulus an die Korinther*, pp. 347-462; Loening, *Die Gemeindeverfassung des Urchristenthums*, pp. 33 ff.; Robinson, *Encyc. Biblica*, 3883 ff.; Gayford, *Hastings' Bible Dictionary*; art. *Church*, i. 434 ff.; Selwyn, *Christian Prophets* (1899); Weinel, *Die Wirkungen des Geistes und der Geister im nachapostolischen Zeitalter bis Irenaeus* (1899)—an extravagant book.

[2] *Didache*, iv. 1.

for the return of Elijah or Jeremiah or another of the prophets;[1] and the apostles could appeal to the prophecies of Joel to explain the outpouring of the Spirit and its universal diffusion on the day of Pentecost.[2] Our Lord too had led His followers to expect a revival of prophecy. He had said that He would send prophets; had foretold that unbelievers would maltreat them when they appeared;[3] and had promised a prophet's reward to those who received His prophets.

We need not wonder then that Christian prophets arose in the Jewish Christian Church, and were to be found there from the very beginning; but what is to be remarked is that prophecy was not confined to the Jewish Church. It appeared spontaneously wherever the Christian faith spread. We find prophets in the churches of Jerusalem and Caesarea among purely Christian Jewish communities;[4] at Antioch where Jews and Gentiles mingled in Christian fellowship;[5] and everywhere throughout the Gentile churches—in Rome, in Corinth, in Thessalonica, and in the Galatian Church.[6] Prophets are mentioned by name in the New Testament writings—Agabus,[7] Barnabas, Saul, Symeon Niger, Lucius of Cyrene, Manaen,[8] Judas and Silas.[9] Women prophesied, among them the four daughters of Philip.[10] Prophecy, with prophets and prophetesses, appears in almost uninterrupted succession from the very earliest times down to the close of the second century, and indeed much longer, although it did not retain its old position. From the beginning too we find the true prophet confronted by the false, who preached a strange Christ, and attempted to turn believers away from the faith.

The primitive Church had its birth at a time when the old

[1] Matt. xvi. 14; Mark vi. 15; viii. 28; Luke ix. 8.
[2] Acts ii. 16; cf. Joel ii. 28, 29.
[3] Matt. x. 41; Matt. xxiii. 34; Luke xi. 49.
[4] Acts xi. 27; xv. 32; xxi. 9, 10.   [5] Acts xi. 27; xiii. 1.
[6] Rom xii. 6, 7; 1 Cor. xiv. 32, 36, 37 ff.; 1 Thess. v. 20; Gal. iii. 3-5.
[7] Acts xi. 28; xxi. 10.   [8] Acts xiii. 1.   [9] Acts xv. 32.
[10] Acts xxi. 9.

religions, whether Jewish or Pagan, had lost their power; when the old religious formulae no longer appealed to the hearts and consciences of men; when an immediate revelation of the mind of the Master was the one pressing religious need for which all craved. Prophecy gave this to the young Christian communities. The effect of the presence of these inspired men, who spoke soberly enough at times, and often burst forth into raptures and recited the visions they had received, can scarcely be overrated. They confirmed the weak, they admonished the lax, they edified the whole society.

The word "prophet," like the term "apostle," was used in a wider and in a narrower sense. In its widest meaning it could be, and it was, applied to all the three classes who were "gifted" to "speak the Word of God." St. Paul himself was called a prophet long after he had begun his apostolic mission.[1] He had the peculiar prophetic gift of speaking in visions and "revelations."[2] The "teachers" also had something in common with the "prophets."[3] In this wider use the whole Church was said to be composed of "saints and prophets,"[4] and the prophets when present, assumed the lead in the local churches (ἡγούμενοι).[5]

---

[1] Acts xiii. 1. Dr. Lightfoot seems to think that Saul was only a prophet until he had received the "call" from the prophets and teachers at Antioch. "The actual investiture, the completion of his call, as may be gathered from St. Luke's narrative, took place some years later at Antioch. It was then that he, together with Baranbas, was set apart by the Spirit acting through the Church, for the work to which God had destined him, and for which he had been qualified by the appearance on the road to Damascus." *Commentary on the Epistle to the Galatians* (7th ed.), p. 98. But this surely contradicts St. Paul's own statements. He claimed to have been an apostle from his conversion, in Acts xxii. 21, and in Acts xxvi. 17. Ramsay, *St. Paul the Traveller*, pp. 66, 67, answers this curious theory very thoroughly. [2] 2 Cor. xii. 1-5.

[3] The "prophet" is continually called a *teacher* and said to *teach*, *Didache*, xi. 10; and the woman Jezebel, who called herself a prophet, is said to have *taught* and seduced many in the church at Thyatira, Rev. ii. 20. [4] Rev. xi. 18; xvi. 6.

[5] Silas and Judas, who were prophets in the church at Jerusalem are called ἡγούμενοι there: Acts xv. 22; cf. Heb. xiii. 7 and above p. 73.

In the narrower sense of the term prophecy had its distinct sphere between apostleship and teaching. St. Paul, following his Master, places it second in his list of the "gifts" which God has bestowed on His Church.[1] It had its place within the congregation, and was part of the preaching ministry of the apostolic Church. In the picture St. Paul gives us of the meeting for edification, prophecy in the order of service[2] comes between the part devoted to instruction and "speaking in a tongue." St. Paul's statements lead us to believe that the prophetic "gift" was not confined to a favoured few. He expected that it should manifest itself in every community of Christians. He desired that every member of the Corinthian Church should possess it, and that all should strive to cultivate it.[3] The Christians in Thessalonica were exhorted to cherish "prophesyings,"[4] and the brethren in Rome to make full use of the "gift."[5] If he criticised the action of prophets at Corinth it was for the purpose of teaching them how to make the best of the "gift" which had been entrusted to them for the edification of their brethren.[6]

What then was prophecy? The new revelation of God in Jesus Christ, the new way of approach to the Infinite Father manifested in the appearance of the Son, had created for the primitive Christians a new life and had illumined them with a new light. It gave them a new insight into the relations between God and man, and a fresh manifestation of the bonds uniting our Father in Heaven with His children on earth. It made them see with new vividness the way of God's salvation and the duties which God required of man. There arose in the midst of the primitive Christian societies men specially filled with all this wealth of insight, and inspired or "gifted" to disclose to their fellows the divine counsels and the hidden mysteries of the faith. These were the prophets.

They were teachers. A large part of what they uttered was

---

[1] 1 Cor. xii. 28.   [2] See above, p. 46.   [3] 1 Cor. xiv. 1, 5, 39,
[4] 1 Thess. v. 20,   [5] Rom. xii. 6,   [6] 1 Cor. xiv. 29-33,

instruction, but their peculiar "gift" was distinct from that of the teacher. He had to make known the new facts and events which the Gospel had disclosed; he had to trace the connexion between these divine events, and to explain the rationale of the divine forces at work for man's salvation. He had to show the bearings of these divine facts and forces upon beliefs and ways of living. The distinctively prophetic task was different. The prophet was a producer, not an expounder simply, not a man whose task was finished when he had taught others to assimilate the divine knowledge which lay at their disposal. The prophet added something more. He was a revealer bringing forth something new. For prophecy presupposed revelation; it rested upon it; and apart from revelation it did not exist.[1] The prophet was a man of spiritual insight and magnetic speech. What he uttered came to him as an intuition of the Spirit, as if he had heard a voice or seen a sight.

This does not mean that the prophet spoke in a state of ecstasy or *amentia*. St. Paul's suggestions in 1 Cor. xiv. 29-33 imply that the prophet retained his consciousness throughout and had the power to control himself. The apostle counselled that whatever number of revelations had been received, not more than two or three should be uttered during one meeting, and that if a brother received a revelation while another was speaking the speaker should give way. Prophecy might be ecstatic, and we have evidence that it frequently was, but it was not so necessarily. Non-ecstatic prophecy lasted in the Church for two centuries, and can be shown to have existed among the Montanists, notwithstanding the accusations of their opponents.[2]

Prophecy might be based on "visions." St. Paul appeals to his own visions as well as to his "revelations."[3] The Apocalypse, which is the great prophetic book of the New Testa-

[1] 1 Cor xii. 3; xiv. 6, 26, 30, 32; Matt. xvi. 17.
[2] Cf. Ritschl, *Die Enstehung der altkatholischen Kirche*, p. 475.
[3] 2 Cor. xii. 1-5.

ment and the most conspicuous relic we have of the prophecy of the primitive Christian Church, is a series of visions seen by a prophet and related by him.[1] Sub-apostolic prophecy had its "visions" also. The *Pastor* of Hermas, a Roman presbyter or elder who was a prophet, is largely composed of "visions."[2] But "visions" were not essential to prophecy, nor do they seem to have been its common accompaniment. All inspired witness-bearing was prophecy, and we may almost say that free, spontaneous discourse about spiritual things was its essential characteristic. We learn, for example, from the *Didache* that, while a definite form of words was prescribed for the celebration of the Eucharist, the prophets were not bound to use it. They were to be allowed to "*give thanks as much as they will.*"[3] At the same time it must be remembered that the prophets were always believed to speak in a very special fashion in the name of God and with His authority. When the prophet spoke God was present, and the prophet was to be listened to as the messenger of God.[4]

There is nothing in the whole series of descriptions of prophecy

---

[1] Rev. xxii. 9.

[2] Compare the very full account of Hermas in the *Dict. of Chr. Biog.* ii. 912-927. It is interesting to notice how many of the "visions" of the sub-apostolic prophets were concerned with some question of Christian life and practice. Hermas had a vision about the restoration of repentant sinners to Church privileges (*Vis.* iii. 7); Cyprian had one about the subject which interested him most—the obedience which ought to be given to bishops; and Eusebius (*Hist. Eccl.* V. iii. 2-3) relates how while the confessors of Lyons were in prison, it was revealed to one of them, Attalus, after his first conflict in the arena, that his companion did not act wisely in prison in keeping to his ascetic living, that he told his vision to his companion Alcibiades, who gave heed to him and left off his ascetic usages, for, it is added "they were not deprived of the grace of God, but the Holy Spirit was their director."

[3] *Didache*, x. 7.

[4] 1 Cor. xiv. 25; Gal. iv. 14; *Didache*, iv. 1: "My child, remember night and day him that speaketh to thee the word of God and honour him as the Lord; for where that which pertaineth to the Lord is spoken, there the Lord is." Acts xiii. 1, 2: "Now there were at Antioch, in the church that was there, prophets . . . and as they ministered to the Lord and fasted, *the Holy Ghost said*, Separate Me Barnabas and Saul. . . ."

which have come down to us from apostolic and from sub-apostolic times to suggest that the prophets held any office, or that they were the recognized heads of local churches. Office-bearers, indeed, might be prophets; for the "gift" might come to anyone, and St. Paul desired that it should be the possession of every member of the Corinthian Church. Office neither brought it nor excluded it ; a prophet was a gift of God to the whole Church, and no community could make exclusive claim to him.

Nevertheless prophets had an important influence within the local churches of primitive times. We can see this from the Epistles of St. Paul and, from sub-apostolic literature, we can discern that their influence grew rather than diminished during the first decades of the second century. This power seems to have been exercised more particularly in the two matters of discipline and absolution or restoration to membership after gross cases of sin. St. Paul does not lend his sanction to any such special powers of interference. When he speaks of ex-communication or of restoration he addresses himself to the whole Christian community, in whose hands he takes for granted that these duties rest.[1] But in writing to the Galatian church about dealing with sinners he uses the words, "Ye that are spiritual" (πνευματικοί).[2] This term "spiritual man" or πνευματικός came to be used, in a fashion quite different from St. Paul's use, almost exclusively of the prophets ;[3] and the phrase of the apostle must have had some effect in leading primitive Christians to believe that the prophets were the persons to deal with these matters. The primitive Church early adopted the idea that certain sins, of which varying lists are given, were

[1] 1 Thess. v. 14 ; 1 Cor. v. 1–8 ; 2 Cor. ii. 5–8.
[2] Gal. vi. 1 : ὑμεῖς οἱ πνευματικοὶ καταρτίζετε τὸν τοιοῦτον.
[3] Pseudo-Clem., *De Virginit.* i. 11 : "With the gift therefore that thou hast received from the Lord, serve the *spiritual brethren*, the *prophets.*" Irenaeus, *Adv. Haer.* V. vi. 1 : "In like manner we do hear of many brethren in the Church, who possess the *prophetic gifts* . . . whom also the apostle terms 'spiritual.'"

of such a grievous kind that the sinner could not be received back again into the Christian society. They did not hold that these sins were beyond the mercy of God; but they did think that, without the direct voice of God commanding them, it was not permitted to them to restore such sinners to the communion of the Christian society. The voice of God they believed that they could hear in the judgment of the prophet; and the prophets could declare the forgiveness which the community felt to be beyond its power. Tertullian, who represents the older view, expresses this very strongly.[1] It was also believed that God dwelt in the martyrs as He did in the prophets, and that confessors and martyrs had the right to declare whether sinners ought to be absolved and restored.[2] There are evidences also that the prophets had a large share in declaring who were to be chosen to fill the posts of office-bearers in the local churches. All these things go to show, that if the statement that the prophets exercised a "despotism"[3] over the primitive Christian churches is too strong, they did possess very great authority—the authority which belongs to one who is believed to utter the Word of God.

The prophets who are referred to in St. Paul's epistles seem to have been members of the communities which they edified with their "gift" of exhortation and admonition, and this was no doubt the case with the largest number of these gifted men.

[1] Tertullian, *De Pudicitia*, xxi.: "The Church it is true will forgive sins; but it will be the Church of the Spirit, by means of a *spiritual man*; not the Church which consists of a number of bishops. For the right and judgment is the Lord's, not His servant's; God's Himself, not the priest's." Hermas, *Pastor, Mandata*, IV. iii.

[2] Sohm has collected the evidence for the right assigned to martyrs to pronounce absolution on the belief that God was specially present in His martyr, in his *Kirchenrecht*, i. 32, n. 9. The office-bearers deprived the prophets of the right of absolution and took it upon themselves in the end of the second and in the beginning of the third centuries; and Cyprian's long struggle with the confessors in North Africa ended in the overthrow of all such rights in the hands of any but the regular office-bearers in the Church.

[3] Harnack, *Theol. Lit. Zeitung*, 1889, pp. 420, 421.

But many who had the "gift" in a pre-eminent way took to wandering from one local church to another, in order to awaken Christian life and service in newly planted congregations; and the wandering habit easily grew when the services of the travelling prophets proved welcome to the infant communities. This custom was foreshadowed by our Lord Himself when He promised a prophet's reward to those who received His prophets,[1] and it evidently existed from the earliest times. Agabus wandered from church to church; we hear of his being at Jerusalem, Antioch and Caesarea.[2] Such wandering prophets might easily become apostles, and we can see an example of this change of work when Barnabas, who did a prophet's work in Antioch, was, at the call of the Spirit, sent, along with Saul, to undertake the work of an apostle or missionary in Cyprus, Pamphylia, Pisidia and Lycaonia. When these wandering prophets settled down for a time with their families,[3] in any Christian community, far from home and employment, it was but right that the community they benefited by their labours should support them. St. Paul had laid down the principle that it was a commandment of the Lord's that "they which proclaim the gospel should live of the gospel,"[4] and had said to the Galatian Christians, "let him that is taught in the word communicate to him that teacheth in all good things."[5] Primitive Christians had also the Lord's promise made to those who received His prophets.[6] Hence the Christian communities made regulations for the support of the wandering prophets who gave them that exhortation and admonition which were the things chiefly sought in the meeting for edification. The prophets were to have the first-fruits of wine and oil, of corn and bread, of oxen and sheep, of clothing and of money.[7] The local churches supported the

---

[1] Matt. x. 41.   [2] Acts xi. 28; xxi. 10.
[3] 1 Cor. ix. 5. [4] 1 Cor. ix. 14; Matt. x. 10.
[5] Gal. vi. 6.   [6] Matt. x. 41.
[7] *Didache*, xiii.: "But every true prophet who will settle among you is worthy of his support. Likewise a true teacher, he also is worthy, like the workman of his support. Every first-fruit then of the products

wandering prophets while they settled among them. In return the prophets exhorted in the meetings for edification and presided at the meetings for thanksgiving.[1]

The conception that a prophet was inspired to speak the Word of God invested him with such a sacred authority that his position would have been completely autocratic had it not been under some controlling power. This power of control lay in the fact that every prophet required the permission or authorisation of the congregation in order to exercise his "gift" among them. This authorisation followed the testing or the recognition whether the supposed prophet had or had not the true spirit of Jesus. The power of testing lay in the witness of the Spirit, which was living in every Christian and in every Christian community. For, as has been before remarked, the prophetic ministry rested on a double "gift," or *charisma*; one, the "gift" of speaking the Word, in the prophet, and the other, in the members of the Christian community, the "gift" of discernment.[2] The possession and use of this "gift" of testing preserved the freedom and autonomy of the local Christian churches in presence of men who were persuaded that they spoke in the name of God. Every prophet had to submit to

---

of the wine-press and threshing-floor, of oxen and of sheep, thou shalt take and give to the prophets; for they are your high-priests. But if ye have no prophet, give it to the poor. If thou makest a baking of bread, take the first of it and give according to the commandment. In like manner also when thou openest a jar of wine or oil, take the first of it and give to the prophets; and of money and clothing and every possession take the first, as may seem right to thee, and give according to the commandment."

[1] *Didache*, x. 7. The mode of conducting the Eucharistic meeting is quite unknown except the one fact that when prophets were present they led. It is easy to conceive a collegiate superintendence of the meeting for edification; but it is hardly possible to think of a collegiate presidency at the dispensation of the Lord's Supper. Did the prophets select one of their number to preside, or did they preside in turn? We do not know. Nor can we get out of this difficulty by supposing that the Lord's Supper was dispensed in the family, when the father would naturally preside; for St. Paul's description clearly implies a common dispensation.

[2] Compare pp. 70-72.

be tested before he was received as one worthy to exhort the brotherhood; and his decisions or admonitions on points of discipline or absolution had to be approved by the congregation ere they were enforced. The right and the duty of Christian communities to test every one who came with a prophetic message was urged repeatedly by St. Paul and in other New Testament writings. The apostle insisted that all prophets, apostles, and even himself, ought to be tested by all Christians to whom they presented themselves. He appealed to their power of judging his own message.[1] The power to discriminate between the true and the false spiritual gifts was a special *charisma* which ought to be used.[2] The Lord had warned His followers against "false" prophets, and had predicted that they would bring evil upon His Church;[3] and St. Paul, after telling the Thessalonians to cherish prophesyings, insists on their using their power of discrimination. The same command is given in 1 John iv. 1.[4] The Church of Ephesus was praised for trying and rejecting men who called themselves apostles and were not.[5] The Churches of Smyrna and Thyatira were blamed for the untested and unrejected teaching which they had permitted.[6]

There was need for testing, for if the genuine Old Testament prophecy was confronted with "gilds" of diviners and soothsayers belonging to the old Semitic naturalist religions, as well as with colleges of Jewish prophets who had retained the external prophetic characteristics, but had lost the true spirit of Jehovah,[7] the prophets of Jesus also had their rivals and their innocent or designing imitators. In that age of crumbling faiths in the Graeco-Roman world, Eastern religions were entering

---

[1] 1 Cor. x. 15; xi. 13; 2 Cor. xiii. 5, 6; cf. Rev. ii. 2; compare H. Weinel, *Paulus als Kirchlicher Organisator* (1899), pp. 18, 19.
[2] 1 Cor. xii. 10; cf. vv. 1, 4.
[3] Matt. vii. 15; xxiv. 11.
[4] 1 Thess. v. 21; 1 John iv. 1-3; cf. *Didache*, x. 1, 2, 11; xiii. 1.
[5] Rev. ii. 2.   [6] Rev. ii. 14, 15; 20.
[7] Deut. xiii. 3; Jer. xxiii. 21-32.

to possess the land. The great imperial system of roads and
sea-routes served other purposes besides the traffic of trade,
the convoy of troops, or the ordinary coming and going of
the population. Bands of itinerant devotees, the professional
prophets and priests of Syrian, Persian, and perhaps of Indian
cults, passed along the high-roads. Solitary preachers of
Oriental faiths, with all the fire of missionary zeal, tramped from
town to town, drawn by an irresistible impulse towards Rome,
the centre of civilization, the protectress of the religions of her
myriads of subject peoples, the tribune from which, if a speaker
could only once ascend it, he might address the world. It was
the age of wandering preachers and teachers, of religious ex-
citements, of curiosity about new faiths,[1] when all who had
something new to teach hawked their theories as traders dragged
about and exposed their merchandise. We need not suppose
that these men were all charlatans or self-conscious impostors.
We must not thrust aside carelessly and without question the
claims made by the prophets and preachers of many of these
Eastern faiths to the possession of a knowledge of hidden powers
and processes of nature, and of a command over them. Above
all, we must not forget the strange assimilative character of so
many Oriental faiths, which was as strong in Syria and Asia
Minor in the early centuries as it is in India now. Christianity
attracted men then as now; they were curious about it; they
seized on sides of the new religion which they could best appre-
ciate, and could so present their beliefs as to be able to plead
that they themselves were Christians of a more sympathetic
character and with a wider outlook than others. The great
cities which were the centres of trade and commerce—the
ganglia of the great empire, as the roads were its nerve-system—
Ephesus, Corinth, Thessalonica, Rome, where we find the Christian prophets most active within the Gentile Christian Church,
were the very places where this pagan Oriental prophecy most

---

[1] Compare Wissowa, *Religion und Kultus der Römer* (1902), pp. 78-83;
Boissier, *La Religion Romaine d'Auguste aux Antonins* (1878), i. 354-403.

abounded. Nothing hindered the presence of such men at the meetings for edification ; nothing prevented them from claiming to speak in the Spirit ; only the διάκρισις lying in the Christian society, only the power of discernment and testing through that " gift " of spiritual insight which was in every true Christian, and therefore in the Christian community, prevented the claims of such men to be inspired guides being admitted.

The testing was for the purpose of finding whether the prophetic " gift " was genuine or not. It had little or nothing to do with the external appearance of the prophet or with the kind of utterance which he selected to convey his message. The question was : Were the contents of the prophetic message such as would come from the spirit of Jesus ? had it the self-evidencing ring about it ? had it the true ethical meaning which must be in a message from the Master ?—something which distinguished it from everything heathenish or Jewish, something which showed that the prophet had drunk deeply at the well of Christ ?

The test that St. Paul gives : " no man speaking in the Spirit of God saith, Jesus is anathema ; and no man can say that Jesus is Lord, but in the Holy Spirit " [1] may seem inadequate and easily eluded ; but St. Paul is not delivering a short verbal creed ; he is setting forth a principle. Prophecy must be filled with the sense of the Lordship of Jesus over the believer's heart, soul and life, if it is true prophecy.[2] In the later days of the *Didache* the need for testing was felt as strongly, if not more so ;

---

[1] 1 Cor. xii. 3.

[2] The test given in 1 John iv. 1 : " Beloved, believe not every spirit, but test the spirits, whether they be of God ; because many false prophets are gone out into the world. Hereby know ye the Spirit of God : every spirit which confesseth that Jesus Christ is come in the flesh is of God ; and every spirit which confesseth not Jesus (annulleth Jesus) is not of God," also looks like a creed ; but what follows makes us see that it is to be taken as a principle which can be felt and which means much more than the form of words in which it is expressed. In both cases the statement of the test is immediately followed by an exposition of the necessity of Christian love permeating the whole Christian life.

the tests, however, took a much more mechanical aspect. The fine spiritual sense which the apostle trusted to has gone into the background and some wooden maxims have taken its place. "Not every one that speaketh in the spirit," says the *Didache* warningly, "is a prophet, but only if he have the ways of the Lord."[1] The phrase "ways of the Lord" does not, taken by itself, suggest anything mechanical, and has a flavour of the old spirituality. But the subordinate tests appear to indicate a degeneracy both in the prophetic office and in the spiritual discernment of the people. For the prophetic office and its discrimination demanded a somewhat high tone of spiritual life, and might very easily deteriorate. In this, as in other things, there is a close parallel to be drawn between the prophets of the New and of the Old Testament.

3. The third class of persons who belonged to this prophetic ministry were the teachers ($\delta\iota\delta\acute{a}\sigma\kappa\alpha\lambda o\iota$).

We can trace their presence along with that of the apostles and the prophets in the promise of Jesus, in the most conspicuous of the "gifts" of His Spirit to the apostolic church, in the records of the sub-apostolic period. Our Lord promised to send "wise men and scribes"—a "gift" to be recognized and appreciated by His followers, and rejected with hatred by those who refused His salvation.[2] St. Paul emphasized their presence, when he said that God had set in the Church "*thirdly* teachers."[3] We find them mentioned throughout the apostolic and sub-apostolic periods, holding an honoured place in the infant Christian communities.

They were not office-bearers necessarily, though there was nothing to prevent their being chosen to office. What made

---

[1] *Didache*, xi. 8: The subordinate tests are: A prophet who orders a meal in the spirit and eateth it; a prophet who does not himself practise what he teaches; a prophet who asks for money—are all false prophets. But a prophet who has the "ways of the Lord," and who practises *more* than he preaches is a true prophet. (*Did.* xi. 9-12.)

[2] Matt. xxiii. 34: "prophets, wise men and scribes." Luke xi. 49: "prophets and apostles." Cf. Matt. x. 41.   [3] 1 Cor. xii. 28.

them "teachers" was neither selection by their brethren nor any ceremony of setting apart to perform work which the Church required to be done. They were "teachers" because they had in a personal way received from the Spirit the "gift" of *knowledge*, which fitted them to instruct their fellow believers. Their more public sphere of work was in the meeting for edification, where, according to St. Paul, they had a definite place assigned to them after the praise and before the prophesyings;[1] but it may be inferred that their work was not limited to public exhortation, and that they devoted time and pains to the instruction of catechumens and others who wished to be more thoroughly grounded in the principles of Christian faith and life.[2] St. Paul gives us some indications of the work of the "teacher." The apostle always brought to the communities he had founded what may be called the "oral Gospel" of the Lord Jesus or the saving deeds of the Evangelical history, and certain institutions and commandments of the Master.[3] These were the things which he "had received," and which he "handed over" to his converts to be stored up in the retentive Oriental memory uncorrupted by reading and writing. He had added others—hidden things revealed to him because he was a prophet—which he called "mysteries," about the Resurrection or the universality of the Gospel.[4] These things he had handed over to them either "by word or by epistle."[5] To these he had added suggestions and opinions of his own.[6] All these things formed the stock of material on which the "gift" of the teacher enabled him to work for the edification

---

[1] 1 Cor. xiv. 26.   [2] Gal. vi. 6.

[3] We can see from 1 Cor. xv. 1-3, how St. Paul had made his converts acquainted with the sufferings, death, and rising again of our Lord; how he had enlarged on His character and ethical qualities (2 Cor. viii. 9; x. 1); etc., etc. He had taught them the institutions of Jesus (1 Cor. xi. 23 ff.). We have references to "commandments" of the Lord in 1 Cor. vii. 6, 25.

[4] 1 Cor. xv. 51: "Behold I tell you a *mystery*: We shall not all sleep, but we shall all be changed, in a moment, in the twinkling of an eye, at the last trump." 1 Cor. ii. 6 ff. Cf. xiii. 2; xiv. 2.

[5] 2 Thess. ii. 15.   [6] 1 Cor. vii. 6, 10, 25.

of the community. St. Paul's own discourses furnished the teachers in his communities with examples of the way in which all these stores of communicated knowledge could be brought to bear upon the faith, life and morals of the members of the local churches. He had given them a " pattern of teaching "[1] which they could strive to imitate, and which they without doubt did copy in their public exhortations or private instructions and admonitions.

From St. Paul's epistles it would appear that the apostle expected that every Christian community would furnish from its own membership, the teachers required to instruct the members;[2] but it is evident, at least when we get beyond the apostolic period, that many gifted men, whose services were appreciated, went from church to church teaching and preaching, and that without having any pretension to the prophetic gift. Justin Martyr and Tatian, well-known apologists of the second century, were wandering teachers of this kind.

Such a wandering master, we learn from the *Didache*, belonged to the class of "honoured" persons ($\tau\epsilon\tau\iota\mu\eta\mu\acute{\epsilon}\nu o\iota$), and at once attained a leading position in the community he entered or to which he belonged. He had to submit to the same tests as the prophet, but like him, when once received, he was honoured as one who spoke the " Word of God."[3]

A position such as this, carrying with it both privilege and support, would be sought after by those who thought more of the honourable position in which the teacher stood than of the serious responsibilities which his office involved, and there are warnings both in apostolic and sub-apostolic literature that the work of a teacher is not to be lightly undertaken.[4] It is perhaps worthy of remark that the " teachers " seem to have maintained their position as a distinct class of men, apart from the office-

---

[1] Rom. vi. 17 : τύπος διδαχῆς.   [2] Eph. iv. 15, 16.
[3] *Didache*, xiii. 2 ; xv. 2.
[4] James iii. 1 ; Barnabas, *Epistle* iv. 9 : " Being desirous to write many things to you, *not as your teacher*, but as becometh one who loves you."

bearers of a local church, much longer than the prophets did. In the general overthrow of the prophetic "ministry" during the second century the office of "teacher" was absorbed by the local ministry; but "teachers" apart from office-bearers seem to have maintained themselves in the Church for some centuries,[1] and some churches, notably that of Alexandria, seem to have possessed large numbers of teachers.[2]

This prophetic ministry and the peculiar place it occupied was the distinctive feature of the organization of the Church of Christ during the apostolic and sub-apostolic periods. It gives this age a place by itself, and separates it from all other periods of the Church's history; for it must be remembered that while this ministry lasted it dominated and controlled. Whatever administrative organization the local churches possessed had to bend before the authority of the members of this prophetic circle. To them belonged the right to lead the devotions of their brethren—to speak the "Word of God" in the meeting for edification, and to preside at the Eucharistic service—and to influence in a large but indefinite manner the whole

---

[1] Compare the curious sentence in the *Apostolic Constitutions* (VIII, xxxii.) which can scarcely be earlier than the beginning of the fifth century: "Let him that teaches, *although he be one of the laity*, yet, if he be skilful in the word and grave in his manners, teach;" where the reference is evidently to the instruction of catechumens. The teachers of the famous catechetical school of Alexandria were laymen during some part of their time as teachers.

The Christian communities, especially in large towns, must have needed teachers for Christian schools; for all teaching within pagan lands is closely associated with idolatry. Tertullian (*De Idolatria*, x.) has discussed the difficulties of schoolmasters amidst a pagan populace; the same difficulties attend native Christians in India now. When a Marathi boy first goes to school he is placed upon a small carpet and a board covered with red tile dust is placed before him. The image of Saravasti, the goddess of learning, is painted on the board. Then the master sitting beside him first worships Ganesa and Saravasti, and teaches the boy to make the letters which form the name Ganesa. The difficulties are exactly those which Tertullian describes.

[2] Eusebius, *Hist. Eccl.* VII. xxiv. 6: "The presbyters and the teachers of the brethren in the villages."

action of the infant Christian communities. Yet they were not office-bearers in any sense of the word. They were not elected, nor were they set apart by any ecclesiastical action to a place of rule. Their vocation was immediate and personal. They could be tested, and their ministry might be accepted or rejected, but there the power of the Church with regard to them and to their ministry came to an end.

They appear on the pages of the apostolic and sub-apostolic literature in the three classes which have been described; but the divisions, we can see, represented functions, not offices, nor can it be said that these functions were separated by any hard and fast line.

The apostle or wandering missionary was also a prophet and a teacher; his vocation required him to be all three. The prophet might become an apostle, if he gave himself permanently to the aggressive creative work which was the characteristic of the apostolic activity; and he was also a teacher, for his prophetic utterances must often have been teaching of the highest and most stimulating kind. But a teacher could fulfil the special work of his vocation without having the "gift" of revelation added to that of knowledge.

In all three classes we can discern the effects of a real outpouring of the Spirit, imparting special spiritual gifts, and creating for the service of the infant Christian communities a ministry which "spoke the Word of God" in the same sense as did the prophets of the Old Testament Dispensation. St. Paul was a prophet in the same sense that Isaiah was, and the author of the Apocalypse had visions as vivid as those of Ezekiel.[1] The one great difference between the prophesying of the two

---

[1] Compare Plumptre, *Theology and Life*, p. 90 : "Strange as the thought may seem to us, there were in that age (the apostolic) some hundreds it may be, of men as truly inspired as Isaiah or Ezekiel had been, as St. Paul or St. Peter then were, speaking words which were, as truly as any that were ever spoken, inspired words of God, and yet all record of them has vanished."

dispensations was that the gift was much more widely bestowed in the New than it had been in the Old Dispensation.

It seems to be impossible to draw any line of demarcation between the prophecy of the Old and that of the New Testament, except that the latter partook of the universalist character of the new revelation of the Kingdom which our Lord proclaimed, and the "gift" was imparted to Gentiles as well as to Jews. The same outstanding features characterized the prophets and prophecy in the two dispensations. In both cases the prophetic "call" came to the prophet personally and immediately in a unique experience; and when the "call" came everything else had to be set aside, and the "word" from God had to be spoken. It is possible to compare narrowly St. Paul and Isaiah, St. John and Ezekiel, Polycarp and Jeremiah. In neither case was the prophetic "call" a call to office in the Church. The New Testament prophets were no more presbyters or bishops in virtue of their "call" than were the Old Testament prophets elevated to the priesthood in Israel; and in both cases the regular office-bearers had to give way to and bow before the men through whom the Spirit of God spoke.

In Old Testament prophecy, as in the prophecy of the New Testament, the Spirit of God was given in a larger measure to some men and in a smaller degree to others, and in each case the natural faculties of the prophet had full play to exert themselves according to the capacities of the man. There were gradations in the prophetic order from men like St. Paul and Isaiah, who stood in the foremost rank, to the nameless prophet whom the lion slew, or the impetuous prophet who interrupted his brother in the meeting of the Corinthian congregation.

In both cases true prophecy was surrounded with a fringe of prophet life which was hostile, and which was inspired by a spirit at variance with the purposes of Jehovah and with the principles of Jesus. In the Old Testament, as in the New, there was a marked tendency towards deterioration within the prophetic order.

In both cases the power to discriminate between the true and the false prophecy, between the man who spoke full of the Spirit of God and the member of the prophetic " gild," was left to the spiritual discernment of the people spoken to. The discerning faculty was often at fault; pretenders were received by and misled the faithful. Jeremiah had to protest against the way in which the people received men who claimed to be prophets, and Origen had to repudiate the prophets, or their caricatures, whom Celsus described with graphic irony.[1] Yet this power of spiritual insight was the only touchstone, and, indeed, there could have been no other in the last resort. For men can never get rid of their personal responsibility in spiritual things.

[1] Origen, *Contra Celsum*, vii. 9: " Again inasmuch as Celsus announces that he will describe from personal observation and an intimate knowledge of the facts, the manners peculiar to the prophets of Phenicia and Palestine, let us consider these statements. Firstly, he declares that there are several kinds of prophesyings, although he gives no list of them . . . . ' The prophets,' he says, ' are many and unknown persons. They are apparently and very readily moved to speak as if in a divine ecstasy without any special occasion both at the time of service and at other times. Some go about as beggars and visit encampments and towns. Every one of them says readily and simply: ' I am God,' or ' I am the Son of God,' or ' I am the Holy Spirit. I have come; for the world is about to be destroyed; you, O men, will be lost through your wickedness. I am willing to save you; and you shall see me again coming with heavenly power. Blessed is he who now worships me. On all others I shall cast eternal fire, on cities and lands and on men. Men who do not recognize their impending judgment will repent and groan in vain; but those who have hearkened unto me, I will protect for ever.' With these threats they mingle words, half-frantic, meaningless and altogether mysterious, whose significance no sensible man could discover. For words that are vague and without meaning give every fool and wizard an opportunity of giving any particular meaning they wish on any matter, to what has been said." One must remember that Celsus was what would now be called a cultured agnostic. His statements are not unlike some criticisms of the Salvation Army preachers.

CHAPTER IV

THE CHURCHES CREATING THEIR MINISTRY

IN approaching the subject of the ministry of the local Christian communities it may be well to note these things at the outset. We have abundant evidence of the thorough independence of the local churches during the apostolic age, whether we seek for it in the epistles of St. Paul or in the Acts of the Apostles.[1] We must remember the uniquely Christian correlation of the three thoughts of leadership, service and "gifts"; leadership depends on service, and service is rendered possible by the bestowal of "gifts" of the Spirit which enable the recipients to serve their brethren.[2] The possession of these "gifts" of the Spirit was the evidence of the presence of Jesus within the community, and gave the brotherhood a divine authority to exercise rule and oversight in the absence of any authoritative formal prescriptions about a definite form of government.[3] We have also to bear in mind the general evidence which exists to show that there was a gradual growth of the associative principle from looser to more compact forms of organization.[4] Nor should it be forgotten that the members

---

[1] Compare what has been said on pp. 32, 33; 54-57.

[2] Compare what has been said on pp. 62 ff.

[3] Compare p. 33 and pp. 69 ff.

[4] This growth of the associative principle is seen in the names given to believers as a united company. The earliest title was *disciples* (μαθηταί), which implied that Jesus, their Lord, was also their teacher, and their only teacher—for Jesus expressly forbade His followers calling any one but Himself Master, Teacher, Father or Lord (Matt. xxiii. 8-10); and the command was repeated by St. Paul when he forbade the Christians of Corinth to call themselves the followers of any of the apostles (1 Cor. iii.

114   THE CHURCHES CREATING THEIR MINISTRY

of these earliest congregations of believers were well acquainted with social organization of various kinds which entered into their daily life in the world. When we remember these facts it need not surprise us that though in the end the organization of all the churches was, so far as we can see, pretty much the same, this common form of government *may* have arisen independently and from a variety of roots which may at least be guessed

3-9); The name *Teacher*, with the corresponding term *disciples*, lingered long in a sporadic way in Christian literature (for example in Justin Martyr, *Apol.* i. 13), and in *Sources of the Apostolic Canons*, vi. p. 23), and the word *disciples* occurs frequently in the Acts of the Apostles. It is a name which suggests a purely personal relationship to Jesus, and it was soon displaced in favour of other designations which implied *association* among the followers of Jesus. Among them we may select the terms *saints*, *brethren*, *the people of the Way*. The last mentioned—οἱ τῆς ὁδοῦ ὄντες—is specially interesting. It suggests a common worship and therefore an organization for worship. It implies groups of men and women, who, though far apart from each other, are united in spite of intervening space by the ties of a common worship. The Christians in Damascus and by implication those in Jerusalem, are so called (Acts ix. 2; xxii. 4). It was the name given to the Christians at Ephesus (Acts xxiv. 14); it was applied by St. Paul to himself when justifying the special services of the Christian worship as distinguished from the Jewish (Acts xxiv. 14). St. Paul himself usually employs the terms *saints* or *brethren* when he speaks of his fellow Christians. The *brethren* or the *saints* who form an independent community, whether in a house or in a town or in a province, are called by St. Paul a *Church*; and he, in his epistles to the Galatians and to the Corinthians, uses the same word to denote *all* the brethren, wherever they may be. These two terms *saints* and *brethren* are, like the phrase *those of the Way*, collective, and imply organization of some kind or other. When the *brethren* or the *saints* met together for worship the meeting or the building in which they met was frequently called a *synagogue* (James ii. 2), and this word was used not only by the judaising Christians (Epiphanius, xxx. 18); but also by the Marcionites, though they were the Christians furthest removed from the Jewish believers in Jesus. The oldest inscription stating that the building on which it is carved was used as a Christian place of worship comes from Syria, and states that the erection was a Marcionist church: Συναγωγὴ Μαρκιωνιστῶν κώμης Λεβάβων τοῦ Κυρίου καὶ Σωτῆρος Ἰησοῦ Χριστοῦ. It dates from 318 A.D. (Compare Le Bas and Waddington, *Inscriptions* No. 2558, iii. 583). Compare Weizsäcker; *The Apostolic Age*, i. 45-8 (Eng. Trans.). Harnack *Texte und Untersuchungen*, II. v. p. 25, or English Translation, *Sources of the Apostolic Canons*, p. 22, n. 10, for the use of *Teacher*. For the general question of designations, cf. Harnack, *Expositor*, 1887, Jan.-June, pp. 322-4.

if they cannot be proved. There are traces of several primitive types of organization within the churches of the apostolic age.

The first notice we have of organization within a local church is given us in the sixth chapter of the Acts of the Apostles when, at the suggestion of the apostles, seven men were chosen for what is called *the service of tables*. This took place probably in the year 34 A.D. These men were selected and set apart to take care of the poor and to administer the charity of the congregation.

It is too often forgotten that this service had not the second-rate importance which now belongs to it in ecclesiastical organization. It is plain that in apostolic times the primary duty overshadowing all others, was that those who had this world's goods should help their poorer brethren who had need. The sayings of our Lord were ringing in their ears: "If thou wouldest be perfect, go, sell all that thou hast and give to the poor, and thou shalt have treasure in heaven"; "Every one that hath left houses and lands for My name's sake shall receive an hundredfold and shall inherit eternal life";[1] "Seek ye His kingdom, and these things shall be added unto you . . . sell that ye have and give alms; make for yourselves purses which wax not old."[2] Their devotion to the invisible God was to manifest itself in practical love to the visible brethren.[3] The first duty of presbyters, according to Polycarp, was to be compassionate and merciful, "visiting all the infirm, not neglecting a widow or an orphan or a poor man";[4] and he calls widows "God's altar"—a phrase repeated by Tertullian.[5]

---

[1] Matt. xix. 21, 23; 29,   [2] Luke xii. 31-33.
[3] 1 John iv. 20.   [4] Polycarp, *Philippians*, 6.
[5] Polycarp, *Philippians*, 4: θυσιαστήριον Θεοῦ. Tertullian, *Ad Uxor.* i. 7: aram Dei. The phrase θυσιαστήριον Θεοῦ is used in the *Apostolic Constitutions* to denote widows, orphans and the poor aided by the congregation. ii. 26: "Let the widows and orphans be esteemed as representing the altar of burnt-offering"; iv. 3: "But an orphan who, by reason of his youth, or he that by feebleness of old age, or the incidence of disease, or the bringing up of many children, receives alms . . . shall be esteemed an altar to God." The phrase is almost always accompanied

These men were chosen to fill the highest administrative position which the Church could give, and were to take charge in the name of the community of the most sacred of all ecclesiastical duties. The office instituted was required by the ordinary and permanent needs of the Christian society, for the Lord had said that the poor were always to be with them.[1]

A few years later we read of money collected outside Palestine and brought for distribution among the poor of the Church in Jerusalem by Barnabas and Saul, who placed it in the hands of men who are called *elders* or *presbyters*. Unless we are to believe that the appointment of the *seven* was a merely temporary expedient, it is only natural to suppose that the duty of distributing money among the poor was performed by the men who were appointed by the Church to do it, or by others appointed in the same way and for the same purpose; and the natural inference is that the *Seven* of Acts vi. were the *elders* of Acts xi., and that we have in the narrative the account of the beginnings of the organization as a whole in the Church at Jerusalem, and not merely the institution of a special order of the Christian ministry.[2]

---

with the thought that those who receive alms are to pray for their benefactors.

[1] Dr. Hatch in his *Organization of the Early Christian Churches*, pp. 32-36 (1st ed.), has, I think, exaggerated somewhat the pauperism of the early centuries throughout the Roman Empire; but the case of Jerusalem must have been peculiar. The population of the city was largely supported by the profits the citizens made from the crowds of pilgrims who came from all parts of the Jewish Dispersion to the great festivals. Conversion to the Christian faith must have deprived the converts of this means of support and brought them into a chronic state of poverty.

[2] Dr. Lightfoot calls the attempt to identify the *Seven* with the *elders* afterwards mentioned in the church at Jerusalem a " strange perversity," although it has the support of Boehmer (*Diss. Jur. Eccl.* p. 373 ff.), of Ritschl (*Entstehung der Altkatholisch. Kirche*, 2nd ed., p. 355 ff.), and of Lange (*Apostol. Zeitalt.* ii. 75), and Gwatkin regards the idea as a possible one (*Hastings' Bible Dictionary*, i. 440, 574); it appears to me that it must be made unless we suppose that the appointment of the *Seven* was a merely *temporary* expedient to provide for an immediate necessity, or discredit the narrative altogether, which is what not even such a destructive critic

THE SEVEN AND THE VILLAGE COMMUNITY 117

The Church in Jerusalem appointed *seven* men. The apostles suggested the number. "Look ye out therefore, brethren, from among you *seven* men."[1] They are never called *deacons*; the *Seven* is the technical name they were known by. Philip, one of them, is not called "Philip the Deacon," but "Philip one of the Seven."[2] Why this name? To say with Dr. Lightfoot that the number is mystical is scarcely an explanation, and it is not likely that it was merely haphazazd. The Hebrew village community was ruled by a small corporation of *seven men*,[3] as the Hindu village is managed by the council of the *Five* or the Punchayat. The *Seven* was a title as well known in Palestine as the *Five* is now in India. The Church in Jerusalem, in founding their official council of administration, created an entirely new organization required by the needs of the young community, but one which brought with it associations which had deep roots in the past social life of the people. Modern missionary enterprise, which has the same problems of organization before it as confronted primitive Christianity, frequently sheds light on the procedure of the latter. The Church of Scotland (Established) missionaries at Darjeeling, who have based the organization of their native church on the Hindu Punchayat; the missionaries of the Presbyterian Church of England, who have laid hold on the village representative system in China; Bishop Patteson, who made a similar use of the native organizations in the South Seas—have all unconsciously followed in the footsteps of the apostles when they suggested the Jewish village government as a basis for the organization of the primitive Church in Jerusalem.

This earliest example of Christian ecclesiastical organization

---

as Schmiedel is inclined to do (*Encyc. Biblica*, art. *Community of Goods*, i. 879, 880).

[1] Acts vi. 3. [2] Acts xxi. 8.

[3] Josephus, *Antiq.* IV. viii. 14, 38; *Bell. Jud.* II. xx. 5. Compare Schürer, *Gesch. d. Jüdischen Volkes im Zeitalt. Jesu Christi* (1898), ii. 178 (3rd ed.). Schürer quotes from the *Talmud*, *Megilla*, 26a, where the "Seven" of the town also appear.

contains in it three interesting elements—apostolic guidance and sanction; the self-government and independence of the community evinced in the responsibility for good government laid upon the whole membership; and, as a result, a representative system of administration suggested by the everyday surroundings of the people.

When we trace the expansion of Christianity and the creation of Christian communities outside Jerusalem, we have no such distinct picture of the beginnings of their organization as is given in Acts vi., but there are indications of what took place. The preaching of the Gospel gave rise to Christian communities in various parts of Palestine which regarded the Church at Jerusalem as their common mother church, and all these communities together made the Church of God which St. Paul persecuted.[1] It is probable also that when this Judeo-Christianity spread beyond the bounds of Palestine throughout Syria and Cilicia,[2] the community in the capital of Judaism, presided over by its college of office-bearers with St. James at their head, was regarded as the mother church and the centre of the whole movement. They had before them the example of Judaism which appeared one visible whole centred in the great council of the elders in Jerusalem.

Further, the Acts of the Apostles relates that Paul and Barnabas left behind them at Derbe, Lystra and Iconium, communities of Christians with *elders* at their head. We are told that the apostles "appointed for them elders in every church."[3] The word, χειροτονήσαντες, means strictly to elect by popular vote. It suggests that Paul and Barnabas followed the example of their brethren at Jerusalem, and suggested and superintended an election of office-bearers, and the title "elders" (πρεσβύτεροι) was probably derived from the Church of Jerusalem. It need not have been so, however, for the word was common enough among the Greeks, and the more mature men in the congregations

---

[1] Gal. i. 13; 1 Cor. xv. 9.   [2] Gal. i. 22.
[3] Acts xiv. 23: χειροτονήσαντες δὲ αὐτοῖς πρεσβυτέρους κατ' ἐκκλησίαν.

would be naturally selected.[1] A second and very different type of organization, though capable of being joined with the first, also comes to us from the primitive Church in Jerusalem. The accounts of the earliest condition of the Church, whether taken from the Acts of the Apostles or from the Epistles of St. Paul, reveal an independent self-governing community under the guidance of the apostles St. Peter and St. John. The leadership of these two apostles is conspicuous throughout the first eleven chapters of the Book of Acts. Then there is a sudden change which is quite unexplained, and in the twelfth chapter (ver. 17) and onwards St. James, the brother of our Lord, is seen to be in a position of pre-eminence.[2] The letters of St. Paul also reveal the change, but equally give no hint of when it took place or of the causes which led to it. But if canonical Scripture tells us nothing about the reasons for the change, tradition and early Church history have a good deal to say about it. It is quite impossible to explain the continuous and marked influence of St. James, on any theory of the organization of the Church at Jerusalem which makes it borrow its constitution from the Jewish Synagogue system. When we read the story of the election of his successors we have suggestions of another and very different organization. The James, who was the recognized and honoured head of the community in Jerusalem, was the eldest male surviving relative of our Lord.[3] We are told by Eusebius, quoting, it can hardly be doubted, from Hegesippus, that after the martyrdom of St. James and the fall of Jerusalem, the remaining apostles and personal disciples of our Lord, with *those that were related to our Lord according to the flesh*, the greater part of them being yet living, met together

---

[1] Deissmann, *Bib. Studies* (Eng. Trans.), pp. 154-157. The names which afterwards came to denote fixed offices in the Church have all general as well as technical uses, and this adds greatly to the difficulty of investigation.

[2] Acts xii. 17; xv. 13; xxi. 18; Gal. i. 19; ii. 9, 12. This is confirmed by later tradition, Eusebius, *Hist. Eccl.* II. i. 2, 3.

[3] Matt. xiii. 55; Mark vi. 3; Eusebius, *Hist. Eccles.* I. xii; 4; II. i. 2, 3; III. xi. 1.

120 THE CHURCHES CREATING THEIR MINISTRY

and unanimously selected Symeon to fill the vacant place.[1] In another passage he says that Symeon was the son of Clopas our Lord's paternal uncle, and adds that " he was put forward by all as the second in succession, being *the cousin of the Lord* " ; in a third he speaks of " the child of the Lord's paternal uncle, the aforesaid Symeon, son of Clopas," and in a fourth he tells us that Hegesippus relates that Clopas was " the brother of Joseph."[2] In short he dwells pertinaciously on the natural kinship between the head of the primitive Christianity in Jerusalem and our Lord. The last glimpse we have of our Lord's kinsfolk has been recorded by the same gossipy writer, who made it his business to preserve such details, and it reveals them at the head of the Jewish Christian community. He tells us that in the fifteenth year of the Emperor Domitian " there still survived kinsmen of the Lord, grandsons of Judas, who was called the Lord's brother according to the flesh." They were dragged to Rome and brought before the Emperor. He questioned them. They showed him their hands horny with holding the plough, and said that their whole wealth amounted to about 9,000 denarii, the value of thirty-nine acres ($\pi\lambda\epsilon\theta\rho a$) of land, which they cultivated themselves and on which they paid taxes. The Emperor contemptuously sent them back to Palestine, and there they were made the rulers of the Church because they had been martyrs and *were of the lineage of the Lord*. They lived till the reign of Trajan, and their names were James and Zoker.[3]

A succession in the male line of the kindred of Jesus, where the eldest male relative of the founder succeeds, where the election to office is largely regulated by a family council, and where two can rule together, has no analogy with any form of

---

[1] Eusebius, *Hist. Eccl.* III. xi. 1, 2.

[2] *Ibid.* xi. 1, 2 ; xxxii. 4 ; IV. xxii. 4.

[3] *Ibid.* III. xx. 1–8 : τοὺς δὲ ἀπολυθέντας ἡγήσασθαι τῶν ἐκκλησιῶν, ὡσὰν δὴ μάρτυρας ὁμοῦ καὶ ἀπὸ γένους ὄντας τοῦ Κυρίου. For the names of the two young men, see the ecclesiastical historian Philippus of Side, in the fragment printed in Cramer, *Anecdota Graeca*, ii. 88.

organization known in the Christian Church. But the type of organization is easily recognizable. It was, and is to this day, a common Oriental usage that the headship of a religious society is continued in the line of the founder's kindred according to Eastern line of succession, from eldest male surviving relative to eldest male surviving relative, whether brother, uncle, son or cousin. Here again we have a Christian community organizing itself, and that under apostolic sanction, on a plan borrowed from familiar social custom.[1]

When we turn to the churches which owed their being to the apostolic work of St. Paul, we find the independence and self-government evidently taken for granted and formulated in principles laid down by the apostle in his epistles. The churches at Rome and at Corinth were churches because the presence and power of Christ were manifested within the Christian fellowship in a series of "gifts," which provided everything necessary for their corporate life as churches, organized according to any form of self-government which recommended itself to them. There is not a trace of the idea that the churches had to be organized from above in virtue of powers conferred by our Lord officially and specially upon certain of their members. On the contrary the power from above, which was truly there, was *in* the community, a direct gift from the Master Himself.

We find in the earlier Epistles [2] of St. Paul traces of men who exercised rule or at least leadership of some kind within the churches.[3] They may have been elected office-bearers or they may have been men who, without being office-bearers in the

---

[1] Dr. Harnack thinks that the position assigned to the "relatives of our Lord" in the choice of the head of the community shows that the thought of Jesus as the "Teacher" had given place to the conception of "king"; but according to Oriental usage it is precisely the position of a religious "teacher" which is transmitted in the line of the founder's kinsfolk. Compare *Expositor*, 1887, Jan.-June, p. 326.

[2] 1 and 2 Thessalonians written about 48-52 A.D.; 1 Corinthians and Galatians written about 53-55 A.D; 2 Corinthians written about 53-56 A.D.; Romans written about 54-57 A.D.

[3] Compare above pp. 60 ff.

strict sense of the words, performed services necessary for the well being of the community such as office-bearers are accustomed to do.

Even in the case of the simplest and smallest Christian communities certain services must always be rendered to the whole fellowship. Some one must provide a room for the meetings, take care of the Scriptures and other books required for the acts of public worship, keep the records of the society. The meetings need a president, if only for the time being. There is also need for services which may be called spiritual. Some one must see that brotherly intercourse is maintained, that quarrels are avoided, and that persons at variance are reconciled. The sick have to be visited, inquirers and the young have to be instructed and encouraged in the faith. Some persons have to see to all these things. They will naturally season their work with advice, admonition, warning, and encouragement. The men who begin to do these things from their love to the cause and the work naturally go on doing them; and their activity which was at first purely personal and voluntary, tends to become recognized and official. This is what may be seen on any mission field in the present day, especially in such lands as China and India, where Christianity is doing aggressive work among a civilized people habituated to work together in a society. The epistles of St. Paul reveal the same state of things. The men who are to be honoured as leaders are those who work for their brethren and put some heart into their labour (οἱ κοπιῶντες ἐν ὑμῖν). Their work might include exhortation and admonition, for the term applied to them by St. Paul is the word he used to describe his own labours,[1] or it might be work of some other kind.[2] Whatever it was, it was necessary for the foundation, growth and stability of the infant churches. The men

---

[1] 1 Cor. xv. 10: "I laboured (ἐκοπίασα) more abundantly than they all." Gal. iv. 11: "Lest by any means I have bestowed labour (κεκοπίακα) upon you in vain."

[2] Rom. xvi. 6, 12; where providing for material wants seems to be the meaning.

who laboured in these ways were the natural leaders of the community, for leadership was to be based on service, and the apostle declared that they were to be " esteemed highly for their work's sake." [1] These workers, as is the case in modern missions, were the first converts, like Stephanas,[2] or the men who had given their houses for the meetings of the brethren.[3] These brethren were to have the pre-eminence, and were to be obeyed for their work's sake.[4]

These natural leaders receive a special name in the epistles to the Romans and to the Thessalonians. They are called " those who are over you in the Lord." The word is προϊστάμενοι; and the term has a history, and would at all events suggest a special kind of relationship between leaders and led. It suggested the relation of patron and client, of προστάτης and μέτοικος, familiar enough in Rome and in Thessalonica, which no longer bore the old strictly legal meaning, but which in a less definite sense permeated the whole social life of the times. The word or a cognate one (προεστώς) lingered long in the Roman Church. It is found in the writings of Hermas, the Roman presbyter, and was used by Justin Martyr when he wished to explain the organization of a Christian congregation to a Roman Emperor.[5]

---

[1] 1 Thess. v. 13.
[2] 1 Cor. xvi. 15, 19, cf. Acts xviii. 2, 26; Clement, 1 *Epistle*, xlii. 4.
[3] Rom. xvi. 5, 10, 11, 14, 15; 1 Cor. xvi. 19; Col. iv. 15; Philem. 2.
[4] 1 Cor. xvi. 16.
[5] We find the series of related words:—προϊστάμενος, προϊστάμενοι (used as a noun), προστάτις, προστάτης and προεστώς, Rom. xii. 8; xvi. 2; 1 Thess. v. 12; Hermas, *Pastor*, Vis. ii. 4; Justin, i. *Apol.* lxv; lxvii. The term προστάτης was used technically in Greek city life (and Thessalonica in Paul's time was a Greek city which had been permitted by the Romans to retain its ancient Greek constitution) to denote those citizens who undertook to care for and rule over the μέτοικοι, or persons who had no civic rights. It denoted technically the Roman relation of patron and client and what corresponded thereto in Greek social life. The word was used by Plutarch to translate the Latin *patronus* (Plutarch, *Rom.* 13; *Mar.* 5). Clement, in his *Epistle to the Corinthians*, applies the word in three different places to denote our Lord: " the Patron and Helper of our weakness " (xxxvi. 1); the Highpriest and Patron of our souls " (lxi. 3; lxiv.). It was the custom that the Roman

Archaeological investigation has proved how families among the privileged Roman aristocracy were the patrons of their poorer Christian brethren. The "church in the house" was not necessarily a "kitchen meeting." The investigations of the late Commendatore de Rossi have shown us that the Christian faith made its way at a very early period into the families of some of the noblest and wealthiest Romans. They could, and probably did, open their houses to their poorer brethren and give their great audience halls (*basilica*) for the worship of the common brotherhood, interposing the protection of the legal sacredness of their private life as a shield on all who joined in their devotions.[1] Congregational meetings of this kind had the appearance of an assembly of powerful patrons and their humble clients, and thus took the form of a well recognized condition of Roman social life in all its ramifications. This idea is confirmed by the shape of the earliest Roman churches, which, as has been before remarked, resemble the audience hall of the wealthy Roman burgher. When buildings were erected for the exclusive use of the Christian worship in happier days, the architects naturally copied the arrangement of the buildings they had been used to, and unconsciously transmitted architectural proof of the churchly organization of earlier times. Here, for a third time, we can see the Christian fellowship organizing itself under social usages well understood by the members of the infant brotherhood.

confraternities, especially those among the poorer classes, had a " patron ": or " patrons," who were frequently ladies of rank and wealth ; compare Liebenam, *Zur Gesch. und Organis. d. roem. Vereinswesens.* pp. 213,-18. The Jewish synagogues in Rome, which externally resembled the pagan confraternities for religious cults, not only had patrons but called their synagogues by their names ; Schürer, *Die Gemeindeverfassung der Juden in Rom in der Kaiserzeit*, p. 15 f., 31. It is probable that Phoebe, who is called by St. Paul a " patroness of himself and of many " (Rom. xvi. 1-3). had a position of this kind at Cenchrea, and that this was the *service* she had rendered.

[1] " Nam servis, respublica et quasi civitas, domus est,": Plin. *Ep.* viii. 16.

THE HEATHEN CONFRATERNITIES

In the Epistles to the Corinthians, while we find exhortations to *obey*, we do not find any words which designate those to whom obedience is due; nor have we any description of the organization which prevailed in the Corinthian Church, nor any advice given by the apostle about what it ought to be. The Christians of Corinth lived amidst so many forms of associated life that if organization was to be worked out by the congregation for itself, they would naturally have more aptitude for it than most Christian communities. For the people of Corinth were accustomed to confraternities of all kinds, and above all to private religious associations for the practice of special cults. Under the universal state religion of the Roman Empire there were innumerable religions with their different forms of worship. The state religion had its colleges of priesthoods, its great temples and its public sacrifices; these private religions had their associations for the performance of their peculiar rites. The Jewish synagogues of the Dispersion were enrolled as private religious societies, and seemed to their heathen neighbours to be one out of many kinds of institutions for the practice of a religion admitted to be lawful (*religio licita*), although it was the faith of only a small minority of their neighbours.

The organization of these confraternities, as far as the western division of the Empire is concerned, is known in a general way; and although it differed in details in different societies, certain common features can be recognized. The confraternities were thoroughly democratic to the extent of admitting slaves to be members provided their masters gave consent. The confraternity was regarded as a great family, and the associates called each other "brothers" and "sisters." They had a common meal at stated times. They paid a monthly subscription to the common fund (*stips menstrua*). They were permitted to make their own laws provided nothing was enacted which came into collision with the regulations of the State. These confraternities elected their own office-bearers, who were commonly called *decuriones*; and the society was strictly divided into office-bearers and commons, though occasionally we find an intermediate class of honoured persons.[1] The confraternities exercised discipline over their members and inflicted fines in money and in kind for offences. A book was kept (*album*) containing the names of all the associates. Women were members of a large number of these confraternities, more especially of the burial clubs.[2] Their places of meeting were generally called *scholae*,[3] because they were the scenes of leisure and recreation, though the words *curia* and *basilica* are sometimes found (the Greek word is almost always οἶκος). There they had their common meals and their business meetings; the two were never held together. "Item," says a *decretum*, "placuit si quis quid queri aut referre volet, in conventu referat, ut quieti et hilares diebus solemnis epulemur." Almost all these confraternities had a patron or a patroness, who was always elected by acclamation and never by a mere majority of votes. Sometimes we hear of confraternities belonging to or having their seat in a private house,[4] consisting probably of the servants or slaves of the mansion. Almost all these confraternities, like their lineal descendants the "gilds" of mediaeval times, whether in England or on the Continent, had a distinctly religious side even when they were not formed for the express purpose of practising a foreign cult. They placed themselves under the protection of some deity or deities—merchants honoured Mercury; the dealers in grain, Ceres and the Nymphs; the wine-

[1] This finds its parallel in the honoured class which existed in the Christian congregations of the early centuries, and who ranked between the clergy and the people—the confessors, martyrs, widows, virgins.

[2] This peculiarity has descended to modern times; it is not very easy, those who have tried it say, to induce women to form trades unions, but they are always ready to become members of burial clubs.

[3] "The σχολὴ Τυράννου" (Acts xix. 9) was probably such a place—the meeting place of a confraternity, and named after the patron of the "gild" according to a usual practice, with a hall which could be hired when not needed for the meetings of the society.

[4] The "collegium quod est in domu Sergiae Paulinae" corresponds to "the church which is in the house of Philemon."

dealers, Liber; the weavers and spinners, Minerva; and the fishermen, Neptune, etc.—and paintings of the protecting deity and images of the emperors adorned the walls of the *Schola*.[1]

A large number of the Christian converts must have belonged to these confraternities before their conversion; many maintained their places as members after their entrance into the Christian Church in spite of all the efforts of masterful ecclesiastics, like Cyprian of Carthage and some bishops of Rome, to prevent the practice.[2] They must have known how the associations were

---

[1] For the confraternities which existed in the Graeco-Roman world, compare: Foucart, *Des Associations Religieuses chez les Grecs* (1873); Lüders, *Die dionysischen Künstler* (1873); Ziebarth, *Das Griechische Vereinswesen* (1895), the fullest and most accurate for the Greek associations; Mommsen, *De collegiis et sodaliciis* (1843); Gérard, *De corporations ouvrières à Rome* (1884); Boissier, *La religion romaine d'Auguste aux Antonins* (1878), ii. 292 ff.; Cohn, *Zum römischen Vereinsrecht* (1873); Liebenam, *Zur Geschichte und Organisation des römischen Vereinswesen* (1890), the fullest and most accurate.

For the relation of these confraternities to the primitive Christian organization, compare: Renan, *Les Apôtres* (1866), p. 351 ff.; Heinrici, *Zeitschrift für wissenschaftlichen Theologie* (1876), pp. 465 ff.; (1877) pp. 89 ff; *Theologischen Studien und Kritiken* (1881), pp. 556 ff.; Weingarten, in his preface to Rothe's *Vorlesungen über Kirchengeschichte* (1876), p. xiv.; and in Sybel's *Historische Zeitschrift*, vol. xlv. (1881), pp. 441 ff.; Hatch, *The Organization of the Early Christian Churches* (1881), p. 36 ff.; Holtzmann, *Die Pastoralbriefe* (1880), pp. 194-202; Loening, *Die Gemeindeverfassung des Urchristenthums* (1889), p. 8 ff.; and *Geschichte des deutsches Kirchenrechts* (1878), i. pp. 195-210; Liebenam, as above, pp. 264-274; Schmiedel, *Encyclopædia Biblica* (1902), pp. 3110-1; Ziebarth, as above, pp. 126-132; Réville, *Les Origines de l'Episcopat* (1894), pp. 180-194.

[2] Cyprian's *Epistles*, lxvii. 6: "Martialis also, besides frequenting the disgraceful and filthy banquets of the Gentiles in their collegium, and placing his sons in the same collegium, after the manner of foreign nations, among profane sepulchres, and burying them together with strangers . . . such persons attempt to claim for themselves the episcopate in vain; since it is evident that men of that kind may neither rule over the Christian Church, nor ought to offer sacrifices to God, especially since Cornelius, our colleague, a peaceable and righteous priest, and moreover honoured by the condescension of the Lord with martyrdom, has long ago decreed with us, and with all the bishops appointed throughout all the world,

organized, and they must have carried that knowledge with them into Christianity. They were likely to make use of that knowledge in the interests of the new faith to which they had attached themselves.

This line of argument may easily be pressed too far. Scholars like Renan, Heinrici, Hatch and Weingarten, to say nothing of Schmiedel,[1] have pushed the relation which they think subsisted between the heathen confraternities and the organization of the primitive Gentile Christian communities much further than the evidence seems to warrant. Nothing that they have brought forward bears out the idea that the Christian societies were framed on the model of these pagan confraternities. On the contrary, all the evidence laboriously accumulated to establish the similarity between the Christian organization and that of the pagan confraternities, has not produced many points of resemblance which are not the common property of all forms of social organization.[2] The primitive Christian communities

that men of this sort might indeed be admitted to repentance, but were prohibited from the ordination of the clergy and from the priestly honour." Martialis was bishop of Astorga or of Merida in Spain, and was a *libellaticus*.

[1] *Encyclopædia Biblica*, iii. 3110-3111. Schmiedel seems to exaggerate the connexion between the confraternities and the Christian societies when he refuses to see any connexion between the latter and the Jewish communities and their synagogue system.

[2] The points of similarity which Heinrici has endeavoured to establish between the Christian community at Corinth and the pagan confraternities do not amount to more than this; Hatch has certainly overrated the evidence he has brought forward that *episcopi* were finance officials in the confraternities; points of resemblance found in the records of Greek associations for religious purposes are almost entirely taken from pre-Christian times, and it is forgotten that under the imperial rule the constitutions and formations of confraternities for all purposes were entirely altered and that we know almost nothing about these confraternities in the eastern provinces of the Empire during the first century and a half of the imperial rule. What can be shown is, that to an outsider there was an external resemblance of the most general kind between the Christian communities and the confraternities; and this can be proved only in a general way: Pliny wrote to Trajan that he had meant to proceed against the Christians of Bithynia as belonging to an illicit confrater-

organized themselves independently in virtue of the new moral and social life that was implanted within them; but they did not disdain to take any hints about organization which would be of service from the pagan associations to which they had been accustomed.

Here then we have, not a fourth type, but a fourth root of early Christian organization.

A fifth may be found in the Jewish synagogues of the Dispersion; for many of the converts must have been Jews, or Gentiles who had become Jewish proselytes. The communities of the Jewish people scattered over the Roman Empire occupied very different positions in different places. In Alexandria and in Cyrene they had acquired almost complete political independence, and formed one large and separate community distinct from the surrounding population. In Rome, they had no rights that could be called political, and were divided into a number of separate communities apparently quite independent the one of the others.

Everywhere however throughout the Roman Empire, thanks to the legislation of Julius Caesar and Augustus, the Jews had acquired complete legal protection for their religion.[1] This had been held to include the right to administer their property within their own communities according to their own laws, and to have a limited jurisdiction over their own members.

---

nity (*Ep.* 96 (97)); Tertullian in his *Apology* plainly pleads for the recognition of the Christian Churches as lawful confraternities; Bishop Zephyrinus succeeded in getting the Roman church recognized as a burial club in the end of the second century; and Lucian, in his *Peregrinus Proteus*, describes Peregrinus while a Christian in words which would be applicable to the official of a Greek confraternity for religious purposes ($\theta\iota\alpha\sigma\acute{\alpha}\rho\chi\eta s$), which would imply that he looked on the Christian community as $\theta\acute{\iota}\alpha\sigma os$ or an association for the promotion of a private cult. Compare Liebenam, *Die Geschichte und Organisation des römischen Vereinswesen*, pp. 264-74, and Ziebarth, *Griechische Vereinswesen*, pp. 126-32.

[1] Both Julius Caesar and his nephew and successor began legislation against the confraternities that abounded; but the Jewish communities were recognized by them as *lawful* confraternities.

Thus even where they had the fewest political rights the Jewish communities were always recognized as lawful associations permitted to practise the rites of a *religio licita*. The unit of the Jewish organization was the synagogue. In Alexandria the syngagogues seem to have been united under a common council; but in Rome, as has been said, the synagogues were independent associations, each having its own council, its own president, and its own office-bearers.[1] The privileges of administering their own property and of exercising jurisdiction over their own members, made these synagogues as much civil as religious communities, and it is very difficult, if not impossible, to distinguish between the two sides. At the head of each community was a council, the γερουσία, with a president, the γερουσιάρχης; the official leaders of the community were called ἄρχοντες, and these *archons* were commonly elected for a term of years and sometimes for life.[2] They were purely civil officials; they decided questions of property; they had some criminal jurisdiction; and they were permitted to punish disobedience. The communities had also almoners—at least three, who are commonly classed among the ecclesiastical office-bearers, but whose work was almost purely civil. The only purely ecclesiastical office was that of ἀρχισυνάγωγος. All the actions of public worship, reading the Scriptures, preaching, praying,

---

[1] These synagogue communities were sometimes named after their *patrons*—the "synagogue of the clients of Augustus," of Agrippa, of Volumnus; sometimes after the quarter of Rome where they stood—the synagogue of Campus Martius, of the Subura, etc.; sometimes after the occupations of the members—the synagogue of the burners of lime. Schürer, *Geschichte des jüdischen Volkes im Zeitalter Jesu Christi* (3rd ed. 1898), iii. 44-7.

[2] The term "elder," which one expects, is not found in inscriptions nor in laws until the fourth century; *archon* is found almost universally. Schürer seems to think that the members of the *gerusia* were the *elders* and that they were not office-bearers, but the honoured heads of the community by whom the *archons* were appointed. If so this would be a parallel to what Harnack believes to be the organization of the early Christian communities, where the *elders* were not office-bearers but honoured persons from whom the *episcopi* were chosen.

were performed by the private members, and it was the duty of the official to select those who were to take part in the services. Some synagogues had more than one ἀρχισυνάγωγος, and in later times the title must have become an honorary one, for we find it given to women and to boys. Besides this purely ecclesiastical official there was the "servant of the synagogue" (ὑπηρέτης), who seems to have combined the offices of schoolmaster, beadle and public executioner; he taught the children, brought in and removed the copies of Scripture used in public worship, and corporal punishment for misdeeds was administered by him.[1]

However the internal organization of these Jewish communities differed from the pagan confraternities, their external appearance was such that they were undoubtedly classed among them, and by the names they gave their officials and by some of their customs they would appear to have tried to carry out the likeness as far as possible.[2]

This synagogue organization has some points in common with that of the early Christian communities, and these were probably taken over into Christianity, but the differences were so great that it is impossible to say that the one organization comes from the other. Whether we regard its connexion with the pagan confraternities on the one hand, or with the Jewish synagogues on the other, it may be said that the organiza-

[1] For the organization of the Jewish synagogue system, compare Schürer, *Geschichte des jüdischen Volkes im Zeitalter Jesu Christi* (3rd ed. 1898), ii. pp. 427-463 (Eng. Trans. ii. 55-68, 243-270); also his *Gemeindeverfassung der Juden in Rom in der Kaiserzeit* (1879); Vitringa, *De Synagoga vetere* (1696).

[2] Schürer notes these customs among others: the Greek communes were accustomed to honour with garlands and with special seats at the public entertainments their public benefactors, the leaders of the synagogues voted garlands and front seats in the synagogues to theirs; slaves were set free in the temples, among the Jews they were brought to the synagogues; women were honoured with titles—*presbytera, mater synagogae, archisynagogos*. As for the names of office-bearers, none of them are exclusively Jewish; even ἀρχισυνάγωγος has a pagan use so common that it is impossible to say that it is of strictly Jewish origin.

tion of the Christian communities proceeded by a path peculiar to themselves. Starting from the simplest forms of combination they framed their ministry to serve their own needs in accordance with what they saw was best fitted for their own peculiar work.[1] This did not mean that the training acquired in pagan confraternity or in Jewish synagogue was altogether without effect on the members of the infant Christian churches, or that usages suitable for their purposes were not adopted; but it does mean that the organization of the primitive Gentile churches was not a copy either of pagan confraternity or of Jewish synagogue. What is to be insisted upon is that, on the supposition that the apostles did not prescribe any definite form of Church government (and there is not only no evidence that they did, but the indications are all the other way), the Christians of Corinth and of other cities in the East and in the West were sufficiently acquainted with forms of social organization to be able to organise their communities in such a way that the possibilities of rule and service which lay in the possession of those gifts of the Spirit that manifested the presence of Christ, could find free exercise for the benefit and edification of the whole community.

One thing, however, in this connexion must not be forgotten, as it often is. The infant Christian churches came into being in the Graeco-Roman world at a time when the imperial policy was extremely jealous of any forms of social organization, and when its officials were on the watch to prevent any new development of the principle. Julius Caesar, on political grounds, had suppressed all confraternities except those of ancient origin,[2] but, also from motives of policy, had expressly excepted the Jewish synagogues.[3] His nephew and successor Augustus

[1] Schürer, *Theologische Literaturzeitung* for 1879, pp. 544-6.

[2] Suetonius, *Caesar*, 42: Cuncta collegia, praeter antiquitus constituta, distraxit.

[3] Josephus, *Antiquitates*, XIV. x. 8: "Julius Caius, praetor of Rome, to the magistrates, senate and people of the Parians, sendeth greeting. The Jews of Delos, and some other Jews that sojourn there, in the pre-

followed in his uncle's footsteps, and in addition had ordered all religious associations to be placed under the strictest control and surveillance.[1] The well-known contempt which the first emperor entertained for Oriental religions was doubtless partly responsible for this.[2] The Jewish synagogues were again specially exempted. All new confraternities had to get a special permit from the senate, if they were in the senatorial provinces, and from the emperor, if they belonged to the imperial ones. The only associations which were *perhaps* exempted were the *collegia tenuiorum*, when they were also burial clubs; but it is doubtful whether there was ever a general concession made till the time of Severus. There existed, however, throughout the empire a multitude of confraternities which had not received the sanction of either senate or emperor, and which were therefore illicit, but which were undisturbed although under police supervision. They could be suppressed at any time, and it was provided that no very serious punishment accompanied the suppression.[3] Christianity was never recognized as a *religio licita*

sence of your ambassadors, signified to us, that, by a decree of yours you forbid them to make use of the customs of their forefathers and their way of sacred worship. Now it does not please me that such decrees should be made against our friends and confederates, whereby they are forbidden to live according to their own customs, or to bring in contributions for common suppers and holy festivals, while they are not forbidden to do so even in Rome itself; for even Caius Caesar, our imperator and consul, in that decree wherein he forbade the Bacchanal rioters to meet in the city, did yet permit these Jews, and these only, both to bring in their contributions, and to make their common suppers. Accordingly when I forbid other Bacchanal rioters I permit these Jews to gather themselves together, according to the customs and laws of their forefathers, and to persist therein. It will therefore be good for you, that if you have made any decree against these our friends and confederates, to abrogate the same, by reason of their virtue and kind disposition towards us."

[1] Dio Cassius, lii. 36; Suetonius, *Augustus*, 32.   [2] Dio Cassius, liv. 6.

[3] "Collegia si qua fuerint illicita, mandatis et constitutionibus et senatusconsultis dissolvuntur; sed permittitur eis, cum dissolvuntur, pecunias communes si quas habent dividere pecuniamque inter se partiri: *Dig.* XLVII. xxii. 3.

134   THE CHURCHES CREATING THEIR MINISTRY

till the time of Constantine, and could never have received official sanction for its assemblies; but it was not impossible for the Christian churches to take the place of an illicit confraternity provided they had such an external resemblance to some well recognized confraternities as would permit the police to connive at their existence. It is undoubted that the Christian Church was at first believed by the Romans to belong to the tolerated and protected Judaism. Tertullian meets the charge that Christianity was "hiding something of its presumption under the shadow of an illustrious religion (Judaism), one which has at any rate the authorization of law." [1]   So long as the Roman Government did not perceive the difference between the Christians and the Jews, the infant Christian churches could remain sheltered under the laws which permitted legalized confraternities; [2] but when the difference became manifest, and when Jews themselves began to denounce the Christians, some other shelter was required.[3]   This could be and no doubt was furnished by the general external resemblance of the Christian societies to the pagan confraternities for religious practices.   Hence con-

---

[1] Tertullian, *Apology*, 21.

[2] De Rossi, *Roma Sottereana*, iii. 509 ; *Bulletino di Archaeologia Cristiana* (1865), pp. 90-94 ; Liebenam, *Zur Geschichte und Organisation des römischen Vereinswesen*, 268.   Holtzmann, *Die Pastoralbriefe*, 197.   The protection was not restricted to those who were Jews by birth ; it extended to proselytes (σεβόμενοι) ; cf. *Bulletino di Archaeologia Cristiana* (1865), p. 91.

[3] Authorities differ about the date when the Roman officials first recognized the difference.   Ramsay (*The Church in the Roman Empire*, p. 266 ff.) differs from most German authorities in thinking it to been have much earlier than the time of Domitian ; I agree with him thoroughly. When we remember the wise political dread of religious combinations which the emperors from Augustus downward showed ; their discernment that religion was the most powerful political motive power in the East ; the presence in every province of men trained to note the beginnings of all movements which might disturb the state ; and when we glance at the objective picture of that old system of ruling provinces which modern India furnishes—none but an arm-chair critic would deny it.   British officials in India know of all the small beginnings of religious movements in their districts long before the public know anything about them, if they ever acquire the knowledge.

formity with the usages of a pagan confraternity gave the Christians the best means of escaping the attention of the authorities, alert to notice any attempts to start altogether new associations.[1] It is evident that the Christian communities had some usages in common with the confraternities, and precisely those which would be the most likely to attract attention. They met together for a common meal (which was one of the things that Pliny noticed) ;[2] they made a distinction between the meetings for the common meal and those for edification and for business ; they honoured the *dies natalis* of a martyr as the confraternities celebrated the birthdays of benefactors ; they exhibited a reverence for their dead brethren in ways that could be compared with the practices of the confraternities ;[3] above all, after the time of the Emperor Nerva they tried to assimilate themselves to the *collegia tenuiorum*, which obtained an easier recognition on the part of the authorities, and this came to a head when Bishop Zephyrinus was able to get the Roman Church registered as a burial club.[4] There was sufficient external resemblance between the confraternities to enable Tertullian to plead that the Church should be recognized as a legally permitted association, and to make Pliny suggest that he might proceed against the Christians as members of an illicit collegium.[5] All these things enable us to see how the Christian churches during the earliest part of their existence could maintain a

[1] Schmiedel, *Encyclopædia Biblica*, 3111; Holtzmann, *Die Pastoralbriefe*, 197 f. Schmiedel, however, is not warranted in making the deductions he does from the external conformity ; there must have been the same outward conformity between the Christian communities and the Jewish synagogues.

[2] Pliny, *Epist.* 96 (97).

[3] For the burial usages of the confraternities, compare Liebenam, *Zur Geschichte und Organisation des römischen Vereinswesens* (1890), p. 254 ff. ; Schultze, *Katacomben* (1882), pp. 9-14, 48-53 ; De Rossi, *Roma Sottereana*, iii. 501-507.

[4] This is commonly inferred from the fact mentioned by Hippolytus, that Zephyrinus " appointed him (Calixtus) over the cemetery "; *Refutation (Philosophumena)*, ix. 7.

[5] Compare above p. 128, n. 2.

position of precarious security in face of the imperial policy of not permitting new associations. But we are scarcely warranted in drawing conclusions about the inward organization of the primitive Christian communities. What we can infer is, that the Christians of the primitive Gentile churches had the ordinary experience to enable them to make use of all the divine gifts of rule and service in creating for their churches from their midst a ministering service.

Churches like that of Corinth and Philippi, whatever may have suggested their forms of organization, and whatever bands held them together, had within them persons with the "gifts" which enabled them to offer wise counsels, to assist their neighbours, to lead the devotions and to manage the affairs of the community. If it be said, as it is sometimes done, that the churches of Corinth and Rome were not properly organized because we do not hear of bishops or presbyters or deacons, then that means that a Christian community could be addressed as a Christian church, could be called "Christ's Body," could admit catechumens by the sacred door of baptism, could assemble together for public worship, could partake together of the Holy Supper, could exercise Christian discipline, and all this without office-bearers set apart for the purposes of the ministry in regular and ecclesiastical fashion. It shows, as nothing else can, that the Church comes before the ministry, and that it creates for itself and its own needs its ministering service; the natural leaders led, the people followed, the organization grew and the new moral and social life had full liberty to develop itself in all manner of Christian service. The two types of the earliest local ministry, the *serving* and the *leading*, the ἀντιλήψεις and the κυβερνήσεις, the διακονεῖν and the ἐπισκοπεῖν appeared first as forms of doing what service was required of them, and then as permanent offices.

Hitherto, with one exception, we have been working at those portions of the New Testament whose dates are well ascertained. Our material has been drawn chiefly from the earlier

Epistles of St. Paul, all of which belong to the years before 57 A.D. When we come to the material given in the Epistle of James, 1 Peter, and the Pastoral Epistles, we are at once confronted with questions of date and authorship, on which modern scholars hold very varying opinions.

For our purposes, however, these questions are by no means so important as might at first be supposed. No critic, whose opinions deserve serious consideration, denies the truth of the pictures of the ecclesiastical organization exhibited in the Pastoral Epistles or in the later chapters of the Acts of the Apostles. While they may refuse to admit that St. Paul or St. Luke was the author and while they may relegate the composition to the last decade of the first or to the second or third decades of the second century, they all admit that the representations of ecclesiastical polity found in these documents are true for this later period and *may* be true for a much earlier one. The Church, it is held universally, did pass through the stage of organization shown in these documents. The only question is the date of the stage. No reasonable critic would affirm that a special feature of ecclesiastical organization may not have been in existence long before it is mentioned, or that the date when we first hear about it is the date of its origin, unless there is the express statement that it took its beginning at that time. For example, when it it said that Paul and Barnabas did not see *elders* set over the churches of Derbe, Lystra and Iconium (Acts xiv. 23), no one denies that the passage is evidence for the existence of *elders* in these churches in the beginning of the second century. Only some critics believe that the statement so conflicts with St. Paul's own account of his conduct towards his missionary churches that it is impossible to accept the idea that the office of *eldership*, which was certainly present when the document was written, dates as far back as the planting of the churches. They say that the writer, not unnaturally, attributes the polity of his own time to the earlier period. Others, who accept the late date of the document, find certain corroborative evidence of the existence of *elders* in these churches long before this date, and have no difficulty in believing that the institution of the office may have come from the missionary journey of St. Paul, whatever the date or authorship of the document which relates the circumstance. The same remark applies to the Pastoral Epistles. If the late date of the documents be accepted, *and* if it is also believed that the accounts of the organization of the churches given in them indicate a difference of polity from what appears in the undisputed Epistles of St. Paul, the result is not to discredit the information the documents give us about ecclesiastical organization, but to accept it as evidence for what existed in the first and second decades of the second century. If the late date of composition be maintained, and if it is held that the information given is not inconsistent with what existed in earlier days, then nothing compels us to conclude that the beginnings of the polity described are as late as the accepted date of the documents describing them. In either case the documents are held to describe truly the condition of the ministry of the Church at an earlier or at a later period—the question of time being settled not by the date of the document but by a comparison between the information it gives with what we know of the earlier period. The matter involved does not concern a general conception of ecclesiastical organization, but whether a certain stage of development, which did exist sometime, was of an earlier or of a later appearance—a question which, when we consider the utmost limits of time involved, is comparatively unimportant.

We need not, therefore, concern ourselves here with the problems which the date and authorship of the Book of Acts and of 1 Peter suggest.[1] But prevailing critical opinions about

---

[1] Personally I am not disposed to brush aside the difficulties which the Book of Acts presents; they relate *chiefly* to the limited time which the Eusebian chronology (and it appears to me to be the most trustworthy) allows for the events recorded down to the conversion of St. Paul; but difficulties seem to me to be increased and not lessened by any proposed reconstruction. So far as our subject of investigation is concerned all

the Pastoral Epistles place the portions which concern our subject so very late that it is necessary either to dissent from them or to relegate the information these documents give to the period which produced the *Epistles of Ignatius* and the *Sources of the Apostolic Canons*.[1] These Pastoral Epistles were

"critics" recognize the election of the "Seven" as an historical fact; and the only remaining question of organization is the statement that "elders" were appointed (not "ordained," for that is not the word) in the churches of the Galatian mission by Paul and Barnabas; and this it seems to me is rendered highly probable by evidence which is altogether independent of the date and authorship of the Acts of the Apostles. As to the date of the book, I follow Professor Sanday who believes the book to have been written about 80 A.D. and that its author was St. Luke. Dr. Harnack on the other hand declares that the date of the book is some time between 79 and 93 A.D. *Geschichte der altchristliche Literatur bis Eusebius*, II.; *Chronologie*, i. 246-50.

[1] The "critical view" of the date of the *Pastoral Epistles* may perhaps be best taken from the short summary in Harnack's *Geschichte der altchristliche Literatur bis Eusebius*, II., *Chronologie*, i. 480-5, supplemented from Holtzmann, *Die Pastoralbriefe* (1880). It is as follows:—The three Epistles, 1 and 2 Timothy and Titus, go together and are to be treated as a whole; the same arguments and the same results apply to all. These epistles contain some genuine sayings of St. Paul—a few verses in 2 Timothy scarcely a third of Titus, but not a verse of 1 Timothy —enough to say that the writings are founded on genuine apostolic letters. But in the state in which they have come to us they represent an entirely different authorship. The reasons given for this judgment may be classed under three heads: the language is different from St. Paul's, and in particular the epistles contain a very large number of words and phrases quite unlike what St. Paul uses in his authentic works; warnings are given against erroneous beliefs and especially against Gnostic opinions which were not in existence before the death of St. Paul; the description of the ecclesiastical organization is entirely different from what we find in the authentic letters of St. Paul. When it is sought to determine the date of the epistles two definite points of time present themselves. Polycarp distinctly quotes 2 Timothy ii. 12; and the redaction cannot be later than 110 A.D. On the other hand the kinds of errors which the author denounces and warns against had no existence until the close of the first century. Hence the probable date of the letters must be sometime between 90-110 A.D. But, it is said, portions must be much later; the closing verses, 17-21, of 1 Tim. vi. were evidently added after the real end of the epistle at verse 16. Of these verses 17-19 contain warnings which find a parallel in the admonitions of the *Pastor* of Hermas and belong to a period later than 100 A.D.; while verses 20-21 have no con-

extensively used in the Primitive Church as a document giving directions about ecclesiastical organization and discipline. The Muratorian Fragment tells us this.[1] Like all documents used in this way, they were apt to be interpolated to suit the needs of time and place. Statements about prevailing errors

nexion with the rest of the epistle, are directed against the "antitheses" of Marcion and cannot be earlier than 130 A.D. Similarly verses 1-13 in 1 Tim. iii. and verses 17-20 in 1 Tim. v. 17-20, and verses 7-9 in Titus i., have little connexion with the context and are portions of an ancient book of discipline. They present striking parallels to the *Sources of the Apostolic Canons* and cannot be much earlier than 130 A.D. This is what "criticism" makes of the Pastoral Epistles. It places those portions which concern our subject as late at 130 A.D. and forbids us to use them to describe the organization of the Churches within the first century. The reasons given are briefly these: a quotation from St. Luke's gospel is called a *scripture* and that of itself, it is said, is sufficient to show the late date of the document; Timothy is represented as the president of a college of elders and in this capacity is the judge and administrator of justice—functions which are much later than even 100 A.D.

A few remarks may be admitted in the way of briefly indicating why I refuse to accept the "critical" theories about these epistles. While I gratefully acknowledge Dr. Harnack as the greatest living authority on early Church history, I never read what he has to say about the two subjects of Gnosticism and ecclesiastical organization without longing that he could spend a few months in the mission field where aggressive work is being done among educated pagans whose minds are full of the same curious oriental faiths and their allied philosophies as were present to the earliest Christian converts in the first and second centuries. I am convinced that if this experience were his he would modify much that he has said both about Gnosticism and about ecclesiastical organization. The Oriental mind, tenacious of its own beliefs and at the same time curiously receptive in religious conceptions, strives *from the first* to weave Christian thoughts into its system of Oriental beliefs and is surprised that the amalgam thus produced is not accepted as Christian doctrine by the missionary. The very errors denounced by the Pastoral Epistles may be found among Hindu inquirers who never get further than inquiry and a certain measured sympathy with Christian teaching. They are the beginnings of Gnosticism apparent to the missionary long before they have acquired the definite shape of such a system as the *Arya Somaj*, to take one of the forms which

---

[1] "Ad Filemonem una, et ad Titum una, et ad Timotheum duas, pro affecto et dilectione in honore tamen ecclesiae catholice in ordinatione ecclesiastice descepline sanctificatae sunt."

to be shunned were liable to be altered in order to be more sharply descriptive of existing heresies or tendencies to heresy and disciplinary directions might easily have taken a more technical language to suit a later period. But when due allowance is made for these natural effects of the primitive use of these documents, there does not seem to be evidence strong

modern Indian gnosticism has assumed. If the living picture were studied fresh insight would be acquired about ancient documents. It would be seen for example, that if Timothy or Titus were acting as deputy for an apostle or missionary it does not follow that he must be president of a college of elders in order to be obliged to listen to accusations against "elders" or to act as the one who rebukes in public and in private. The more I study these pastoral epistles the more evident it becomes to me that they are just what every experienced missionary has to impart to a younger and less experienced colleague when he warns him about the difficulties that he must face and the tasks, often unexpected, he will find confronting him. It is scarcely to be wondered at then that the Pastoral Epistles are always among the earliest portions of the scriptures translated in almost every Christian mission. A study of the living picture would also teach students that while the declaration of Hegesippus may be accepted that gnosticism did not trouble the Church till about the time of Trajan (which is the deduction usually drawn from his statements given in Eusebius, *Hist. Eccles.* III. xxxii. 7) that need not prevent our believing that incipient gnosticism had to be guarded against from the very beginning. At the same time it is very probable that the Pastoral Epistles contain many interpolations in which statements about errors and even directions about discipline have been somewhat altered to suit the requirements of the middle of the second century. That is what would naturally happen to a document which was used, as we know these epistles were used, for a manual of ecclesiastical procedure (the Muratorian Fragment tells us that). The insertion of "scripture" ($\gamma\rho\alpha\phi\dot{\eta}$) might easily have come in in this way. But all this does not prevent me accepting these epistles as the work of St. Paul or of a companion who wrote for him. It may be said that the supposition that these letters come from St. Paul requires us to believe that the apostle was released from his first captivity, and made missionary journeys of which no record has remained; but this is rendered more than likely by the statement of Clement (I. v. 7) that St. Paul visited the furthest parts of the West ($\tau\grave{o}$ $\tau\acute{\epsilon}\rho\mu\alpha$ $\tau\hat{\eta}\varsigma$ $\delta\acute{v}\sigma\epsilon\omega\varsigma$)—an expression which, notwithstanding all that has been said against the idea, seems more naturally applicable to Spain than to Rome. As for the language—" Tous ceux qui ont l'expérience de la parole en publique ne savent-ils pas que le ton n'est plus le même quand on parle à une assemblée que lorsqu'on s'adresse à une personne en particulier " (Réville, *Les Origines de l'Episcopat* (1894), p. 497.)

enough to warrant our refusing to believe that they are what they declare themselves to be—letters from St. Paul to two of his most trusted fellow-workers, instructing them how to carry on his missionary work, which he was not able to superintend personally. If this be the case these letters show us what St. Paul was in the habit of doing in the mission fields which belonged peculiarly to himself. Titus[1] had accompanied the apostle, released from his Roman captivity, to Crete, and had been left there to complete the work which the apostle, pressed for time, could not stay to finish. His duty was to see that "elders" were chosen in every local church. The charge recalls the account given in the Acts of the Apostles of the missionary journey of Paul and Barnabas through the district which included the cities of Derbe, Lystra and Iconium. On that missionary tour the apostles did not see to the appointment of " elders " when their converts were first gathered from Judaism and heathenism. They allowed the believers in the new faith some little time to prove themselves. It was on their return journey, when they were "confirming" their converts, that the *elders* were appointed. So here Titus was left till the sufficient time had elapsed, and then he was to see to the selection of *elders* in the local churches of Crete. His work was one that could be finished within a comparatively short time, for the apostle expected him to follow to Nicopolis, where St. Paul was to pass the winter. There is no suggestion that his function was anything like a permanent office in the Church. The work given him to do is perfectly familiar to modern missionaries.

---

[1] Titus had been one of the earliest gentile converts from heathenism —a convert or spiritual son of St. Paul himself (Titus i. 4). The apostle had esteemed him so highly that he had taken him up to Jerusalem when he went there to plead the cause of gentile liberty. Titus went with St. Paul to be shown as a specimen of what these gentile converts of his were like (Gal. ii. 3); and he had passed the test so well that the leaders of the Church at Jerusalem had not required that he should be circumcised. He had been employed by St. Paul on work involving tact and confidential discretion (2 Cor. xii. 18), and had acquitted himself well.

The other deputy was Timothy.[1] He had come with the apostle to Ephesus, and circumstances, we know not what, had required that one of the two should remain and "confirm" the Church there. St. Paul had other work to do; Timothy was selected to remain, and he received two letters advising him how to act. Such is the setting of these Pastoral Epistles as related in the writings themselves.

In these letters to Titus and to Timothy we find, as we might expect in such documents, much more detailed references to the organization of the churches than in the Epistles addressed to the churches themselves. We find unmistakably an official ministry which appears to consist of two grades. We see evi-

---

[1] Timothy was the favourite fellow-worker with the great apostle. When we piece together his story from the Acts of the Apostles and from St. Paul's epistles, we find something like the following. When St. Paul left Antioch with Silas on his second visit to the Galatian Churches, feeling sadly, no doubt, that Barnabas was no longer with him, either he or his companion had an assurance given in "prophecy" that St. Paul would find in a brief time a helper who would be to him as another Barnabas (1 Tim. i. 18; iv. 14). When St. Paul reached Lystra he suddenly recognized in a young man there the fellow-worker who had been divinely promised to him. "And *behold*," says Luke, "a certain disciple was there, named Timothy, the son of a Jewess who believed; but his father was a Greek. Him Paul *would* have to go forth with him." The apostle received him with the kindly Jewish benediction, laying his hands on his head (2 Tim. i. 6); and the *elders* of the Church also gave the young man their benediction before he set out on his new life-work (Acts xvi. 1-4; 1 Tim. iv. 14). There is a striking parallel between the "call" of Timothy and the earlier "call" of the great apostle himself—the vision of Ananias and the prophetic intuition of St. Paul; Ananias' benediction, when he laid his hands on the future head of the Apostle to the Gentiles, and the benediction of Timothy by St. Paul; the blessing of Saul and Barnabas by the "prophets and teachers" at the head of the Church at Antioch, when they started on their first mission tour, and the blessing of the *elders* of Lystra when Timothy started on his life work as an apostle or evangelist. From this time he and St. Paul were almost always together; they were like father and son. Timothy's name occurs frequently in the epistles of St. Paul. When difficult questions arose in St. Paul's mission Churches which needed delicate handling and when the Apostle could not go himself to settle them Timothy was his favourite deputy (1 Cor. xvi. 10; 1 Thess. iii. 2). The apostle saw himself living his life over again in the person of his son Timothy.

dence of a congregational roll on which the names of the poor, who are to receive the support of the congregation, are entered. There are also traces of a ministry of women. We find the apostle laying down rules to guide his deputies in the selection of office-bearers and in the removal of ecclesiastical excommunication. In short, we find a great deal more definite information about the organization and the ministry of the primitive churches than in any other of the New Testament writings.

If we believe that the apostle was above all things a *missionary*, and that his deputies were to do the work of missionaries, which seems to be the only view which is consistent with the nature of the function and the description of their work which is given in the New Testament writings, these Pastoral Epistles may be expected to show us the organization of the primitive Gentile churches from the inside, while in the Epistles of St. Paul, written either before or during the Roman captivity, we see the same organization from the outside. They tell us how the apostle personally superintended the building into churches of the communities of believers his preaching had gathered together. The two sets of letters are complementary. In the earlier letters we see the apostle encouraging every form of spontaneous action, and how he made the infant communities feel that the whole responsibility lay upon their shoulders. In the later epistles the master-builder shows his deputies how carefully he was accustomed to guide the exercise of that responsibility with scarcely felt touches of the hand.

The duties of the two deputies varied with the wants of the places in which they were set. Timothy had to do with an older community whose special circumstances demanded special care; Titus had to deal with comparatively newly-established congregations, and to guide them carefully but unobtrusively to organize themselves. Both had to do the work which the apostle was himself accustomed to do in similar circumstances. It was the most difficult and delicate work that falls to the lot of a missionary—to guide into right channels of self-government communities comparatively young in the faith, and to do it in such a way that the community may feel that it is doing the work itself, and will be able to sustain itself when the guiding hand shall be removed. In modern times nothing tests the ability of a missionary for his work like this very task.

The apostle gave both Titus and Timothy a master-thought to guide them. The infant Christian communities were to be looked on as *Households of God*, and as every great household needs servants who superintend, so *the Household of God* needs men who have the oversight. He that has proved faithful in small things is the most likely to prove faithful in all-important work, and the man who has shown that he can guide and rule his own household well is declared to be the best fitted to superintend the Household of God. Hence we are told very little about the special duties of the *presbyters* or *bishops*, or whatever their usual name was, and find little mention of qualities fitted for special functions. What the apostle insists on is *character*, and that kind of character which is shown in family relationships.

Titus is told that a *presbyter* or *elder* must be a man who is above suspicion, who is a faithful husband [1] and whose children are Christians of well regulated lives. He is *not* to be self-willed, nor soon angry, nor given to wine, nor turbulent, nor given to money; he *is* to be a lover of strangers, a lover of what is good, sober-minded, upright, pious and temperate in all things. Besides, he ought to be so well-grounded in the principles of Christian morality and religion that he can exhort the brethren and answer the common Jewish and heathen objections to the Christian faith.

Timothy was placed in temporary charge in a district where the Christian community had existed for a longer period; and the differences in the advice given all gather round this fact.

---

[1] "A faithful husband" appears to be the best translation of μιᾶς γυναικὸς ἄνδρα—one who acts on the principles of Christian morality and is not led astray by the licentious usages of the surrounding heathenism.

146   THE CHURCHES CREATING THEIR MINISTRY

The office-bearers selected by the community were not to be taken from the most recently converted, but from men who had some experience of Christianity, and whose character had stood the test of time.[1] The office of "oversight" had become sought after, and there was the more need for careful selection.[2] But as in the letter to Titus what St. Paul insists on is *character*, as that has displayed itself within the family, for rule in the human household is the best training for management within the Household of God.[3] The list of qualifications is practically the same as was given to Titus, with this added, that he who has the oversight ought to be a man respected by the heathen[4] as well as by his fellow Christians.[5]

---

[1] 1 Tim. iii. 10; 2 Tim. ii. 2.   [2] 1 Tim. iii. 1.
[3] 1 Tim. iii. 5.   [4] 1 Tim. iii. 7.
[5] Harnack, who thinks that the verses in 1 Tim. which relate to the organization of the Church are an interpolation and represent an old book of the Church Order not unlike the *Sources of the Apostolic Canons* and perhaps derived with these fragments from a common source, points out a number of interesting coincidences:—"Let a woman learn in quietness with all subjection." (1 Tim. ii. 11): "in order that it (the congregation) may be at rest without disturbance, after it has been first proved in all subjection" (*Apost. Can.* ii); "I permit not a woman to teach" (1 Tim. ii. 12): compare with the whole of *Apost. Can.* viii., especially "How then can we, concerning women, order them services?" "The bishop must therefore be without reproach, the husband of one wife, temperate, sober-minded, orderly, given to hospitality, apt to teach, no brawler nor striker, but gentle, not contentious, no lover of money . . . moreover he must have good testimony from them that are without" (1 Tim. iii. 2-7); "If he (the bishop) has a good report among the heathen, if he is without reproach, if a friend of the poor, if sober-minded, no drunkard, nor adulterer, not covetous nor a slanderer . . . it is good if he is unmarried; if not, then the husband of one wife; educated . . . if unlearned, gentle" (*Apost. Can.* i.); "Deacons, in like manner, must be grave, not double tongued, not given to much wine . . . and let these also be first proved, then let them serve as deacons . . . let the deacons be husbands of one wife, ruling their children and their own houses well" (1 Tim. iii. 8, 9, 12); "The deacons shall be approved in every service . . . husbands of one wife, educating their children, sober-minded . . . not double-tongued . . . not using much wine" (*Apost. Can.* iv.); (of deacons) "Not using much wine, not greedy of lucre" (1 Tim. iii. 8); (of widows) "Not greedy of lucre, not using much wine" (*Apos. Can.* v.); "For they that have served well as deacons gain to themselves a good

The qualifications demanded of deacons also practically consist of character tested by behaviour in the household—faithfulness to wife, and evidence of parental control over children and wise dealing with servants.[1] It is also interesting to notice a ministry of women.

Presbyters or *elders* who rule well are to be honoured, and those who in addition assist in the ministry of the Word are to be doubly honoured, or perhaps to receive a double honorarium from the free-will offerings of the people. *Elders* who do not rule well are to be looked after; but the apostle charges his deputy not to accept accusations against them rashly, but to follow the old Jewish rule which required at least two grave witnesses to any accusation affecting character. But if an *elder*, or indeed any member of the congregation, did fall into sin, public rebuke was to be given without respect of persons.[2] The apostle also insists that his deputy is to be very cautious in admitting to Church Communion those who have lapsed. He is not "to lay hands hastily,"[3] according to the usual form in

---

standing " (1 Tim. iii. 13); " For they who have served well as deacons . . . purchase to themselves the pastorate " (*Apost. Can.* vi.); and so on. It appears to me, however, that the interesting series of parallels affords striking evidence that the statements in the Pastoral Epistles are much older than those in the *Sources of the Apostolic Canons*. In the former it is *women* who are to be in *subjection*, and the phrase corresponds to 1 Cor. xiv. 34; while in the *Sources of the Apostolic Canons* it is the congregation who are to be *in subjection* to the office-bearers: the leaders and the led of the Pauline Epistles have given place to the clergy and the laity of a later period. Then in the Pastoral Epistles the deacons who have served well gain to themselves " a good standing "; in the later document they are promised *clerical promotion*, which is a very different idea and suggests a much later period. Again in the former document the senior office-bearers are to be *faithful husbands* (husbands of one wife); in the latter it is said that it is better that they be not married, which shows either a growth in ascetic sentiment or perhaps difficulties in a fair distribution of the offerings of the congregation and the desire for distributors who have no claims on themselves to influence their judgment, or both of these conceptions. Compare *Chronologie*, pp. 483, 484.

[1] 1 Tim. iii. 8-10, 12, 13.   [2] 1 Tim. v. 17-20.
[3] 1 Tim. v. 22. Compare Hort, *The Christian Ecclesia*, p. 175 ff.

restoration, " on any man, neither to be a partaker of other men's sins."

The picture of the relief of the poor of the community is both vivid and homely. It brings before our eyes not merely that far-off primitive Christian Church of Ephesus, but also the present work of a Scottish country kirk-session. When the bread-winner dies careful inquiries are to be made, whether the bereaved widow and orphans have any means of support, or can receive any aid from their relations, who are to be stirred up to do their duty to those who are left helpless. If the children or grandchildren are able to work they are to be commanded to support her who has been left a widow; but if such help fails, and if the widow is too old to earn her own living and has always borne a good character, then she is to be placed on the poor roll of the congregation and supported by the community.

According to our view, these Pastoral Epistles are to be regarded as complementary to the earlier Epistles of St. Paul, in so far as they give us information about the organization of the Gentile Christian communities. The earlier epistles, written to the various churches, reveal the principles of the growth of the organization lying within the communities themselves; while the Pastoral Epistles, written to guide the men who were to be the apostle's deputies, and had to be instructed in his methods, show how he watched over the communities his preaching had gathered together. The apostle acted like a wise father, who encourages every appearance of independent and responsible action, but at the same time carefully guides it into the proper channels. From one point of view it can be truly said that the churches of St. Paul's mission were thoroughly independent and acted on their own responsibilities; from another the apostle or his deputies watched over and guided this activity. There was control, but it was the control of the missionary, and partook largely of parental monition and guidance.

If we combine what is given us in the earlier Epistles of St. Paul with what we find in the Pastoral Epistles, we can discern the principles of organization within the Pauline communities. According to the ideas of the apostle, a Church of God was thoroughly organized when it found within its membership a variety of persons endowed with various spiritual gifts producing activities helpful to the whole community. That was the real basis of the common life, the divine element without which all else was of little moment, and with which everything else was a matter of executive detail. These gifts were divided into two great classes, those which served for the ministry of the Word, and those which were at the foundation of other kinds of ministry. It was from this second class of "gifts" that the ministry of the local churches proceeded. Among them we find two which crystallise into ecclesiastical office. St. Paul calls them "wise counsels" and "helps" ($\kappa\upsilon\beta\epsilon\rho\nu\eta\sigma\epsilon\iota\varsigma$ and $\dot{\alpha}\nu\tau\iota\lambda\dot{\eta}\psi\epsilon\iota\varsigma$, 1 Cor. xii. 28); we may call them "oversight" and "subordinate service." Whatever may have been the original principle of association, whatever suggestions of social combination earliest presented themselves to the minds of the primitive Christians in the Gentile Christian communities, whatever the human bands that bound them together, these two classes of officials were sure to emerge—the one fitted to guide and lead the brethren and the other to render subordinate service.

Some time must have elapsed before active services crystallised into offices, but it need not have been a long period.[1] Things move fast in young communities organizing themselves for the first time, and the spiritual gift of discernment which belonged to the whole community was an instrument of organization lying ready to hand. This gift of "discernment," when applied to teaching, implied that those who were really believed to be the mouthpiece of the Holy Spirit were to be heard with reverence, and that the hearers ought to fashion their lives according to what was taught. The same gift, when applied to the discernment of abilities for rule and service, implied the

[1] Compare the evidences of growth in organization collected by Gayford, *Hastings' Bible Dictionary*, art. *Church*, i. 434.

power to select and bestow office upon men so gifted, and the duty of the community to obey its chosen leaders in all practical matters.

In young communities full of a fresh and active enthusiasm, feeling that the possession of "gifts" of rule and help was the fulfilment of the promise of the Master to be present with them, and that the "gift" of discernment enabled them to select their leaders with something of divine authority, activities helpful to the community would speedily become offices. There is no reason to prevent us from believing that Stephanas and the others whom the Corinthian Church are ordered to reverence were office-bearers in the full sense of the word.[1] Harnack and many others are disposed to deny this. They argue that there is no trace of office-bearers properly so-called in St. Paul's writings composed before his Roman captivity, although they naturally admit there must have been ministries from the very first, and that the ministries took shape under the two conceptions of "oversight" and "subordinate service." It may be so, but the arguments do not convince me.[2] If the προϊστάμενοι of the Epistles to the Thessalonians and to the Romans were not office-bearers they did the work of office-bearers. To assert that a period of fifty years must have elapsed before the προϊστάμενοι of the earlier epistles could become the official πρεσβύτεροι of the Pastoral Epistles (which is practically

[1] Compare Schmiedel, *Encyc. Bibl.*, art. *Ministry*, 3111 (d).

[2] *Expositor* (1887, Jan.–June), 328-31. The arguments put shortly are:—St. Paul addresses his advice about discipline, etc., to the whole community and not to special individuals who are in the position of office-bearers; all the members of the Christian community are exhorted to do what is enjoined upon the leaders (1 Thess. v. 14); the word ἔργον (verse 12) shows that an office is not thought of; while in Rom. xii. 6-8 presidency stands between "liberality" and "showing mercy," and is described as a "gift". The same arguments, it appears to me, would exclude the presence of office-bearers in the *Didache* and in the *Epistle of Clement*; for there the exhortations to exercise discipline are addressed to the whole community. The fact that the congregational meeting is the supreme judge does not exclude the fact of office-bearers. Compare below pp. 171 ff. for the *Didache* and 176 n. for 1 *Clement*.

Loening's contention), or that the development required eighty years (which Harnack requires), seems to me to be quite unwarrantable. As has been said before, things move fast in young communities and, so far as the development in organization goes, there is no reason whatever why the state of matters described in the Pastoral Epistles should not have arrived at a comparatively early date.

It is quite in accordance with what has been said, that in all the New Testament writings, and indeed in all the earlier books of discipline, the work done is always thought more of than the persons selected to do it, and office-bearers are honoured for their work's sake rather than for their rank. The one thought running through all the earlier documents is that the power to render special service to the community—for rule and leadership according to primitive modes of thought are always founded on "service" and never on "lordship"—depends on the possession of "gifts" engrafted by the Spirit on individual character, and the occasion of these particular services is their recognition by the community, who appoint the brethren to serve it in ruling it. One of the chief services which belonged to those who were placed at the head of the Christian communities was to set an example to those under their charge, and what the leaders did all the brethren in their several places were expected to do. Hence in the New Testament writings, as well as in the earlier canons, the qualities which were to determine the selection of men to be leaders were those qualities of stable Christian character which all Christians ought to possess. The function of the missionary or his deputy, as we can see from the Pastoral Epistles, was to advise the community in their selection of those who were to be over them, and to inculcate such principles of selection as would abide permanently in their minds, and thus secure a succession of worthy office-bearers when the first missionaries of the Gospel were no longer present to advise; or to use the words of St. Clement of Rome: "Our apostles knew through our Lord Jesus Christ that there would be strife over the name (dignity) of the overseer's office. For this cause, therefore, having received complete foreknowledge, they appointed the aforesaid persons (i.e. their first converts) and afterwards gave a further injunction that if they should fall asleep, other approved men should succeed to their administration " [1]—a description of what takes place now on every mission field of the whole Christian Church.

The earlier Epistles of St. Paul show us, as has been said, that the services rendered to the local churches by those whom the brethren are commanded to obey for their works' sake were of two kinds, which we have called "oversight" and "subordinate service." I think that we may presume that these were office-bearers, if not from the beginning, at all events from a very early period; but we can at least say that these two different kinds of service were rendered by the leaders to the led. Later writings, both within and without the New Testament Canon, make it plain that these services were rendered by two classes of officials who bore official names, which still exist within the Christian Church. We read of pastors, overseers, elders and deacons ($\pi o \iota \mu \acute{\epsilon} \nu \epsilon \varsigma$, $\acute{\epsilon} \pi \acute{\iota} \sigma \kappa o \pi o \iota$, $\pi \rho \epsilon \sigma \beta \acute{\upsilon} \tau \epsilon \rho o \iota$, $\delta \iota \acute{\alpha} \kappa o \nu o \iota$).[2] The references to the office-bearers of the local churches are always in the plural, and the government must have been collegiate. Whatever the special origin and primitive meanings of the first three names, they appear to have denoted the same office, and the service they gave was what the foremen or the $\pi \rho o \ddot{\iota} \sigma \tau \acute{\alpha} \mu \epsilon \nu o \iota$ of the Epistles to the Thessalonians and to the Romans rendered to their respective communities. The terms "pastors" ($\pi o \iota$—

---

[1] Clement, 1 *Epist.* xliv., 1; cf. xlii. 4; cf. Sanday's *The Conception of Priesthood* (1898), pp. 70-2. The sentence in Clement (1 *Epist.* xlii. 4) is:—"So preaching everywhere in town and in country, they appointed their first-fruits ($\tau \grave{\alpha} \varsigma$ $\dot{\alpha} \pi \alpha \rho \chi \grave{\alpha} \varsigma$ $\alpha \dot{\upsilon} \tau \hat{\omega} \nu$) when they had proved them by the Spirit, to be overseers and deacons unto them that should believe."

[2] Compare Lightfoot, *Philippians* (1881), 6th ed. pp. 95-9.; Loofs, *Theologische Studien und Kritiken* (1890), 628-42; Schmiedel, *Encyc. Bibl.* pp. 3135-9; Loening, *Die Gemeindeverfassung des Urchristenthums* (1889), pp. 58-63. Compare note on 'Presbyters' and 'Bishops' at the end of the chapter.

μένες) and "overseers" (ἐπίσκοποι) describe the kind of work done, and "elder" (πρεσβύτερος) was the title of the office. This name naturally suggests a Jewish origin; for among Jewish people we find "elders" from the earliest to the latest times. The principles of social organization which were current among the Jews no doubt insensibly moulded the earliest ecclesiastical organization in Palestine; and when we find "elders" in charge of the community in Jerusalem, ready to receive the contributions for the relief of those who were suffering from the famine which overtook them in the reign of Claudius,[1] it is impossible to doubt that the name came from their Jewish surroundings. At the same time it must always be remembered that Christian "elders" had functions entirely different from the Jewish, that the vitality of the infant Christian Communities made them work out for themselves that organization which they found to be most suitable, and that in this case nothing but the name was borrowed.[2] The respect which St. Paul always inculcated toward the mother Church in Jerusalem and the reception among the primitive Christian congregations of converts from Jewish synagogues, can easily account for the presence of the name within Gentile Christian churches. This does not mean that every Christian congregation had presbyters designedly copied from the Jewish synagogue. The largest number probably copied their neighbours when they came to make use of the word in a technical fashion. The constant intercommunication between Christian communities which was such a feature of primitive Christianity that the keen-sighted Lucian recognized it as their special possession,[3] promoted

---

[1] Acts xi. 30.

[2] It ought to be remembered that the organization which prevailed among the Judaising Christians, who refused all fraternal intercourse with the Gentile believers, was on the strict Jewish lines and was quite different from the Christian. Epiphanius tells us (*Heresies*, xxx. 18) that their congregations were presided over by archons and an archisynagogos like the Jewish synagogues of the Dispersion; Compare pp. 130-131.

[3] Lucian, *De Morte Peregrini*, 12, 41.

the gradual assimilation of constitution even when the beginnings were of different origins. But it is not necessary to suppose that the Gentile Christian communities took the word from Judaism. The term was common enough to denote rulers in the Graeco-Roman civilization;[1] and the frequent and familiar use of the word to denote a ruling body in the ordinary social life around them, if it did not altogether suggest the use, must have at least facilitated it and ensured its spread. Besides, we must remember that the word "elder," in the sense of ruler, is one of the commonest expressions among all nations. The English have their aldermen and the Romans had their senators, as Dr. Lightfoot has reminded us.[2] We may add to this the well-known fact that in young Christian communities recently won from paganism the word *elder* is applied naturally to those who have been earliest brought to believe in Christ, and that the first office-bearers, or those to whom obedience is due, are usually taken from the first converts, like Stephanas in the Corinthian Church.

All this shows us that during the last decades of the first century each Christian congregation had for its office-bearers a body of deacons and a body of elders—whether separated into two colleges or forming one must remain unknown—and that the elders took the "oversight" while the deacons performed the "subordinate services." These constituted the

---

[1] Deissmann, *Bible Studies*, Eng. Trans. pp. 154 ff. and 233 ff. Deissmann shows that the term πρεσβύτερος was common for the rulers of a a corporation in Asia Minor, and it must have been familiar to the inhabitants of those towns which furnished the Christian communities among which St. Paul saw elders chosen on his return mission journey through Derbe, Iconium and Lystra (Acts xiv. 23). One of the most interesting series of facts which Deissmann has unearthed is that the term "elder" was a religious official name in Egypt, and that the affairs of the whole Egyptian priesthood in the times of the Ptolemies were conducted by an assembly whose members (twenty-five in number) were called πρεσβύτεροι. Milton had very old authority for his saying that "new presbyter is but old priest writ large."

[2] *Commentary on the Epistle to the Philippians* (1881), 6th ed. p. 96.

local ministry of each Christian church or congregation—for these terms were then equivalent. These men watched over the lives and behaviour of the members of the community; they looked after the poor, the infirm, and the strangers; and in the absence of members of the prophetic ministry they presided over the public worship, especially over the Holy Supper.[1]

Before the close of the first century the labours of apostles (and under this name a large number of wandering missionaries must be included) had given birth to thousands of these local churches. They were all strictly independent self-governing communities—tiny islands in the sea of surrounding paganism—each ruled by its session or senate of elders. There is no trace of one man, one pastor, at the head of any community. The ruling body was a senate without a president, a kirk-session without a moderator; and if its members did not themselves possess the "prophetic gift," their authority, however defined, had continually to bend before that of the "prophets" and "teachers," to whom they had to give place in exhortation and even in presiding at the Lord's Table. The organization of the Primitive Christian Church in the last decades of the first century without one president in the community, and with the anomalous prophetic ministry, has no resemblance to any modern ecclesiastical organization, and yet contains within it the roots of all whether congregational, presbyterian (conciliar) or episcopal.

It must not be forgotten that while each Christian community

[1] While everything goes to show that in primitive times the function of teaching was not confined to the office-bearers or rulers it is difficult to believe that leadership and teaching were not frequently associated. The "prophetic" gift was so highly prized that it was only natural that men possessing it in combination with the "gift" of oversight should be selected. The use of the phrase "to shepherd" in connexion with the leaders of the Christian community as in 1 Peter v. 2 ($\pi o\iota\mu\acute{a}\nu a\tau\epsilon$ τὸ ἐν ὑμῖν ποίμνιον τοῦ Θεοῦ) appears to include more than simple oversight, and the word "admonish," applied to the προϊστάμενοι in Thessalonica, seems to point to something more than mere leadership in the very early times.

was a little self-governed republic, the visible unity of the corporate Church of Christ was never forgotten. Although each local church was an independent society, although it was not connected with other Christian communities by any organization of a political kind, it was nevertheless conscious that it belonged to a world-wide federation of equally independent churches. Its self-containedness did not produce isolation. On the contrary, every local church felt itself to be a real part of the universal and visible Church of God to which many hundreds of similar societies belonged. "All the churches of Christ," said Tertullian, "although they are so many and so great, comprise but one primitive Church . . . and are all proved to be one in unbroken unity by the *communicatio pacis, et appellatio fraternitatis et contesseratio hospitalitatis*."[1] They kept the conception of this unity alive in their hearts by the thought that all shared the same sacraments, were taught the same divine mysteries, obeyed the same commandments of God, and shared the same hope of the same kingdom. They made this corporate unity apparent by mutual help in all Christian social work, and by boundless and brotherly hospitality to all fellow-Christians. The picture of this corporate unity was always before their eyes in the fraternal intercourse of church with church by official letters and messengers, and was made vivid by the swift succession of wandering "apostles," "prophets" and "teachers," who, belonging to no one community, were the ministers of the whole Church of Christ—the binding-stones which made it visibly cohere.

[1] *De Praescript.* 20.

NOTE ON "PRESBYTERS" AND "BISHOPS"

The view taken about presbyters or elders at the close of the preceding chapter was for a long time undisputed by all serious students of the conditions of the primitive Church. It may be found stated at length in the late Dr. Lightfoot's Note on "The synonymes 'bishop' and 'presbyter,'" in his Commentary on the *Epistle to the Philippians*.[1] It has been disputed by such distinguished scholars as Harnack, Sohm and Weizsäcker, and their divergence from the opinion which was previously held with great unanimity arose after and in consequence of the publication of the late Dr. Hatch's Bampton Lectures in 1881.

The theory about early ecclesiastical organization which embodies this change of view as to the relation between the "presbyters" and "deacons," will be discussed in an Appendix. The matter which concerns us here is whether "presbyters" were church officials, chosen and appointed as such, in the Church of the first century, and identical with "bishops," or whether Harnack is right when he says that "We meet with chosen or appointed presbyters for the first time in the second century. The oldest witnesses for them are the *Epistle of James*, the *Acts of the Apostles*, the *Pastoral Epistles*, the Original Document of the so-called *Apostolic Ordinances*, and the *Shepherd of Hermas*."[2]

Harnack's opinion, if I do not mistake him, is, when put briefly, as follows. He believes that in the last decades of the first century there was at the head of each Christian congregation what may be called a three-fold organization—a pro-

---

[1] Pp. 95–9 of the 6th ed. (1881).
[2] *Expositor* for 1887. Jan.–June, p. 334. In a footnote Harnack says, "It seems to me very improbable that the Acts of the Apostles was written during the first century."

phetic, a patriarchal and an administrative one. The patriarchal rule was based upon the natural deference of the younger to the older members of the community, and the circle of elders, in all emergencies which affected the congregation, could come forward as their guides; these elders watched over the conduct and the evangelical character of the members, and admonished, punished and exhorted the congregation. The elders were the natural heads of the community, the aged members who were revered on account of age and character, but were not elected or appointed officials. The real officials, who formed the administration, were the bishops and the deacons—men who possessed the "gifts" of government and of public service. They were appointed primarily to preside at public worship. Originally there was no distinction between the bishops and the deacons save what came from age and experience, but their work naturally fell into two divisions, in which the oversight belonged to the bishops and the subordinate services were performed by the deacons. The bishops, in consequence of their position as the officials appointed to conduct public worship, became naturally the custodians and administrators of the property of the congregation, the distributors of the gifts of the faithful, the recognized guardians of the poor, the sick, the infirm and strangers, and the representatives of the society to people outside.

Harnack, therefore, holds that presbyters and bishops were distinct from the first. He believes, besides, that while a circle of elders, in the sense of "honoured" old men, existed from the most primitive times, there were no elected or chosen elders forming a college of office-bearers till the second century; but he thinks that the bishops were usually selected from the circle of honoured old men, were sometimes called "elders," and were invariably classed among them. In reaching this conclusion he rejects as unhistorical the statement in Acts xiv. 23, which tells us that the apostles, Paul and Barnabas, saw to the appointment of elders in the churches, which they had formed in Derbe, Lystra and Iconium; he believes that the "elders" of Acts xx. 17 were bishops; he concludes that the "elders" of 1 Peter v. 1 ff. were not office-bearers; he rejects, as an interpolation, the verses in Titus i. 7-9,[1] which practically assert the identity of bishops and presbyters; and he finds a complete justification of his views in the statements about presbyters and bishops in the Epistle of Clement to the Corinthians.

Let us accept, for the sake of argument, the critical conclusion of Harnack about the dates of documents [2] and the interpolations which may have come into texts, and then see what emerges from an examination of the authorities in which presbyters and bishops are mentioned.

The Epistle of Clement to the Corinthians is the best starting point, for there is practical unanimity among scholars of all schools that this document belongs to about the middle of the last decade of the first century. The letter was sent from the Roman Church to remonstrate with the Corinthian Christians

---

[1] Compare Otto Ritschl in the *Theologische Literatur-Zeitung* for 1885, No. 25.

[2] It is important to bear in mind the dates which Harnack assigns to the various documents he deals with. The following are taken from his *Chronologie der altchristlichen Literatur bis Eusebius* (1897): —1 Peter was probably written, he thinks, some time between the years 83 and 93 A.D., but it may have been written one or two decades earlier, which gives at the extreme limits of time 63-93 A.D. (pp. 454, 718). 1 Clement he dates about 93-95 but perhaps as late as 97 A.D. (pp. 255, 718). The dates he gives for the writings which he says are the first witnesses for presbyters are :—The Epistle of James about 120-140 A.D. (pp. 491, 719); the Pastoral Epistles, or at least those verses in them which are in question about 130 A.D. (p. 483); the original document of the so-called Apostolic Ordinances, about 140-180. Harnack classes the Acts of the Apostles among this set of documents in the *Expositor* (1887, Jan.-June), p. 334, and says that the book belongs to the second century. But in his *Chronologie* which was published ten years later, he says that the Acts of the Apostles was written some time between 80-93 A.D. (pp. 250, 718). There may not be much difference between the year 93 A.D. and the second century; but the change of date lifts the Acts of the Apostles out from the other writings named along with it in the *Expositor*, and places it as early as the Epistle of Clement to the Corinthians and perhaps as early as the Epistle of Peter.

about the dismissal of the leaders of the Church there from their office. We find three names given to these men—ἡγούμενοι, ἐπίσκοποι, πρεσβύτεροι.[1] Harnack's contention is that πρεσβύτεροι invariably denote the members of the circle of revered old men in the community, and that when the term is used to denote office-bearers,[2] they are so called because they were always members of that circle. On the other hand, Lightfoot,[3] in the past, and Loening, Loofs and Schmiedel in the present, declare that πρεσβύτερος is the technical name for the office, while ἐπίσπokos describes what was done (having ἐπισκοπή or oversight), or at all events that πρεσβύτερος and ἐπίσκοπος are synonymous terms for the same officials.

One thing to begin with is significant. Three men were sent from Rome to Corinth with the letter, Valerius Bito, Claudius Ephebus and Fortunatus, "men that have walked among us," says the writer, "from youth to old age unblameably." They belonged, therefore, to that class whom Harnack supposes to have been generally called "presbyters," and if his theory were correct we should expect them to be so designated in an official letter, but they are not.

In the Church in Corinth some men had been thrust from office, and the office is always referred to as ἐπισκοπή.[4] This is what is said: "For it will be no light sin for us, if we have thrust out of the oversight (ἐπισκοπή) those who have offered the gifts (i.e. the prayers of the congregation) unblameably

---

[1] ἡγούμενος and προηγούμενος, I. i. 3; xxi. 6. ἐπίσκοποι, I. xlii. 4, 5. πρεσβύτερος, I. i. 3; iii. 3; xxi. 6; xliv. 5; xlvii. 6; lv, 4; liv. 2; lvii. 1.

[2] I. xliv. 5; xlvii. 6; liv. 2; lvii. 1.

[3] Lightfoot, *Commentary on the Epistle to the Philippians* (1881), 6th ed. p. 95 ff.; Loening, *Die Gemeindeverfassung des Urchristenthums* (1889), p. 58 ff.; Loofs, *Studien und Kritiken* (1890), pp. 628 ff.; Schmiedel, *Encyclopaedia Biblica* (1902) p. 3134 ff. If we apply the well-recognized critical principle that the statement that there were "elders" in Derbe, Lystra and the neighbourhood when the book which describes them was written, this change of date gives us "elected" elders before the close of the first century.

[4] I. xliv. 1, 4.

Loofs of Halle.¹ Dr. Loofs asserts that in his opinion the idea that ἐπίσκοπος is the name of an office, and not the term describing the work done by the official, is the πρῶτον ψεῦδος of many of the modern attempts to investigate and describe primitive ecclesiastical organization.

¹ After declaring that he does not regard ἐπίσκοπος any more than ποιμὴν or ἡγούμενος as a technical term denoting an office, Loofs goes on to say:—" Mir scheint in der vorschnellen Annahme, ἐπίσκοπος sei frühe Amtsname, Titel gewesen, ein πρῶτον ψεῦδος vieler neuerer Konstructionen zu liegen; die ältere Anschauung halte ich durchaus nicht für veraltet; ἐπίσκοπος ist eine Funktionsbezeichnung und bis ins endende zweite Jahrhundert hinein gehen die Spuren davon, dass man ein Bewusstsein davon hat, dass ἐπίσκοπος weniger Amtsname als Amtsbeschreibung ist." *Studien und Kritiken* (1890), p. 628. Compare Professor Sanday, *The Conception of Priesthood*, pp. 61-62.

tried in a very interesting but not quite conclusive manner to show that *episcopi* were officers of administration and finance;[1] Lightfoot has shown that the Attic *bishop* was the commissioner appointed to inspect a newly acquired province, and that the word was used in a similar way outside the sphere of Athenian influence. In the Septuagint *episcopus* means an official set to oversee work, a military officer, a commissioner to carry out the orders of the king.[2] But while all these parallels are interesting much may be said for the more commonplace idea that the word *episcopus* means simply one who has an *episcope*, one who has oversight or superintendence. If so the word is not, during the first century, the technical term for an office-bearer; it is rather the word which describes what the office-bearer, i.e. the elder, does. The elder was the *episcopus*, overseer or superintendent, while the deacon rendered the subordinate services. The office connected itself therefore with the κυβερνήσεις, while deacon was related to the ἀντιλήψεις of 1 Cor. xii. 28.[3] The use of the words in the earliest Christian literature seems to bear out this idea.[4] This leads to the conclusion in the end of the preceding chapter that elder is the name for the office, while bishop is the title describing what the elder has to do. It can claim the support of Professor Sanday of Oxford and of Professor

---

[1] *Bampton Lectures* (1881), pp. 36–46.

[2] *Commentary on the Epistle to the Philippians*, pp. 95, 96.

[3] Compare for example the suggestive phrase in Hermas: ἐπισκέπτεσθε ἀλλήλους καὶ ἀντιλαμβάνεσθε ἰλλήλων (*Vis.* iii. 9).

[4] The word ἐπίσκοπος is used of Christ in 1 Peter ii. 25 and of God in 1 *Clem.* lix. 3. The word ἐπισκοπή is used of the providence of God in Luke xix. 44 and in 1 Pet. ii. 12. In 1 *Clement* ἐπισκοπή, in the sense of exercising oversight, is a much more prominent thought than ἐπίσκοπος. The author speaks of ὄνομα ἐπισκοπῆς, λειτουργία ἐπισκοπῆς, δῶρα ἐπισκοπῆς not ἐπισκόπων; Hermas of ἐπίσκοποι ... ἐπισκοπήσαντες ἁγνῶς. Loofs has collected a number of similar phrases from later authorities in *Studien und Kritiken* (1890), p. 629, showing that there are traces of this way of regarding ἐπίσκοπος as late as the end of the second century. Then in Titus i. 7 the article is prefixed (τὸν ἐπίσκοπον) to denote that a type is spoken of: cf. Lightfoot, *Commentary on the Epistle to the Philippians*, p. 97, n. 1.

8-13) ; in v. 17-19 the former ministers are alluded to as presbyters ; (5) in Titus i. 5-7 we find that " thou shouldest set in order the things that were wanting, and appoint elders in every city . . . for the bishop must be." ; (6) in the Peshito Syriac Version of the New Testament ἐπίσκοπος is usually translated by kashisho—elder or presbyter ; (7) the opinion of the ancient Church, founding on these passages, and voiced by Jerome, unhesitatingly declared that in the apostolic age elders and bishops were the same ; and this idea may almost be said to have prevailed throughout the Middle Ages down to the Council of Trent.[1]

The word *episcopus* had a long and varied history before it was used in connexion with the Christian Church. Hatch has

[1] Compare Lightfoot, *Commentary on the Epistle to the Philippians* (1881), 6th ed. 95-9 ; Loofs, *Studien und Kritiken* (1890), 639-41 ; Lightfoot gives quotations from Jerome, but omits some of his strongest sayings ; it may be useful to quote at greater length from his *Commentary on Titus*, i. 7 :—Idem est ergo presbyter, qui episcopus ; et antequam diaboli instinctu studia in religione fierent, et diceretur in populis : ego sum Pauli, ego Apollo, ego autem Cephae, communi presbyterorum consilio ecclesiae gubernabantur. Postquam vero unusquisque eos, quos baptizaverat, suos putabat esse, non Christi ; in toto orbe decretum est, ut unus de presbyteris electus superponeretur caeteris, ad quem omnis ecclesiae cura pertineret, et schismatum semina tollerentur. Putat aliquis non scripturarum, sed nostram esse sententiam, episcopum et presbyterum unum esse, et aliud aetatis, aliud esse nomen officii ; relegat apostoli ad Philippenses verba, dicentis (then follow the passages quoted above in the text) . . . Haec propterea, ut ostenderemus, apud veteres eosdem fuisse presbyteros, quos et episcopos ; paulatim vero ut dissensionum plantaria evellerentur, ad unum omnem sollicitudinem esse delatam. Sicut ergo presbyteri sciunt, se ex ecclesiae consuetudine ei, qui sibi praepositus fuerit, esse subjectos ; ita episcopi noverint se magis consuetudine, quam dispositionis dominicae veritate, presbyteris esse majores, et in commune debere ecclesiam regere." Gieseler in his *Compendium of Ecclesiastical History*, i. pp. 88-90, n. 1, collects a large number of authorities to show that this opinion of Jerome was held throughout the Mediaeval Church until the time of the Council of Trent. He concludes by saying " Since the Tridentine Council, the *institutio divina* of episcopacy and its original difference from the presbyterate became the general doctrine of the Roman Catholic Church, which the English Episcopalians also followed in this particular, while the other Protestant Churches returned to the most ancient doctrine and regulation on the subject."

flock. Whatever be the date or authorship of the book the fact remains that the author did believe that *the* presbyters (not some of them) were the " overseers " and the " shepherds " of the Church in Ephesus. They were the office-bearers there and were called both presbyters and overseers or bishops.

These statements carry us a long way. They prove to us that before the close of the first century bodies of presbyters existed as ruling colleges in Christian congregations over a great part of the Roman Empire. *The Epistle of Clement* proves this for the Roman Church. The First Epistle of Peter proves it for Pontus, Galatia, Cappadocia, Asia and Bithynia.[1] The Apocalypse confirms the proof for Ephesus, Smyrna, Pergamus, Thyatira, Sardis, Philadelphia and Laodicea.[2] The Acts of the Apostles adds its confirmation for Ephesus and Jerusalem.[3] The writings all imply that the colleges of presbyters at the head of congregations were no new institution. They had evidently existed for a long time. It will be observed that the places include the sphere of the mission-journey of Paul and Barnabas. They seem to me to confirm what the Acts of the Apostles tell us of the institution of presbyters by the apostles.[4] All this has been reached on the dates of the writings as given by advanced critics.

The proofs for the identity of the offices of elders and bishops in the Church of the first century have often been collected. They may be arranged thus : (1) Acts xx. 17 ; St. Paul sent for *the* elders of Ephesus, and in his address to them said that " the Holy Spirit had made them *bishops* ; (2) in 1 Peter v. 1, 2, elders are told to act as pastors and as bishops ($\pi\rho\epsilon\sigma\beta\upsilon\tau\epsilon\rho\sigma\iota \ldots \pi\sigma\iota\mu\acute{a}\nu\alpha\tau\epsilon \ldots \dot{\epsilon}\pi\iota\sigma\kappa\sigma\pi\sigma\hat{\upsilon}\nu\tau\epsilon\varsigma$); (3) in 1 Clement it is made clear that at Rome presbyters or elders and bishops are the same officials ; (4) in 1 Timothy a description of bishops is given (iii. 1-7), then follows what is required of deacons (iii.

---

[1] 1 Peter i. 1.   [2] Rev. iv. 4, 10 ; v. 5, 6, 8, etc.
[3] Acts xx. 17, 28 (Ephesus) ; xi. 30 ; xv. 4, 6, 22 ; xvi. 4 ; xxi. 18 ; (Jerusalem).   [4] Acts xiv. 23.

It appears to me that the *Epistle of Clement*, on which Harnack so firmly relies to establish his conclusion that "elders" had no official position until the second century, fails him utterly, and that his own earlier position is much more in accordance with the facts of the case. In his edition of the *Epistles of Clement*, published in 1875, Harnack said, commenting on the words *episcopi et diaconi* (xlii. 5): "Luce clarius est, duo in clero ordines tum temporis (i.e. in the time of the apostles) fuisse, episcopos (= presbyteros) et diaconos."[1] This seems still to hold good.

When we turn to 1 Peter (v. 1, 2) we find there that, even if we discard the disputed reading "exercising the oversight" (ἐπισκοποῦντες), the elders are told to "shepherd the flock of God which is among you." There is no word in the whole round of primitive ecclesiastical phraseology which is more frequently used to express the relation of office-bearers than "to shepherd" (ποιμαίνειν); and the difference between "shepherds" and "flock" is much greater than between the more aged and the younger members of the society.[2]

In Acts xx. 17, St. Paul summoned *the* presbyters (τοὺς πρεσβυτέρους) of the Church of Ephesus to meet him at Miletus; he charged them to "shepherd the Church of God"; he called the Church a "flock" (ποίμνιον); and he said that the Holy Spirit had made them overseers (ἐπισκόπους) in this

---

[1] *Patrum apostol. opera*, I. p. 132 n. (p. 68, n. 4, in ed. of 1876).

[2] Loofs says that he is so convinced that the presbyters of 1 Peter v. 1 are office bearers, that if the argument needed it (which it does not) he would rather believe with Mosheim and others that the νεώτεροι were deacons; *Studien und Kritiken* (1890), p. 638. Schmiedel, who takes the same view, asserts that the fact that the presbyters have to be warned against "discontent with their office, greed and ambition" points against the early date of the epistle (*Encyclopaedia Biblica*, p. 3134); he would not have said this had he known much about Churches in the mission field; the pregnant remark of Denney (*Hastings' Dictionary of the Bible*, iii. 82 b), that tendencies to antinomianism seem inseparable from every revival of religion, religion transcending even while it guarantees morality, ought to be kept more in mind than it is by students of early Church history.

and holily. Blessed are those *presbyters* who have gone before, seeing that their departure was fruitful and ripe, for they have no fear lest any one should remove them from their appointed place. For we see that ye have displaced certain persons though they were living honourably, from the ministration (λειτουργία) which they had kept blamelessly."[1] Everything implies that the men who had been thrust out from their ἐπισκοπή were called *presbyters*. This inference is strengthened by what follows: "It is shameful . . . that it should be reported that the very steadfast and ancient Church of the Corinthians, for the sake of one or two persons, maketh sedition against its presbyters."[2] "Only let the flock of Christ be at peace with its duly appointed presbyters."[3] "Ye therefore that laid the foundation of the sedition, submit yourselves unto the presbyters."[4] The only sentence in the epistle which lends itself to the theory of Harnack is: "Let us reverence our rulers (προηγούμενοι), let us honour our elders (πρεσβύτεροι), let us instruct our young men in the lesson of the fear of God; let us guide our women toward that which is good";[5] where 'elders' evidently mean old men. Schmiedel's remark on the rhetorical effect of substituting "elders" (πρεσβύτεροι) for "old men" (πρεσβῦται) is a sound explanation of the use of the words.[6]

---

[1] I. xliv. 4-6.   [2] I. xlvii. 6.   [3] I. liv. 2.   [4] lvii. 1.   [5] xxi. 6.

[6] "In iii. 3 allusion is made to the deposition of certain Church leaders, but in dependence on Isaiah iii. 5, where of old age it is said: "the child will press against the old man." Clement can very well have preserved this meaning in his words "the young are stirred up against the elder," as he has also retained the other general antithesis from Isaiah. "the base again the honourable." Yet the selection of the word "elders" (πρεσβύτεροι) instead of "old men" (πρεσβῦται) points to the fact, only too well known to the readers, that it was against official presbyters that the rising was. "Elders" (πρεσβύτεροι) in this case has a double meaning which rhetorically is very effective; and so also young men. For since according to xlvii. 6 only one or two persons had given occasion to the offence, it is possible that these were young persons, but at the same time also that they stood in the position of laymen towards the presbyters in so far as these were official persons." *Encyclopaedia Biblica*, p. 3135.

CHAPTER V

THE MINISTRY IN THE SECOND CENTURY

DURING the first century we can see the local churches creating their ministry. The same independence marks their action in the second century. They can be seen changing the ministry they have inherited. The beginnings of the change date from the early decades of the second century; by the end of the century it was almost complete. The change was twofold, and concerned both the prophetic and the local ministry. Stated in the briefest manner it may be described thus: the "prophetic" ministry passed away, its functions being appropriated by the permanent office-bearers of the local churches; and every local church came to supplement its organization by placing *one* man at the head of the community, making him the president of the college of elders. The one part of the change which came about in the second century, that which gave the senate of the congregation its president, was simple, natural and salutary; it came about gradually and at different times in the various portions of the Empire; it was effected peacefully, and we hear of no disturbances in consequence.[1] The other change, which meant the overthrow of the "prophetic" ministry of the apostolic and immediately subsequent period, was a revolution, provoked a widespread revolt and rent the Church in twain.

[1] Ritschl's idea that the dissensions in the Church in Rome witnessed to in the *Pastor* of Hermas arose from the attempt to force on this change finds little acceptance. Compare Ritschl, *Die Entstehung der altkatholischen Kirche* (1857), pp. 403, 535.

170 THE MINISTRY IN THE SECOND CENTURY

To understand the change in the ministry of the local churches it is to be kept in mind that at the close of the first century every local church had at its head a college or senate or session of rulers, who were called by the technical name of elders, and were also known by names which indicated the kind of work they had to do—pastors, overseers (ἐπίσκοποι). This was the ministry of oversight. To each congregation there was also attached a body of men who rendered "subordinate service," and who were called deacons—but whether they formed part of the college of elders, or were formed into a separate college of their own, it is not easy to say. The change made consisted in placing at the head of this college of rulers one man, who was commonly called either the pastor or the bishop, the latter name being the more usual, and apparently the technical designation. The ministry of each congregation or local church instead of being, as it had been, two-fold—of elders and deacons—became three-fold—of pastor or bishop, elders and deacons. This was the introduction of what is called the three-fold ministry. It is commonly called the beginning of episcopacy; but that idea is based on the erroneous conception that a three-fold ministry and episcopacy are identical.[1]

In order to show what the change was and what it meant, three relics of the oldest Christian literature may be taken, the *Didache* or the *Teaching of the Twelve Apostles*, certain fragments which are sources of the *Apostolic Canons*, and the *Letters of Ignatius of Antioch*. Authorities differ about the dates of these documents, but it may be taken as well ascertained that they all belonged to the years between 100 and 180 A.D.[2]

In the first mentioned we find the Christian society ruled by a college of office-bearers who are called "overseers and

---

[1] The Presbyterian or Conciliar system of Church government is as much a three-fold ministry as episcopacy.

[2] My own opinion inclines to the following dates: The *Epistles of Ignatius*, about 116 A.D.; the *Didache*, not earlier than 135 A.D.; the *Sources of the Apostolic Canons*, between 140-180 A.D. Compare note on next page.

deacons "; in the second we see one bishop or pastor (the terms are synonymous in the document), a session of elders and a body of deacons, but the elders rule over the bishop as they rule the congregation, and the bishop is not their president; in the third we have the three-fold ministry of bishop, elders and deacons constituting a governing body[1] at the head of the congregation or local church.

The *Didache* or *Teaching of the Twelve Apostles*[2] is a short

---

[1] In the Ignatian Epistles the bishop, elders and deacons are named together twelve times: *Magn.* ii., vi., xiii.; *Trall.* vii.; *Philad.* pref., iv., vii.; *Smyrn.* viii., xii.; *Polyc.* vi.,; *Trall.* ii.; *Philad.* x.; and, in the first ten at least, the three classes of office-bearers form an inseparable unity.

[2] The manuscript of the *Didache* was discovered in 1873 in the library of the monastery of the Holy Sepulchre in the Phanar or Greek quarter of Constantinople by Philotheus Bryennios, Patriarch of Nicomedia. It was published by him in 1883. It is now known by numerous editions. Of these by far the best comes from the pen of Professor Harnack of Berlin, and it is to that edition that the references in the notes here are made. It is difficult to say what country gave birth to this manual. The external evidence is all in favour of Egypt; and Harnack and Lightfoot conclude that it came from that land. The only evidence worth mentioning which seems to invalidate this conclusion is the sentence in the eucharistic prayer :—" Just as this broken bread was scattered over the hills and having been gathered together became one, so let Thy Church be gathered together from the ends of the earth into Thy kingdom "—words which cannot refer to Egypt but which might appropriately describe the corn of the Lebanon or the regions beyond the Jordan. But there is no reason why the eucharistic prayer might not come from Palestine and be received into the Churches of Egypt. The external evidence proves the use and the knowledge of the manual in Egypt, and the internal, with the exception of the sentence quoted, confirms the idea. A few Anglican scholars have done their best to minimise the value of the book and its evidence. A good example of this depreciation is to be found in Bishop Gore's *The Ministry of the Christian Church* (1893), 3rd ed., App. L. p. 410. It is very difficult to determine the *date*. The *Didache* quotes the *Epistle of Barnabas* and is quoted by Clement of Alexandria, and the date assigned is practically determined by the date fixed for the *Epistle of Barnabas*. The probable date of this epistle depends on whether the events referred to in the sixteenth section describe the condition of things in the time of Domitian or of Hadrian. Personally I am inclined to think that the references in the *Epistle of Barnabas* are to the later period. If this be the case it is scarcely possible to place the *Didache* earlier than 135 A.D., i.e.

Christian manual, of composite character, containing rules for the conduct of individual men and women, and regulations for the guidance of small Christian communities, hundreds of which must have been scattered over the wide face of the Roman Empire in the second century. The sixteen paragraphs of this little manual are well-arranged when compared with most manuals of the same kind. The first six contain simple directions for living the Christian life, based upon the Beatitudes of our Lord and the Ten Commandments. They seem to have formed the instruction administered to catechumens before baptism. Then follow directions about baptism, fasting and prayer and the Eucharist. Three sections are devoted to injunctions which concern the " prophetic ministry." Then follow instructions about the Lord's Day services, and the selection of office-bearers. The whole concludes with a warning about the last days.

Tertullian has said: " We Christians are one body knit together by a common religious profession, by a unity of discipline and by the bond of a common hope." [1] This little manual reads like a commentary on the saying. Every wayfaring stranger seeking food and lodging was to be received and fed if he came with a profession of the Christian faith. The letter of commendation which was in use among the Jews and to which St. Paul refers, was not required to ensure a hos-

---

later than the Ignatian letters. The majority of scholars place it very much earlier. The commonest date is about 100 A.D.—Wordsworth, Hitchcock and Brown, Spence, Bonwetsch, Massebieau; a few place it earlier—Funk and Loening, between 80 and 100 A.D.. Zahn dates it 80-120 and more exactly about 110 A.D.; Bryennios, its first editor, gives 120-130, and Harnack 130-160 A.D. as the probable date. Hilgenfeld, who finds traces of Montanism in the writing, places it later than 160. For our purposes an exact determination of date is unnecessary; all that we have to deal with is that the *Didache* describes the condition of a Christian organization some time between the Epistles of S. Paul and the third century.

[1] *Apology* 39; elsewhere (*De Praescrip.* 20) he speaks of the *contesseratio hospitalitatis* which linked all Christians together.

pitable reception [1] for one night at least. It was better to be imposed upon sometimes than to miss the chance of entertaining a brother Christian. But this hospitality was not to be without discrimination. "Let every one coming in the name of the Lord be received, but afterwards ye shall test him and know the true from the false; for ye shall have insight. If he cometh as a traveller, help him as much as you can; but he shall not remain with you unless for two or three days if it be necessary. If he will take up his abode with you and is an artizan, let him work and so eat; but if he has no trade provide employment for him, that no idler live with you as a Christian. But if he will not act according to this he is a Christ-trafficker; beware of such." [2] The brotherly love of these early Christians was a real and practical thing which no experience of imposition seems to have damped. Their simple rules are witness to the fact that they were sometimes imposed upon, and Lucian's account of the impostor Peregrinus, shows how a heathen could see that their charity was often abused. [3]

One does not naturally expect to find an elaborate ecclesiastical organization among these simple folk, and there are no traces of it. The *Didache* reveals a state of matters not unlike what we see in the Epistles of St. Paul. The control in all things evidently rested with the community met in congregational meeting. It is to the community as a whole that all the directions are addressed. It receives, tests, finds work for or sends away the travelling strangers who ask assistance or hospitality. It discharges all these duties of Christian benevolence which we find elsewhere laid upon the president. [4] It is the community, in congregational meeting, which tests and receives or rejects the members of the "prophetic ministry" when

---

[1] Compare 2 Cor. iii. 1. These commendatory letters became the rule at a later period in the Christian Church. Compare Smith's *Dictionary of Christian Antiquities*, I. 407.

[2] Chapter xii.   [3] *Peregrinus Proteus*, 13.

[4] In Justin Martyr's *Apology* it is the president ($\pi\rho o\epsilon\sigma\tau\grave{\omega}\varsigma$) who succours strangers and travellers: *Apology*, i. 67.

they appear. The injunctions about baptism, fasting, prayers, are all given to the whole community,[1] and not to the office-bearers; and yet office-bearers did exist among them whom the community are required to elect and to honour.

The manual bears evidence to the value of the "prophetic ministry." Its members are to be honoured in a very special fashion. If a prophet is present he is to preside at the Lord's Table, and his prayers are to follow his heart's promptings;[2] if no prophet was present, one of the office-bearers presided; but he had to use a fixed form of prayer. The duty of obeying the members of the "prophetic ministry" who speak the Word of the Lord is laid down in the most solemn manner. Prophets and teachers who happen to be residing within the community are to be supported by the members; the first fruits are to be set aside for them; and in this respect they are like the high priests of the Old Testament.[3]

The figures of these prophets, true and false, which are somewhat shadowy in the New Testament, take definite shape in this ancient church directory. We see the stir in the community when the prophet arrives. The women hasten to set apart the first baking of bread, the first cup of the newly opened wine-skin or jar of oil, the first yard or two of the newly spun cloth[4] for the use of these men, gifted with magnetic speech,

---

[1] "Now concerning baptism, thus baptize ye: having first uttered all these things (i.e. the instructions given in cc. i.-vi.), baptize into the name of the Father and of the Son and of the Holy Ghost in living (running) water. But if thou hast not living, baptize in other water: and if thou canst not in cold then in warm. But if thou hast neither, pour water thrice upon the head unto the name of the Father, the Son and the Holy Ghost. But before the baptism let the baptizer and the baptized fast and whatever others can; but the baptized thou shalt command to fast for one or two days before," c. vii.

[2] "But permit the prophets to give thanks as much as they will," x. 7.

[3] "Every first fruit . . . thou shalt take and give to the prophets; for they are your high-priests," xiii. 3.

[4] "Every first fruit then of the produce of the wine-press and of the threshing-floor, of oxen and of sheep, thou shalt take and give to the prophets. . . . If thou bakest a baking of bread, take the first of it and

who have come to edify the little society and instruct them in the ways of the Lord.

Not that every one who comes among them saying that he is a prophet is to be received as such. If he asks for money, if he does not practise more than he preaches, if he has not the ways of the Lord—then he is a false prophet and is to be sent away.[1] For the Christian communities felt that they had the presence of their Lord with them according to His promise, and had the gift, however rudely it might be shown and exercised, of testing even " prophets " and " apostles." When the members of this prophetic ministry were received they were the only persons permitted to abide within the community without earning their living by artisan or other labour. *Their labour was the instruction and edification of the members of the society.*[2]

Although the community was honoured with the presence of these gifted men, and although the congregational meeting was, as in the Churches of Corinth and Thessalonica, the centre and seat of rule, the brethren were directed to elect office-bearers. The context gives the reason. " But on the Lord's Day do ye assemble and break bread and give thanks, after confessing your transgressions, in order that your sacrifice may be pure. But every one that hath controversy with his friend, let him not come together with you until they be reconciled. . . . Therefore appoint for yourselves bishops and deacons worthy of the Lord, men meek and not avaricious, upright and proved, for they too render you the service of the prophets and teachers."[3] The office-bearers are needed to act as judges in quarrels within

---

give according to the commandment. In like manner when thou openest a jar of wine or oil, take the first of it and give to the prophets; and of money and clothing and every possession take the first, as may seem good unto thee, and give according to the commandment," xiii. 3-7.

[1] xi.

[2] " But every true prophet who will settle among you is worthy of his support. Likewise a true teacher, he also is worthy, *like the workman*, of his support " ; xiii. 1, 2.   [3] xiv. 1-2; xv. 1, 2.

the community, and to act as the "wise men" whom St. Paul asked the Corinthians to appoint.[1] They are also, whether in turn or otherwise we do not know, to preside at the Holy Supper and to edify the community, for they are to serve as "prophets and teachers."[2] There is no division of labour indicated between the bishops (presbyters) and the deacons; and the same qualities of meekness, uprightness, proved Christian character and the absence of avarice are demanded of both.

What went on in the smaller took place in the larger Christian communities; the outlines of the picture sketched for us in the *Didache* appear also in the *Epistle of Clement*[3] and in the quaint *Pastor* of Hermas. At the head of the community, as regular office-bearers, were a number of men presbyter-bishops

---

[1] 1 Cor. vi. 5.

[2] "They render you the service of the prophets and teachers. Therefore neglect them not; for they are your honoured ones along with the prophets and the teachers": xv. 1, 2. This passage is rightly regarded by Harnack, and in this Sanday follows him, as of the utmost importance to enable us to trace the development of the Christian ministry in the primitive Church. It must be referred to later. It is sufficient to say here that we see the change taking place whereby the ministry of the local Church secured the place at an earlier period possessed by the prophetic ministry. Compare Harnack's edition of the *Didache* in *Texte und Untersuchungen*, II. i. 58 note; ii. 140 ff.; Sanday, *Expositor* (1887), Jan.-June, p. 14 ff. The word τιμή was specially used to denote the respect due to spiritual guides (compare Harnack's note for references); it is a question whether the "honoured ones" are also those who "receive an honorarium" (for the Greek word has the double reference); the prophets and teachers received the firstfruits in preference to the poor. Did the bishops and deacons who are placed among the honoured spiritual guides partake of these first fruits also? The *Didache* does not answer the question.

[3] In the Epistle of Clement we find that the congregation is the supreme authority; the letter is addressed to the whole Church:—"To the Church which sojourneth in Corinth" (preface); the evil-doers are urged to do "what is ordered by the people" (liv. 2). The office-bearers are a number of presbyter-bishops and deacons (compare above pp. 159 ff.). The epistle says little or nothing about a "prophetic ministry" but that is not to be wondered at as it was written for a definite purpose which had nothing to do with the question. In Hermas we have the same organization and the distinct traces of prophets and their ministry

with deacons as their assistants, but the congregation is seen to be the supreme judge in the last resort. The people rule and form a little democracy; they choose their office-bearers who lead their devotions and act as arbiters in all disputes. They are a self-governing community. They can even reject the services of men who assert that they are members of the prophetic ministry. They can do this in God's name. They are a theocracy as well as a democracy. The "gifts" of the Spirit are present in their midst and are manifest in the power of judging.

Our second document is what Harnack calls the *Original Sources of the Apostolic Canons*.[1] These sources are but fragments, preserved because they have been incorporated in a much later law-book of the Christian Church. We do not know from what land they came nor how wide or narrow was the sphere of their authority. They show us, however, what a small Christian community was in the last decades of the second century, and they describe the way in which it was created out of a number of Christian families. We can see the birth and growth of a Church with its complete organization. In many respects the process described can be seen now in any mission field, especially among peoples of ancient civilization. Perhaps

[1] A summary of the critical history of the *Apostolic Canons* (to be distinguished from the *Apostolic Constitutions*) will be found in Harnack's edition of the *Didache* (*Texte und Untersuchungen*, II. ii. p. 193-209) followed by Harnack's critical reconstruction based on the discovery of the *Didache* (pp. 209-25), and lastly the full text of the canons (pp. 225-37), tables and summary (pp. 237-41). According to generally accepted critical opinions the compiler of the Canons used four sources, the *Epistle of Barnabas*, the *Didache* (or more probably an abridgement of the *Didache*), and two fragments from an old ecclesiastical law-book. It is with these fragments that we have now to do, or rather with the first of them. Harnack dates it at some time between 140 and 180 A.D. These fragments, with commentary and excursus, have been published by Harnack in the *Texte und Untersuchungen*, II. v. Professor Sanday appears to agree with Professor Harnack about these fragments: *Expositor* (1887), Jan.-June, pp. 20, 21, 106. Harnack's edition of the *Sources* has been translated into English by L. A. Wheatley under the title *Sources of the Apostolic Canons* (1895).

the most interesting thing about it is that every body of Christians however small is ordered to form itself into a congregation, and the implied thought that the Christian life must be lived within an orderly Christian society before the full benefits which accompany it can be enjoyed.

The document takes us back to a time when a few Christian families found themselves the only believers in the midst of a surrounding paganism. Few or many, they are commanded to organize themselves as a *church*.[1] If the families number less than twelve, or rather if they include fewer than twelve persons entitled to vote in the election, it is supposed that they need aid in the first important step in the organization, which is the selection of some one to be their pastor or bishop—the names are synonymous in the document.[2] In this case they are to apply to a neighbouring Christian community which has been established for some time, and ask them to appoint three men to assist them to select their pastor.[3] Along with these three,

---

[1] "If there are few men, and not twelve persons who are competent to vote at the election of a bishop, the neighbouring Churches should be written to, where any of them is a settled one, in order that three selected men may come thence and examine carefully if he is worthy." *Sources of the Apostolic Canons*, pp. 7, 8. (Here and elsewhere I quote from the English translation of Harnack's edition in the *Texte und Untersuchungen*, II. v.)

[2] The word $\dot{\epsilon}\pi\acute{\iota}\sigma\kappa o\pi os$ occurs in i. 4, 22; ii. 15, 19; and $\pi o\iota\mu\acute{\eta}\nu$ in ii. 18.

[3] The phrase is $\dot{\epsilon}\kappa\lambda\epsilon\kappa\tau o\grave{\iota}\ \tau\rho\epsilon\hat{\iota}s\ \ddot{\alpha}\nu\delta\rho\epsilon s$. Various parallels may be found to the employment of *three* chosen men to conduct together work requiring tact and experience. The most obvious is the mission of the three men Claudius Ephebus, Valerius Bito and Fortunatus to Corinth from Rome (1 Clem. lxiii. 1). Harnack finds in the three men selected to assist the small congregation in the selection of a bishop the anticipation of the much later rule that the consecration of a bishop required the presence and co-operation of the three neighbouring bishops. He finds a middle point in the fact evidenced by the letter of Cornelius of Rome to Fabius of Antioch (Euseb. *Hist. Eccl.* VI., xliii. 8, 9) that by the middle of the third century it was the custom that bishops were consecrated by three neighbouring bishops (*Sources of the Apostolic Canons* (1895), pp. 36 ff.). This afterwards became the law and is found in canons of many

presumably experienced Christians, but not necessarily office-bearers, they are to select some one (whether from their own number or from the outside is not said) to be their bishop. A list of qualifications is given them to direct their choice, from which it appears that character and Christian experience are the things really needful for the office.[1] A pastor or bishop is to be one whose character stands so high that no one may be expected to bring any charge of misconduct against him. He is not to be given to drinking, nor to covetousness nor to foul living. He must not be a respecter of persons. It is better that he should be unmarried, but if he has a wife he must be a faithful husband. It is advisable that he should be an educated man and able to expound the Scriptures, but that is not indispensable. If he is unlearned he must at least be gentle and full of love towards all persons. He has to represent the community to the outside world, and must therefore be a man whom the heathen respect. He is to be the leader in public worship, and the elders are to support him, seated on his right hand and on his left. He must be a valiant fighter against sin, and the elders are to aid him in this duty also. He is, under the control of the elders, to administer the property of the Church, which in these early days consisted of the gifts brought by the faithful to the meeting for thanks-

councils (the Council of Arles in its twentieth canon being the first). Hence comes the saying "All Christendom becomes presbyterian on a consecration day." It is evident from the continual repetition of the law that the Churches found it somewhat difficult to enforce their regulation.

[1] The qualifications are divided into two classes those indispensable and those desirable. "That is if he has a good report among the heathen, if he is faultless, if a friend of the poor, if honourable—no drunkard no adulterer, not covetous nor a slanderer, nor partial or such like" (i. 10-15). These are the necessary qualifications. Then follow the desirable: "It is good if he is unmarried; if not then a man of one wife; educated, in a position to expound the scriptures; but if he is unlearned, then he must be gentle and filled with love to all, so that a bishop should never be as one accused of anything by the multitude" (i. 10-23); *Sources of the Apostolic Canons*, pp. 8-10.

giving. They were handed over to him, and distributed under the watchful supervision of the elders.

Besides the pastor the congregation is required to appoint at least two elders or presbyters.[1] They are to be men advanced in years and presumably unmarried (the meaning of the phrase is somewhat doubtful).[2] They must not be respecters of persons. They are to be ready to assist the pastor at all times in the conduct of public worship and in dealing with sinners. They are the rulers in the strict sense of the word. They are responsible for summoning the people to public worship, and it is their place to preserve order during Divine Service. The women who visit the sick are to report to them and not to the bishop. They are to see that the bishop distributes in a proper manner the offerings of the faithful. They have charge of the discipline of the congregation including the pastor.[3]

Every church must have at least three deacons, who are to be the ministers of the people in their private and home life. They are to report on any unseemly conduct which may call

---

[1] "Hence the presbyters must be already advanced in life, abstaining becomingly from communication with women, willingly sharing with the brotherhood, not having regard to the person, companions in consecration with the bishop (συμμύσται τοῦ ἐπισκόπου), and fighting on his side, collecting the congregation together, kindly disposed towards the pastor. The elders on the right should look after the bishops at the altar, in order that they may distribute the gifts and themselves receive the necessary contributions (ὅπως τιμήσωσι καὶ ἐντιμηθῶσιν, εἰς ὃ ἂν δέῃ). The elders on the left shall look after the congregation in order that it may be at rest and without disturbance, after that it has been first proved in all submission. But if one who is admonished should answer rudely; those at the altar should unite and condemn such an one to the punishment deserved by a general resolution, so that the others may be in awe, in order that they (the elders) look not at the person of any one, and that it may not spread as a cancer and be taken up by every one" (ii.).

[2] The phrase is τρόπῳ τινὶ ἀπεχομένους τῆς πρὸς γυναῖκας συνελεύσεως.

[3] The relation of the elders to the bishops is expressed by the word προνοήσονται; this has been translated in the English version "shall assist," which cannot be right, for the same word is used to express the relation of the elders to the people, and it is evident that the power of discipline is meant (ii. 19, 23).

for discipline at the hands of the elders. They are to be men well esteemed in the congregation, faithful husbands, with well-behaved families.[1] It is their duty to move among the people, " and carefully give heed to those who walk disorderly, warning one, exhorting another, threatening a third, but leaving scoffers entirely to themselves." They were to be men of generous disposition, for part of their duty was to insist that the wealthier members of the *Brotherhood*, as the congregation is called, " open their hands " to support the poor and for other ecclesiastical needs, and example is better than precept. In short their duties, as laid down in these ancient canons, are almost identical with those of the deacons in presbyterian churches now, both in what they do and in what they are to refrain from doing.

Every church was also to have a ministry of women. Three were to be appointed. They are called *widows*, and a curious division of duties is enjoined.[2] One of them is to act as a combination of nurse and Bible-woman. She is to assist the sick women of the congregation. To this end she " must be ready for the service, discreet and not avaricious, nor given to much love of

---

[1] " They shall be approved in every service, with a good testimony from the congregation, husbands of one wife, educating their children, honourable, gentle, quiet, not murmuring, not double-tongued, not quickly angry, not looking on the person of the rich, also not oppressing the poor, also not given to much wine, intelligent, encouraging well to secret works, while they compel those among the brethren who have much to open their hands also themselves generous, communicative, honoured with all honour and esteem and fear by the congregation, carefully giving heed to those who walk disorderly, warning the one, exhorting the other, threatening a third, but leaving the scoffers completely to themselves " (iv.). *Sources of the Apostolic Canons*, pp. 17-19.

[2] " Three widows shall be appointed, two to persevere in prayer for all those who are in temptation, and for the reception of revelations where such are necessary ; but one to assist the women visited with sickness. She must be ready for service, discreet, communicating what is necessary to the elders, not avaricious, not given to much love of wine, so that she may be sober and capable of performing the night services and other loving services if she will ; for these are the chief good treasures of the Lord " (v.). *Sources of the Apostolic Canons*, pp. 19-21.

wine, so that she may be sober and capable of performing the night services and other loving ministry if she will." The duty of the other two was to "persevere in prayer for all who are in temptation"; and they were also to pray for the reception of revelations where these were necessary. They took the place in the congregation of the old prophetic ministry, and were among the number of the New Testament prophetesses.

There was another official. The congregation is told to appoint a *Reader*. He is to be an experienced Christian. His duty is to read the Scriptures during Divine Service, and it is required that he should have a good voice and a clear delivery. He is told to come early to the church on the Lord's Day. He is to be able to expound the Scripture that he has read. He is to remember that "he fills the place of an evangelist." The *Reader* in these ancient times did what the pastor or bishop was expected to do in later times. There was the more need for the office when we remember that the bishop might be an unlearned man, and by unlearned was frequently meant one who did not know the alphabet.

Such is a picture of a small Christian Church in the last decades of the second century. It may be taken as the type of hundreds. It is independent and self-governing, but it is not isolated. It is a brotherhood ($\dot{\alpha}\delta\epsilon\lambda\phi\acute{o}\tau\eta\varsigma$), consisting of brethren organized under office-bearers chosen by themselves, but it has relations with, and a knowledge of, a wider brotherhood of which it is a minute part. When need comes it can appeal for and get help in the selection of its pastor. Its ministry need not be learned; Christian character, saintly behaviour, the power to exhort and teach which comes from deep Christian experience, are more highly valued than ability to read. The *Brotherhood* has the *Wise Men* whom St. Paul desired to see in the Corinthian Church in its elders or presbyters who share the responsibilities of the pastor's work, and in this respect are his assistants, but whose superintendence and rule extends over the pastor himself in other respects. We see the deacons going out and in among the members of the society, encouraging, warning, rebuking, if need be, and endeavouring to excite to Christian liberality by precept and example. We descry through the mists of seventeen hundred years the homely and simple ministry of women; on the one hand an active motherly woman, able to nurse her sick sisters, strong enough to endure, as women only can, long periods of night-watching, giving wholesome motherly advice to the women and girls of the community; and on the other two solitary women, in the weakness and loneliness of their sex and of their widowhood, powerful to wrestle with God in prayer, and to assist with their supplications the whole congregation and the strong men who are tempted and tried in the daily battle of life. The strong supporting the weak; and the weak, powerful in prayer, helping the strong; the picture is one which only a Christian community could show, and there it often appeared. Early Christian literature abounds in references to the prayers of the widows of the congregation. They are expected to bear the whole burden of the brethren upon their hearts, and to entreat the Lord in prayer. The prayers of believers are *the* sacrifice of primitive Christianity, and because the widows abound in prayer they are the altar of sacrifice.[1]

These ancient fragments of old ecclesiastical canons are, however, specially interesting, because they represent the transition stage between the organization of the churches, shown in the *Epistle of Clement to the Corinthians* or in the *Didache*, and the three-fold ministry of the third century. They do this in

---

[1] Compare Polycarp, *Epistle to the Philippians*, 4; in the *Canons of Hippolytus* (ix. 59) widows are to be highly honoured because of their *copiosas orationes et infirmorum curam*. In *Apostolic Constitutions*, iii. 12, 13, it is said: " For it becomes widows when they see that one of their fellow widows is clothed by any one or receives money or meat or drink or shoes, at the sight of the refreshment of their sister to say: Thou art blessed O God, who hast refreshed my fellow widow. Bless O Lord, and glorify him that has bestowed these things upon her, and let his good work ascend in truth unto Thee and remember him for good in the day of his visitation." Compare *Apost. Constit.* iii. 5, 7.

two ways. The prophetic ministry has departed, but its memories linger in the prayers of the widows for revelations and in the exhortation to the *Reader* that he holds the place of an *evangelist*. For our immediate purpose, however, it is most interesting to have in the fragments an organization lying between that of a church or congregation, ruled by a college of presbyter-bishops as in the *Didache*, and one where the bishop or pastor is the president of a compact circle of elders and deacons, and where these office-bearers have their fixed places under their head. In these fragments the bishop or pastor has neither the power nor the position he afterwards came to occupy almost universally in the third century.

But there is this advance on the older organization. There is now one man who has a distinct position which he occupies by himself. He is the recognized leader of the congregation or church in several definite ways. He represents the congregation to those outside, else why should it be a necessary qualification for office that he is respected by the heathen? He leads the congregational worship in the meeting for thanksgiving at any rate, and if he is learned and can expound the Scriptures, probably at the meeting for edification also. The gifts of the congregation are given into his hands for distribution, and he is the almoner. He stands alone and separate from the other office-bearers in all this. In these respects also he stands forth as the representative of the unity of the congregation or church.

On the other hand, he has not yet been placed in the position which the bishop or pastor afterwards held. In the *Apostolic Constitutions* it is the bishop who calls the congregation together for worship; here that duty belongs to the elders, who also watch over the behaviour of the people while in Church.[1] In later ecclesiastical manuals the deacons and deaconesses report to the bishop; there they, or at least the deaconesses, report to

---

[1] *Apostolic Constitutions*, ii. 57; cf. *Sources of the Apostolic Canons*, ii. 15: the same word συναθροίζειν being used in both as the technical term to summon to Church.

the elders, who have the responsibilities for the sick and infirm of the congregation, which in later days belonged to the bishop.¹ All these things show that the discipline of the congregation is in the hands of the elders exclusively, and that the bishop is not the president of their court. If any doubt remained on this head it must vanish when we consider the unique regulation that the bishop himself is under the supervision of the elders in one of the most important of his functions.² When he acts as almoner they are to see that he acts rightly, and, what is of the highest importance for understanding the situation, the word used to express the control of the elders over the bishop is the same word ($\pi\rho o\nu o\epsilon i\sigma\theta a\iota$), which describes their power of discipline over the congregation. The bishop has emerged from the circle of presbyters, but he is not their president; and while he is the leader of the congregation in many respects he is, in one respect at least, like the members of the congregation, amenable to the discipline of the elders.

Probably had we other relics of ecclesiastical manuals belonging to this transition period we should find other instances of organizations on the road towards the three-fold ministry,

---

[1] *Apostolic Constitutions*. iii. 19 orders the deacons and deaconesses: "Tell your *Bishop* of all those that are in affliction; for you ought to be like his soul and senses." *Sources of the Apostolic Canons*, v. 8, 9, directs the *Widows* to "communicate what is necessary to the presbyters or elders." In the *Canons of Hippolytus*, c. 5, the deacons are ordered to report to the bishop. Cf. Riedel, *Die Kirchenrechtsquellen des Patriarchats Alexandrien* (1900), p. 203.

[2] *Apostolic Constitutions*, ii. 25, 35, make it plain that the bishop was accountable to no one but God in his duty as almoner. The bishop is thus addressed: "Let him use those tenths and first fruits, which are given according to the command of God, as a man of God; as also let him dispense in a right manner the free-will offerings which are brought on account of the poor, to the orphans ... as having that God for the examiner of his accounts Who has committed the disposition to him" (ii. 25). And in the thirty-fifth section the people are enjoined: "Thou shalt not call the bishop to account nor watch his administration, how he does it, when or to whom, or where, or whether he does it well or ill or indifferently; for he has One Who will call him to account, the Lord God."

186 THE MINISTRY IN THE SECOND CENTURY

but travelling by different paths. We know that the threefold ministry grew more rapidly in some places than in others, and the organization probably passed through several transition stages, of which this is one, before it attained to maturity.

Our third group of writings consists of the famous *Letters of Ignatius of Antioch*—a series of documents which have provoked an immense amount of criticism which cannot be said to be ended. Without entering into the controversy we may accept the results of the scholarly criticism of the late Dr. Lightfoot in this country, and of Dr. Zahn in Germany, according to which the *Seven Epistles* in the shorter recension are genuine documents. These letters came from the head of the Christian community in Antioch in Syria. Ignatius had been seized in an outburst of persecution and was being dragged across Asia Minor, a prisoner in charge of a band of Roman soldiers. He wrote to the Christians of Ephesus that he was on his way from Syria, in bonds for the sake of the common Name and hope, and was expecting to succeed in fighting with wild beasts at Rome, that by so succeeding he might have power to become a disciple.[1] The journey was an apprenticeship in suffering; for the ten soldiers, who guarded him, treated him as ten leopards might have done, and only waxed worse when they were kindly entreated.[2] The churches of Asia Minor had sent him comforting messages by special delegates. The letters are his answers.[3]

---

[1] *To the Ephesians*, 1. [2] *To the Romans*, 5.

[3] The letters of Ignatius were generally known during the later Middle Ages in the form of seventeen epistles, of which fifteen were believed to come from the pen of Ignatius while two (one from the Virgin and another from a Mary of Cassobola) were addressed to Ignatius. Renascence criticism disposed of the claims of four of these letters. There remained thirteen, twelve from the pen of Ignatius and one (from Mary of Cassobola) addressed to him. This collection is now known as the *Long Recension*, and it was this collection which was the subject of fierce controversy in the end of the sixteenth and during the seventeenth century. At the basis of these attacks made on the genuineness of these letters lay two facts: that Eusebius knew of seven letters only and that these thirteen contained passages evidently unknown to Eusebius or to any of the ancients.

They exhale the fragrance of a saintly and impassioned Christian life. They dwell on the need that the sin-sick children

The learned Englishman, Ussher, afterwards archbishop of Armagh and primate of all Ireland, observed that the quotations made from Ignatius by some English writers from the thirteenth century onwards corresponded with those found in Eusebius, Theodoret, etc., and concluded that there must exist in England a manuscript which would represent the Ignatius known to the ancients. After a prolonged search two such manuscripts were brought to light, both of them in Latin. They contained seven letters but in a form shorter than the generally received letters. Ussher accepted six of these shorter letters as the genuine epistles of Ignatius (he refused to accept the letter to Polycarp). His book was published in 1644. Soon afterwards (1646) Isaac Voss published six letters from a Greek MS.—his MS. did not give the *Epistle to the Romans*; and in 1689 the full Greek text of the seven letters was published by Ruinart. It was generally admitted that, if any genuine letters of Ignatius had descended to the present time, they were these seven in the shorter form; but many critics still refuse to admit the genuineness of any of the letters.

The controversy was raised again in 1845 by the publication of Cureton's *Ancient Syriac Version of the Epistles of S. Ignatius to S. Polycarp, the Ephesians and the Romans*. The author had found two Syriac MSS. in the library of the British Museum containing the three epistles mentioned in his title and in a still shorter form than those published by Ussher. He maintained that these three short letters were the genuine remains of Ignatius. He defended his position in a second work, *Vindiciae Ignatianae* (1846), and in his most complete treatise, *Corpus Ignatianum* (1849). His views at once attracted attention and were very largely adopted, though many distinguished scholars still defended the seven letters, while others refused to accept even Cureton's three in the brief form. This controversy was almost ended by Zahn, who, in his *Ignatius von Antioch* (1873), showed very successfully that Cureton's three Syriac letters were epitomes of the three in what were called the *Short Recension*. This opinion was supported by the late Dr. Lightfoot's elaborate work, *Apostolic Fathers*, part II., *S. Ignatius, S. Polycarp* (1885). The result of these two works has been that in Germany, France and England the seven letters, in the shorter form published by Ruinart in 1689, are generally accepted as the genuine remains of Ignatius. Many critics still refuse to accept the letters in any form as genuine, but their criticism is mainly of the subjective and unconvincing kind. The only writer whose book deserves serious consideration and who dissents from the conclusions of Zahn and Lightfoot is Bruston, who, in his *Ignace d'Antioche* (1897), refuses to admit the genuineness of the *Epistle to the Romans* and combines his critical opinions with the theory that Ignatius was not the Bishop of Antioch but a deacon in the Church there.

Many scholars are of the opinion that the letters of Ignatius were known

of men have for the One great Physician of souls.¹ The Christian preacher of the second century lives in them still, embalmed there and treasured up for a life beyond life. We find in them bursts of poetic fancy: the Lord was a Star which shone forth in the heaven above all stars; and its light was unutterable; and its strangeness caused astonishment; and all the rest of the constellations, with the sun and the moon, formed themselves into a chorus about the star; but the Star itself far outshone them all.² They abound in simple but striking metaphors, such as the lyre and its strings, the athlete and his training; the chorus with its keynote; the wheat ground in the hand-mill.³ We find quaint emblems: "Ye are stones of a temple, which were prepared beforehand for a building of God, being hoisted up to the heights through the engine of Jesus Christ, which is the Cross, and using for a rope the Holy Spirit; while your faith is your windlass, and love is the way that leadeth up to God." ⁴ They show deep knowledge of the human heart: "No man professing faith sinneth, and no man possessing love hateth" ⁵—a sentence which might have come from Thomas à Kempis. Sometimes the words seem insensibly to take the form of a prophetic chant, and have a rhythmic cadence all

---

to Lucian and that he used his knowledge in writing his story *De Morte Peregrini*. They think that the imprisonment of Peregrinus, the visits paid to him by delegates from the Churches of Asia Minor, and the letters written by him to the Churches which were received with reverence, were all incidents suggested by the letters of Ignatius. The idea seems to me somewhat far-fetched; the points which Lucian seizes and makes use of may easily have been suggested by a general observation of usages common to early Christianity and need not be attached to any particular person however famous; but compare Lightfoot, *S. Ignatius, S. Polycarp*, i. pp. 331 ff.

¹ *To the Ephesians*, 7.
² *Ibid.* 19.
³ *To the Ephesians*, 4; *To the Philadelphians*, 1; *To Polycarp*, 1, 2; *To the Romans*, 4.
⁴ *To the Ephesians*, 9.
⁵ *Ibid.* 14.

their own.¹ Throughout there is that taste of Oriental extravagance which makes them so natural.²

The letters breathe the storm and strain of a time of persecution. The rallying cry which rolls from the first to the last is union! Keep united! Close the ranks! Intimate union with Christ; that is the main thing, and that which comes first. This is how he puts it. "For being counted worthy to bear a most godly name, in these bonds, which I carry about, I sing the praise of the churches; and I pray that there may be in them union of the flesh and of the Spirit which are Jesus Christ's, our never-failing life—an union of faith and of love which is preferred before all things, and—what is more than all—an union with Jesus and with the Father, in whom, if we patiently endure all the despite of the prince of this world and escape therefrom, we shall attain unto God."³

Varying pictures of the Christian Churches rise in his imagination. Now they are ships driven and tossed in the storm of persecution; there must be a strong man at the helm and discipline in the crew; they need a favouring wind and a sheltering haven.⁴ Or they are so many households of God: the office-bearers are the upper servants set there by the Master to rule, and the other members obey the Master Himself when they are submissive to those whom He has set over them.⁵

---

¹ Compare especially the *Epistle to the Philadelphians*, 7 :—

Χωρὶς τοῦ ἐπισκόπου μηδὲν ποιεῖτε·
Τὴν σάρκα ὑμῶν ὡς ναὸν Θεοῦ τηρεῖτε·
Τὴν ἕνωσιν ἀγαπᾶτε·
Τοὺς μερισμοὺς φεύγετε·
Μιμηταὶ γίνεσθε Ἰησοῦ Χριστοῦ,
Ὡς καὶ αὐτὸς τοῦ Πατρὸς αὐτοῦ.

Ignatius had evidently visited Philadelphia and had addressed the brethren there, and in his address he had felt the prophetic afflatus, had interrupted himself with a loud cry, and these sentences were part of what he had said. They are an example of the prophetic utterances.

² As where he says :—"These men ye ought to shun as wild beasts for they are mad dogs, biting by stealth," *To the Ephesians*, 7.

³ *To the Magnesians*, 1.

⁴ *To Polycarp*, 2.   ⁵ *To the Ephesians*, 6.

Or they are disciple companies, cherishing an imitation of Christ, not in the solitary fashion of Thomas à Kempis, but in companionship. The pastor represents Jesus, the elders are His apostles,[1] and the deacons and the faithful those who followed Him in Galilee—and all, pastor and elders and people, look for the footprints the Master has left, and try to set their steps where He trod. Perhaps this picture of a disciple company is his favourite one. It has been a thought tenderly cherished through the centuries, and has often been set forth with a certain quaint realism. Columba and twelve companions came from Ireland to Iona. Columbanus with twelve companions appeared among the Franks and the Burgundians to preach the Gospel. Bernard and twelve companions left Citeaux to found his new dwelling at Clairvaux. In each case the chronicler lovingly adds: " a disciple company."

We miss the main thought in Ignatius if we neglect to see that the unity which is his passion is primarily and fundamentally something spiritual and mystical. The Person of Christ is the centre round which the Church crystallizes. By His death on the Cross and by His Resurrection our Lord has elevated a standard round which His troops of believers can rally and form a disciplined army.[2] This sacred mystical attraction is the inward essence and source of that union which he has always in view. So strong is it that all believers may be said to have one mind, a godly concord and one spirit of perseverance.[3] The unity which he insists upon is first of all a union with Christ Jesus, and then, and arising from that, a common religious

---

[1] *To the Magnesians*, 6 ; *To the Trallians*, 2, 3 ; *To the Smyrnaeans*, 8.

[2] *To the Smyrnaeans*, 1:—" Truly nailed up in the flesh for our sakes under Pontius Pilate and Herod the Tetrarch . . . that He might set up a standard unto all ages through His resurrection, for His saints, whether among Jews or among Gentiles, in one body of His Church."

[3] *To the Magnesians*, 7, 15 :—" But let there be one prayer in common, one supplication, one mind (νοῖς), one hope, in love and in joy unblamable which is in Jesus Christ. . . . Fare ye well in godly concord, and possess ye a stedfast spirit which is in Jesus Christ."

belief and a common affection diffused throughout all believers who ought to live in a harmony of love. The unity Ignatius yearns after is first of all a unity of faith and love.[1]

But this unseen mystical unity ought to make itself manifest according to the ordinances of Jesus and of His apostles. It can make itself seen in the best way in the attachment of believers to the visible local church which is the assembly of believers for prayer, exhortation, and for the celebration of the Holy Supper and for baptism. Those who are truly the Lord's, and who share in the invisible mystical union, cannot fail to assemble together with one heart and mind, nor to unite in one common prayer. Ignatius addresses himself more than once to men who seem to think that the Christian life can be lived apart from the Christian visible fellowship;[2] and he declares that apart from the office-bearers there is not even the name of a Church.[3] Christians ought to manifest this inward unity which they have in an external unity, which can best show itself in the manifestation of mutual respect for each other, in reverencing each other and in loving one another *in* Jesus Christ.[4]

This submission which is due by all believers to each other is specially due to those who have been placed at the head of the Christian communities, and who are there to be examples to their flocks.[5] Submission to one another and to the office-

---

[1] " Run in harmony with the mind of God " (*Ephesians*, 3); " In your concord and harmonious love Jesus Christ is sung; do ye, each and all of you, form yourselves into a chorus, that being harmonious in concord and taking the key-note of God ye may in union sing with one voice through Jesus Christ to our Father " (*Ephesians*, 4); cf. *To the Magnesians*, 1.

[2] *To the Ephesians*, 5, 13, 20; *To the Magnesians*, 7.

[3] *To the Trallians*, 3.

[4] " Therefore do ye all study conformity to God, and pay reverence one to another " (*Magnesians*, 6). " Attempt not to think anything right for yourselves apart from others " (*Magnesians*, 7). " Be obedient to the bishop *and to one another* " (*Magnesians*, 13).

[5] " Let there be nothing among you which shall have power to divide you, but be ye united with the bishop and with them that preside over

bearers—a submission founded on love—is the outward manifestation of the inward mystical union which all true believers have with Christ, who is the true centre of the union. For Ignatius never loses sight of the mystical union fed by faith and love.[1]

The real centre of this unity is God and Christ Who is God; the real oversight lies with Him. In his fervent Oriental way which expresses abstract thoughts in defective, though picturesque, material and external representations, Ignatius sees this Divine and invisible unity manifest in the bishop (or in whatever may be the visible centre of the ecclesiastical rule).[2] For it must not be forgotten in attempting to interpret the thoughts of Ignatius that he belonged to what has been called the "enthusiastic" age of the Church, and that he shared in an exalted degree in the spirit of his times. He claimed to be a prophet and to possess the prophetic gift. "I am in bonds," he says, "and can comprehend heavenly things and the arrays of angels and the musterings of principalities, things visible and invisible."[3] He describes how, when he was preaching at Philadelphia, the prophetic afflatus suddenly possessed him, and he felt compelled to cry out "with a loud voice, with God's own voice, Give ye heed to the bishop and the session and the deacons." His hearers thought that this had been a studied reference to persons accused of causing division in the Church, but Ignatius assured them that was not so. The Divine afflatus had possession of him, and it made him cry out:

you as an example and a lesson of incorruptibility" (*Magnesians*, 6). The office bearers in this sentence are called προκαθήμενοι, which may be compared with the προϊστάμενοι of the Epistle to the Romans and to the Thessalonians.

[1] He calls a church τὸ πολυεύτακτον τῆς κατὰ Θεὸν ἀγάπης (*Magnesians*, 1).

[2] "Give place to him (the bishop) as to one prudent in God; yet not to him, but to the Father of Jesus Christ, even to the Bishop of all. ... For a man doth not so much deceive this bishop who is seen, as cheat the other Who is invisible" (*Magnesians*, 3).

[3] *To the Trallians*, 5.

"Do nothing without the bishop; keep your flesh as a temple of God; cherish union; shun divisions; be imitators of Jesus Christ, as He Himself also was of His Father."[1] With the prophetic eye he *saw* the invisible and mystical unity which lay hidden within the actual visible Christian community, and every little local church was a symbol of what existed in the Heavenly Places where God was the centre and source of unity. It is from this mystical standpoint that we must view the impassioned exhortations to obey the office-bearers,[2] remembering also that obedience to the rulers in the Church is only the superlative of the submission of love which all Christians owe to one another.

When due allowance is made for the exaltation of the writer, and for the Oriental extravagance of language natural to a Syrian, the exhortations of Ignatius do not differ so widely from the calm injunctions issued in the measured language of Rome to the church of Corinth which we find in the *Epistle of Clement*: "Let us mark the soldiers that are enlisted under our rulers, how exactly, how readily, how submissively, they execute the orders given them. All are not prefects, nor com-

---

[1] *To the Philadelphians*, 7.

[2] "The bishops established in the furthest parts of the world are in the counsels of Jesus Christ" (*Ephesians*, 3). "Every one whom the Master of the House sendeth to govern His own household we ought to receive, as Him that sent him. Clearly therefore we ought to regard the bishop as the Lord Himself" (*Ephesians*, 6). Those who "obey the bishop as Jesus Christ" live a life after Christ" (*Trallians*, 2). "It is good to know God and the bishop; he that honoureth the bishop is honoured of God; he that doeth anything without the knowledge of the bishop serveth the devil" (*Smyrneans*, 9). To obey the bishop is to obey "not him, but the Father of Jesus Christ, even the Bishop of all," while to practise hypocrisy towards the bishop is "not to deceive the visible one, so much as to cheat the One who is invisible" (*Magnesians*, 3). "As many as are of God and of Jesus Christ, are with the bishop" (*Philadelphians*, 3). Compare Lightfoot, *Apostolic Fathers, S. Ignatius, S. Polycarp*, i. 375 f.; *Commentary on the Epistle to the Philippians* (1881), 6th ed. pp. 236, 237), for a complete list of passages. Almost equally strong language about obedience to elders or presbyters and deacons will be found on the same pages.

manders of thousands, nor of hundreds, nor of fifties, and so forth; but each man in his own rank executeth the orders given by the prince and the government."[1]

It is also to be remembered that Ignatius is writing to churches in Asia Minor, exposed to the temptations to division caused by the presence of men teaching the separative doctrines of a Judaising Christianity and of Doketism. The epistles themselves afford abundant evidence that these sources of division existed and had proved strong temptations in the communities to which he was writing.[2] His passionate anxiety was that each local church should present an unbroken front and manifest a complete unity. The simple means which he believed would effect this was that all Christians should rally round the office-bearers who were at the head of the little Christian societies. Most, though not all, of the churches he addressed had the three-fold ministry in some form or other, and he enforced obedience to that form of ecclesiastical rule. "There is no indication that he is upholding the episcopal against any other form of Church government, as for instance the presbyteral (i.e. the government by a college of presbyters without a president). The alternative which he contemplates is lawless isolation and self-will. No definite theory is propounded as to the principle on which the episcopate claims allegiance. It is as the recognized authority of the churches which the writer addresses, that he maintains it. Almost simultaneously with Ignatius, Polycarp addresses the Philippian Church, which appears not yet to have had a bishop, requiring its submission

---

[1] Clement, 1 *Epistle* xxxvii.

[2] "But I have learned that certain persons passed through you from yonder, bringing evil doctrine" (*Ephesians*, 9); "It is better to keep silence and to be, than to talk and be not" (*Ephesians*, 15). "It is monstrous to talk of Jesus Christ and to practise Judaism.... I would have you be on guard betimes, that ye fall not into the snares of vain doctrines" (*Magnesians*, 10-11); compare the *Epistle to the Trallians*, 6-11, where the brethren are warned against Doketism; the *Epistle to the Philadelphians*, 6, where the warning is against Judaism; and the *Epistle to the Smyrneans*, 5-7, where the error is Doketism.

'to the presbyters and deacons.'[1] If Ignatius had been writing to this church, he would doubtless have done the same. As it is, he is dealing with communities where episcopacy (the three-fold ministry) had been already matured, and therefore he demands obedience to their bishop."[2] He makes no attempt certainly when writing to the Roman Church, which was still under the government of a college of presbyter-bishops without a president, to insist that the three-fold ministry is an essential thing to the well-being of a Christian community.[3] What is more, he evidently regards union with the college of elders as the same thing as union with the bishop; for he invites the malcontents at Philadelphia, who had repented, to return " to the unity of God and of the council of the bishop."[4]

We can scarcely look for a calm statement about the organization of the Christian churches in letters of this kind. They were the impassioned outpourings of a man on his way to death; full of fears, not for himself, but for the brethren he was leaving behind in a persecuting world. It is pathetic to see the fiery, impassioned words of the martyr used as missiles by some reckless preacher of episcopal supremacy, or subjected to the scalpel of a cold-blooded critic, neither of whom seem to recognize the Oriental extravagance of language which makes them so natural. Yet the letters do give us a good deal of information about our subject.

Ignatius insists that the unity of the society has for its centre and source of strength the supremacy of the pastor, who is always called the bishop. His writings are a proof that the three-fold ministry *in some form or other* did exist, early in the second century, in some parts of the Church though not in others.

---

[1] Compare Réville, *Les Origines de l'Episcopat* (1894), p. 497 f.
Lightfoot, *S. Ignatius, S. Polycarp*, i. 382.

[3] The three-fold ministry developed much more slowly in Rome than in Asia Minor. Compare Lightfoot, *Commentary on the Epistle to the Philippians* (1881), 6th ed. p. 217 ff.; Réville, *Les Origines de l'Episcopat* (1894), p. 420 ff.

[4] *Epistle to the Philadelphians*, 8.

But they are not to be taken as proof that the Ignatian *conception* of what the three-fold ministry ought to be existed in any part of the Church whatever.[1]

According to the conception of Ignatius, every Christian community ought to have at its head a bishop, a presbyterium or session of elders, and a body of deacons. These constitute its office-bearers to whom, jointly and severally, obedience is due. Ignatius regards these three elements as going together to form one whole. He mentions the three classes of officials together twelve times in his seven epistles, and in ten out of the twelve they form an inseparable unity—presumably they do so also in the remaining two, but that is not evident from the passages themselves.[2] There is not a trace of sacerdotalism in the sense that the Christian ministry is a special priesthood set apart to offer a special sacrifice; there is a great deal about the sacredness of order, but not a word about the sanctity of orders. Ignatius only once refers to priests and high priests, and he does so in the thoroughly evangelical fashion of contrasting the imperfect Old Testament priesthood with the perfect priesthood of the Redeemer.[3] The bishop is not an autocrat. There is a "council of the bishop," which includes

---

[1] In some form or other or in some stage of its growth. Lightfoot has drawn a distinction between chief over the presbyters and chief of the presbyters, and the second phrase, he says, suits very well the beginning of the *Epistle of Polycarp*:—"Polycarp and the presbyters that are with him." Then there is the form given in the *Sources of the Apostolic Canons*, cf. above pp. 183 f.

[2] *To the Magnesians*, 2, 6, 13; *To the Trallians*, 7; *To the Philadelphians*, preface, 4, 7; *To the Smyrnaeans*, 8, 12; *To Polycarp*, 6; *To the Trallians*, 2; *To the Philadelphians*, 10. Compare Réville, *Les Origines de l'Épiscopat* (1894), p. 496:—"L'exaltation du pouvoir épiscopal qui se donne libre cours à travers les Épitres d'Ignace fait trop souvent perdre de vue aux commenteurs cette intime association de l'autorité presbytérale et de l'autorité épiscopale, qu'un examen plus attentif dégage très clairement."

[3] *To the Philadelphians*, 8, 9. Compare Lightfoot, *Apostolic Fathers, S. Ignatius, S. Polycarp* (1885), i. 381, 382; ii. 274, 275. Zahn, *Ignatii et Polycarpi Epistulae* (1876), p. 79.

the bishop himself.[1] The people are told to obey all the office-bearers, bishops, elders and deacons.[2] The ruling body is a court in which the bishop sits as chairman surrounded by his council or session of elders; and the one is helpless without the other, for if the bishop is the lyre the elders are the chords, and both are needed to produce melody.[3] There is no apostolic succession in any form whatsoever; even in the poetic conception of the disciple company it is the elders who represent the apostles.[4] Lastly, there is no trace of diocesan rule. We undoubtedly find the phrase τὸν ἐπίσκοπον Συρίας; but as Lightfoot and Zahn, to say nothing of others, have pointed out, it must be translated "the bishop from Syria." A bishop of Syria would have been an anachronism in the fourth century, and is

[1] *To the Philadelphians*, 8. Compare Lightfoot, *S. Ignatius*, i. 380; ii. 269.

[2] Obey the bishop:—*Ephesians*, 6; *Trallians*, 2; *Smyrnaeans*, 8, 9; *Magnesians*, 3, 4; *Polycarp*, 4, 6; *Philadelphians*, 7. Obey the elders:— *Ephesians*, 2, 20; *Magnesians*, 2, 7; *Trallians*, 13. Obey he deacons: *Polycarp*, 6,; *Magnesians*, 6; *Trallians*, 3; *Philadelphians*, 7; *Smyrnaeans*, 8.

[3] *To the Ephesians*, 4.

[4] "It is worthy of notice that though the form of government in these Asian Churches is in some sense monarchical, yet it is very far from being autocratic. We have already seen that in one passage the writer in the term 'council of the bishop' includes the bishop himself as well as his presbyters. This expression tells its own tale. Elsewhere submission is required to the presbyters as well as to the bishop. Nay sometimes the writer enjoins obedience to the deacons as well as to the bishop and to the presbyters. The 'presbytery' is a 'worthy spiritual coronal' (ἀξιοπλόκου πνευματικοῦ στεφάνου) round the bishop (*Magn.* 13). It is the duty of every one, but especially of the presbyters 'to refresh the bishop unto the honour of the Father and of Jesus Christ and of the apostles' (*Trall.* 12). They stand in the same relation to him 'as the chords to the lyre' (*Ephes.* 4). If obedience is due to the bishop as to the grace of God, it is due to the presbytery as to the law of Jesus Christ (*Magn.* 2). If the bishop ocupies the place of God or of Jesus Christ, the presbyters are as the Apostles, as the council of God (*Magn.* 6; *Trall.* 2, 3; *Smyr.* 8). This last comparison alone would show how widely the idea of the episcopate differed from the later conception, when it had been formulated in the doctrine of the Apostolic succession. The presbyters, not the bishops, are here the successors of the apostles." Lightfoot, *S. Ignatius*, i. pp. 382, 383.

much more so in the second.¹ It is unquestionable that the bishop is made the centre of everything in the Church or congregation. "It is not permitted without the bishop either to baptize or to hold a love feast," ² and the love feast must include the Holy Supper. It is even declared that when men and women marry they should unite themselves with the consent of the bishop, that the marriage should be after the Lord and not after concupiscence.³ But this only means that in such a solemn action as matrimony the blessing of the Church should be joined to the civil contract.

But if there be no sacerdotalism, no apostolic succession, no one-man rule, and no diocese; if every Christian community is to be organized under a leader, who is called a bishop and sometimes a pastor, who presides over a court of elders,⁴ and has under him a body of deacons; further, if, as the *Sources of the Apostolic Canons* inform us, every small Christian community, even when consisting of fewer than twelve families, is to have its bishop, its elders and its deacons; if nothing is to be done without the consent of the pastor or bishop, neither sacrament nor love-feast, nor anything congregational—then while the resemblance to modern episcopacy, with its diocesan system, is but small, there is a very great amount of resemblance to that form of ecclesiastical organization which re-emerged at the Reformation and which is commonly called the presbyterian, though it might be more appropriately named the conciliar system of Church government.

A more minute examination of the letters reveals some details

---

¹ Lightfoot, *S. Ignatius*, i. 383; ii. 201, 202; Zahn, *Ignatii Epistulae*, p. 59 n.; and his *Ignatius von Antioch*, p. 308.
² *To the Smyrnaeans*, 8.
³ *To Polycarp*, 5.
⁴ The πρεσβυτέριον or court of elders, i.e. kirk-session, is mentioned frequently by Ignatius:—*To the Ephesians*, 2, 4, 20; *To the Magnesians*, 2, 13; *To the Trallians*, 2, 7, 13; *To the Philadelphians*, 4, 7; *To the Smyrnaeans*, 8, 12. It is called the "council of God" in the *Epistle to the Trallians*, 3 (συνέδριον θεοῦ).

of the organization of the churches which were familiar to Ignatius.

For one thing, it seems clear that whatever the authority of the bishop may have been, it did not extend beyond his own church or congregation. The corporate unity of the Churches of Christ was still a sentiment, strongly felt no doubt, but not yet expressed in any kind of polity. Ignatius did not write as a bishop of the Catholic Church; he says expressly that he was no apostle.[1] He wrote as a confessor of Christ to brethren who might soon be required to confess Christ in the same way of threatened martyrdom. Nor does Polycarp claim to write as a superior to the Philippians. He wrote because he had been asked for advice.[2] The various churches were still independent units in fraternal intercourse with each other, but without any signs of inter-congregational jurisdiction.

The *Epistle to Polycarp* show what Ignatius believed to be the duties of a bishop within his own community. He was the administrator of the finances of the Church; to him the widows and the poor of the congregation had to look for their support, and the funds to buy the manumission of slaves were in his hands;[3] he had the moral oversight of the whole congregation, and was therefore the president of the court of discipline;[4] he had the right to call, and presumably to preside over, the congregational meetings;[5] he had the sole regulation of the sacraments of

---

[1] " I did not think myself competent for this (writing more sharply), that being a convict I should order you as though I were an apostle " (*To the Trallians*, 3). Throughout the letters there are constant references to his impending martyrdom.

[2] *Epistle of Polycarp to the Philippians*, 3.

[3] *To Polycarp*, 4.   [4] *To Polycarp*, 3, 5.

[5] *To Polycarp*, 4; Ignatius evidently thought that Polycarp did not hold congregational meetings often enough:—" Let the meetings be held more frequently." It is interesting to notice that all the duties which Ignatius supposes to belong to the bishops in the Church at Smyrna are supposed by Polycarp to belong to the elders in the Church at Philippi, with the exception of presiding at public worship, which is not mentioned; Polycarp, *Epistle to the Philippians*, 6-12

Baptism and of the Holy Supper and of everything congregational.[1] But large as were the bishop's powers, he had to exercise them under serious limitations. There is not a hint that the bishop can by himself, or even in conjunction with his session or elders, excommunicate an offender. The power which Ignatius urges Polycarp to use is only that of moral suasion.[2] It is more than probable that the final power in all cases of discipline lay with the congregational meeting, as was the case in Corinth in the time of St. Paul. It is the congregation who are warned against false teachers and evil-minded persons, and they are directed to act in certain ways with regard to them.[3] The passages, however, do not warrant us in drawing any distinct conclusion. On the other hand, it is clear that the congregational meetings had powers. It was they who appointed delegates and messengers. The Christians at Smyrna are asked directly to send a delegate into Syria, whereas the bishop is only asked to convene a meeting of the congregation in order that the messenger may be appointed; and elsewhere it is made plain that this power belonged to the whole Church, who could order on a mission their bishops as well as their elders or their deacons.[4]

Readers who know something about the work of Church extension at home and on the mission field, may wonder how it was possible in these early centuries that the smallest bodies of Christians could have had, and were commanded to have, such a complete ecclesiastical organization as these *Epistles of Ignatius* and the *Sources of the Apostolic Canons* require,

---

[1] *To the Smyrnaeans*, 8, for the bishop's duties with regard to the eucharist, baptism, and the love-feasts; *To Polycarp*, 5, with regard to marriage. Yet the advice to meet more frequently for the eucharistic service is given to the Ephesian community (*Ephesians*, 13).

[2] *To Polycarp*, 2, 3, 5.

[3] *To the Ephesians*, 7; *To the Magnesians*, 11; *To the Philadelphians*, 6; *To the Smyrnaeans*, 4.

[4] *To the Smyrnaeans*, 11; *To Polycarp*, 7; *To the Philadelphians*, 10; *To the Ephesians*, 1, 2; *To the Magnesians*, 2, 6; *To the Trallians*, 1

and how they could be at the same time so independent and self-supporting. A large part of the problem of ecclesiastical extension in our own days, at home and on the mission field, has to do with money. Churches and other buildings have to be erected, and a salaried ministry has to be supported. But it must be remembered that in those early days the ministry was not paid as we understand payment, and that money for buildings was not needed. Church buildings did not exist until the second century was drawing to a close, and then only in large and populous centres. The only property which the Church had besides its copies of the Scriptures, its congregational records and perhaps a place of burial, were the offerings, mostly in kind, which the faithful presented during the meeting for thanksgiving, and which were almost immediately distributed. Justin Martyr gives the earliest description in his *Apology*. "On the day called Sunday, all who live in town or country gather together in one place, and the memoirs of the apostles or of the prophets are read as long as time permits ; then when the reader has ceased the president verbally instructs, and exhorts us to the imitation of these good things. Then we all stand together and pray, and, when prayer is ended, bread and wine are brought and the president offers prayers and thanksgivings, according to his ability, and the people assent, saying Amen. Then there is a distribution to each of that over which thanks has been given, and a portion is sent by the deacons to those who are absent. Then they who are well to do and are willing, give what each thinks fit ; and it is collected and deposited with the president, who succours orphans and widows and those who, through sickness or any other cause, are in want, those who are in bondage and the strangers sojourning among us—in a word all who are in need."[1]

The gifts so bestowed and distributed were the property of the early Church—all that it had. Both Justin and Tertullian insist on the fact that these offerings were of free-will,

[1] Justin, *Apology*, i. 67

contrasting them, it is probable, with the monthly compulsory payments made by the members of confraternities; but this did not hinder indications being given about these offerings. We find a continuous series of recommendations that the first fruits of all the necessaries of life ought to be given. All the oldest ecclesiastical manuals, from the *Didache* downwards, contain injunctions to the people about these first fruits. In the *Didache* these offerings went to support the prophets, and failing them the poor of the community; and the Pastoral Epistles[1] mention a church roll of members who ought to share because of their poverty. In the quotation just made from Justin Martyr these first fruits are distributed among the widows, orphans, poor strangers and so on; Tertullian describes a similar mode of distribution; so do the Canons of Hippolytus, which expressly prohibit any claim on the part of the ministry to share.[2] In the ancient *Sources of the Apostolic Canons* the elders superintend the bishop, while he makes the distribution,[3] but in Justin and in the *Canons of Hippolytus* the full control of this distribution lies with the president or bishop. It is probable that the members of the ministry from the beginning had some share in these offerings, but not in the way of stipend, and only if they could be classed among the poor. The ancient *Sources of the Apostolic Canons* teach us that the pastor may share if need be, but not by way of stipend. Dr. Hatch has only summed up what the history of the whole period teaches when he says: "The funds of the primitive communities consisted entirely of voluntary offerings. Of these offerings those office-bearers whose circumstances required it were entitled to a share. They received

---

[1] *Didache*, xiii. 1; 1 Tim. v. 9. The Pastoral Epistles perhaps teach us that the ministry have a share; cf. 1 Tim. v. 17, 18; 2 Tim. i. 4-7, but the seventh verse of the latter passage suggests that the share is not by way of stipend.

[2] Tertullian, *Apology*, 39. *Canons of Hippolytus*, Canon xxxii. (Riedel) *Kirchenrechtsquellen des Patriarchats Alexandrien*, p. 221.

[3] *Texte und Untersuchungen*, II. v. 13-15, or *Sources of the Apostolic Canons*, p. 13.

such a share only on account of their poverty. They were, so far, in the position of the widows and orphans and helpless poor."[1]

The idea that when men are once set apart for the function of office-bearers in the Christian Church it becomes the duty of the Church to provide them with the necessaries of life does not belong to the times of primitive Christianity. The office-bearers of the early Church were clergy in virtue of their call, election, and setting apart by special prayer for sacred office; but they worked at trades, carried on mercantile pursuits, and were not separate from the laity in their every-day life. We find bishops who were shepherds, weavers, lawyers, shipbuilders,[2] and so on, and the elders and deacons were almost invariably men who were not supported by the churches to which they belonged. An interesting series of inscriptions was found on the gravestones of the cemetery of the little town of Corycus, in Cilicia Tracheia, records of the Christian community there. They can scarcely be older than the fifth, and not later than the sixth century. One of them marks the burial place of a master potter and another that of a goldsmith, both of whom were elders or presbyters of the Church there.[3] The power of the laity in the early Church did not depend simply on the fact that they chose the office-bearers and had some indefinite influence over councils, as some modern writers put it,[4] but on the

---

[1] *The Organization of the Early Churches* (1881), p. 147.

[2] A shepherd, Socrates, *Eccles. Hist.* i. 12; a weaver, Sozomen, *Eccles. Hist.* vii. 28; a shipbuilder, S. Gregorii Magni *Epistolae*, xiii. 26; a lawyer, S. Gregorii Magni, *Epistolae*, x. 10. Compare Cyprian *De Lapsis* 6. Basil, *Epistolae*, 198. Compare Hatch, *The Organization of the Early Christian Churches* (1881), p. 148, who, besides giving the well-known individual instances quotes regulations from the *Theodosian Code* and from the *Statuta Ecclesiae Antiqua* proving the general practice. The eighty-seventh of the *Canons of Basil* says that " none of the clergy are to engage in merchandise but that they are to learn a handicraft and live of the labour of their hands." Riedel, *Die Kirchenrechtsquellen des Patriarchats Alexandrien* (1900), p. 270.   [3] *Bull. de Corr. Hell.* vii. 230 ff.

[4] As for example the Rev. R. B. Rackham in *Essays on Church Reform* (1898), p. 30 ff.

fact that in the earliest times none of the office-bearers, and for many centuries few of them, depended upon the Church as a whole to provide them with the necessaries of life. They were clergy, as has been said, in virtue of their selection for office and of their solemn setting apart to perform clerical functions; but they had daily association with the laity in the workshop, on the farm, in the warehouse, in the law-courts, and in the market-place. They held what must seem to be a very anomalous position to mediaeval and modern episcopalians. When the ancient practice is revived, as it was by the Reformed Church at the Reformation, episcopalians speak disdainfully of lay-elders and lay-deacons, as if an ecclesiastical stipend and not consecration by prayer and the laying on or giving of hands were the true and essential mark of ordination. But the practice had its value in the early centuries and has its importance now. It knit clergy and laity together in a very simple and thorough fashion, and brought men, whose life and callings made them feel as laymen do, within the circle of the hierarchy which ruled, and so prevented the hierarchy degenerating into a clerical caste.

During the last decades of the second and throughout the third century the conception of Ignatius, to him perhaps only a devout dream,[1] dominated the whole Church, or at least a great part of it. Every Christian community had at its head a single president who is almost always called the bishop. He presided over the session of elders, over the body of deacons, and over the congregation. The whole Christian activity of

[1] Compare Ramsay, *The Church in the Roman Empire*, pp. 370-1, where he says that Ignatius is not an historian describing facts but a preacher giving advice; and adds that he does not find in Ignatius proof that bishops were regarded as *ex-officio* supreme, that his language is quite consistent with the view that the respect actually paid to the bishop in each community depended on his individual character, and that his reiteration of the principle of the authority of the bishop, which came to him as a revelation, makes it evident that he did not find his ideal in actual existence. Compare also Sanday in the *Expositor* (1888, July-Dec.), p. 326.

the community found its centre in him, as it does in presbyterian congregations in the present day. He presided over the public worship in all its parts ; had chief charge of the sick and of the sinful ; he was over the discipline and over the administration of the property of the community whatever that happened to be. This was his position as a matter of fact. On the other hand, his position theoretically was by no means so unique. There is many a trace in the ancient canons, as we shall afterwards see, that the bishop was only *primus inter pares* in the session of elders, and that he was distinguished from them by two things only—a special seat in the church and the power to ordain elders and deacons. The practice made him the centre of the whole congregational life and the ruler ; the theory recalled the earlier days when every congregation was governed by a council of elders who had no president. We find the theory in such law-books as the *Canons of Hippolytus* ;[1] it was repeated by Jerome ; it never lacked supporters during the Middle Ages, of whom Thomas Aquinas was one ; it re-emerged at the Reformation when the Reformed Church revived the ecclesiastical organization of the early centuries ; and the same difference between theory and practice exists among the Reformed Churches in the present day.

The great change in the ministry which we have seen evolving itself in the three documents selected, and which belonged to the second and third centuries, was that the ruling body in every congregation changed from being a session of elders without a president and became a session with a president. The president, sometimes called the pastor, but usually the bishop, became gradually the centre of all the ecclesiastical life of the local Christian church and the one potent office-bearer. We have now to ask how this came about. In answer one thing only can be asserted with confidence. The change came gradually. It provoked no great opposition. It was everywhere, or almost everywhere, accepted. But when we seek for the causes that

[1] Compare below, p. 248.

produced the change, or ask what were the paths along which the change manifested itself—then we can only give conjectural answers.

Probably the main impulse came from the pressure of temptation—intellectual and moral—and persecution, and the feeling that resistance to both would be strengthened by a more thorough unity than could be attained under the leadership of a number of men who had no individual head. One man can take a firmer grip of things. Divided responsibility continually means varying counsels. What is the business of many is often the work of none. A divided leadership continually brings with it fickle and impotent action. The need for an undivided front in time of danger was what inspired Ignatius, when, with the eye of a statesman and the fire of a prophet, he pleaded for the union of the congregation under one leader. The circumstances of the times and the voices of those who led in the movement, all suggest that the supreme need of the moment was unity; and that unity could be best won and maintained by the change which was made.

The paths along which the change progressed probably differed in various places. It is quite unnecessary to suppose that the process was everywhere the same. It is much more natural that there should have been several at work simultaneously. Differences in racial temperament and in experience in the art of governing; greater or less exposure to the disruptive influences of strange teaching; more or less capacity to endure temptations; differences in local environment and in inherited political usages, might easily produce different modes in the evolution of the ecclesiastical organization. Dr. Lightfoot has shown, with his usual careful minuteness, how the threefold ministry came into being much sooner in some parts of the Empire than others, and that it appeared first in Asia Minor,[1] which differed in the fact that it was more exposed to the divisive influences of strange teachings, and that the people had been

[1] *Commentary on the Epistle to the Philippians* (1881), 6th ed. p. 206 ff

THE THREE-FOLD MINISTRY

long accustomed to the rule of one man in secular affairs. It well may be imagined that the different social surroundings which belonged to Rome, to the cities of Greece, and to Asia Minor, bred different ecclesiastical conditions, which led to the selection of differing paths in the development of the ecclesiastical organizations.

Professor Ramsay has suggested, ingeniously, one way in which the change may have come. His idea is that any member of the session of presbyters or elders became an *episcopus* or *overseer* when he was given the oversight of any special duty by his brethren. The *episcopus* who did his work well would naturally continue to do it, and the tendency was for his function to become permanent. One of the most important duties which fell to the college of elders was correspondence with other Christian churches and the reception and entertainment of the delegates who came from other churches to visit them. The elder who had the oversight of, or was the episcopus for this work, naturally became a very important man. He was the representative of his own church to all Christians outside it. He might easily come to represent the unity of the Church to those who also were inside it, more especially as he was the official who would naturally be selected to hold the property of the congregation when it became possessed of a place of burial. Thus he came to stand forth from among the other elders as the *episcopus par excellence*. Thus gradually one of the presbyters or elders became the *episcopus* for everything within the community, and the session of elders received its permanent head.[1] There is a great deal to be said for this conjecture. For one thing, there is evidence that the appointment of one of the elders to look after the communications with other churches was actually a custom;[2] for another it gives a reasonable explanation of

[1] *The Church in the Roman Empire* (1893), p. 367 ff.
[2] In the *Pastor* of Hermas, the old lady who represents the Church and who has given Hermas a revelation orders him to make two books and give one to Clement and the other to Grapte, "and Clement will send his to

those lists of bishops in various churches dating back to times when all the evidence shows that there was no real permanent president in existence. They are the lists of the men who, being the foreign correspondents, represented the unity of their respective churches to all Christians outside, and were therefore regarded as the most prominent members.

It is also probable that the celebration of the Holy Supper suggested one permanent president. It is easy to conceive how the meeting for "exhortation" could be conducted by a session of elders, but it is very difficult to imagine a collegiate superintendence of the meeting for "thanksgiving." Did the members of the session of presbyter-bishops or elders take it in turn to preside, or in what way was it done? We do not know. But we do know that in the second century there was one official who presided at the Lord's Supper, and that he, the προεστώς or president of Justin Martyr,[1] is clearly the anticipation of the later bishop. There was evidently some close connexion in thought between the *one* bishop and the *unity* of the congregation or church at the Holy Supper. One bishop, one place of celebration (θυσιαστήριον) and one Eucharist are almost equivalent terms in Ignatius. This thought would lead us to imagine that the *episcopus* was the presbyter or elder selected by his brethren to preside at the Eucharist, and that he was bishop while he was so presiding.[2] The presbyter

---

the foreign countries, *for commission has been given him to do so*, and Grapte will admonish the widows and the orphans; but you (Hermas, who was a presbyter) will read the words in this city along with the elders who preside over the Church," *Visiones*, ii. 4.

[1] *Apology*, i. 67.

[2] Tertullian in his *De Praescriptione Haereticorum*, 41, speaking of the condition of the Gnostic or Marcionite Churches, says:—"itaque alius hodie episcopus, cras alius." Sohm (*Kirchenrecht*, i. 119 n.) takes this as a proof of the condition of things in the most primitive days. He infers that in the earlier times when there were several bishops in each community the one who presided at the Eucharist was *the* bishop for that day, and gave place to another on another day who thus became *the* bishop in his turn. It is doubtful whether we can infer anything about primitive ages from these references in Tertullian.

who had a special gift for this sacred work would naturally be frequently called to undertake it, and the duty might easily become a permanent one. In the *Sources of the Apostolic Canons* it is the bishop or pastor who presides at the Holy Communion, although he is under the disciplinary authority of the elders.

It may also be said that the need for one authority in doctrinal matters led to the selection of one man, and to placing on him the responsibility of seeing that the members of the congregation were not tempted away from the true faith by irresponsible teachers, who offered themselves to instruct the community. This conception, as we shall see later, was developed in a special way with reference to the office-bearer by Irenaeus, and some critics see it foreshadowed in the letters of Ignatius.

No one way needs to be selected as the only path by which the organization advanced, and the college of elders received a president who was the permanent head of the community, and the living and personal representative of its unity. They might all have their effect and that simultaneously.

It must always be remembered that the duty of presiding at the Holy Supper, which is invariably seen to belong to the bishop as soon as he emerges from the college of presbyters or elders, brought with it the control over the gifts of the faithful which were presented after the Eucharistic service, and formed for long the only property of the congregation. If we add to this that the presbyter or elder chosen for this highest portion of the worship was frequently a man possessed of the prophetic gift as Ignatius was, additional reverence and obedience would not fail to be bestowed upon him; and we can see how the old reverence for the " prophetic ministry " could easily be transferred to the new authority.

Whatever paths led to the change in the ministry whereby the rule was transferred from a college of elders without a president to a college with a president, when once the change was made the power of the *episcopus* grew rapidly; and one source of this increase of authority lay in the fact that he was always the administrator of the property of the local church.

Without any apostolic sanction, in virtue of the power lying within the community and given to it by the Master, the Church of the second century effected a change in its ministry quite as radical, if not more so, as that made by the Reformed Church in the sixteenth century, when it swept away mediaeval excrescences, restored the bishops to their ancient position of pastors of congregations, and vested the power of oversight in councils of greater and lesser spheres of authority. What was within the power of the Christian people of the second century belongs to it always when providential circumstances seem to demand a change in the organization, for the ministry depends on the Church and not the Church on the ministry.

CHAPTER VI

THE FALL OF THE PROPHETIC MINISTRY AND THE CONSERVATIVE REVOLT

THE prophetic ministry of the apostolic and immediately sub-apostolic times passed away in the course of the second century, and its overthrow was a much greater alteration of the organization of the churches than the institution of a three-fold ministry, important as that was. The difference may be seen from two extracts. "Every prophet," says the oldest ecclesiastical manual, "who speaketh in the Spirit, ye shall neither try nor judge; for every sin shall be forgiven, but that sin shall not be forgiven."[1] That comes from a time when the prophetic ministry was the great controlling power. "Wretched men," says Irenaeus, "who wish to be false prophets . . . holding aloof from the communion of the brethren"; and the test of being in communion with the brethren is "to obey the elders who are in the Church."[2] That comes from the end of our period.

The change between the time when the prophet was not to be judged, but to be obeyed, and when disobedience to his commands was believed to be "an unpardonable sin"; and the time when the test of a true prophet was obedience to the office-bearers of the local church, whose superior he had once been, amounted to a revolution. It was so, and the overthrow of the supremacy of the prophetic ministry rent the Church in twain.

[1] *Didache*, xi. 7.
[2] Irenaeus, *Contra Haereses*, III. xi. 9 and IV. xxvi 2.

It was inevitable. The more close and firm the organization of the local churches became the less room remained for the exercise of the prophetic ministry, which in the nature of things claimed at once freedom for itself and the power of ruling in some indefinite way over the churches which admitted its exercise among them. A careful examination of the scanty records of the second century reveals that the early prophetic ministry was active within the churches down till the Montanist revolt, and that in the churches which shared in that movement it was continued, and its place within the Church became accentuated. It is also possible to show in what way the office-bearers of the local churches could gradually come to take the place of the prophetic ministry, and how with the great body of Christians this could be done naturally and without any strong feeling that there was a real breach with the past.

In St. Paul's summary of the gifts which the Spirit bestows, and which when manifested within a community of Christians make it a Church, it can be seen that all these gifts may be divided into two classes—those which enable their possessors to edify the brethren by speaking the word of God, and those which fit them for serving the community in many practical ways. Two of these practical gifts, "pilotings" ($κυβερνήσεις$) and "aids" ($ἀντιλήψεις$) foreshadow in the abstract the concrete offices of overseer and servant; and from them the office-bearers of the local churches derive their origin. The task of edifying by speech belonged primarily to the first class of gifted persons, and the work of edifying by wise counsels and all manner of brotherly services belonged to the two branches of the second class out of which the local office-bearers developed. Edification by the Word of God was the most important need of the churches; and if the "gifted" apostles, prophets and teachers failed any community their services had to be supplied somehow.

The *Didache* shows us the transition stage, and explains how this need was supplied in an ordinary way when the extraordinary means failed. "Appoint, therefore, for yourselves bishops and deacons worthy of the Lord, men that are meek and are not covetous, upright and proved ; *for they also render you the service of the prophets and teachers. Therefore neglect them not, for they are your honoured ones, together with the prophets and teachers.*" These words in italics show us at once the point of junction between the prophetic and the local ministry, and indicate how the latter could fulfil the duties of the former. They also reveal the possibility of the abolition of the prophetic ministry as a permanent part of the organization (to use the word in its widest sense) of the local churches. When the wave of spiritual enthusiasm and illumination which came with the earliest proclamation of the Gospel had somewhat spent itself, there was need to supply through the ordinary office-bearers of the churches that exhortation and instruction which in the earliest times had been left to the inspiration of those gifted with the power of speaking the Word of God. Hence the *Didache*[1] counsels the community to select men for its office-bearers in the knowledge that they may be called upon to supply this need. But when once the local churches began to have their spiritual needs satisfied within their own circle and the bands of association grew stronger, it is easy to imagine that the power

---

[1] "The peculiar value of the *Didache* consists in this, that it reveals to us the process in the moment of transition. It brings down the bird as it were upon the wing. The sentence italicized explains why the permanent officials of the Christian Churches did not possess at first all the functions which they possessed later. They did not possess them because the more prosaic duties which they themselves discharged were supplemented by that extraordinary wave of spiritual exaltation which swept over the whole primitive Church. In that age the wish of Moses was well-nigh fulfilled, that 'all the Lord's people were prophets.' The difficulty was not to incite to the attainment of such gifts, but to regulate and control them. One by one they became rarer, and disappeared. The apostolate was the first to go. Prophecy lasted until it was finally discredited by Montanism. The class of teachers survived still longer into the third century ; indeed, it would hardly be wrong to regard the Catechetical School of Alexandria as a systematizing of this office, with learning and philosophy substituted for the primitive enthusiasm." Sanday, *Expositor* (1887, Jan.-June), p. 17.

216   THE FALL OF THE PROPHETIC MINISTRY

of the office-bearers grew strong enough to withstand the members of the prophetic ministry unless the prophets were content to take a secondary place. The very fact that the office-bearers could " render the service of the prophets and teachers " inevitably tended to place them, the permanent officials of the local churches, permanently in the position of the exhorters, instructors, and leaders of the public worship of the communities. Hence, while we can trace the presence and the power of the prophetic ministry during a great part of the second century, we can also see that complaints against false prophets became more and more common, and that there was a tendency to make the test of true prophecy subordination on the part of the prophets to the control of the permanent office-bearers of the churches.[1]

We can see that the transition from the time when the prophets were supreme to the days when they were expected, if true prophets, to be subordinate to or at least deferential towards the office-bearers of the community, was the more easily effected when we remember that it is highly probable that some men among those chosen to lead the brethren by their gifts of governing had also the power of exhortation and instruction. This was probably the case from the earliest times. The προϊστάμενοι of 1 Thessalonians v. 12, not only laboured among the brethren but "admonished"; and to "admonish" (νουθετεῖν) seems to imply more than mere leading. Whatever be the date of the Pastoral Epistles, it is clear that by the time they were written, the functions of instruction and leadership were conjoined; and few critics, even among those who dispute the Pauline authorship, will be inclined to place them as late as Harnack does.[2] Then, as before remarked, those office-bearers

---

[1] Perhaps the earliest trace of this is to be found in Clement, 1 *Epistle*, xlviii. 5 :—" Let a man be faithful, let him be able to expound a deep saying, let him be wise in the discernment of words, let him be strenuous in deeds, let him be pure ; so much the more ought he to be lowly in mind, in proportion as he seemeth to be greater ; and he ought to seek the common advantage of all, and not his own."

If leadership implied instruction in the earliest times (1 Thessalonians)

who stand forth most clearly in these ancient times were almost all men who had the prophetic gift. We have already seen how the divine afflatus descended on Ignatius while he was preaching in Philadelphia, and made him cry forth words which the Spirit put in his mouth. The prophetic gift was to be found among the office-bearers of the local churches before the conflict of jurisdictions arose, and the office-bearers who possessed it had all the divine authority which was supposed to belong to the prophetic order.

All these circumstances have to be taken into account in attempting to describe the great change in the ministry which the second century witnessed; and the last-mentioned is useful in enabling us to see how, while the overthrow of the prophetic ministry was sufficient to provoke a disruption of the Church, it could nevertheless be accepted by the great mass of the Christian people.

We have no specific information in the documents of post-apostolic Christianity to tell us how and by what steps the great revolution was brought about; but the conditions and needs of the time enable us to put ourselves to some extent in the place of the men who carried out the change.

Several distinct sets of circumstances require to be kept in mind.

In the first place, the second century was a time of great fermentation in the world of intellectual paganism. In the east of Europe and among the Greek inhabitants of Asia Minor the old religions had lost almost all their real power. The same may be said of the people of Italy also, and especially of the more cultured classes of Rome. It is something pathetic to learn that the only one of the ancient Greek deities whose cult was still practised with something of the old reverence and fervour was Esculapius, the god of bodily health, and that he was called Soter, the Saviour, as if men had despaired of salvation of soul

the fact that in the Pastoral Epistles leadership involves instruction does not imply that these epistles are late.

and could hope for no more than the health of the body. On the other hand, worships strange to Greek or Roman, coming from the far East, with painful initiations and purifications for those who felt the power of sin or the fickleness of imperfection within them, and weird philosophies for the cultured, spread far and wide, counting their votaries by thousands and permeating all classes of society.

Among them were systems of cosmical speculation and mystic theosophy, curiously similar to what we find in Hinduism, and possessing that strange power of absorbing and assimilating religious ideas foreign to themselves, which is still such a feature of Oriental speculation. Votaries of these theosophies were attracted towards the doctrines of Christianity, caught at the Christian conceptions of redemption and of the Person of Christ, and tried to find room for them among the medley of their fantastic beliefs. They set redemption within the circle of their thoughts about the inherent evil in matter, and the Person of Christ found its place among the doctrines of emanation. Christianity attracted them as it still attracts cultivated Hindus. The Brahma Somaj, the Prathana Somaj, the Arya Somaj, strange attempts to absorb some features of Christianity into Hinduism in the nineteenth century, had their parallels in some of the Gnostic speculations of the earlier centuries.

Strange as it may seem to us, those weird speculations had an attraction for many cultivated persons who had embraced the Christian faith; for if the whole phenomenon of Gnosticism was, as it seems most likely to have been, a scheme of thought essentially pagan, trying to assimilate some leading Christian ideas, there were sides to the movement which show us men who were really Christians attempting to make use of these speculations as the metaphysical framework on which to stretch their Christian thoughts and to give them the shape of a rationalized theology. These metaphysics of "wonderland," where the categories of Aristotle and the ideas of Plato assumed bodily shapes, married and begot a fantastic progeny, filled the intellectual atmosphere of the times, and were the air which thinkers breathed. The Church was face to face with the danger of seeing its historical verities dissolve into the shadowy shapes of a metaphysical mythology. For when Gnosticism entered into the Christian societies, and claimed to be a philosophical Christianity, the very life of the Church was threatened.[1]

Nor were these the only difficulties of intellectual speculation which the Church of the second century had to face. We are apt to think that the apparent contradiction between an Almighty Maker of all things and the miseries of life is the peculiar property of our own age. That is not so. Men felt keenly the contrasts which trouble modern minds. They lived in a civilization as intellectually trained as our own. How could the God and Father of our Lord Jesus Christ, the Father of Mercies and the God of all Love, inspire the Old Testament, where the Jews were ordered to exterminate their enemies and threaten and practise all kinds of cruelties? How can creation, groaning and travailing in pain, be the work of that God Who has manifested Himself in Jesus Christ? Nature is not merciful. It seems hard and pitiless. The mystery of pain broods over it and in it. History is full of battle and pestilence, of turmoil and misery.

Among men who had ideas like these Marcion was a leader. His solution of the problem was that the God of the Old Testament and the Creator of the Universe were very like each other and very unlike the God and Father of our Lord Jesus Christ. The Being who had created scorpions and sent venomous creeping things into the world was not unlike the God Who had commanded the slaughter of the Amalekites and had inspired the imprecatory Psalms. An old world Count Tolstoy, Marcion said that Christ's Christianity had nothing to do with any part of the Old Testament, nor with much of the New. The New

[1] Compare Hatch, *The Organisation of the Early Churches* (1881), pp. 91, 92.

Testament had indeed come from Jesus Christ, but it had been sadly corrupted by the votaries of the God who created the Universe. He constructed a Canon of Scripture for himself and for his disciples, and into his Scriptures no portion of the Old Testament was admitted, and from them much of the New was excluded. He went back to the Pauline Epistles, the earliest literary creations of the Christian inspiration, to seek in them the purest records of the teaching of that Saviour, Who, unheralded, as he thought, by any partial anticipations, had come suddenly to reveal to the world the hitherto absolutely unknown God of Love and Mercy. Marcion was a man of deep and genuine religious character, of an intensely practical nature, and without any tendency to speculation. He stood forth in that age of mixed faiths, of eclectic paganism and Gnostic Christianity, as a teacher who had mastered a clear and definite, if narrow, creed. His sincerity, his piety, his energy and his wonderful powers of organization, created not merely bands of devoted followers, but a church which, according to the ideas of those who belonged to it, was a reformation and a purification of the existing Christianity. Within it asceticism was practised in a manner hitherto unknown within Christianity. No married persons could ever rise to be more than catechumens, and members were required to abstain from all sexual relations; rigid laws about meats and drinks were laid down and enforced; martyrdom was to be welcomed, not shunned, and the hatred of the great mass of their fellow-Christians was an additional burden to be endured. Wherever Christianity had spread the followers of Marcion appeared, formed themselves into separate churches, with the same ceremonies of worship, the same ecclesiastical organization, or one very similar, the same, if not greater, strictness of moral living, and an intenser joy in martyrdom. The dogmatic unity of the Church, if it ever had been truly and thoroughly one, was broken. Other bodies of Christians, with separate organizations, appeared standing between the Marcionite and the parent churches, and pagans could sneer at a divided Christianity and ask the Christians which God, they who preached His Unity, really worshipped ?[1]

Can we wonder then, that in face of these anxieties the leaders of the Christian churches felt the need for a closer fellowship and a firmer grasp of what they believed to be the verities of the faith ? Irenaeus voiced the clamant need of the Church. His rallying cry is familiar enough. It is one which has arisen always in such crises. It was practically this : " Back to the Christ of history ; back to the fixed verities of the Christian faith."

But how was it possible to get back to these fixed verities of the Christian faith, and by a path that all could tread ? All the more important writings of the New Testament were already recognized as Scripture in the West, but the prevailing attitude of mind was towards allegorising, and the Epistle of Barnabas shows how unhistorical this mystical interpretation could become. If Barnabas could find a text and proof for the Cross and for Baptism in Psalm i. 3,[2] the Gospels might be drawn upon for proofs as satisfactory for the Gnostic metaphysical mythology. Tertullian confesses as much, and naïvely remarks that he does not risk contradiction in saying that the Scriptures were " even arranged " by the will of God in such a manner as to furnish materials for heretics.[3] The bent of the philosophy of the day was to dissolve facts into theories, and the Platonists in their expositions of Homer had taught orthodox Christian and Gnostic alike their elusive methods of exegesis. Then, apart from the impossibility of using a sound exegesis which

---

[1] Compare especially Origen, *Contra Celsum*, v. 59-64.

[2] " Again He saith in another prophet 'The man who doeth these things shall be like a tree planted by the courses of waters, which shall yield its fruit in due season ; and his leaf shall not fade, and all he doeth shall prosper. . . . Mark how He has described at once both the water and the cross. For these words imply, Blessed are they who, placing their trust in the cross, have gone down into the water ; for, says He, they shall receive their reward in due time : then He declares, I will recompense them.' " *Epistle of Barnabas*, xi.

[3] *De Praescriptione Haereticorum*, 39 ; cf. 19.

yielded a common method of interpretation, the question of what was the canon of the New Testament Scripture was one of the matters in dispute between the organized Christian Church and those believers in Christ who were outside its pale. Marcion had a canon of his own, as we have already seen; the various Gnostics had theirs, not always the same—for what we call the apocryphal Gospels and Acts were received by many. Nor could an appeal be made to any short common creed. There was none as yet common to all Christendom, although what lies at the basis of the *Apostles' Creed* was received throughout the Church and had become fixed in a form of words in the West.[1] Various Gnostics had their creeds differing from each other, and to them they appealed.[2] Disputes also existed about the true apostolic tradition; whether Jesus had or had not entrusted His apostles with a secret doctrine in addition to what He openly taught, and whether that "secret teaching" had been communicated to any by the apostles, and if so to whom.[3]

[1] The Apostles' Creed in its earlier form, the old Roman Creed, can be traced as far back as 150 A.D.

[2] We can reconstruct the creed of the Gnostic Apelles from Hippolytus (*Refutation of all the Heresies*, vii, 26); "We believe, That Christ descended from the Power above, from the Good, and that He is the Son of the Good; That He was not born of a Virgin and that when He did appear, He was not devoid of flesh; That He formed His Body by taking portions of it from the substance of the universe, i.e. hot and cold, moist and dry: That He received cosmical powers in the Body, and lived for the time He did in the world; That He was crucified by the Jews and died; That being raised again after three days He appeared to His disciples; That he showed them the prints of the nails and (the wound) in His side, being desirous of persuading them that He was no phantom, but was present in the flesh; That after He had shown them His Flesh He restored it to the earth; That after He had once more loosed the chains of His Body He gave back heat to what is hot, cold to what is cold, moisture to what is moist and dryness to what is dry; That in this condition he departed to the Good Father, leaving the Seed of Life in the world for those who through His disciples should believe in Him." Cf. Tertullian, *Adversus Marcion*, i. 1 (Marcion's *regula fidei*); *De Praescriptione Haereticorum*, 42; Irenaeus, *Against Heresies*, III. xi. 3.

[3] *The Pistis Sophia*, the only complete Gnostic treatise which has decended to us, has a great deal to say about this secret teaching of our

Amidst this medley of beliefs and assertions Irenaeus assured the faithful that it was easy to know what the simple and fixed verities of the Christian faith really were. They are everywhere the same. Ask Christians of the most different classes, whether cultured inhabitants of centres of civilization or nomade Scythians roaming over the steppes in waggons and unable to read or to write, and the answer will be everywhere the same. He describes what the answer will be, and gives a short string of sentences resembling the *Apostles' Creed*.[1] The Church, he says, though scattered throughout the world, preserves this creed, " as if it were some precious deposit in an excellent vessel."[2] Varieties of language do not interfere with the meaning of the truths of the faith; "the churches which have been planted in Germany do not believe nor hand down anything different, nor do those in Gaul, nor those in the East, nor those in Egypt." [3] He declares that the sentences which he gives as containing the simple verities of the Christian belief can be proved to be what he has said, because there are in the Christian Church successive generations of men who go back to the time of the apostles who were the companions of Jesus. His argument is always: I know a man who knew a man who knew an apostle.[4]

There are in the various churches scattered throughout the world successions of men who have been taught generation by

Lord and how it was given and transmitted and was the teaching which the author of the book accepted. The book has been translated into English by G. R. S. Mead (1896). Compare Irenaeus, *Against Heresies*, III. ii. 1.

[1] *Against Heresies*, I. x. 1; cf. III. iv. 2.

[2] III. xxiv. 1; elsewhere, "The apostles, like a rich man in a bank lodged in the hands (of the Church) most copiously all things pertaining to the truth: so that every man, whosoever will, can draw from her the water of life" (III. iv. 1).

[3] *Against Heresies*, I. x. 2.

[4] The sentence condenses his argument; but it is interesting to remember that he uses the words himself:—"I have heard from an aged elder who had heard it from those who had seen the apostles, and from those who had been their disciples" (IV. xxvii. 1).

generation what the fixed verities of the Christian faith are. In some of these churches the successions go back to the times of the primitive apostles themselves, who taught the first generation of believers. If questionings arise, if speculations trouble, if plain men are bewildered by the gorgeous phantasy of Gnostic theosophy or by the sincere if narrow logic of Marcion, if the canon of New Testament Scripture is doubtful or if the original documents have been tampered with, if the allegorising exegesis makes the whole of Scripture of doubtful interpretation, there is a commn-sense remedy for all these evils and one which has been constantly used. Apply to the men who are in the best position for knowing what the apostles really taught, what words they used, and what meaning they attached to these words. "If there arise a dispute about any ordinary question among us, should we not have recourse to the most ancient churches with whom the apostles held constant intercourse, and learn from them what is certain and clear with regard to it it?"[1] This is no new means of arriving at the truth, he urges. It is what is constantly done. There are believers in Christ who cannot read, who cannot make use of any written documents which the apostles have left, but who "have salvation written in their hearts by the Spirit, without paper or ink," and who have received orally the ancient tradition, and have become very wise in doctrine, morals, and tenor of life.[2]

Irenaeus proposed to give to this old and much used method of finding out what were the primary and fixed verities of the Christian faith the sanction of an ecclesiastical usage. Here we meet for the first time, outside the Roman Church, the thought of a succession from the apostles in the office-bearers of the local churches; but it is a very different thing from the "gigantic figment" of an Apostolic Succession which dominates the Anglican and is a law in the Roman Church of the present day. It is meant to be a simple and clear way to find out what the real faith of the Church is in a time of more than usual

[1] *Against Heresies*, III. iv. 1. [2] *Ibid.* iv. 2.

perplexity. This is evident from the application Irenaeus makes of his principle, and it is also clear from the manner in which Tertullian, who adopts the principle, illustrates the use to be made of it. " Run over the apostolic churches, in which the very chairs (*cathedrae*) of the apostles still guard their places (*suis locis praesident*), where their own unmutilated (*authenticae*) writings are read, uttering the voice and representing the face of each of them individually. Achaia is near you; you find Corinth. You are not far from Macedonia; you have Philippi; you have the Thessalonians. You are able to cross to Asia; you find Ephesus. You are close upon Italy: you have Rome."[1] In all these churches apostles once taught; to all these churches they sent epistles which are to this day read; their voices are still living there, and their very presence seems still to haunt them. From their days until now, such is the argument, men with the gifts of leadership and of wisdom had been office-bearers in these communities and in others founded, if not by apostles, by "apostolic men";[2] each generation had been carefully trained in the apostolic doctrine by their predecessors, and they were able to judge what the simple verities of the Christian faith were. What Irenaeus proposes is that the office-bearers who are in the succession are to be made the judges of what wholesome Christian teaching is. It is the fact of an uninterrupted succession of responsible men that is the natural and historical guarantee that the doctrines once transmitted to the fathers have been retained in the memory of the sons. For some generations it is probable that individual men had presided at the head of the Christian communities, and Irenaeus might have simply spoken of a succession of bishops, but he does not; it is the whole body of elders and bishops that Irenaeus has in view. This can be seen only when all his allusions to the matter are read. They will be found in the footnote.[3]

[1] Tertullian, *De Praescriptione Haereticorum*, xxxvi. [2] *Ibid.* xxxii.
[3] " When we refer them to that tradition which originates from the apostles and which is preserved by means of the successions of elders in

Tertullian, who is twenty years later than Irenaeus, always speaks of successions of bishops or chief pastors.[1] In both cases, however, the main thought is that there are in the various local churches actual successions of men who, because these successions go back to the actual times of the apostles, can be

the Churches," Irenaeus, *Against Heresies*, III. ii. 2. "It is therefore within the power of all, in every Church, who may wish to see the truths to contemplate the tradition of the apostles manifested throughout the whole world; and we are in a position to reckon up those who, by the apostles, were instituted bishops in the Churches, and the succession of these men to our own times," III. iii. 1. Irenaeus then gives the succession of bishops in Rome, and proceeds: "In this order and by this succession, the ecclesiastical tradition from the apostles and the preaching of the truth have come down to us," III. iii. 3. "Wherefore it is incumbent to obey the elders who are in the Church—those who, I have shown, possess the succession from the apostles; those who, together with the succession of the oversight (episcopate) have received the charisma of truth according to the good pleasure of the Father; but to hold in suspicion others who depart from the primitive succession and assemble themselves together in any place whatsoever," IV. xxvi. 2. "It behoves us to adhere to those, who, as I have already observed, do hold the doctrine of the apostles, and who, together with the order of the presbyterate (presbyterii ordine), display sound speech and blameless conduct for the confirmation and correction of others," IV. xxvi. 4. "Such elders does the Church nourish, of whom also the prophet says: 'I will give thy rulers in peace, and thy bishops in righteousness,'... where therefore the gifts of the Lord have been placed, there it behoves us to learn the truth—from those who possess that succession of the Church which is from the apostles," IV. xxvi. 5. "As I have heard from a certain elder, who had heard it from those who had seen the apostles and from those who had been their disciples," IV. xxvii. 1. "Then every word shall also seem consistent to him, if he for his part read the scriptures diligently in company with those who are the elders in the Church, among whom is the apostolic doctrine, as I have pointed out," IV. xxxii. 1. "Agnitio vera est apostolicorum doctrinae, et antiquus ecclesiae status in universo mundo et character corporis Christi secundum successiones episcoporum quibus illi eam, quae in unoquoque loco est, ecclesiam tradiderunt: quae pervenit usque ad nos custoditione sine fictione scripturarum tractatio plenissima, neque additamentum neque ablationem recipiens," IV. xxxiii. 8. Eusebius quotes Irenaeus (*Ecclesiastical History*, V. xx. 4) addressing a friend, Florinus, who had lapsed into Valentinianism. "These opinions, those elders who preceded us, and who were conversant with the apostles did not hand down to thee."

[1] Tertullian, *De Praescriptione Haereticorum*, 32, 36.

THE CHARISMA VERITATIS OF OFFICE-BEARERS 227

said to have known men who knew apostles or apostolic men, and who are therefore able to know what the apostles really meant to teach. With both writers the succession they speak of as a guarantee of the correctness of the Church's creed and as a pledge of her dogmatic unity, is an historical succession, and the conception is a matter of fact and not of dogma.

Yet with both something is added to this purely historical conception of the succession. There is an addition, the thought somewhat indefinitely formulated that these men who are office-bearers in the succession have a *charisma veritatis* because of their official position.[1] The thought is not very strongly

---

[1] *Against Heresies*, IV. xxvi, 2:—"certum veritatis charisma." In IV. xxvi. 5, Irenaeus speaks of the "gifts" of God bestowed upon the Church in the apostles, prophets and teachers, i.e. the old prophetic ministry always believed to have been specially charismatic, and then adds, "where therefore the 'gifts of the Lord' have been placed, there it behoves us to learn the truth from those who possess that succession of the Church which is from the apostles"; and in the preface to Book III. he applies to the apostles, and presumably to those who are in the succession from them, the words of our Lord in addressing the Seventy, "He that heareth you, heareth Me; and he that despiseth you, despiseth Me and Him that sent Me" (Luke x. 16; cf. Matt. x. 40). At the same time it is very doubtful if the thought of an official *charisma veritatis* is definitely and distinctly before the minds of either Irenaeus or Tertullian in the sense of something which belongs to the office-bearers exclusively and as something coming to them from their office. Both writers were too strongly posessed with the idea that the whole Church is the sphere of the Spirit to limit the action of the Spirit of Truth to the office-bearers, and the idea that a *charisma* was something which was given to the individual and not to the office was powerfully felt not only in their time but much later. Irenaeus says expressly: "'For in the Church,' it is said, 'God hath placed apostles, prophets and teachers,' and all the other means through which the Spirit works; of which all those are not partakers who do not join themselves to the Church, but defraud themselves of life through their perverse opinions and infamous behaviour. For where the Church is there is the Spirit of God; *and where the Spirit of God is there is the Church and every kind of grace;* but the Spirit is truth" (III. xxiv. 1). The Spirit of Truth was in the whole Church and not confined to any class in it; and it is possible to argue that according to Irenaeus the special charisma of those in office was the advantage that their position in the succession gave them of knowing the truth transmitted. Both Irenaeus and Tertullian asserted that members within the Church might

dwelt on by Irenaeus; but it is present in one or two passages quoted in the note below, and in the second it is plain that whatever use he makes of it with reference to office-bearers what he has in his mind is the "gift" which in earlier days was exclusively associated with the prophetic ministry.[1]

It is evident that this new official task of guaranteeing the true apostolic teaching, which is laid upon the office-bearers in general, and on the pastors or bishops in particular, must have had a very restraining effect upon the prophetic ministry, and on the unlimited freedom of exhortation which characterized the churches in the first century and in many decades of the second century. The office-bearers who were in the succession

and did possess the "gift" of true prophecy (Irenaeus, *Against Heresies*, I. xiii. 4; II. xxxii. 4; xxxiii. 3; III. xi. 9; V. vi. 1), and Tertullian's so-called Montanist period is simply his recoil from where he perceived this theory of an official *charisma veritatis* was leading him (cf. specially his *De Pudicitia*). Even in Cyprian's days this idea of an official inspiration was not accepted without some misgivings; and although the bishops at his North African Councils in recording their votes gave their opinion and that of the Holy Spirit, the idea that the inspiration was after all personal is evidenced in the part which dreams and visions play (*Epist.* lvii. 5).

[1] This indefinite thought (for with Irenaeus it is indefinite) that in addition to the natural means of knowing the true Christian doctrine which comes from being in the regular succession of office-bearers in places where the apostles themselves taught, there is a *charisma veritatis* which is *official*, is the germ of the Romanist doctrine of tradition; and although the road may be long between the *certum veritatis charisma* and the utterance of Pope Pius IX., "Io sono la tradizione," the milestones may be marked. Some Anglicans make much of the thought that there is a *charisma veritatis* attached to the succession of office-bearers (they say bishops), and put a great deal more into it than Irenaeus ever intended; but it is somewhat dangerous for their own theories to do so. It is part of the conception of Irenaeus that the Church which has the surest claim to know what are the verities of the Christian faith is the Church in Rome, and he insists that every other Church ought to agree with the Christian society in the capital city. "It is a matter of necessity," he says, "that every Church should agree with this Church *propter potiorem principalitatem*" (III. iii. 2), and however the words *propter principalitatem* be translated the idea in the mind of Irenaeus is the simple historical one that the two greatest apostles both taught there and that their teaching had been remembered by means of the succession of office-bearers; place the dogmatic instead of the historical idea and you have papal infallibility.

were now made the judges of what ought to be taught to the people in exhortation and in instruction ; and they were therefore set in the position of judging all who undertook the function which was the peculiar work of the prophetic ministry. Besides, it was suggested that the peculiar *veritatis charisma*, the " gift " which gave them their unique and distinguished position, belonged to the office-bearers of the churches as well as the " gift " of government. The indications are that the suggestion of Irenaeus had been acted on long before he placed it on record. Whenever it came to be the accepted rule in the Church the revolution became an accomplished fact ; and the men who had been supreme (the prophets), and whom to disobey had been accounted an unpardonable sin, became the servants of the office-bearers whose superiors they once had been.

The need for some authority to express the dogmatic unity of the Church, and the idea that this authority lay in the office-bearers of the churches, must have placed the prophetic ministry in an inferior position and tended to destroy it altogether. For though the position assigned to the heads of the churches meant practically that they were to be the judges of what the proper instruction was, and did not necessarily mean that they were in every case to take the instruction in their own hands, still that was bound to come out of the idea in the end. The office-bearers, and especially the bishops, would inevitably become the instructors as well as the judges of the instruction that was given.

Another set of circumstances was working to the downfall of the prophetic ministry. The Rescript of the Emperor Hadrian to Minucius Fundanus, who was Proconsul of Asia sometime about 124 A.D., was rightly regarded by the Christians as the beginning of an era of comparative toleration.[1] The

---

[1] On this Rescript of Hadrian's compare Ramsay, *The Church in the Roman Empire* (1893), pp. 320 ff. ; Lightfoot, *Apostolic Fathers : S. Ignatius, S. Polycarp* (1885), i. pp. 460-4 ; Mommsen, *Der Religionsfrevel nach römischen Recht* in the *Histor. Zeitschrift*, vol. lxiv. (xxviii.), pt. iii.

character of the great Emperor, his curiosity, half cynical half hopeful, about all kinds of religious faiths, made them expect great things from him. Christian literature struck a bolder note. The writings of the apologists began to appear, who demanded on behalf of their brethren to be treated like their fellow-subjects, free to live, so long as they did not transgress against the laws of morality, under the shelter of the wide-spreading *pax Romanorum*. Christianity found a voice and demanded to be heard, pleading for the toleration which was granted to all other religions. The earliest of these writers was probably Quadratus. Aristides, Justin Martyr, Miltiades, Melito, Tatian, Athenagoras and others followed in succession. From our modern standpoint these documents are but feeble expositions of the Christian faith; Tertullian alone, with his lofty elevation of sentiment and his stern moral enthusiasm, seems to be an apologist for all time. But if these writings are looked upon, as they ought to be, in the light of pleas for some way of living quietly and peaceably under the imperial rule,[1] they are very interesting documents. They almost invariably take the same line of argument. Christianity, they say, can have no quarrel with good government; its morals are purer than those of paganism, and are therefore a better protection to the State; Christians cannot pray *to* the Emperor, but they always pray *for* him; they are and they mean to be loyal citizens of the great commonwealth to which they belong. It is strange to observe an undertone of admiration for the imperial rule under which they live, and a conviction that all would be well if the emperors could only learn what Christianity really is,[2]

---

i.: 389 ff.; Harnack, *Die Chronologie der altchristlichen Literatur* (1897), pp. 256, n. 6. These authors all believe in the genuineness of the Rescript. Keim and others reject it on very superficial grounds. The Rescript itself is to be found at the end of the *First Apology* of Justin Martyr.

[1] "Grant us the same rights, we ask for nothing more, as those who persecute us," Athenagoras, *Plea for the Christians*, 3.

[2] Athenagoras, *Plea*, etc., 37; Theophilus, *To Autolycus*, i. 11; Tertullian, *Apology*, 1; "If in this case alone you are ashamed or afraid

and to notice how they almost invariably distinguish the imperial ruler from those who persecute them. Tatian seems even to discern that there is a universal humane aim in the imperial rule, that it has proclaimed in some shadowy way the brotherhood of mankind, that there is a measure of resemblance between the empire and Christianity, and that the two ought to be allies and not foes.[1] They all look forward to a possible accommodation between the imperial government and the Christian societies. Tertullian indeed pleads that the Christian churches ought to be allowed to enrol themselves as associations for practising a lawful religion.

But the more thoughtful and politic among the leaders of the Christian societies could not help seeing that if there was to be any accommodation with the empire there must be some change on the part of the Christian societies, and that Christians must to some extent change their habits of life if they were to mingle more freely with their fellow-men who were not Christians. In the earlier times Christianity was held to be a "mode of life," to use the expression of Tatian;[2] Christians were men and women who had little or nothing to do with this world; who were not to conform themselves to it in any way, and were not to mingle in its pursuits nor in its pleasures. They were little separate secluded societies, awaiting on the threshold the opening of the new heavens and the new earth. The earliest Christians were content with this, and asked for nothing more.

The middle of the second century, however, witnessed a change which may be best indicated by saying that the Christian faith was attracting to it multitudes of people drawn from all classes and ranks in society—imperial officials, merchants,

---

to exercise your authority in making public inquiry with the carefulness which becomes justice."

[1] The design of Christianity is to put an end to slavery and to "rescue us from a multiplicity of rulers and from ten thousand tyrants" (*Address to the Greeks*, xxix.); "there ought to be one common polity for all" (xxviii.). [2] Tatian, *Address to the Greeks*, xlii.

character of the great Emperor, his curiosity, half cynical half hopeful, about all kinds of religious faiths, made them expect great things from him. Christian literature struck a bolder note. The writings of the apologists began to appear, who demanded on behalf of their brethren to be treated like their fellow-subjects, free to live, so long as they did not transgress against the laws of morality, under the shelter of the wide-spreading *pax Romanorum*. Christianity found a voice and demanded to be heard, pleading for the toleration which was granted to all other religions. The earliest of these writers was probably Quadratus. Aristides, Justin Martyr, Miltiades, Melito, Tatian, Athenagoras and others followed in succession. From our modern standpoint these documents are but feeble expositions of the Christian faith; Tertullian alone, with his lofty elevation of sentiment and his stern moral enthusiasm, seems to be an apologist for all time. But if these writings are looked upon, as they ought to be, in the light of pleas for some way of living quietly and peaceably under the imperial rule,[1] they are very interesting documents. They almost invariably take the same line of argument. Christianity, they say, can have no quarrel with good government; its morals are purer than those of paganism, and are therefore a better protection to the State; Christians cannot pray *to* the Emperor, but they always pray *for* him; they are and they mean to be loyal citizens of the great commonwealth to which they belong. It is strange to observe an undertone of admiration for the imperial rule under which they live, and a conviction that all would be well if the emperors could only learn what Christianity really is,[2]

---

i.: 389 ff.; Harnack, *Die Chronologie der altchristlichen Literatur* (1897), pp. 256, n. 6. These authors all believe in the genuineness of the Rescript. Keim and others reject it on very superficial grounds. The Rescript itself is to be found at the end of the *First Apology* of Justin Martyr.

[1] "Grant us the same rights, we ask for nothing more, as those who persecute us," Athenagoras, *Plea for the Christians*, 3.

[2] Athenagoras, *Plea*, etc., 37; Theophilus, *To Autolycus*, i. 11; Tertullian, *Apology*, 1; "If in this case alone you are ashamed or afraid

In the end the leaders of the Christian societies seem to have spontaneously and gradually come to see that it was their duty to bring their followers into what accommodation was possible with the conditions of existing society. It was this feeling that rendered the writings of the apologists possible. The time of enthusiasm had passed away for the great majority of Christians. Unimpassioned conviction took the place of the earlier almost unrestrained passion of faith. One can scarcely fancy Ignatius of Antioch writing in the tone of cool argument which characterises the apologists.

The change of moral and intellectual atmosphere did not suit the prophetic ministry, which had been the enthusiastic element from the beginning, and had become the element of asceticism. It was unavoidable that it should lose its old place and its ancient power. Pleasant things continued to be said about prophets, provided only they accepted a position under the office-bearers of the local churches. Curious regulations appear in some of the ancient canons, enjoining the people to respect their utterances. In the ancient Syrian collection known as the *Testamentum Jesu Christi*, for example,[1] those who despise prophecy are debarred from coming to the Holy Supper, but the prophets were no longer the superior ministry in the churches.

There is also evidence leading us to believe that the prophetic ministry had been deteriorating. From the very beginning men had claimed to be included within its ranks who were not true prophets. Warnings against such persons are to be found within the New Testament writings,[2] and they occur, and with increasing strength, in writers of the second century. We have

---

[1] *Testamentum Jesu Christi*, edited by Rahman (1899), p. 37. Among the proclamations made by the deacon before the Eucharistic service is: *Si quis prophetas despicit, semet segreget.* The *Testament* also says:—*Si quis autem verba prophetica dicit, mercedem habebit*, p. 79.

[2] Matt. vii. 15; xxiv. 11, 24; Mark xiii. 22; Acts xiii. 6; 2 Peter ii. 1; 1 John iv. 1-3; Rev. ii. 2, 14, 15, 20.

seen them in the *Didache*.[1] Justin Martyr cites their presence in the Church as a proof that Christianity is the true development of Judaism, because the Christians have among them false prophets as well as true ones like the ancient Israel.[2] Hermas has given expressive pictures of the true and the false prophets.[3] All this was a sign of the times.

---

[1] Justin Martyr, *Dialogue with Trypho*, 82 ; Irenaeus, *Against Heresies*, I. xiii. 3 ; III. xi. 9 ; Eusebius, *Hist. Eccles.* V. xvii. 1–4 ; *Apostolic Constitutions*, VII. xxxii. ; VIII. ii. ; *Didache*, xi. 1, 2, 8.

[2] *Dialogue with Trypho*, lxxxii.:—"For the prophetical gift remains with us even to the present time. Hence you ought to understand that the gifts formerly among your nation have been transferred to us. And just as there were false prophets contemporaneous with your holy prophets, so there are many false teachers among us, of whom our Lord forewarned us to beware ; so that in no respect are we deficient, since we know that He foreknew all that would happen to us after His resurrection from the dead and ascension to heaven. For He said that we would be put to death and hated for His Name sake ; and that many false prophets and false Christs would appear in His name and deceive many ; and so it has come about. For many have taught, too, and even yet are teaching those things which proceed from the unclean teaching of the devil and which are put into their hearts."

[3] Hermas, *Pastor, Mandata*, xi :—" He showed me some men sitting on a seat, and one man sitting on a chair. And he says to me, ' Do you see the persons sitting on the seat ? ' ' I do,' I said. ' These,' he says, ' are the faithful, and he who sits on the chair is a false prophet, ruining the minds of the servants of God. It is the doubters, not the faithful, he ruins.' . . . ' How then,' sir,' I say, ' will a man know which of them is the prophet, and which is the false prophet ? ' ' I will tell you,' he says, ' about both prophets, and then you can test the true and the false prophet according to my directions. Test the man who has the Spirit of God by his life. For he who has the Divine Spirit proceeding from above, is meek and peaceable and humble and refrains from all iniquity and the vain desire of this world and contents himself with fewer wants than those of other men, and when asked he makes no reply ; nor does he speak privately, nor when a man wishes the Spirit to speak does the Holy Spirit speak, but it speaks only when God wishes it to speak. When, then, a man having the Divine Spirit comes into an assembly of righteous men who have faith in the Divine Spirit, and this assembly of men offers up prayer to God, then the angel of the prophetic Spirit, who is destined for him, fills the man ; and the man being filled with the Holy Spirit, speaks to the multitude as the Lord wishes. Thus then the Spirit of Divinity becomes manifest. Whatever power therefore comes from the Spirit of Divinity

These various influences combined to help forward the revolution which excluded the prophetic ministry from its earlier position of supremacy and installed the local official ministry in the supreme place of rule. They worked slowly and surely during the second century, and especially during the first half of the period.

But while this movement was going on, and its effects on the prophetic ministry were gradually manifesting themselves, protesting voices were raised. This movement fostered by the official ministry of the local churches was a departure, it seemed to many, from the traditions of the Church which they had in reverence; and it was accompanied by a relaxation of the stern rule of Christian life under which the earlier generations had lived and died. The prophetic ministry had always been considered as the direct gift of God to the Church. *It* was the ministry *from above*. It had been placed by St. Paul second only to the apostolate. Souls had been won from heathenism through its ministrations. The lives of believers had been braced by it to endure the hardships and persecutions which their Master had foretold them would fall upon them, and which they had been taught to regard as their blessed lot while this life lasted. They saw that with the neglect of the prophetic ministry

---

belongs to the Lord. Hear then,' he says, 'in regard to the Spirit which is earthly and empty and foolish and powerless. First the man who seems to have the Spirit exalts himself, and wishes to have the first seat, and is bold and impudent and talkative, and lives in the midst of many luxuries and many other delusions, and takes reward for his prophecy; and if he does not receive rewards he does not prophesy. Can then the Divine Spirit take rewards and prophesy? It is not possible that the Spirit of God should do this, but prophets of this character are possessed of an earthly spirit. Then it never approaches an assembly of righteous men but shuns them. And it associates with doubters and the vain, and prophesies to them in a corner and deceives them, speaking to them, according to their desires, mere empty words. . . . This then is the mode of life of both the prophets. Try by his life and by his deeds the man who says that he is inspired. But as for you, trust the Spirit which comes from God, and has power; but the spirit which is empty and earthly trust not at all, for there is no power in it; it comes from the devil.'!'

there went hand in hand an attempt at conformity with the world and a relaxation of the more rigid rules of the Christian life. It was by no means the worst kind of Christians who called upon the Church to halt in this rapid approach to the usages of the world, in this relaxation of the severer maxims of the Christian life, in this neglect or undervaluing of the prophetic ministry, and in this exaltation of the office-bearers of the local churches. They grew increasingly alarmed and uneasy in the presence of the silent movement above described. It was taking from them some of their most precious possessions. They began to feel that there was no room for them in the Church which had hitherto sheltered them. All this was felt most strongly, as was to be expected, in the regions more remote from the great centres of public life, where the pressure of coming to some terms with the State was lighter. The standard of revolt was raised in the mountainous region of Phrygia—a land not thoroughly incorporated within the Roman administration. The movement was headed by a presbyter or elder, called Montanus, and became known as Montanism. It was natural that the crisis should emerge in these regions of Asia. No portion of the empire was so peopled by Christians. Christian prophecy had flourished in the neighbouring regions. The daughters of Philip had lived in the great city of Hierapolis. The Christian prophets Quadratus and Ammia had belonged to Philadelphia.[1] Attalus of Pergamos had been taught in visions.[2] Polycarp, the most distinguished Christian of the whole of Asia, was a prophet. Ignatius had exhibited his prophetic gifts in Philadelphia.[3] On the other hand, if the country had produced many Christian prophets, its churches had been the earliest to organize themselves under the threefold ministry. The prophetic and the local ministries confronted each other there as they did nowhere else.

This Phrygian movement was the centre and exaggeration

---

[1] Eusebius, *Ecclesiastical History*, V. xvii. 3. [2] *Ibid.* V. iii. 2.
[3] *Epistle to the Philadelphians*, 7.

of a wide-spreading revolt and separation from the great Church of the second and third centuries. It has been represented as an attempt at innovation on the old usages and habits of primitive Christianity. This is a mistaken view. At the same time if we confine our attention to the actions and claims of Montanus himself and the circle of Phrygia immediately surrounding him, there was much that was entirely new. Montanus' idea seems to have been that he had been commissioned by God to gather all true Christians into a community, which would be ready by its renunciation of all the claims that social life presented and by an absolute self-surrender to the requirements of the higher Christian life, to meet the Lord Who was about to come and inaugurate His millennial kingdom in the immediate future. He seems to have believed that the Church had reached its final term of existence in the world. He and his fellow prophets therefore represented the last stage of prophecy, and consequently possessed an inspiration such as none of their predecessors could lay claim to. They in their own persons and with their special prophetic gifts, were the literal fulfilment of the promise given by our Lord in the Gospel of St. John, that the Father and the Son would take up their abode in true believers, and that the Paraclete had come to abide with them.[1] Hence when they spoke under the influence of the divine afflatus it was not they, but the Spirit, that uttered the words. So entirely were the prophets separated from the Spirit, who made use of their organs of speech, that the oracles were uttered in the first person,[2] and the Spirit, speaking through the mouth of a woman, used the masculine forms of speech.[3] All this was new.

[1] Compare *St. John's Gospel*, xiv. 16-26; xv. 7-15. It ought to be remembered that the most strenuous opponents of the Montanists denied the authenticity and authority of the *Gospel of St. John* and also of the *Apocalypse*.

[2] Compare the prophetic utterances as collected by Bonwetsch in his *Geschichte des Montanismus*, pp. 197 ff., Oracles 1, 3, 4, 5, 12, 18, 21. It ought to be remembered however that this applies only to some of the utterances.

[3] Compare oracle 11; it is from Epiphanius, *Heresies*, xlviii. 13.

On the other hand, if the Phrygian movement be connected, as it must be, with the strenuous action of Christians in Gaul, North Africa, and indeed throughout most parts of the empire, these novelties were toned down in such a way that very little that was new remained. We may mis-read the Montanist utterances which belong to its earliest period if we interpret them as Tertullian and others did;[1] but there is no misreading the feelings, thoughts and strivings of that great mass of Christians that welcomed the movement as something which encouraged them to resist that secularising of the Church which was being pressed forward by the heads of so many of the more powerful Christian communities.

When Dr. Salmon[2] says that the bulk of what Tertullian taught as a Montanist he probably would equally have taught if Montanus had never lived, the statement, thoroughly correct, shows that Tertullian and the conservative Christians he represented saw in the Montanist movement something which was no innovation, but a strong assistance in preserving the old condition of the Church with its prophetic ministry, its rules for daily life, its separation from the world, and its expectation of the nearness of the coming of the Lord to found His millennial kingdom. The real question between these conservative Christians and the majority of their brethren was not about the government of the local churches. They all accepted the threefold ministry, and both parties professed to accept and to honour prophecy. But the advanced party, which in the end triumphed, would subject the prophets to the official ministry; while the conservatives insisted that prophecy should be free as in the old days, and specially free to interfere with and rebuke the

---

[1] Harnack, whose view of Montanism is very much his own, insists strongly upon this. Compare his *History of Dogma*, ii. 95 n. 2 (Engl. Trans.). On the other hand it must be remembered that the Montanist sayings recorded have all, save those which have come to us from Tertullian, been transmitted by their bitter enemies who may have exaggerated.

[2] *Dictionary of Christian Biography*, iii. 943b.

growing desire for conformity with the world and for coming to terms with the State.[1]

A conservative reaction can scarcely avoid exaggerating the phases of Church life or organization for which it contends and perhaps suffers. This was probably true of the reaction in the second and in the beginning of the third centuries; but the conception that Montanism in the larger sense of the word (i.e. in the sense which includes Tertullian) was an innovation, and that the party in the Church which it attacked were carrying on the old line of Church life and usages, is untenable and in face of all the facts of history. The distinctive features of Montanism: its appreciation of the prophetic ministry, its conception of the Gospel as the new law, its refusal to entrust the officebearers of the local churches with the restoration of those who had lapsed into grievous sins unless on the recommendation of a prophet speaking in the Spirit, and its views about the near approach of the millennial kingdom of the Lord, were all characteristic of the earlier Christianity.

The question of prophecy may be taken as an example.

It is true that *after* the separation between the Montanists and the "great" Church, Christian theologians vehemently opposed the Montanist theory of the nature of prophecy, and especially protested against the idea that true prophecy was ecstatic. But this was an afterthought for the purpose of discrediting the Montanist movement and claims. This can be shown by a comparison of the statements made about the prophecy which existed and was honoured within the Christian Church before the Montanist movement arose and while the earlier stages of the antagonism lasted.[2] The nature of the

---

[1] Compare Ramsay, *The Church in the Roman Empire*, p. 435.

[2] For Montanism compare:—Ritschl, *Die Entstehung der altkatholischen Kirche* (1857), 2nd ed. pp. 462-554; Bonwetsch, *Geschichte des Montanismus* (1881); also article in the *Zeitschrift für kirchliche Wissenschaf. und kirchliches Leben* (1884) on *Die Prophetie im apostolischen und nachapostolischen Zeitalter*; Renan, *Les Crises du Catholicisme Naissant, Revue des Deux Mondes* (1881), Febr. 15; also in his *Marc Aurèle* (1882), pp. 208 ff.;

Christian prophecy remains the same down to the time of Irenaeus, whose descriptions are not different from those of Justin Martyr. Justin declares that prophetic gifts existed in the Church in his time. "For one receives the spirit of understanding, another of counsel, another of healing, another of strength, another of foreknowledge, another of teaching, and another of the fear of God."[1] "The prophetic gifts remain with us even to the present time,"[2] he says. They abide in fulfilment of the Old Testament promise quoted by St. Peter on the day of Pentecost.[3] Irenaeus declares that prophecy existed in the Church in his days. "For some (believers) do certainly cast out devils, so that those who have thus been cleansed from evil spirits do frequently both believe and join the Church. Others have knowledge of things to come; they see visions and utter prophetic expressions."[4] He goes on to say that these things come about not by performing incantations, but by praying to the Lord in a pure, sincere and straightforward spirit. Tertullian has given us a vivid picture of what this kind of prophecy was like. He says:[5] "We have now among us a sister whose lot it has been to be favoured with sundry gifts of revelation, which she experiences in the Spirit by ecstatic vision amidst the sacred rites on the Lord's Day in the Church. She converses with angels and even with the Lord. She both sees and hears mysterious communications (*sacramenta*). Some men's hearts she understands, and to them who are in need

---

Voigt, *Eine verscholl ne Urkunde des antimontanistischen Kampfes* (1891); articles on Montanism in the *Dictionary of Christian Biography* by Salmon, in the *Encyclopædia Britannica* by Harnack, and in *Herzog's Real-Encyclopaedie* by Möller; Harnack's *Das Monchthum, seine Ideale und seine Geschichte* (1886), 3rd ed.; and his *History of Dogma* (1896), ii. pp. 94-108 of the Engl. Transl. The monograph of Bonwetsch is the most complete. He has collected in an appendix (p. 197) all the recorded utterances of the Montanists, and an elaborate statement of all our sources of information appears on pp. 16-55.

[1] Justin Martyr, *Dialogue with Trypho*, 39.
[2] *Dialogue with Trypho*, 82.   [3] *Ibid.* 39, 82.
[4] Irenaeus, *Against Heresies*, II. xxxii. 4, 5.
[5] Tertullian, *De Anima*. 9.

she distributes remedies. Whether it be in the reading of the Scriptures, or in the chanting of Psalms, or in the preaching of sermons, or in the offering up of prayers—in all these religious services matter and opportunity are afforded to her of seeing visions. . . . After the people are dismissed, at the conclusion of the sacred services she is in the regular habit of reporting to us whatever things she may have seen in vision—for all her communications are examined with the most scrupulous care that their truth may be probed."

Besides, the theory of the nature of prophecy ascribed to the Montanists was the theory of the second century. Prophecy was described as ecstatic. It is difficult, perhaps, to understand exactly what was meant by the word. This, however, is clear, that it meant that what came from the prophet was something given him, and was not the result of his ordinary powers of intelligence; also that the prophet could not prophesy at will, but had to wait for the divine afflatus, which might come quite unexpectedly or in answer to prayer. If this be all that is meant by ecstasy it is plain that the Church of the second century believed that its prophecy was ecstatic. Hermas declares that in true prophecy the spirit " speaks only when God wishes it to speak," and that the " man filled with the Spirit of God speaks to the multitude as the Lord wishes." [1] The statements of Irenaeus about true prophecy are exactly the same. He says that the gift of prophecy comes from the grace of God alone, and "that only those on whom God sends His grace from above possess that divinely-bestowed power of prophesying." Prophets " speak where and when God pleases." [2] We have seen how the prophetic afflatus came upon Ignatius when preaching to the Philadelphians, and how he cried out, speaking things quite unpremeditated which he felt had been given him to speak.[3] It was afterwards maintained that the Montanist theory of prophecy meant more than this, and the famous

---

[1] Compare p. 234 n. [2] Irenaeus, *Against Heresies*, I. xiii. 4.
[3] *Epistle to the Philadelphians*, 7. Compare pp. 189 n., 129.

dictum of Montanus is continually quoted to mean more and to be repudiated. Montanus has said: "Behold the man is as a lyre, and I sweep over him as a plectrum. The man sleeps, and I wake. Behold it is the Lord who estranges the souls of men from themselves and gives them souls"; and the metaphor suggests that man is a merely passive instrument in the hands of God.[1]

But even if we are to argue from a metaphor (always a dangerous kind of reasoning), it should be remembered that the same or similar metaphors were used to describe non-Montanist prophecy. Athenagoras speaks of the Spirit of God moving "the mouths of the prophets like musical instruments," and of the Spirit making use of the prophets as "a flute-player breathes into his flute."[2] The author of the *Cohortatio ad Gentes* uses the famous metaphor of Montanus and speaks of the "divine plectrum descending from heaven and using righteous men as an instrument like a harp or lyre," in order to reveal to men things divine and heavenly.[3] It is impossible to say that Montanist prophecy was a new thing, and that Montanism in exalting the prophetic ministry was not thoroughly conservative in its endeavour.[4]

The same result is reached when we consider the Montanist discipline. The whole movement was a protest against that growing conformity with the world which the Church of the second century had felt constrained to attempt, under the leadership of the office-bearers of the local churches. Like all conservative reactions, it exaggerated the characteristics it had arisen to conserve, but that was the only great difference.

It is probable that the movement in Phrygia had continued

[1] Bonwetsch, *Geschichte des Montanismus*, p. 197.
[2] *Plea for the Christians*, 7, 9.
[3] Pseudo-Justin, *Cohortatio ad Gentes*, 8.
[4] It may be said that this second century theory of prophecy abandoned St. Paul' great principle that the spirits of the prophets are subject to the prophets, and perhaps that is so. But the point here is that the Church and Montanism had to begin with the same *theory* of prophecy.

for some years before there was any break with the "great" Church: and after the separation did take place efforts were made to bring the leaders on both sides together again. The Martyrs of Lyons wrote urging peace, and the Roman Church had serious thoughts of interfering on the side of unity.[1] Such attempts would probably have been unsuccessful. The separation came; and in Phrgyia at least, the great proportion of the Christian people sided with the party of Montanus. It became the Kataphrygian Church (the Church-according-to-the-Phrygians), and continued so for long. When the Emperor Constantine recognized the Christian religion the Marcionite and Montanist Christians did not share in the peace of the Church. The persecutions against them were rather intensified. The Phrygian Montanists, however, were not overwhelmed; but according to Sozomen Montanists disappeared elsewhere.[2] Penal laws of increasing severity were enacted against them by Christian emperors. Their churches were confiscated; a rigorous search was made for their religious writings, which were destroyed when discovered; the ordination of their clergy was made a penal offence; the power of disposing of their property by will was denied them, and their nearest Catholic relatives were allowed to seize their possessions—and still they remained true to their church and to the prophetic ministry.[3] At last in the sixth century the Emperor Justinian resolved to stamp them out, and the historian Procopius tells us that in their despair the Montanists gathered themselves, with their wives and

---

[1] Eusebius, *Eccles. Hist.* V. iii. 4; Tertullian, *Adversus Praxean*, 1:— "For after the bishop of Rome had acknowledged the prophetic gifts of Montanus, Prisca and Maximilla, and, in consequence of the acknowledgment, had bestowed his peace on the Churches of Asia and Phrygia (i.e. had declared himself in communion with them), Praxeas, by importunately urging false accusations against the prophets themselves and their Churches and insisting on the authority of the bishop's predecessors in the see, compelled him to recall the pacific letter which he had issued, as well as from his purpose of acknowledging the said gifts."

[2] *Eccles. Hist.* ii. 32; cf. vii. 12.

[3] Imperial edicts of 398 A.D. and 415 A.D.

children, into their churches, and setting fire to the buildings perished in the flames [1] rather than submit to the bishops' Church which had urged the persecution through all these centuries, and had forbidden the members to have any communion with Montanists, even when confined in a common prison for a common faith. All this bitterness and all this bloodshed because some Christians would insist that the prophetic ministry should be kept in the position assigned to it by St. Paul, and should not be subject to the rule of the elders "who are in the Church—those who possess the succession from the apostles."

The "Great Church," as it then began to be called, separated from her daughters, the Marcionite and the Montanist churches, went forth to her task of subduing the Roman world under the guidance of a three-fold ministry which ruled in every Christian community within the Empire. In its efforts to do its work thoroughly the organization of the great Empire, and especially its religious organization, became, as we shall afterwards see, a study growing in attractiveness and presenting points for imitation by the leaders of the society.

In this changed organization of the second and third centuries the old prophetic ministry was completely abandoned, and the local or congregational ministry had now no superiors to interfere with them and to supersede them in exhortation, in the dispensing of the Holy Supper, and in prescribing how Christians ought to live in the fear of God. The revolt against the changes made had ended in the conservatives, zealous for that ministry which had come down from apostolic days, and which St. Paul had placed at the head of the gifts bestowed by God upon His people, being driven out of the Church, and in their forming separate societies. The ministry which remained is what represented the "helps" and "pilotings" which God had placed in the Church. It was the spontaneous creation of the individual local churches. The ministry "from above" had

[1] Procopius, *Historia Arcana*, 11.

disappeared; but what remained was not the less divine because it had been the creation of the congregation, for it was based on the possession and the recognition of "gifts" of service and rule which God had bestowed according to His promise upon His worshipping people.

Pictures of this ministry which ruled in the end of the second and in the earlier part of the third century, have been preserved for us in early ecclesiastical manuals. Perhaps the *Canons of Hippolytus* may be most fitly selected to furnish them.[1] These canons are thoroughly representative. They were the work of a western ecclesiastic, and they form the basis of almost all the later ecclesiastical discipline of the Eastern Church. They are also especially interesting, because they contain the clearest description of Christian public worship which we have between the Epistle of St. Paul to the Corinthians and the much later *Apostolic Constitutions*.

The Christian society consisted of believers and their children, with a fringe of catechumens or candidates for baptism, and those who were still only inquirers into the truths of the Christian faith. The community was sharply divided into clergy and laity,[2] with a number of persons who stood between the two

[1] *Texte und Untersuchungen*, VI. iv., *Die aeltesten Quellen des orientalischen Kirchenrechts, erstes Buch, Die canones Hippolyti*, Dr. Hans Achelis (1891). Riedel, *Die Kirchenrechtsquellen des Patriarchats Alexandrien* (1900), pp. 193-230:—*Die Canones Hippolyti*. Compare Funk, *Die Apostolischen Constitutionen* (1891), pp. 265-80 ; Wordsworth, *The Ministry of Grace* (1901), pp. 18-42 ; de Lagarde in Bunsen's *Analecta Ante-Nicaena*, ii. 37 ; Sohm, *Kirchenrecht*, i. 287 n. 20. Achelis gives in parallel columns extracts from Ludolf's *Ethiopic Statutes*, from the Coptic *Heptateuch* (a new translation made by Steindorf), and from the eighth book of the *Apostolic Constitutions*.

[2] The division of the congregation into clergy and laity and the common mode of making the difference apparent in daily ecclesiastical life were both borrowed from the usages of the civil society round them. The laity were called *plebs* and the clergy the *ordo*—the names applied to the commons and the senate of the Italian and provincial towns. As the members of the senate or the ordo had a special bench, called the *consessus*, in the basilica or court-house, so the clergy had special seats in church. "It is the authority of the Church," says Tertullian, "that

sections, and who were specially honoured for their services or character—the confessors, the widows (honoured for their abundant prayer and for their nursing the sick),[1] and celibates and virgins. The office-bearers included the pastor (now invariably called the bishop), elders, deacons, readers, and, perhaps, subdeacons. At the head of all stood the bishop, in whom the whole congregational life centred. He was chosen by the whole congregation, who assembled in church for the purpose. The people were taught to recognize that God was with them while they selected their pastor. When they had made their choice known and had clearly intimated the man whom they had elected, they were enjoined to say, "Oh God, strengthen him whom *Thou* hast prepared for us."[2]

It was the rule, when the bishop was set apart to his office, that the neighbouring bishops should be present; but this was not essential. The congregation possessed within itself the power and authority to carry out the ordination of their chief office-bearer. When all things were ready, and the whole congregation had assembled in Church, one of the bishops or one of the elders of the congregation, was selected to perform the act of ordination, which consisted in laying his hands on the head of the bishop-elect and praying over him.[3] The beautiful prayer of consecration is given.[4] God was asked

makes the difference between the ordo and the plebs—this and the honour consecrated by the special bench of the ordo " (*De Exhortatione Castitatis*, 7).

[1] " Viduis propter copiosas orationes, infirmiorum curam et frequens jejunium praecipuus honor tribuatur," Can. ix.

[2] " Episcopus eligatur ex omni populo . . . dicat populus : nos eligimus eum. Deinde silentio facto in toto grege post exhomologesin omnes pro eo orent dicentes : O Deus, corrobora hunc, quem nobis preparasti," Can. ii.

[3] " Deinde eligatur unus ex episcopis et presbyteris, qui manum capiti ejus imponat, et oret dicens," Can. ii.

[4] " O Deus, Pater domini nostri Jesus Christi, Pater misericordiarum et Deus totius consolationis . . . .Respice super N., servum tuum, tribuens virtutem tuam et spiritum efficacem, quem tribuisti sanctis apostolis per dominum nostrum Jesum Christum, filium tuum unicum ; illis, qui

to fill the bishop with the Spirit possessed by the apostles who founded the churches everywhere; to bless him in permitting him to rule a blameless flock; to make him a pattern in all holy living; to make him powerful in prayer; to give him grace to declare the pardon of sins; and to make him able to break the chains in which the evil spirits held any of his flock. The prayer makes us see what the duties of the bishop were. He led the public devotions of his people; he presided over the exercise of discipline; he had the care of the poor and of the sick; he was to drive out the evil spirits who troubled the bodies and the souls of members of his flock. The congregation was a Church of Christ because they were endeavouring to live the life of new obedience to which their Lord had called them, and the man at their head, their representative, was expected to be the saintliest man among them. If he had not learning, the reader was there to read and expound the Scriptures; if he possessed few administrative gifts the elders and the deacons were beside him to aid him; but a man of prayer and of holy life he *must* be—there could be no substitute for that.

Nothing is said about the election of elders, and it is impossible to say whether they were chosen by the people or nominated by the bishop or co-opted by the session. But we have two interesting bits of information which show from what classes of men the elders were often drawn. Martyrs and confessors were to be made elders. The martyr was one who, for

fundaverunt ecclesiam in omni loco ad honorem et gloriam nominis tui sancti. Quia tu cognovisti cor uniuscujusque, concede illi, ut ipse sine peccato videat populum tuum, ut mereatur pascere gregem tuum magnum sacrum. Effice etiam, ut mores ejus sint superiores omni populo sine ulla declinatione. Effice etiam, ut propter praestantiam illi ab omnibus invideatur, et accipe orationes ejus et oblationes ejus, quas tibi offeret die noctuque, et sint tibi odor suavis. Tribue etiam illi, O Domine, episcopatum et spiritum clementem et potestatem ad remittenda peccata; et tribue illi facultatem ad dissolvenda omnia vincula iniquitatis daemonum, et ad sanandos omnes morbos, et contere Satanam sub pedibus ejus velociter, per dominum nostrum Jesum Christum, per quem tibi gloria cum ipso et Spiritu Sancto in saecula saeculorum. Amen." Can. iii.

the faith's sake, had stood before the civil tribunal and had been punished. He became an elder at once; "his confession was his ordination." If a man had made a confession before the court and had not suffered, he was to be made an elder by the bishop, and the same was to be done to a Christian slave who had confessed and had suffered. Only, the bishop in these two cases was to omit the petition for the bestowal of the Holy Spirit.[1] The other case is even more interesting. Those men who possess the "gift" of healing are to be ordained presbyters after careful investigation be made that the "gift" is really possessed and that the cures do really come from God.[2] The leaders of the churches seem to be anxious to enrol within the regular ministry of the congregation, and to prevent them overshadowing its authority, all who are possessed of "gifts," or whom Christ has honoured by permitting them to be witnesses for Him. The elder was ordained by the bishop, who used the same prayer of consecration which was employed in the ordination of bishops, substituting only the word *presbyteratum* for *episcopatum*, for according to the theory of the Canons the elder was the equal of the bishop in all things save a special seat

---

[1] "Quando quis dignus est, qui stet coram tribunali et afficiatur poena propter Christum, postea autem indulgentia liber dimittitur, talis postea meretur gradum presbyteralem coram Deo, non secundum ordinationem quae fit ab episcopo. Immo, confessio est ordinatio ejus. Quodsi vero episcopus fit, ordinetur. Si quis confessione emissa tormentis laesus non est, dignus est presbyteratu; attamen ordinetur per episcopum. Si talis, cum servus alicujus esset, propter Christum cruciatus pertulit, talis similiter est presbyter gregi. Quamquam enim formam presbyteratus non acceperit, tamen spiritum presbyteratus adeptus est; episcopus igitur omittat orationis partem, quae ad spiritum sanctum pertinet," Can. vi.

[2] "Si quis petitionem porrigit, quae ad ipsius ordinationem pertinet, quod dicit: Nactus sum charisma sanationis, non prius ordinetur, quam clarescat ea res. Imprimis inquirendum est, num sanationes, quae per eum fiunt, revera a Deo deriventur," Can. viii. We see in this an echo of the verse in the Epistle of James:—"Is any one among you sick? let him call for the elders of the Church; and let them pray over him, anointing him with oil in the name of the Lord; and the prayer of faith shall save him that is sick, and the Lord shall raise him up; and if he have committed sins, it shall be forgiven him" (v. 14, 15).

in the church and the right to ordain elders and deacons.[1] The elder was therefore to be filled with the spirit of the apostles; to be an example to the flock; to be powerful in prayer; to care for the sick; to attend to discipline. The elders assisted the bishop in the conduct of public worship; they placed their hands on the offerings while the bishop prayed the prayer of thanksgiving; they stood on either side of the catechumens when they were baptized, and they introduced them into the congregation.[2] The visitation of the sick, the power to drive out by means of prayer the evil spirit which was believed to produce disease, the care of the young and the exercise of discipline, were the peculiar duties of the elders, as they appear in these Canons.

The deacon, on the other hand, is the official who does the subordinate services. He is told to remember that he is the servant of God, the servant of the bishop and the servant of the elders. The deacons visit the congregation, report cases of sickness to the bishop and to the elders; they have special charge over the poor, especially of the " secret poor," widows, orphans and strangers. They undertake the instruction of the catechumens and report to the bishop when they are ripe for baptism.[3]

Not much is said about the duties of the " widows " and the " virgins," but they seem to look after the women and the girls as the deacons care for the men. The " widows " are the sick-nurses of the community, and are to be honoured for these loving services and for their prayers for the whole congregation.

[1] " Si autem ordinatur presbyter, omnia cum eo similiter agantur ac cum episcopo, nisi quod cathedrae non insideat. Etiam eadem oratio super eo oretur tota ut super episcopo, cum sola exceptione nominis episcopatus. Episcopus in omnibus rebus aequiparetur presbytero excepto nomine cathedrae et ordinatione, quia potestas ordinandi ipsi non tribuitur," Can. iv. It should be noted however that a martyr or one who has confessed the Lord and suffered for his confession and who *ipso facto* becomes an elder does not become a bishop unless by regular ordination; and the equality in theory is not one of fact.

[2] Canon xix.   [3] Canons v., xvii.

250   THE FALL OF THE PROPHETIC MINISTRY

The picture of the Christian community presented in these Canons is that of a single congregation ruled by a pastor or bishop with his session of elders, who, theoretically of the same ecclesiastical rank as himself, are in practice his assistants. The laity are in the position of loving subordination which Ignatius contemplated and urged. The brotherhood of the members of the community is expressively shown in the way in which newly baptized catechumens, introduced formally by the elder, are greeted with the kiss of welcome and received with expressions of joy;[1] in the care for the sick and the poor; in the provisions for nursing suffering women by the "widows" and the "virgins"; and in the thought that it is the duty of the widows to pray for the whole congregation.

The little society is thoroughly self-governing and independent. It contains within itself the power to perform all ecclesiastical acts from the selection and ordination of its bishop[2] to the expulsion of offenders;[3] but it nevertheless belongs to a wide society or larger brotherhood, and this is expressed in the usual but not essential practice of associating neighbouring bishops with its elders in the ordination of its bishop.[4]

The acts of worship are described with greater detail in these Canons than in any earlier Christian document save the First Epistle of St. Paul to the Corinthians. St. Paul has given us more information about the meeting for Exhortation; these Canons tell us more about the meeting for Thanksgiving—indeed, they present us with the earliest complete description of this crowning act of Christian worship. As in apostolic times, we find two separate meetings for public worship—the meeting for Exhortation and the meeting for Thanksgiving—but the latter is no longer associated with a common meal. No forms of prayer are given for use at the former, but there is a set form of service prescribed for the latter. Both are held on the Lord's

---

[1] "Jam cum toto populo orant, qui eos osculentur gaudentes cum iis cum jubilatione," Can. xix.
[2] Canon ii.   [3] Canons i. xi.-xvi.   [4] Canon ii.

THE MEETING FOR EXHORTATION

Day—the meeting for Exhortation early in the morning, and the Eucharistic service in the afternoon.[1]

The exercises at the meeting for Exhortation were prayers, singing of psalms and hymns, reading portions of Scripture and exhortation in sermon and address.[2] No details are given us about the order of the service save that there was a prayer between the reading of each portion of the Scripture. The early freedom of worship no longer existed. The reading, prayers, and exhortation were all in the hands of the clergy. The people shared in the singing only. It was expected that they should join heartily in this part of the service, for one of the questions put to candidates for baptism was whether they had sung heartily in the service of praise.[3] This service was held not only on the Lord's Day, but on every day of the week. It was the daily worship of the great Christian family. The Canons order that the elders, deacons, readers and people are to come to church at cock-crow (*quo tempore canit gallus*), and to consecrate the day by a service of prayer, praise, and reading the Word. All the clergy, save the bishop, are strictly ordered to be present. Only sickness or absence on a journey are to be taken as excuses. The catechumens,[4] whose instructions in the faith by the deacons seems to have been given just before the service began, were

[1] It must have been in the afternoon: for although the rule was that the whole service must end before sundown, there was often an *Agape* or *Supper* afterwards and it had to be finished before darkness had come. Can. xxxii.

[2] "Congregentur quotidie in ecclesia presbyteri et diaconi et anagnostai omnisque populus tempore gallicinii, vacentque orationi, psalmis, et lectioni scripturarum cum orationibus. . . . De Clero autem qui convenire negligunt, neque morbo neque itinere impediti, separentur." Can. xxi.
"Porro autem tempore, quo canit gallus, instituendae sunt orationes in ecclesiis," Can. xxvii.

[3] Catechumenus baptismo initiandus si ab iis, qui eum adducunt, bono testimonio commendatur, eum illo tempore, quo instruebatur, infirmos visitasse et debiles sustentasse seque ab omni perverso sermone custodisse, *laudes cecinisse*, numque oderit vanam gloriam, num contempserit superbiam, sibique elegerit humilitatem," Can. xix.

[4] "Quando vero doctor quotidianum pensum docendi terminavit, **orent separati a christianis**," Can. xvii

required to be present, and had a special place assigned to them. If any members of the congregation were unable to be present at this morning worship they are enjoined to read the Scriptures at home, so that the first thing that the sun sees when it shines into their windows in the morning may be the long roll of Scripture unfolded on their knees.[1]

The Eucharistic service is described at much greater length, and the details have to be collected from instructions scattered throughout the Canons.[2] It had three parts—an introductory service, the actual Holy Supper, and the receiving and distributing the thankofferings. Most of the details are clearly enough stated, but it is impossible to say with any certainty whether a sermon was part of the introductory service. It was so in the time of Justin Martyr,[3] and his account is so like an outline whose details can be filled in by what is directed in these Canons, that it is improbable that this very important portion of the service had fallen into disuse. It may be, however, that the sermon, which must have been given at the morning service on the Lord's Day,[4] was considered to suffice, and that

---

[1] "Quocunque die in ecclesia non orant, sumas scripturam, ut legas in ea. Sol conspiciat matutino tempore scripturam super genua tua," Can. xxvii. 1.

[2] The canons have been carefully analyzed and the information they convey on the services and organization brought together by Dr. Achelis in his admirable edition. I have made full use of his labour. In one rather important point, however, I fail to follow his arguments. He believes that the bishop alone was entitled to conduct the eucharistic service when it took place on a Sunday, and that the provisions for an elder or a deacon presiding refers only to week-day celebrations. The statements made in the Canons are not distinct and our conclusions are only inferences. The reasons for the delegation seem to me to be the necessary absence of the bishop and the necessary absence of the elders; and apply equally well to the Sunday as to other celebrations. It was natural that provision should be made where Christian congregations were scattered and far from each other.

[3] Justin's order of service is:—Prolonged reading of the scriptures, sermon by the pastor or bishop, prayer, the Bread and Wine brought in. *Apology*, i. 67.

[4] Compare Canon xii.

the service described by Justin had been divided into two parts.

The Eucharistic service, held in the evening or in the late afternoon,[1] began by the readers, placed at an elevated desk, reading portions of Scripture one after another, the readers taking turns and relieving each other. This went on for some time while the congregation were gradually assembling.[2] If there was a sermon by the bishop it would be delivered after the reading was over and all had taken their places. A prayer including confession of sins followed. The bishop stood behind a table, called the "Table of the Body and Blood of the Lord," the elders on his right hand and on his left. The elements, bread and wine, which had been furnished by intending communicants, were then brought in by the deacons,[3] and were placed on the Table before the bishop. The elders, deacons and readers were all dressed in white—the colour of festival times.[4] Then the bishop and the elders placed their hands on the bread and on the cup, and the bishop began the responsive prayers :—

The bishop . . .	*The Lord be with you all.*
The congregation .	*And with Thy spirit.*
The bishop . . .	*Lift up your hearts.*
The congregation .	*We have, to the Lord.*
The bishop . . .	*Let us give thanks to the Lord.*
The congregation .	*Worthy and righteous.*[5]

The bishop then prayed over the elements (no form of prayer being given).[6] The bishop himself distributed. He stood by

---

[1] The whole service had to be over before sundown; and there was frequently a common meal late in the evening.

[2] "*Etiam anagnostai habebant festiva indumenta,* et stent in loco lectionis et alter alterum excipiat, donec totus populus congregetur," Can. xxxvii.

[3] Canons iii. xix.

[4] "Quotiescunque episcopus mysteriis frui vult, congregentur diaconi et presbyteri apud eum, induti vestiment is albis pulchioribus toto populo potissimum autem splendidis. Bona autem opera omnibus vestimentis praestant," Can. xxxvii.

[5] Canon iii.

[6] It is probable that this prayer was extempore; no form is prescribed

the "Table of the Body and Blood of the Lord." The people came one by one to the bishop, who first gave the Bread, saying, "This is the Body of the Lord," and then the Cup, saying, "This is the Blood of the Lord," and the people answered "Amen."[1] At the celebration at which the newly baptized communicants partook, the elders who stood beside the bishop had cups of milk and honey in their hands, and the communicants partook of these also from the hands of the elders to show that they had become as little children and fed on the food of infants;[2] but whether this ceremony accompanied every celebration of the Holy Supper is uncertain. The deacons who brought in the elements were required to sing a psalm as they entered, and the sound of the singing is compared to the tinkle of the bells on the robes of Aaron.[3]

After the celebration the faithful, who all remained in the church, came forward to the "Table" and presented their offerings, the firstfruits. These consisted of all kinds of useful things—oil, wine, milk, honey, eatables of all kinds, the fruit of trees and the fruit of the ground (apples and cucumbers being specially mentioned), wool, cloth and money. They were all placed at or on the table.[4] The bishop prayed the prayer of

in the Canons, and many forms for other parts of the service are given in the text; the prayer of consecration was extempore in the time of Justin Martyr (*Apology*, i. 67 :—" The president offers prayers and thanksgivings according to his ability ").

[1] " Communicat populum stans ad mensam corporis et sanguinis Domini . . . Deinde porrigat illis episcopus de corpore Christi dicens : Hoc est corpus Christi ; illi vero dicant : Amen ; et ei, quibus ille calicem porrigit dicens : Hic est sanguis Christi, dicant : Amen," Can. xix.

[2] Canon xix. :—" Et presbyteri portant alios calices lactis et mellis ut doceant eos, qui communicant, iterum eos natos esse ut parvuli, quia parvuli communicant lac et mel."

[3] Canon xxix. :—" Et sint illis psalmi pro tintinabulis, quae erant in tunica Aaronis."

[4] This offertory or collection in *kind*, which the records of the early centuries bring vividly before us, can be seen in village churches in India at present. The offerings there include many things not mentioned in the text. Great baskets are deposited in which the people place small parcels of all kind of grain, the produce of their fields, fruits, cooked food.

DISTRIBUTION OF THE OFFERINGS

thanksgiving over the gifts and the givers—a special thanksgiving being said over the oil, probably because it was so much used in ecclesiastical services. The bishop then pronounced the Benediction, and the people responded with the Doxology: Glory to Thee, Father, Son, and Holy Ghost, for ever and ever.[1]

This did not end the service, however. The offerings had to be distributed before the going down of the sun. The poor, the widows and the orphans rose from their places, and came to the bishop, who distributed to them the offerings which had been received, and also the bread and wine which had remained after the Communion.[2] Portions were no doubt reserved for those in prison, for strangers who might arrive during the week, and for the sick who were unable to come to church.[3] The Canons forbid any of these offerings being reserved for the clergy, as was the custom in later times, and those of them who required assistance were reckoned among the poor.[4]

It was the custom for one of the wealthier members of the congregation to give a supper on the evening of Sunday to the poor of the congregation. Members who had come from a distance, as Justin Martyr tells us they did, were doubtless included.[5]

eggs, flasks of oil and live poultry. I once saw a portion of the offertory running away with the beadle! It was a lively young sheep, and when the beadle tried to hold it, it pulled him round the corner of the church. Missionaries from Ceylon have assured me that the Christian matrons are accustomed to put aside every tenth handful of the rice or other things to be cooked and thus collect during the week what is given on Sunday. They say that when the people were heathen they did the same in order to present offerings to their priests; and they carry the practice over into Christianity. It was probably the same in heathen antiquity, and this is no doubt the reason why in the Canons the bishop is called " priest " *in connexion with receiving these offerings* and *not* in connexion with his presiding at the Holy Supper (Canon xxxvi.). The title " priest " (*sacerdos*) is given to the bishop alone and that only when he performs the two functions of exorcising the sick (Canon xxiv.), and of receiving and blessing the offerings (Canon xxxvi.); both actions done by the heathen priests with which the early converts from paganism were quite familiar.

[1] Canon iii.   [2] Canon xxxii.
[3] Canon v., cf. also Justin, *Apology*, i. 65, 67.
[4] Compare above, p. 201.   [5] *Apology*, i. 67.

The bishop presided, and the clergy (one deacon at least) were present. The bishop prayed for the host and for the guests, and the prayer of thanksgiving which was said during the Communion service was repeated. When it became dark the deacon had the charge of lighting the lamps, but the supper came to an end before it got very dark. The president generally gave the guests a short address, which he delivered sitting, and which was " for their benefit and for his own." The people were told to eat their fill, but not to drink to excess; not to speak too much; not to shout; and above all not to bring disgrace on their host by indulging in mischievous gossip.[1]

It is pleasant to learn that occasional suppers were given to the widows of the congregation. The poor bodies, who are elsewhere praised for their fasting,[2] seemed to have enjoyed a good supper, where they could eat and drink *ad satietatem neque vero ad ebrietatem*, and to have been inclined to prolong the feast as much as possible, for they need to be warned thrice over within four short sentences that they are to end their supper by the going down of the sun.[3] These suppers are called *Agapae* by Dr. Achelis. Dr. Riedel, on the other hand, refuses to translate the word in this way.[4] This is to be said, however, in justification of Dr. Achelis' translation that the entertainments

---

[1] Canons xxxii.-xxxv.   [2] Canons xxxii. ix.

[3] "Si quis viduis coenam parare vult, curet, ut habeant coenam et ut dimittantur, *antequam sol occidat.* Si vero sunt multae, caveatur, ne fiat confusio neve impediantur, quominus *ante vesperam dimittantur.* Unicuique autem earum sufficiens cibus potusque. *Sed abeant antequam nox advesperascat*," Can. xxxv.

[4] Compare Riedel, *Die Kirchenrechtsquellen des Patriarchats Alenandrien* (1900), p. 221 n. He thinks that they correspond with feasts which are still the custom among the Christians of the Levant, and quotes Wansleben:—" Ils ont encore la coûtume de faire des Agapes ou des repas de charité après les Bâtêmes, et les enterremens, pour tous ceux qui veulent s'y trouver; donnant à un chacun un plat de bouillie, avec un morceau de viande dedans, et du pain autant qu'il en peut manger; et ces repas se font ou dans l'église même ou sur le toit de l'église, qui est, selon la coûtume des Levantins, toujours plat, et capable de contenir un grand nombre d'hommes."

have all a religious significance, that there seems to have been a symbolical breaking of bread at all of them, that one of them, which was a memorial feast in honour of a martyr, was preceded by the celebration of the Holy Supper, and that at all of them the prayer of thanksgiving which was included in the Eucharistic service was recited.[1] The Lord's Day supper, at any rate, has all the appearance of the older Agape, separated from the Holy Supper, and coming after it instead of preceding it.

It is very interesting to observe that there is nothing in the Canons which implies that the Holy Supper has any special and unique sacrificial conceptions attached to it. Such ideas are markedly absent. The word *altar* occurs in the Canons; but in those portions which refer to the act of celebrating the Lord's Supper, the phrase used is "Table of the Body and Blood of the Lord."[2] The term *offering* is certainly used of the Bread and the Wine in the Holy Supper, but it is equally employed to denote the firstfruits given to the bishop by the people.[3] The term *priest* is never found in connexion with ordination or with the celebration of the Holy Supper. It occurs in two references only, and is used of the bishop when he is described as receiving the firstfruits and as exorcising the sick; and since both of these acts were performed by the pagan priesthood it is easy to conjecture why the word is applied to the bishop in these acts.[4]

Reverence in all the actions of public worship is carefully inculcated. The Church is the house of God and the place of prayer with fear; women are not to come there in gaudy apparel,

---

[1] These memorial feasts were called *Anamneseis*; the custom of celebrating the birthday of an honoured martyr with a memorial feast was one of the usages of primitive Christianity which gave the early Christian societies a superficial resemblance to the pagan *collegia*; compare above p. 126.

[2] *Altar* occurs in the Canon which tells the clergy to keep the vessels clean, etc. (Canon xxix.); *mensa* is used when the act of communicating is described (Canon xix.).

[3] Canons xvii. xxxii. xix.   [4] Canons xxxvi. xxiv.

and they are not to laugh nor chatter there. A worthy matron was made an "inspectress," to see that the women and girls behaved themselves properly.[1] The clergy are to see that the communion elements are kept with care from all impurity, and specially that flies do not get into the wine of the sacrament. Great care is also to be taken that no drop of the wine nor crumb of bread falls to the ground while the elements are partaken of by the communicants. In short, the Canons contain many a little suggestion, familiar to all missionaries, for the purpose of teaching that reverence in worship which is almost always lacking in heathen religious rites.

These early Christians were men of their generation, however. They believed that the air around them was full of evil spirits bent on their discomfiture, whose malignity had to be guarded against;[2] but while the traces of such superstitions appear, one cannot fail to see how the attempt is continually made to wean the Christians from pagan superstitions which they have brought over with them into Christianity. To take only one example, sick persons are prohibited from continuing beyond the hours of prayer in the Church or from sleeping there.[3] When it is remembered that sick folk were taken to the heathen temples in order that the dwelling in a sacred place might cure them, it is easy to see what the meaning of the prohibition is. One can perceive the doors by which pagan ideas might enter into Christian worship, but the sorry mixture of paganism and Christianity which was to follow Cyprian's conceptions of priesthood and sacrifice were still in the future.

[1] "Mulier libera ne veniat veste variegata ... neve crines demittat solutos, habea: potius capillos complexos in domo Dei, neve faciat cirros frontales in capite quando vult participare in mysteriis sacris (Canon xvii.). It is one of the marks of a good woman that if she excels male beings in knowledge she does not let any one see that she does!

[2] The fear of demons appears most strongly in the exorcisms at baptism, in exorcising the bread at the feasts, and in the reason given why no drop of wine or crumb of bread was to be allowed to fall to the ground: the demons might get hold of it. Compare Canons xix. xxix. xxxiv.

[3] Canon xxiv.

Such were the ordinary services, and such the organization of a Christian Church in the earlier decades of the third century, before accommodation to imperial points of view and imitation of pagan organization had invaded the Church of Christ.

Perhaps a brief comparison of this organization of the ministry with modern types may bring it more distinctly before us. It had some relation with all modern types of ecclesiastical organization, and was identical with none.

The organization had a certain resemblance to modern Congregationalism, for the vast majority of communities called churches were simply self-governing and independent congregations. The bishop was the pastor of the congregation, and in him, as in a modern congregationalist Church, all the ecclesiastical life centred. On the other hand, this does not apply to all these primitive churches; for the independent unity was the community large or small, and before the close of the second century the larger communities must have included several congregations, and all were served on the collegiate principle by the one bishop and his body of elders and deacons—the *one* pastor or bishop representing the unity of the community. These primitive independent churches all cherished the essential idea that they belonged to, and were portions of, a common visible Church—the Great Church it was called, to distinguish it from the Marcionite and Montanist Churches; but they had not yet discovered the way to express this idea of a visible catholicity in a definite political organization. We have the beginnings of the polity in the common though not universal custom that all the neighbouring bishops assisted at the ordination of a bishop.

The organization had a much greater resemblance to what is commonly called the Presbyterian, and ought properly to be called the Conciliar, system of Church government. The points of agreement are very many. There is common to both the conception of the three-fold ministry of pastor or bishop, elder or presbyter, and deacon, and both have the theoretical equivalence of the offices of bishop and elder (save only a special seat in the Church and the right to ordain elders and deacons), while in practice the bishop or pastor is the real head of the whole of the ecclesiastical life. In both there is the idea that the unit of organization is the Christian community of the place, and the conception that the unity can be preserved by a collegiate administration.[1] Both have the thought that the whole congregational activity centres in the bishop or pastor, who is the leader in public worship and who celebrates the sacraments. Both believe strongly that each congregation is a portion of the visible Catholic Church, that catholicity can best be reduced to a polity by means of representative councils with gradually widening areas of control, and that the ordination of a bishop or pastor is to be performed by the pastors or bishops of the bounds as representatives of the Church Catholic.[2] The two great differences are: that the modern system of organization insists that the bishop or pastor cannot, of his own authority, delegate to a presbyter or to a deacon the right to celebrate

---

[1] This characteristic has almost faded out of most English-speaking portions of the great Presbyterian Church, but it remains in the Dutch-speaking parts. The traces remaining in Scotland are the almost forgotten, but still existing, "General Kirk-Sessions" of the larger towns.

[2] Dr. Sanday has said (*Expositor*, Jan.–June, 1887, p. 113) that in the earlier centuries "every town of any size had its bishop; and if there were several churches, they were served by the clergy whom the bishop kept about him: they were in fact like our (Church of England) present 'chapels of ease,' and the whole position of the bishop was very similar to that of the incumbent of the parish church in one of our smaller towns. The tendency at first, as Ignatius shows, was towards complete centralization: the whole serving of the *paroikia* was directly in the hands of the bishop. The parish system in the later sense, with an extended diocese, and a number of more or less independent clergy circling round the bishop, did not grow up until the 6th–9th centuries, when it took shape mainly in France under the Merovingian and Carolingian kings. In some respects the Nonconformist communities of our own time furnish a closer parallel to the primitive state of things than an Established Church can possibly do." This is all true so far as it goes; but it takes no account of the three-fold ministry, which is not exhibited in an English parish. The primitive three-fold ministry appears however as soon as the Border is crossed into Scotland or over into Holland.

the sacraments, and that the bishop or pastor of the early centuries had almost unlimited control over the ecclesiastical finances and property of the congregation. This characteristic of primitive Christian organization arose from the fact that at first the sole property was the firstfruits given to the bishop at the close of the Holy Supper and distributed afterwards by him, and it was strengthened when the churches were able to hold buildings and burial places by the Roman laws regulating the property of corporations.[1]

The modern episcopal system, apart from the retention of the name "bishop," has fewest points of resemblance to what we find in the ancient ecclesiastical manuals we have been studying; but the germs of the mediaeval and modern episcopacy are there in the power which the primitive bishop possessed of delegating functions which were peculiarly his, such as baptizing and celebrating the Holy Communion, to his elders and even to his deacons.

[1] Compare Ramsay, *The Church in the Roman Empire*, p. 431. Many illustrations of the legal principles and their effects on the tenure of Church property laid down by Professor Ramsay may be found not only within the Turkish Empire, but in the Tributary Indian States, such as the Nizam's Territories, where the Mohammedan law rules.

CHAPTER VII

MINISTRY CHANGING TO PRIESTHOOD

DURING the third century, it may be said during the middle third of that century, there are clear traces of a general change insinuating itself into men's minds and finding expression in language, in the way of thinking of the Church and of the relation of the ministry to the Church. This is commonly spoken of as the change of the ministry into a mediating priesthood, standing between the people and God. But this manner of regarding the whole silent movement gives a very inadequate and one-sided representation of the real meaning of the change, and of the conceptions which it embodied. The idea that the ministry is a priesthood was there, but the main thought was much more the *power* of the priest than his *mediation*. The power and the authority of the ministry and especially of the chiefs of the ministry over the Christian people was the central conception. It finds expression in Cyprian's repeated quotation of the Old Testament text: "And the man that doeth presumptuously, in not hearkening to the priest that standeth to minister there before the Lord thy God, or unto the judge, even that man shall die; and thou shalt put away the evil from Israel. And all the people shall hear and fear, and do no more presumptuously."[1] It is this change and what it implies that concerns us now.

It may be briefly expressed by saying that the two separate

---

[1] Deut. xvii. 12, 13; Cyprian, *Epist.* iii. 1 (ixiv.); iv. 4 (lxi.); xliii. 7 (xxxix.); lix. 4 (liv.); lxvi. 3 (lxviii.).

conceptions of local "Church" and of "Church universal" became more precise, and that precision of thought was given by new ideas about the relation in which the office-bearers stood to the community. The Church was defined by the ministry in a way that it had not been in earlier times.

So far as the local "church" is concerned the Christian thought, which in earlier times had dwelt upon the picture of saints and brethren living together the Christian life, now dwelt upon the controlling power of those who governed. The Church, which was in earlier days a "brotherhood of saints," became a community over whom a bishop presided. It was defined, not so much by the manner of life led by its members, as by the government which ruled over them. The train of thought was reversed. It was no longer—people worshipping and some of them leading the common devotions, saints believing and some among them instructing and admonishing; it became—teachers who imparted and pupils who received, priests who interceded and sinners who were pardoned through the intercession, rulers who commanded and subjects who were bound to obey.

The thought of the universal visible Church underwent an analogous transformation. It was no longer the wide brotherhood of all who professed the name of Jesus, and lived the life of new obedience demanded from His disciples. It became a federation of local churches, who believed in the same verities, the truth of which was guaranteed by legitimate rulers, and whose members yielded an implicit obedience to the bishop at the head of every local "church." It was the federation of churches which excluded heretics and rebels.

In the earlier days the local Christian communities were companies of men and women who called themselves the brethren and the saints or holy persons, and these words expressed the relations in which they stood to each other and to the world around them. Fellowship as with brothers, and a fellowship united in holiness, were the main thoughts present to the minds of the earliest Christians when the word Church was used to denote either the individual community or the wide brotherhood of believers.

The idea in the minds of Christians united together in a local community was that they were called upon to live a new and a holy life. They had marked out for themselves what was meant by this holy life, with its duties to be lovingly fulfilled and sins to be resolutely shunned; and this chart of the Christian life is to be found in manuals like the *Didache* with its two ways, all of which treat of the private as well as of the communal life. There was also a feeling throughout the churches that, while for the ordinary and lesser sins to which men are prone, there must be confession, sorrow, and certain external signs of sorrow, and while for others there was to be suspension for longer or shorter time from the Holy Supper, some sins were so very heinous that those who committed them had placed themselves outside the communion of the brethren so long as life lasted. No limits were placed on the forgiveness of God, but Christians believed that if any of their number fell into sins of more than ordinary gravity, no amount of penitence, however sincere, entitled the Church to permit these fallen brethren to return to the inner fellowship of the Christian brotherhood. Such sinners had to manifest a life-long repentance, and could never hope to be more than catechumens. Tertullian has given a list of these deadliest sins, but it is not likely that such lists were always the same, for there is no trace of any settled rule or theory. Only, each Christian community felt that it must keep itself pure and merit its title of "the saints."[1] Ordinarily

[1] Compare Tertullian, *Against Marcion*, iv. 9. *The Canons of Basil*, though very much later than the period now described, retain ideas which may enable us to conceive the attitude of the early Christian society. They declare that a murderer must be excluded from the society for twenty years; a homicide for ten years, which are to be spent in the following way—two years in mourning, three years admitted to the meeting for exhortation, and five years admitted among the faithful but not allowed to come forward and partake of the Holy Communion. For one who has been baptized and has lapsed from the faith, the penitence must be life long, and the penitent is to be allowed to communicate only when he

those who were guilty of such heinous sins had to remain for life in the condition of catechumens, and could never hope to be re-admitted to the inner circle of believers. If, however, a brother, believed to have the prophetic gift, spoke on behalf of a penitent, and announced that it was the will of God that he should be pardoned, then, and then only, an exception was made.[1]

All the Christian communities, although they felt that they belonged to one great Church, were not linked together by any distinctive polity, however indefinite. All the churches of Christ, Tertullian tells us, were one great Church, because they gave each other the salutation of peace, because they regarded each other as brethren, and because they practised the interchange of familiar hospitality.[2] That was what bound them together, and made them feel and be one; not any external polity, however slight. They maintained a close fellowship by means of intercommunication, by the interchange of letters and messengers, and by their hospitality towards all Christian travellers who passed their way. This constant intercourse no doubt led to a similarity in the rules for holy living and in modes of dealing with backsliders; but there was nothing of

---

is on his deathbed. Compare Riedel's *Kirchenrechtsquellen des Patriarchats der Alexandrien* (1900), pp. 243, 244. The sins named by Tertullian are:—Idolatry, blasphemy, murder, adultery, fornication, false-witness and fraud.

[1] Hermas, *Mandata*, iv. 3 ; *Visiones*, iii. 7 ; Tertullian, *De Pudicitia*, 21.

[2] Tertullian, *De Praescriptione Haereticorum*, 20 :—" They then (the apostles) in like manner founded Churches in every city, from which all the other Churches one after another, derived the tradition of the faith and the seeds of doctrine, and are every day deriving them, that they may become Churches. Indeed it is on this account only that they will be able to account themselves apostolic, as being the offspring of apostolic Churches. . . . Therefore the Churches, although they are so many and so great, comprise but the one primitive Church founded by the apostles from which they all spring. In this way all are primitive, and all are apostolic, whilst they are all proved to be one, in unity, by their salutation of peace (communicatio pacis), and title of brotherhood, and bond of hospitality (contesseratio hospitalitatis)—rights which no other rule directs than the one tradition of the self-same mystery."

a common polity to unite them as the various parts of civil society are united within one state. No doubt the advice of one Church was frequently asked, and acted upon by another in matters of difficulty and in times of trial. We have an example of such a thing in the letter of the Roman Church to the Corinthian, which goes by the name of the First Epistle of Clement. No doubt such advice was received and attended to in proportion as the Church, offering its advice or appealed to for its counsel, had showed itself worthy of deference by its brotherly conduct and by its eminence. No Church in those early centuries showed such generosity to its poorer brethren as the Roman Church; besides it inhabited the world's capital; it was believed to inherit the traditions of the two greatest of the apostles —St. Paul and St. Peter. It held the position of the wise and generous elder brother in the brotherhood of churches, but there was no acknowledged ecclesiastical pre-eminence.[1]

The situation, therefore, may be thus expressed: there were thousands of churches, most of them single congregations, which nevertheless were one Church, not because they had agreed in any formal way to become one, not because there was any polity linking them together in one great whole, but because they had the unmistakeable feeling that they belonged to one brotherhood.

They lived in the immediate presence of eternity, on the threshold of the blessed and real life which awaited them, when the period of their probation in this world was ended; and every Christian community had the feeling that it was its business by a strict discipline to preserve, in the pure life of the members of the little brotherhood, a foreshadowing of the life which awaited them when the Father should call them home to Himself. Meanwhile they were in the presence of a hostile and evil world-

---

[1] Clement, 1 *Epist.* v. 4-6; Ignatius, *Epistle to the Romans*, preface; Eusebius, *Hist. Eccles.* II. xxv. 8; IV. xxiii. 10; V. xxiii., xxiv.; VII. v. 2; Irenaeus, *Against Heresies*, III. i. iii.; Tertullian, *De Praescript.* 24; *Scorpiace*, 15; *Against Marcion.* IV. 5.

power, which was under the dominion of sin, and which manifested itself to them in the persecuting pagan state. That was the first stage. Doctrine could scarcely be said to exist, and doctrinal divisions were therefore almost impossible. No doubt their teachers and leaders occasionally warned them against strange teachings, but these were limited to individuals or to small companies, and hardly impressed the imagination.

When the Gnostic teachers gathered their followers into companies large enough to attract attention, and above all when Marcion, with his organizing genius, had established Marcionite Christian communities almost everywhere, the situation became changed. The Christians were now divided among themselves. The Christian brotherhood was set over against, not simply the pagan state, but also against false brethren who did not accept the traditions of the apostles nor the common simple verities of the faith. Christianity now implied more than a life lived in the presence of God and Christ; it meant a doctrine to be protected by a creed or a form, more or less fixed, of intellectual beliefs. The possession of a common form of creed in which the simple verities of the faith were stated could not fail to give the " great " Church accepting it something more of an outward polity. The succession of office-bearers in the churches was the guarantee for the correctness of the tradition suggested by Irenaeus, urged by Tertullian, and apparently accepted by all who were neither Gnostics nor Marcionites, nor any of the smaller separate bodies of Christians. Tertullian in the *De Praescriptione*, as may be seen in the quotation given in the note,[1] links the common tradition, its guarantee in the succession of office-bearers, the name of brethren, the salutation of peace, and the bond of hospitality all together, and there are, though in a very indefinite kind of way, the beginnings of a polity.

Still the existence of the creed did not give the churches which accepted it an homogenous external polity in any thing like the modern sense. The creed was the law for the individual

---

[1] See above, p. 268.

local church, and the local church was not joined to the other churches in a definite federation, still less in a corporate union. The old thought of St. Paul[1]—fellowship (κοινωνία)—still prevailed. The churches refused to have fellowship with professing Christians and with communities of professing Christians who did not accept the same verities that they did, and they had fellowship and intercommunion with societies who accepted these verities. The increased powers given to office-bearers, when they were made the guarantee of the orthodox faith, were powers to be exercised within the communities over which they presided, and did not give them any rule outside the local churches they governed, whether these were large or small. Still the fact that it was recognized that all Christians had a common set of convictions, which could be expressed in a more or less definite way in propositions, gave the whole brotherhood of churches something of a polity; and the thought that in times of doubt or difficulty guidance could be got from what Tertullian called "apostolic" churches, or churches where the original apostles had actually taught,[2] gave these churches and their office-bearers a certain pre-eminence which claimed and received the deference of all the rest.

The separation and secession of the Montanists, in the wider meaning of the term,[3] still further altered and made more precise the conception of the Church. It must always be remembered that the Montanists were not driven out, but separated themselves from the main body of Christians. They claimed to represent the apostolic Church; and their claim was based quite as much on the persuasion that they had preserved the prophetic ministry in the position within the churches in which it had been placed by the apostles, as on their belief that they were preserving the character of the true church by their strictness

---

[1] Compare above, p. 24.
[2] Compare Tertullian, *De Praescriptione*, xx., xxxii. and especially xxxvi.
[3] That is the Montanism which included men like Tertullian. Compare above p. 238.

of discipline. To the succession of office-bearers, descended from the *secondary* ministry of apostolic times, they opposed the succession of prophets representing the *superior* ministry of the apostolic days. The Montanist movement had this result that men who professed to live according to the commandments of Jesus, who adhered to the traditional teaching of the churches, who had the three-fold ministry, were nevertheless found outside. They had separated on the question of the power of the office-bearers at the head of the local churches; they had insisted that the time-honoured prophetic ministry should retain its old supremacy; they had especially declared that in the case of heinous sins it belonged to the prophetic ministry, and not to the bishops, to declare whether such sins could receive the churches' pardon.[1] Their opponents had joined issue with them on these two points. They asserted that a true prophet would submit himself to the "elders who were in the succession," and that, while the Montanist prophets had positively refused to admit of the church's pardon being extended to heinous sinners,[2] yet these sinners might be pardoned on confession

---

[1] Tertullian, *De Pudicitia*, 21:—"The power of loosing and binding committed to Peter had nothing to do with the *capital* sins of believers; and if the Lord had given him a precept that he must grant pardon to a brother sinning against *him* even seventy times seven-fold, of course He would have commanded him to 'bind'—that is to retain—*nothing* subsequently, unless perchance such sins as one may have committed against the Lord and not against a brother. For the forgiveness of sins committed in the case of a man is a prejudgment against the remission of sins against God. What now about the Church—your psychic Church? For in accordance with the person of Peter, it is to spiritual men that this power will correspondingly appertain, either to an apostle or else to a prophet. For the Church itself is, properly and principally the Spirit Himself. . . . And accordingly the 'Church,' it is true, will forgive sins; but the Church of the Spirit, by a spiritual man; not the Church which consists of a number of bishops. For the right and arbitrament is the Lord's, not the servant's; God's Himself and not the priest's." Tertullian's argument is that the power was given to Peter because he was *inspired* of the Father to confess Christ. He was a spiritual man. Cf. Döllinger, *Hippolytus and Callistus* (Eng. Trans.), pp. 116 f.

[2] Tertullian tells us (*De Pudicitia*, 21), that the new prophecy, speak-

and signs of sincere repentance. The great majority of the members of the churches had followed the office-bearers, and the Montanist movement had failed to arrest the course of the local ministry on the path they had chosen to pursue. It was only natural that an unsuccessful revolt would strengthen the position of the ministry which it had conspired against. All these things combined to place the office-bearers in a position of authority they had never before occupied, and to give peculiar powers to the bishops who were the chief office-bearers. The tendency was to think that the churches were summed up in their bishops, and these officials thus acquired a new position with reference to the whole Church.

The most potent cause producing this change of sentiment with regard to the character of the ministry and its relation to the Church was the attempt to come to some accommodation with the world lying round the Christian communities in order to justify the plea that Christians were entitled to the toleration extended to all other religions. This consideration was always accompanied by the other that the Church wished to keep hold on crowds of adherents, who in the years of peace from persecution [1] were flocking to join it, and who could not be retained if the old hard conditions or, perhaps one ought to say, the earlier high standard of Christian life, were insisted upon. These two motives invariably acted together, and are to be found working in such churches as those of Rome and Corinth in the beginning of the third century.[2] The first practical consequence of these ideas was to alter the thought and conditions of penitence. In the earlier times, as has been said, when a Christian fell into such grievous sins as idolatry, murder, adultery, fornication and some others, he could never be received again into full

ing in the name of the Spirit had said "The church has the power to forgive sins; but I will not do it lest they commit others."

[1] That is in the years between the persecution under Severus and that under Decius.

[2] Earlier in the Corinthian Church, if we are to believe Eusebius. Compare his *Hist. Eccl.* IV. xxiii. 6.

communion, but had to remain in the position of a catechumen, permitted to wait in the ante-chamber but never admitted within the family abode until death was at hand. Gradually the practice was softened to the extent that, on due manifestation of sorrow, a second trial of the full Christian life was allowed, but a second fall was not to be forgiven.[1] In all probability this remained the general rule till the third decade of the third century, when Calixtus, the bishop of Rome, introduced a change which met with the fierce opposition of Tertullian and Hippolytus.[2] He, or rather the Roman Church of which he was the head, entered on a policy of relaxation.[3] It was asserted that the church, through its office-bearers, was entitled to proclaim God's pardon for any sins, however heinous, due signs of sorrow being accepted by the office-bearers as sufficient.[4] It was announced by an edict posted up in the church, that pardon would be bestowed on these terms for all sins of the flesh, and that penitents would be restored to Church communion. It appears to be almost certain that this innovation contained

---

[1] This statement appears to be borne out by what Tertullian says in his tract on *Repentance* :—" In the vestibule God has stationed repentance the second to open to such as knock ; but *now once for all*, because now for a second time ; but never more, for the last time it had been in vain " (7).

[2] Tertullian's attack is to be found in his work on *Modesty* (*De Pudicitia*), and Hippolytus' in his work against *Heresies* (*Philosophumena*), ix. 6, 7. It has been commonly said that the bishop of Rome attacked by Tertullian was Zephyrinus ; compare Langen, *Geschichte der röm. Kirche*, i. 217 ff., and Döllinger, *Hippolytus and Callistus* (1876), Eng. Trans., p. 117 ; but see Harnack, *Herzog's Real-Encyclopaedie*, x. 656, and in the *Zeitschrift für Kirchengeschichte* (1876–77), p. 582.

[3] There is no doubt that as Döllinger says (*Hippolytus and Callistus* (Eng. Trans.), p. 117) the power of a bishop in the beginning of the third century was anything but absolute, being limited by both the elders and the laity. "No one who knows the life of the Church at that time will believe that Callistus introduced a practice previously unknown in Rome against the will of his presbytery (session)."

[4] Calixtus openly claimed this power to pardon, because he was the successor of St. Peter, to whom Christ had given power to remit sins (Tertullian, *De Pudicitia*, 21).

two things; the first being the general statement of the power of the Church exercised through its office-bearers to restore all persons to Church communion, no matter how heinous the sin had been into which they had fallen, and the second being the resolution on the part of the Roman Church to make use of this general power in respect to sins of the flesh. Of course there was no attempt to coerce other churches to follow the example of the Roman Church, and many churches did not:[1] Some North African churches kept to the old practice on to the time of Cyprian,[2] but it is undoubted that the Roman example was largely followed. The statements in Hippolytus and Tertullian seem to warrant the conclusion that this relaxation from the older sternness was made because without it large numbers of Christians could not be restrained from going back to heathenism.[3]

There was no doubt a thoroughly evangelical element in this manifesto of the Roman Church.[4] It was based on the evangelical truth that God has commanded to his ministering servants to proclaim that He is not willing that any should perish, that

---

[1] As late as the beginning of the fourth century the Spanish Church insisted on visiting certain sins with perpetual excommunication, while the council of Ancyra held about the same time in the east set a limited penalty on the very sins for which the council of Elvira had decreed a perpetual excommunication—so impossible is it to make general statements about ecclesiastical usages in the early centuries.

[2] Cyprian, *Epistle*, lv. 21 (li.).

[3] Compare Tertullian's phrases in the *De Pudicitia*:—"A profitable fickleness . . ."; "easier to err with the majority" (1); his statement of sins for which it is proper to provide repentance (7), etc. Compare Hippolytus on *Heresies*, ix. 7. Although the account of Hippolytus must be taken with some caution as the statements of a bitter opponent, yet it seems clear that Calixtus expected to detach many from the churches of his opponents in Rome by this policy of relaxation from the old strictness; and that his policy was successful. There must have been four or five different bodies of Christians in Rome at this time, each esteeming itself to be *the* Church of Christ.

[4] An interesting parallel might be drawn between the evangelical root in the sixteenth-century doctrine of indulgence and the evangelical basis of this manifesto. Compare my *Luther*, p. 62.

His promises in Christ can be trusted in by the most heinous sinners and backsliders. But in all the circumstances of the times and of the case, it took a very unevangelical shape, and was worked out by Cyprian into the beginnings of the mediaeval doctrine of penance. In the shape it took it inevitably led the people to regard the office-bearers of the Church, and especially the bishops, as if they were in God's place, and it ascribed to the bishops the power of actually pardoning and not simply of proclaiming the pardon of God.[1] On the other hand, the Church lost her old idea that she was the company of the saints or the actively holy people; and the new feeling grew that the Church was the institution within which God had placed the means of acquiring holiness, and that these means were at the disposal of the bishops or the heads of the Christian communities, and could be reached only through them. Hence the office-bearers, and more especially the bishops—the men who had already been declared to be the guardians of the essential Christian verities—now came to be regarded also as the keepers or guardians of that peace of God which comes from the pardon of sin. They were the persons to whom it was necessary to go in order to know with certainty the truths of the Christian religion, and only through them could be acquired that saintly character which was desirable, but which was no longer a necessary condition of membership within the Christian Church. So the beginnings of a wide gulf were dug between the clergy and the laity, and the conception began to grow that the one duty of the laity in the presence of the clergy was that of simple obedience. Add to this the ever-present expectation that the day was approaching when the Church was to enter into an alliance with the hitherto persecuting state and to find a peaceful shelter under its protection; the growing conviction that the action of all the various Christian Churches ought to be as harmonious

---

[1] The proclamation of Calixtus, as quoted by Tertullian, was: *I remit to such as have discharged repentance, the sins of adultery and fornication* (*De Pudicitia*, 1)

as possible, and that whatever step was taken by one ought to be taken by all; and the feeling that the Christian Churches ought to be divisions of a well-drilled army marching in step towards the earthly paradise of an alliance with, and therefore of a conquest over, the hitherto persecuting power, and it is possible to have some estimate of the changes which the conception of the Church and of the ministry were undergoing in the middle of this third century. At the same time it is easy to make too much of the power exercised by the bishops of the first half of the third century. The bishops of these days were not the great potentates that one is apt to imagine them to be from the language and phrases used by many modern historians. They, all of them, had to carry their people, and, above all, their elders or presbyters with them, in any change they suggested.

Canons which belong to the early part of the third century, like the Canons of Hippolytus, may say little about the rights and much about the duties of the laity. They may concern themselves with the layman's duty to pray in private, to come to Church regularly, to offer the firstfruits, and may enjoin his wife to be careful to prepare the oblations. They may prohibit him from taking any part in public worship or from presiding even at an *agape*. They may appear to leave him no rights in the Church whatsoever save that of choosing his pastor. But we know that long after this few things were done in any local church without their being approved by a council of the whole people and clergy, *plebs* and *ordo*; and that this congregational meeting existed and exercised its powers from the days of St. Paul to those of Cyprian. The modern associations connected with the word "bishop" impose upon us, and the misleading phrase "monarchical bishop" adds to our illusions. The fact was that this "monarch" was in the vast majority of cases the pastor of a congregation of a few score of families, that no imperial legislation had as yet compelled the payment of tithes by law, nor had conferred a high social position upon any pastor or bishop who happened to be at the head of the Christian societies in cities which had been the provincial centres of the imperial cult.[1] When Christianity became the recognized religion of the Roman Empire; when imperial edicts confirmed ecclesiastical legislation; when imperial troops were employed to hunt down Marcionite, Montanist or Donatist nonconformists, the state of things became different. But until we get to the middle of the fourth century the Christian pastors were too dependent on their people to be great potentates and irresponsible rulers. It was the theory that was changing—that is the important thing to be remembered.

This new theory of the position and authority of the office-bearers in the Christian churches was so novel, and so opposed to the old traditions of primitive Christianity, that an extraordinary sanction was needed to support it, and in the nature of things the sanction had to come down from the earliest days. It is here that the idea of an "Apostolic Succession," in the modern Roman and Anglican sense, first makes its appearance. It is a conception which had its origin in the brains of leaders of the Roman Church, and although it was adopted and defended by Cyprian, it has never ceased to be associated with Roman claims and to fit most naturally into Roman theories. To understand it one must remember, what is continually forgotten, that the great men who built up the Western Church were almost all trained Roman lawyers. Tertullian, Cyprian, Augustine, to say nothing of many of the most distinguished Roman bishops, were all men whose early training had been that of a Roman lawyer—a training which moulded and shaped all their thinking, whether theological or ecclesiastical. The framework of Roman law supported their thoughts about Christian organization and about Christian doctrines. They instinctively regarded all questions as a great Roman lawyer would. They had the lawyer's craving for regular precedents, for elaborate legal fictions to bridge time and connect the present

[1] Compare below, p. 352 ff.

with the past. They had the lawyer's idea that the primary duty laid upon them was to enforce obedience to authority, and especially to that authority which expressed itself in external institutions. Apostolic succession, in the dogmatic sense of that ambiguous term, is the legal fiction required by the legal mind to connect the growing conceptions of the authority of the clergy with the earlier days of Christianity. It served the Christian lawyer in much the same way that another curious legal fiction assisted the pagan civilian. The latter insisted that the government of the Emperors from Augustus to Diocletian was the prolongation of the old republican constitution; the former imagined that the rule of bishops was the prolongation through the generations of the inspired guidance of the original apostles who were the planters of the Church.

A legal fiction has generally some historical basis to start from. The basis of the fiction in civil law was the fact that the emperors, while wielding almost absolute personal authority, did so in accordance with republican forms inasmuch as they were invested by the senate with almost all the offices which under the republic had been distributed among a number of persons. The fiction in ecclesiastical government had also its basis of fact. The apostles had founded many of the churches, and their first converts or others suitable had become the first office-bearers. There had been a succession of leaders, the characteristics of leadership, as has been explained, undergoing some striking changes in the course of the second century. All these successions of office-bearers could be traced back to the foundation of the churches in which they existed, and therefore to the missionaries, whether apostles or apostolic men, who had founded them. This was the historical thread on which, in the end, was strung the gigantic figment called apostolic succession—a strange compound of minimum of fact and maximum of theory.

The beginnings of the theory are easily discernible, and have been already explained. Irenaeus seized upon the undoubted fact of successive generations of office-bearers going back to the apostolic founders of certain churches in order to find a guarantee for the true Christian doctrine. To make assurance doubly sure, he added a theory to his fact—this, namely, that these office-bearers who were in the succession had a *charisma veritatis*. According to the ideas of the time there was a minimum of fact in the added theory, for many of the pastors of these primitive churches were prophets and had the *charisma*. This made it easier to suppose that what belonged to some pastors personally was the property of all officially. The result was that Christian leaders had a short and easy method of dealing with Gnostics and others.[1] Moreover, when the leaders became the guardians of sound teaching they acquired additional magisterial powers within the communities over which they presided. But neither Irenaeus, nor Tertullian who adopted and extended his theory, ever claimed that the leaders of the churches who were in the succession stood in the same position to the churches of the end of the second and beginning of the third centuries as that held by the apostles in the middle of the first. If they believed that the apostles were the mediators between Jesus and the Church they were also firmly convinced that the Holy Spirit was imparted to the whole membership, and was not the peculiar possession of the leaders of the communities because they were in the succession from the apostles. The idea appeared earliest in the Roman Church. So far as I am aware, the earliest claim of this kind was made by Hippolytus in his struggle with Calixtus in Rome; and Calixtus, the head of one of the rival factions, was not slow to adopt the same arrogant position. The former made use of the idea of an apostolic succession to strengthen his position when he tried to show that his rival was a heretic; and the latter used it to warrant him in issuing decrees which relaxed the ancient discipline in the hope of attracting to his own congregation men who felt the rules of Christian living laid down by Hippolytus too hard for their weakness. These were the edifying surroundings from amidst

[1] Compare above, p. 224 ff.

which came the first full statement of the claim to apostolic succession.[1] The theory may be older in the Roman Church than this its first distinct statement.[2]

From the time that this doctrine of apostolic succession comes into being in the West on to its full statement by Cyprian, its use is the same. It is appealed to as the ground for the assumption of powers of command on the part of the bishops or pastors. It is interesting to notice that while the idea of a succession is to be found in the East, it took an altogether different shape from the formal legal Roman dogma. There is no mention of an apostolic succession of chief pastors in the first six books of the *Apostolic Constitutions*. It does not appear in the definition or description of the Church which is given in the first book.[3] Yet the office of bishop or pastor is dwelt upon at length. He is always looked upon as the minister of a congregation, and frequently of a very small congregation,[4] but that does not prevent the authors heaping up phrases to

---

[1] "But none will refute these (heretics), save the Holy Spirit bequeathed unto the Church, which the apostles having in the first instance received, have transmitted to those who rightly believed. But we, as being their successors, and as *participators* in this grace, high-priesthood, and office of teaching, as well as being reputed guardians of the Church, will not be found deficient in vigilance, or disposed to suppress correct doctrine," *Refutation of all Heresies* (*Philosophumena*), I., proemium. Hippolytus attacks Calixtus in IX. vi. vii. He says of his discipline :—"For he is in the habit of attending the congregation of any one else, who is called a Christian ; should a man commit any transgression, the sin, they say, is not reckoned to him, provided only he hurries off to the school of Calixtus," IX. vii. Calixtus is the bishop of Rome whom Tertullian attacks in his *De Pudicitia*, and whose proclamation he quotes :—"*I* remit, to such as have discharged repentance, the sins of adultery and fornication " (1).

[2] Harnack, whose careful chronological investigations have led him to believe that the Roman list of bishops or pastors may be trusted from Anicetus (about 155 A.D.) or from Soter (about 166), while no Oriental list can be trusted before the third century, regards this as an indication that the theory of apostolic succession in its beginnings at least had become established in Rome at a comparatively early date. Compare *Die Chronologie der altchristlichen Literatur*, pp. 144-230 ; and his *History of Dogma*, Eng. Trans. (1894-99), ii. 70 n.

[3] *Apostolic Constitutions*, I. i.   [4] *Ibid*. II. i

describe his importance and the respect which is due to him from his people.[1] The elders, "the counsellors of the bishop" —his Kirk-Session—"sustain the place" of the apostles of the Lord.[2] The formal legal Roman mind needed a precedent, in the shape of this legal fiction, for the unwonted domination which the chief pastors were beginning to claim. The Oriental, accustomed to arbitrary government, did not feel that usurpation of power required to be cloaked under legal fictions. Yet in the East we find a trace of a succession. Clement of Alexandria conceives the number of the apostles continually recruited from age to age by the enrolment of men who have attained to a "gnostical perfection,"[3] and who are, therefore, the true

---

[1] The bishop is told to sustain the character of God among men, "as being set over all men, over priests, kings, rulers, fathers, children, teachers, and in general over all who are subject" to him ; *Apostolic Constitutions*, II. xi. ; " It is thy privilege (O bishop), to govern those under thee, but not to be governed by them" (II. xiv.) ; the laic is to "honour him, love him, reverence him as his lord, as his master, as the high-priest of God, as a teacher of piety ; for he that heareth him heareth Christ ; and he that rejecteth him rejecteth Christ" (II. xx.) ; "the bishop, he is the minister of the word, the keeper of knowledge, the mediator between God and you in the several parts of your divine worship ; he is your ruler and governor ; he is your king and potentate ; he is, next after God, your earthly god, who has a right to be honoured by you" (II. xxvi.) ; and so on in Oriental luxuriance of phrases. It is not that there was no sense of the continuity of office in the East :—"It is also thy duty, O, bishop, to have before thine eyes the examples of those who have gone before, and to apply them skilfully to the cases of those who want words of severity or of consolation" (II. xxii.).

[2] "Let also a double portion (of the firstfruits) be set apart for the elders, as for such as labour continually in the word and doctrine, upon the account of the apostles of our Lord, whose *place they sustain*, as the counsellors of the bishop and the crown of the Church (II. xxviii.).

[3] Speaking of those who attain to "gnostical perfection," Clement says (*Stromata*, VI. xiii.) :—" Luminous already, and like the sun shining in the exercise of beneficence, he speeds by righteous knowledge through the love of God to the sacred abode, *like as the apostles*. . . . Those then also, who have exercised themselves in the Lord's commandments, and lived perfectly and gnostically according to the Gospel may be now enrolled in the chosen body of the apostles. Such an one is in reality an elder of the Church, and a true deacon of the will of God if he do and teach what is the Lord's ; not as being chosen by men, nor regarded as righteous because

teachers of the Church, for the Christian Neo-Platonist of Alexandria was as familiar with the thought of a succession of inspired teachers,[1] as the minds of the Roman lawyers who built up the Church in the West were saturated with legal precedents and the need for the visible continuity of government even though a legal fiction had to be invented to show it. The great Alexandrian conceives the continuity of the Church to exist in the succession of Christian generations, and to be made evident by the appearance among them from time to time of saintly men of apostolic character who are known to God, and whose supreme importance in preserving the true character of Christianity will be revealed in the future. This he deems to be a much better guarantee than a succession of office-bearers, chosen and ordained by fallible men.

Although the conception that the heads of the Christian churches were the successors of the apostles, in the sense that they possessed the gifts and the powers of the original apostles (now thought of as Twelve only), was really the creation of the Roman Church, it is intimately connected with Cyprian of Carthage,[2] who gave it definiteness as a dogmatic idea. This

a presbyter, but enrolled in the eldership because righteous. And although here upon earth he be not honoured with the chief seat, he will sit down on the four-and-twenty thrones, judging the people, as St. John says in the Apocalypse. For in truth the covenant of salvation, reaching down to us from the foundation of the world, through different generations and times, is one, though conceived as different in respect of gifts."

[1] The Neo-Platonists believed that the true philosophy was preserved to the world through a succession of divinely inspired teachers.

[2] The best edition of Cyprian's works is that of J. Hartel (1868-71) in the Vienna *Corpus Scriptorum Ecclesiasticorum Latinorum*, where the letters are to be found in the second volume. The numbering of the letters in this edition is the same as in the Oxford edition of 1682; Migne's edition has a different numbering. In our quotations Migne's numbering is given in brackets. A very suggestive account of Cyprian's work in constructing the polity of the Church is given by Albrecht Ritschl in his *Die Entstehung der altkatholischen Kirche*, 2nd ed. (1857), pp. 555-73. Otto Ritschl, his son, has written *Cyprian von Karthago und die Verfassung der Kirche* (1885)—a careful and elaborate work. Other monographs on Cyprian are:—Rettberg, *Thascius Caecilius Cyprianus, Bischof von*

great ecclesiastical statesman, like Gregory I., has left behind him a collection of letters which reveal the working of his mind,

Carthago, dargestellt nach seinen Leben und Wirken (1831). Fechtrup (Roman Catholic), *Der Heilige Cyprian; sein Leben und seine Lehre* (1878). Pearson's *Annales Cyprianici* are valuable; they are published in Fell's (Oxford) edition of Cyprian's works (1682), and have been republished in Pearson's *Minor Theological Works* (1884). The latest book on Cyprian is from the pen of Dr. Benson, the late archbishop of Canterbury, who was the author of the article on Cyprian in the *Dictionary of Christian Biography*. The book is entitled *Cyprian, his Life, his Times, his Work* (1897). From one point of view it is impossible to praise this book too highly; but it has very grave defects. It displays fine scholarship, unwearied research, and an historical imagination which enables the author to reconstruct the secular society of the times when Cyprian lived. The framing is excellent; but the portrait framed is scarcely so good. The author exhibits to us a pious, suave, courteous, far-seeing ecclesiastical statesman, whose letters and speeches were seasoned with a sarcastic humour; but the real Cyprian had other characteristics which are either hidden out of sight or relegated to an obscure background. We see nothing whatever of the prophet whom the Spirit inspired in dreams and visions when moments of difficulty in life or in ecclesiastical policy arose, and whose dread of demons changed spiritual sacraments into magical rites; little of the canonist who measured the deep promptings of the heart's repentance by stereotyped expressions, and paved the way for the degradation of sorrow into the mechanism of penance; little of the fiery Roman African who launched envenomed phrases at ecclesiastical opponents; and nothing of the ruthless Roman lawyer who condemned a Christian martyr, who had survived the tortures which had covered her poor body with blood, to eternal perdition (for this he thought he could do as a successor of the apostles), when she crossed the path of his ecclesiastical policy. Then a curious colour blindness or perhaps an amiable propensity to see all things ecclesiastical through the coloured glass of the modern institutions of the communion over which he so worthily presided, prevents the author from seeing the ecclesiastical situation which existed in the middle of the third century. Dr. Benson had evidently great difficulty in stating an opponent's argument fairly, and seldom succeeds in doing so. He had no acquaintance with the organization of any branch of the Protestant Church save his own, and yet makes continual allusion to other organizations. We have such phrases as "Presbyterian Teutonism" (this is applied to the greatest living authority in early Church history, Dr. Harnack of Berlin); "heavy pages," "laborious pages" (phrases which mean that an opinion Dr. Benson does not like is supported by a plentiful supply of quotations from Cyprian's writings), "Calvinism" (used at random, for Calvinists agree with Cyprian and Augustine on the matter discussed); and many others of the same kind. They are useful to warn the unwary reader of the bias in the book.

and enable us to see how his thoughts took sharper outline in a controversy which he had to maintain with his own office-bearers in Carthage, and how he aimed at and partly succeeded in giving the Christian Church a polity which enabled it to be one in practical activity as it was one in devotional conception.

Thascius Cyprianus was the most eminent of the many distinguished converts whom Christianity was drawing from the learned and wealthy classes during the second third of the third century, during that long period of " peace " which preceded the outbreak of the Decian persecution in 250 A.D. He was a Roman whose ancestors had settled in Africa. Such men were called Roman Africans. They belonged to a race which had given the capital some of its most distinguished lawyers, and which furnished to the Church such men as Tertullian, Minucius Felix, Cyprian, Lactantius and Augustine. By training and profession he was a *pleader*, and therefore of the highest social standing.[1] His wealth was great; his house, with its " gilded ceilings " and " mosaics of costly marble,"[2] and his gardens, were famous in the city of palaces. He became a Christian in middle life, drawn by the persuasion of the in-

[1] " Far from any shade of unreality resting on them, the teachers of oratory were courted leaders in society. The publicity in life, the majesty of national audiences, the familiarity of the cultivated classes with the teaching of the schools, required the orator to be not only perfect in the graces of life, but to be versed in ethical science; to be armed with solid arguments as well as to be facile of invention; not less convincing than attractive; in short to be a wit and a student, a politician and an eclectic philosopher. At the age of nearly thirty Cicero was still placing himself under the tuition of the Rhodian Molon. Augustine's fourth book on Christian doctrine shews us that five centuries and a changed religion did not abate the value placed on technical perfection. No statesman's name had for generations commanded such reverence as was paid in Cyprian's times to the life and memory of Timesitheus the Rhetorician, whose daughter the young African Emperor had espoused, and whose honour and universal cultivation had for a brief interval restored purity to the Court, dignity to the senate, and discipline to the camps of Rome "; Benson, *Cyprian, his Life, his Times, his Work*, pp. 2, 3.

[2] Cyprian, *Ad Donatum*, 15:—" Auro distincta aquearia et pretiosi marmoris crustis vestita domicilia."

tellect as well as by the pleadings of the heart. We may see the path he trod towards conversion in his *Treatise to Donatus* and in the *Book of Testimonies* he wrote for a friend. After a brief space of time he probably became a deacon; he was certainly an elder when Donatus, the Bishop of Carthage, died. The Christians at Carthage resolved that the most distinguished Christian in the city, although two years had scarcely passed since his baptism, should be their bishop. His reluctance only increased their ardour. "A crowded brotherhood besieged the doors of his house, and throughout all the avenues of access an anxious love was circulating."[1] Cyprian yielded and was ordained, the bishop, the Papa, the spiritual Father of the Christian community in Carthage. We must forget many of the associations which the word "bishop" inevitably brings with it to understand his position. He was simply the chief pastor of the Christian congregation at Carthage and of its outlying mission districts. He had no diocese and never exercised diocesan rule. He had no cathedral, not even a church. His congregation met in the audience hall of a wealthy Carthaginian burgher.[2] It was the man who made the position he occupied one of such commanding importance as it soon attained to.[3]

---

[1] Pontius, *Life and Passion of Cyprian, Bishop and Martyr*, 5.

[2] Benson, *Cyprian, his Life, his Times, his Work*, p. 41 and note.

[3] It may be useful to give the principal dates known proximately about Cyprian. He was baptized probably in the spring of 246 A.D.; became a member of the Session of Carthage in 247 A.D.; and was consecrated bishop some time after June in 248 A.D. It is not quite certain that he was a deacon; the evidence lies in the phrase used by his biographer Pontius, who was a deacon :—"Erat sane illi etiam *de nobis* contubernium viri justi et laudabilis memoriae Caeciliani" (*Life*, 4); and in the sentence in sect. 3 :—"quis enim non omnes honoris gradus crederet tali mente credente." The outbreak of the Decian persecution being imminent, Cyprian retired from Carthage to his unknown hiding-place in January 250 A.D.; the persecution began in April of the same year. It raged fiercely until November, and was then relaxed; but it was not considered safe for Cyprian to return. He came back to Carthage in 251 A.D., some time after Easter. Then followed a series of councils at Carthage where

Eighteen months of quiet rule were vouchsafed him. During this period he had conciliated the few who had been opposed to the choice of so recently baptized a Christian for the important place of chief pastor. They became, says Pontius, his biographer, "his closest and most intimate friends."[1]

Decius was one of those stern upright emperors who believed that Christianity was a source of menace to the empire, and that it had to be stamped out. His edict against it was published early in the year 250 A.D. It had been expected by the heathen population of Carthage, and threats against the wealthy and well-known head of the Christian community were freely uttered by the mob. Cyprian, thinking less of his own safety than of the welfare of his people, believed it to be his duty to go into retirement, and a large part of his correspondence deals with the management of his congregation from his place of safety. We find three distinct questions of ecclesiastical organization raised and in the end settled—the right of men supposed to be specially possessed by the Spirit to interfere in the discipline of the local

---

the African bishops met under the presidency of Cyprian;—the first in April 251 A.D.; the second in May 252 A.D., the third in September 253 A.D., the fourth in the autumn of 254 A.D., the fifth in 255, and the sixth and seventh in 256; in 257 Cyprian was banished to Curubis; he returned to Carthage in 258 and was martyred there in September 258.

[1] It is commonly said and has been repeated by Dr. Benson that the five presbyters who were at variance with Cyprian in the question of the influence of confessors and martyrs on the discipline of the Church were among those persons who disliked his elevation to the episcopate and that they continued to bear a grudge against him. This idea seems to me to have no basis in fact. Dr. Benson adduces as his only proof the sentence: "retaining that ancient venom against my episcopate, that is against your suffrage and God's judgment, they renew their old attack upon me" (*Ep.* xliii. 1 [xxxix.]); but the "ancient venom" and "old attack" it is clear from section three and other epistles, was their first siding with the confessors against Cyprian's judgment not to accept the certificates of the confessors; while the word "suffrage" means here as elsewhere that Cyprian held that all his acts as bishop were to be justified by the fact that he had been validly called to office. There is no trace of any difficulties between Cyprian and his presbyters until the dispute about what was due to the wishes of the martyrs and the confessors in the matter of the lapsed.

church, the seat of the one supreme authority in the local church, and the best means of giving a practical expression to the unity of the whole Church of Christ. The occasion which demanded solution of all three questions was the fact that many Christians had lapsed and were asking to be restored to the communion of the Church at Carthage. The ecclesiastical questions are so connected with the course of events that these last must be briefly noted.

The persecution resolved upon by the Emperor Decius was begun in swift ruthless Roman fashion. It attacked the Christian Church everywhere simultaneously—in Rome, Egypt, Syria, Armenia, Spain, and North Africa. It aimed at breaking up the Christian communities by destroying their leaders and then coercing their followers. Cyprian speaks of bishops proscribed, imprisoned, banished, and slain.[1] Persecution had been almost unknown in Africa for thirty-eight years, during which time of "peace" the Christian communities had been growing rapidly in numbers and in influence; the results of its renewal seemed at first sight to be disastrous to the Christian faith. Multitudes relapsed into heathenism.[2] The larger half of the Christian community in Carthage and at least one presbyter had been unable to face the terrible risks in which the profession of Christianity had involved them. They relapsed. They appeared before the imperial commissioners, five of whom, called *The Commissioners of the Sacrifices*, were appointed to act along with the magistrates of the district. They made a declaration that they worshipped the gods and in the presence of the commissioners they took part in the pagan worship, either joining in a sacrifice, tasting the wine and eating of the sacrificial victim (the *sacrificati*) or throwing incense on the altar of the emperor (the *thurificati*). This done they received a certificate (*libellus*), certifying that they had done so. This was registered, and then a copy was posted up in the market place or *forum*. Some found a way of appearing to comply and yet of escaping from

[1] Cyprian, *Epist.* lxvi. 7 (lxviii.).   [2] Cyprian, *De Lapsis*, 8.

actual participation in the pagan rites. They bribed officials to give them certificates declaring that they had taken part in sacrifices which they had not done (the *libellatici*).[1] Thus poor Etecusa,[2] a Roman Christian, while she sadly and fearfully was climbing the ascent to the Capitol, where she had to make her declaration and take part in the sacrifices, found an official near the small temple to the Three Fates, who sold her a certificate and she went home again without sacrificing. Many sought safety in flight, hoping to find freedom from persecutions in cities where they were unknown.

[1] Two of these *libelli* were actually discovered in 1893 and 1894, brought from Egypt among bundles of papyri dug out of Egyptian sands. They show us how thorough this persecution of Decius was, how systematically arranged, how minute in its searching out Christians—little villages being included and the women peasants as well as the men interrogated. The first runs:—" To the Commissioners of sacrifices of the village of Alexander's Island from Aurelius Diogenes (son of) Satabus. About 72. Scar on right eyebrow. I was both constant in ever sacrificing to the gods and now in your presence according to the commands I sacrificed and drank and tasted of the victims, and I beseech you to attach your signature. May you ever prosper. I Aurelius Diogenes have presented this." (Then follow the signatures of the magistrate and witness. "I Aurelius . . . saw him sacrificing. I Mys(thes, son of) . . . non have signed. (First) year of the Emperor Caesar Gaius Messius Quintus Trajanus Decius, Pius Felix Augustus. 2nd day of Ephiphi." The second, in every way similar, bears the name of Aurelius Syrus, his brother Pasbeius, and Demetria and Serapias their wives. They were unable to write and the scribe Isidorus appended his name. The signatures of the magistrates have been torn off.

[2] Etecusa belonged to a Carthaginian family which had suffered much. Her grandmother Celerina had been martyred in an earlier persecution; so had her uncles, the son and son-in-law of Celerina, both in the army. Her brother Celerinus was a noted confessor, who had come forth alive out of the severest tortures without denying his faith. Her sister Candida had faltered and had sacrificed. We see the *confessor*, the *sacrificata* and the *libellatica*, in one family. The two sisters were overwhelmed with remorse and endeavoured to make atonement for their fall by waiting on the arrivals of travellers at Rome and at Portus, and when they found any Christian refugees from Carthage they took them home, hid them, and tended them. They had no less than sixty-five of these refugees in their house at Rome. Compare Cyprian, *Epistles*, xxi. (xx.), and xxxi. 3 (xxxiii.).

Those Christians who were of sterner stuff were imprisoned, awaiting torture and probably death. The torture was repeated over and over again. Even if it produced recantation a second torture was applied. If the confessor stood firm it might be applied time after time until the sufferer expired under it. Such men and women were called *confessors* before they had suffered, and *martyrs* after they had been done to death, or had suffered tortures without expiring. The *martyrs* and *confessors* were carefully tended while they were in prison by their fellow-Christians; and many of the *lapsed*, repenting of their weakness, thronged the prisons in Carthage and lavished all manner of attentions on the heroic confessors. These lapsed Christians, especially those of them who had purchased exemption from suffering by means of false certificates, were anxious to be reconciled with the Church, and besought the good offices of the confessors and martyrs to intercede on their behalf with the office-bearers, and beg them to restore them again to communion. The result was that many of the confessors, from the prison where they lay, gave letters (which were also called *libelli*) to the elders of the Church, the bishop being absent in hiding, asking that the bearers might be restored to the Church which they had abandoned in a moment of weakness. This Decian persecution differed from all preceding ones to this extent, that it had fallen on the whole Church of Christ, and was not confined to any one portion. The question of what was to be done in the case of lapsed members who wished to return to the faith they had abjured was one which was forced upon the whole Church everywhere and at the same time.[1] It was a question of discipline which had to be inevitably faced by every church.

So far as our information goes, the leaders of the Roman Church were the first to see the importance and the urgency of the question. The Bishop Fabian had been one of the first martyrs; to meet and appoint a successor would have been to

---

[1] Cyprian, *Epistle*, xix. 2 (xiii.).

offer new victims to the persecuting government. The elders of the church took the burden of leadership on their own shoulders; they saw the universal situation and the need for an immediate understanding with sister churches about what it was possible to do at once. They put aside matters that could wait until their church had again its lawful head; but the one matter which pressed for an immediate decision was what ought to be done in the case of lapsed Christians who earnestly desired reconciliation with the Church, and *who were on the point of death.* They accordingly wrote to the elders in Carthage, advising them to follow a definite rule with regard to the lapsed who were repentant—that if any were taken with sickness, and repented of what they had done and desired communion, it should be granted to them. In the same letter these Roman elders speak not obscurely of Cyprian as the hireling shepherd who deserts his sheep when peril draws near. They in Rome and the elders in Carthage are both deprived of their chief; persecution makes all work difficult, but it must be done. This letter reached Cyprian, who treated it in a very lofty way, and sent it back to the writers with a few grimly sarcastic remarks; but it had a marked effect on him nevertheless.[1] It altered his attitude towards his own elders. Before he had read it he had sent a letter to his elders and deacons, in which he had said: "I beg you by your faith and your religion to discharge

[1] Harnack and Ritschl think that Crumentius carried this letter to the office-bearers in Carthage for whom it was certainly intended, and that they manifested their loyalty to Cyprian by making Crumentius take it on to their bishop. Benson asserts that the elders in Carthage never saw the letter; that it was put into Cyprian's hands and that he sent it back to Rome without permitting it to reach its destination. Benson may be right. Cyprian suppressed a more important letter on a more important occasion and he might have suppressed this one also. The archbishop justifies the one suppression by calling Cyprian a "benevolent despot"; and the other by praising his sense of humour! Otto Ritschl, *Cyprian von Karthago* (1885), p. 9; Benson, *Cyprian, his Life, his Times, his Work* (1897), p. 149. It does not matter which view is the correct one; the important thing is the effect of the letter on the mind of Cyprian, not its effect on the elders of Carthage.

both your own office and mine, that there be nothing wanting either to discipline or diligence." [1] He left the whole work unreservedly in their hands—all his work as well as theirs. The two words used, *disciplina* and *diligentia*, are employed by Cyprian to denote the two great divisions of a bishop's work—the term *disciplina* including everything which belonged to the office of judging and punishing, and *diligentia* including all that belonged to his work as the head of the religious administration of the congregation, the care of the poor and such matters. In a letter following, however, he distinctly limited the work of his elders and deacons to the *diligentia* or to the religious administration.[2] "I exhort and command you, that those of you whose presence there is least suspicious and least perilous, should in my stead discharge my duty in respect of doing those things which are required *for the religious administration.*"[3] In the same letter he refuses to answer a question sent him by four presbyters, which evidently concerned matters of discipline on the ground that in such matters he did nothing on his own private opinion without the advice of his elders, deacons, and people.[4] From this time onwards Cyprian shows himself more and more irritated with his elders. He wrote to the martyrs and the confessors complaining that some of his elders had admitted some of the lapsed to communion;[5] he wrote to his elders and deacons complaining that some of the elders, "remembering neither the Gospel nor their own place, and, moreover, considering neither the Lord's future judgment nor the bishop now placed over them, claim to themselves entire

---

[1] Cyprian, *Epist.* v. 1 (iv.); compare *Epist.* xx. 1 (xiv.).

[2] Dr. Benson rather vehemently declares that there is no change of attitude in Cyprian's two letters. He gives an abstract of Ritschl's arguments and says that his "abstract will be as just as he can make it"; and yet he omits entirely the strongest argument Ritschl has adduced! Compare Benson, *Cyprian*, etc. pp. 148-50; Otto Ritschl, *Cyprian von Karthago*, pp. 9-13, 216, 217.

[3] Cyprian's *Epist.* xiv. 2 (v.).

[4] *Epist.* xiv. 4 (v.).   [5] *Epist.* xv. 1 (x.).

authority (a thing which was never done in anywise under our predecessors) with discredit and contempt of the bishop." Their fault was that the elders blamed had communicated with some of the lapsed, and offered and given them the eucharist, "disregarding the honour which the blessed martyrs, with the confessors, maintain for me, despising the law of the Lord, and that observance which the same martyrs and confessors order to be maintained."[1] He wrote to the people complaining of the action of the elders in almost the same terms, and promised that when he could return a meeting of bishops would be convened and that in the presence of the confessors, and with their opinion, the letters and wishes of the "blessed martyrs" with reference to the lapsed would be carefully considered.[2]

We do not know whether Cyprian got any answer to these letters; but the probability is that he received none, and that people and clergy felt sore that the bishop would neither return and act himself nor allow his elders to do anything in the pressing question of the lapsed. He wrote again to the elders and deacons and for the first time suggested some immediate action. If any of the lapsed had a certificate from one of the martyrs and were in sore sickness they were to be allowed to communicate.[3] This letter brought an answer, which assured him that the elders and deacons had hitherto done their best to follow his instructions, and to restrain the people and especially the lapsed; and Cyprian reiterates the command that if any of the penitent lapsed had a certificate from one of the martyrs, and were at the point of death, they were to be received back into the communion of the Church.[4]

Then comes a curious letter.[5] Cyprian, whose last dealings with Rome had been to send back the letter of advice which the Roman elders had addressed to their brethren at Carthage, now wrote to these Roman elders; justified to them his actions in Carthage; complained bitterly of the way in which the

[1] *Epist.* xvi. 1, 3 (ix.).   [2] *Epist.* xvii. 2, 3 (xi.).
[3] *Epist.* xviii. (xii.).   [4] *Epist.* xix. 1, 2 (xiii.).   [5] *Epist.* xx. (xiv.).

libellatici had pestered the martyrs for certificates; bemoaned the weakness of some of his clergy in admitting some of the lapsed to communion; and declared that he had followed the advice given in the letter from Rome which he had treated so scornfully when it reached him. His letter, however, contains one interesting fact. Cyprian says distinctly that although some of his presbyters had acted rashly in communicating with the lapsed, they had refrained as soon as he had remonstrated with them.[1] Rome, however, had not forgotten his earlier action, and he had to write four times ere he got an answer. When it came it was practically a repetition of what had been written to the elders of Carthage, at least so far as immediate action was concerned: If the lapsed are in severe sickness and are penitent, admit them to communion, whether they have certificates from martyrs or not. But as regards the larger, statesmanlike policy, which belonged to the immediate future, the Roman elders adopted the proposals laid before them by Cyprian, and by intercourse and correspondence they obtained the adhesion of many bishops in Sicily and in some parts of Italy.[2] Cyprian himself had meanwhile gained the adoption of his policy by a large number of bishops in Africa, with whom he had been in correspondence.[3]

Having thus secured the support of the Roman elders and of so many bishops throughout the West for his conception of arriving at a common mode of dealing with the lapsed, Cyprian at once took measures to subdue all resistance in Carthage. He superseded his elders by a commission of five, three bishops and two elders, to whom he entrusted not merely the discipline, but also the relief of the deserving poor. They were to be his vicars. It was this action that produced the subsequent schism in the Church at Carthage,[4] a result scarcely to be wondered at. Why such an arbitrary step should have been taken it is difficult

---

[1] *Epist.* xx. 2 (xiv.).   [2] *Epist.* xxx. 5, 8 (xxx.); xliii. 3 (**xxxix.**).
[3] *Epist.* xxv. (xix.); **xxvi.** (xvii.).
[4] *Epist.* xl. 1 (xxxvii.); xlii. (xxxviii.).

to say. Cyprian himself testifies that his clergy were at one with him; they had with his approval excommunicated Gaius of Didda, a presbyter who had insisted on communicating with the lapsed. However it is to be accounted for it remains a witness to what Cyprian believed to be the power of the chief pastor; and it also seems to imply that at this juncture Cyprian stood very much alone, separated in sympathy both from his clergy and his people.

Such was the situation in Carthage immediately before Cyprian was able to return, and to hold the successive councils of African bishops which exhibited his ecclesiastical statesmanship. Through the whole course of these events one question thrusts itself into prominence—the possibility of the restoration to Church communion of Christians who had lapsed during the persecution, and who penitently begged to be allowed to return. Cyprian had one opinion on this matter and some of his elders had another.

If the earlier usages of the Church be kept in mind, there was much to be said on both sides. Idolatry had always been considered one of the worst sins into which the baptized Christian could fall. It was one of those heinous sins against God which, it was believed, the Church could never pardon. No limits were set to the mercy of God; He might pardon and in the end receive; but the Church could only accept such repentant sinners as catechumens, who could never again approach the Lord's Table. On the other hand, it had been held that such sins could be pardoned in the Church if a revelation was received from God authorizing the restoration in any particular case. So long as the prophetic ministry lasted, it was believed that a prophet might receive such a revelation.[1] The opinion which silently spread through the Church that deadly sins might receive forgiveness once but not on a second lapse, can be traced back to a prophetic utterance.[2] It was also believed that, besides the prophets, the martyrs were the very men to whom it was

[1] Tertullian, *De Pudicitia*, 21.   [2] Hermas, *Pas'or, Mandata*, iv.

likely that God would vouchsafe such a revelation of His mind and will.[1] They too had the right to speak the word of pardon which the office-bearers of the Church dared not do. To speak such pardons, then, was the prerogative of prophets and martyrs;[2] and it was theirs because the Spirit of God dwelt in them in larger measure than in any other Christians, whether office-bearers or not. Martyrs had used this prerogative of theirs in the past. The martyrs of Lyons had pronounced the pardon of the penitent lapsed around them;[3] and we can see from Tertullian,[4] how common a practice it was for men who, by reason of some great sin, were "outside the peace of the Church," to supplicate the martyrs to procure this peace for them. Hence the elders of Carthage might well plead that they were acting according to the ancient traditions of the Church when they were induced to give communion to those who came with the letters of the martyrs in their hands.

On the other hand, Cyprian felt that the Decian persecution was a crisis which might make or mar the Church of God. The long rest from persecution had made conversion a comparatively easy thing, and the persecution, with the wholesale defections

---

[1] The Holy Spirit had entered the prison along with them, Tertullian declared (*Ad Martyras*, 1). It was the constant belief that the Lord had taken up His abode in His martyr, speaking in him and suffering with him; compare the collection of evidence in Sohm, *Kirchenrecht*, i. 32 n. 9.

[2] Eusebius, *Hist. Eccles.* V. xviii. 7.

[3] Eusebius, *Hist. Eccles.* V. ii. 5, 6:—"They *loosed all*, they bound none. . . . They did not arrogate any superiority over the lapsed; but in those things wherein they themselves abounded, in this they supplied those that were deficient, exercising the compassion of mothers, and pouring forth prayers to the Father on their account." Cf. Eusebius, *Hist. Eccles.* xlii. 5.

[4] Tertullian, *Ad Martyras*, 1:—"You know that some not able to find this peace in the Church, have been used to seek it from the imprisoned martyrs." In his tract *De Pudicitia* he denounces the practice in the case of those who had been guilty of sins of the flesh (22). The martyr, he says, is no sooner in prison than sinners beset and gain access to him; "instantly prayers echo round him; instantly pools of tears of all the polluted surround him; nor are any more diligent in purchasing entrance into prison than those who have lost the Church."

it had produced, had shown how bad these easy conversions had been for the stability of the Church. To make restoration an easy matter might do more harm to Christianity than the persecution itself. He was unwearied in urging, in his earliest letters, that lapsing into idolatry was a heinous sin against God, which must be bitterly repented in protracted sorrow. Hasty restoration was a profanity in his sight, and the demand for it did not seem to him to be a sign of the depth of sorrow that should exist. He knew that the churches had relaxed their former rigid attitude with regard to sins specially heinous; he had no word of disapproval for the practice; he believed that the churches had authority to forgive even the sin of idolatry—at least he must have come to believe that they had;[1] but with that strong view of authority which was his characteristic and with his ideas of orderly Church procedure, he was determined that the whole question of the lapsed ought to be gone into with the greatest deliberation. The dominant idea in his earliest epistles is that after the persecution had ceased the bishop, elders, deacons, confessors and people ought to meet together, and the question of the lapsed, their repentance and their pardon be deliberately dealt with.[2] The scene suggested by his words is what we know was the mode of discipline in the Roman Church after Calixtus' proclamation that the office-bearers at Rome were prepared to grant pardon for sins of the flesh on due signs of sorrow. Tertullian's description of the scene, although a caricature by a bitter opponent, conveys a not unfair impression of what must have frequently taken place.[3] Cyprian's later declaration that he meant to ask the

---

[1] In his *Testimonies* (iii. 28), Cyprian says distinctly that "remission cannot be granted in the Church to him who has sinned against God"; but he does not say whether this "sin against God" is idolatry or not.

[2] *Epistles*, xi. 8 (vii.); xiv. 4 (v.); xv. 1 (x.); xvi. 4 (ix.).

[3] *De Pudicitia*, 13:—"You introduce into the Church the penitent adulterer for the purpose of melting the brotherhood by his supplications. You lead him into the midst clad in sackcloth, covered with ashes, a compound of disgrace and horror. He prostrates himself before the widows,

assistance of other bishops in the determination of so grave a matter is not incompatible with his earlier promises.[1]

Suddenly he was brought face to face with a question of *authority*. To the grave Roman lawyer who had become a Christian bishop, the question of authority was the question of questions. Another authority suddenly confronted him within his own congregation. He could afford to be sarcastic in a dignified manner when the elders of the Church of Rome compared him to a hireling shepherd and then proceeded to give advice to his own office-bearers. That was from without; but this was from within; and had moreover some sanction from ancient usage. He felt bound to resist, and he did with all his powers.

Thus this struggle successfully maintained by Cyprian against the right of the martyrs or confessors to pronounce pardon of one who had lapsed, may be looked upon as the last stage of the long contest waged by the office-bearers of the local churches against the ancient supremacy of the prophetic ministry. His success established the complete supremacy of the local office-bearers; it was never again questioned. Carthage had therefore a peculiar place in the development of the idea of the centre of authority in the Church of Christ in addition to the prominence given to it by the genius of its bishop. The martyrs and confessors do not seem to have contested the supremacy of the bishop or office-bearers anywhere else. At Rome,[2] at Alexandria and at Corinth, they all supported the ordinary ecclesiastical

---

before the elders, suing for the tears of all; he seizes the edges of their garments, he clasps their knees, he kisses the prints of their feet. Meanwhile you harangue the people and excite their pity for the sad lot of the penitent. Good pastor, blessed father that you are, you describe the coming back of your goat in recounting the parable of the lost sheep. And in case your ewe lamb may take another leap out of the fold—as if that were not lawful for the future which was not really lawful in the past—you fill all the rest of the flock with apprehension at the very moment of granting indulgence."

[1] *Epistle*, xvii. 3 (xi.).
[2] Cyprian, *Epistle*, xxxi. 6, 7 (xxv.).

authorities.¹ In Carthage alone the confessors and martyrs strove to exert their power against that of the bishop, and found some of the office-bearers ready, at first at least, to accept their decisions as the commands of God.

Felicissimus could say: "God speaks through His martyrs as He spoke in the old days through His prophets, and where God speaks there is His Church"; and the lapsed could send letters to Cyprian written in the name of the Church, because they were written by martyrs; while Cyprian could reply: "God speaks through the bishop as he formerly spoke through His apostles, and the Church is founded on the bishops, and every act of the Church is controlled by these same rulers."² Thus the two authorities faced each other in Carthage—at first within the one community—then, when the tension became too strong, in two separate congregations, in one of which Felicissimus and the five elders represented the old idea of authoritative divine utterance in the midst of the congregation; while in the other Cyprian insisted on the new thought, first proclaimed by Hippolytus and Calixtus in their mutual quarrels, that the bishops speak the divine decisions as the apostles had done.³

Cyprian took this position from the first:—No one can be

---

[1] Compare the account given by Eusebius of the way in which Dionysius of Corinth persuaded his people to admit the lapsed there to communion (*Hist. Eccles.* VI. xlii. 5, 6);—"But these same martyrs, who are now sitting with Christ and are the sharers of His kingdom, and the partners in His judgment, and who are now judging with Him, received those of the brethren that fell away and had been convicted of sacrificing, and when they saw their conversion and repentance, and having proved them as sincere, they received them and assembled with them. They also communicated with them in prayer and at their feasts. What then, brethren, do ye advise concerning these? What should we do? Let us join in our sentiments with them, and let us observe their judgment and their charity; and let us kindly receive those who were treated with such compassion by them. Or should we rather pronounce their judgment unjust, and set ourselves up as judges of their opinions, and thus grieve the spirit of mildness, and overturn established order?"

[2] Compare the whole of *Epistle* xxxiii. (xxvi.).

[3] Otto Ritschl seems to think that Cyprian, if he did not during the course

received back into the communion of the Church until penance has been performed, confession made, and the hands of the *bishop* and clergy are laid upon their heads. This cannot be done in the absence of the bishop, and therefore there can be no restitution of the lapsed until the " peace " comes and the bishop is able to return. But he was too great a man to be a doctrinaire theorist. When he found the strength of the martyrs' position in Carthage, when his humanity was touched with the thought of really penitent lapsed dying without the reconciliation they longed for, he permitted his elders to communicate with those invalids who had martyrs' certificates, although he could not be present himself to receive them formally,[1] and by nomina-

of the Decian persecution alter his conception of what the Church was, held it in a more rudimentary form before the persecution arose, and that it took shape during his experiences while the persecution lasted. He is therefore of opinion that he sees these more rudimentary ideas in the letter lxiii. (lxii.), which he accordingly places at the head of the list. The argument from the expressions in the letter does not appear to be very conclusive. Cyprian is there speaking of the cup in the Holy Supper. He says that the water in the mixed chalice represents the baptized people and the wine is the symbol of Christ ; and that when the cup is given the Church becomes united with Christ. He calls the Church which is thus united to Christ in communicating " the people established in the Church faithfully and firmly persevering in what they have believed." He is not speaking about what makes a Church, but about how the people who are in the Church are united to Christ in partaking of the cup in the communion. It is true that Cyprian tells us that the Church is in *episcopo et clero et in omnibus stantibus constituta* ; but this definition does not prevent him asserting in the previous sentence that the Church is founded on the bishops (*Epist.* xxxiii. 1 (xxvi.). Cyprian held from the beginning that the bishop is the keystone of the arch ; without him nothing remains but a heap of ruins. At the same time, his theory grew more and more distinct as he had to accept consequences which followed from his premises in the discussions which the controversies about the lapsed evoked. Compare Ritschl, *Cyprian*, etc. pp. 86 f. and 241 ; Benson, *Cyprian*, pp. 39, 186 f.

[1] *Epistle*, xviii. (xii.); xx. 3 (xiv.); lvii. 1 (liii.). Cyprian, like his master, Tertullian, evidently thought that it ought to "suffice to the martyr to have purged his own sins ; it is part of ingratitude or of pride to lavish upon others what one has obtained at a high price. Who has redeemed another's death by his own, but the Son of God alone ? " He also knew that beneath the noble constancy which endured tortures there was a nervous excitement on the part of some at least which was leading

ting a distinguished martyr to be one of his commission of five, he managed to show the people that the whole strength of the martyrs was not on the side opposed to him.[1] Never from beginning to end did he acknowledge an *authority* in the local church superior or even equal to that of the bishop. He went the length of superseding his elders, the ancient counsellors of the bishop, when he thought that the influence of the martyrs over them was likely to weaken his. He was the despot, generally a benevolent despot, of the local church. His position might be due to his people, but he never imagined that his authority came from them; it came from God directly. That was his idea from first to last. The old theory that the bishop did not differ from the elders save in having a special seat of honour in the Church and in having the power to ordain, was not his. He was a Roman lawyer, and the analogies of imperial government were always before him. The governors of the imperial provinces, large or small, were nominated by the emperor and were responsible to him alone. It was their duty to govern for the benefit of the people over whom they were set, to take counsel with them and their leaders on the affairs of the province, but they were responsible to the emperor alone from whom their authority came. The Church had begun to copy the imperial organization in many things, as we shall see hereafter, and the analogy of the imperial government was never absent from the thoughts of the leaders during the second half of the third century. The bishops were the *dispensatores Dei et Christi*, as the governors were the deputies of the emperor. They were in God's place, set there by His authority, and responsible to Him alone. If their authority was recognized then they might take their people and their subordinate office-bearers into their confidence and

---

them to practise unnatural tests of continence—tests which should never have been used, which might prove dangerous and which in some cases did prove dangerous in the end. Compare *Epistles*, xi. 1 (vii.); xiii. 5 (vi.); *De Unitate Ecclesiae*, 20.

[1] *Epistles*, xl. (xxxiv.); xli. (xxxvii.); xliii. (xxxviii.).

into their counsels, but if it was in any way questioned, then they were alone with God against all gainsayers.[1]

According to Cyprian's idea, the bishop entered upon the rights and duties of his office through ordination, which was the indispensable gate to all office in the Church.[2] His selection was commonly the act of the people, but neighbouring bishops might select him and present him to his people, whose assent must always be obtained before installation.[3] Whatever the mode of selection and of consecration, Cyprian saw in these acts the hand of God. It was God and God alone who made bishops,

---

[1] *Epistles*, iii. (lxiv.); lxviii. (lxvi.).

[2] *Epist.* lxix. 3 (lxxv.):—"Habere namque aut tenere ecclesiam nullo modo potest qui ordinatus in ecclesia non est."

[3] Cyprian describes the appointment of a bishop thrice—the one being his own, the others that of a bishop in Spain and of Cornelius of Rome. Of his own he says:—"When a bishop is appointed into the place of one deceased, when he is chosen in time of peace by the suffrage of an entire people, when he is protected by God in persecution, faithfully linked with his colleagues, approved to his people by now four years' experience in his episcopate; observant of discipline in time of peace; in time of persecution, proscribed with the name of his episcopate applied and attached to him; so often asked for in the circus, ' for the lions ' in the amphitheatre; honoured with the testimony of the divine condescension," *Epist.* lix. 6 (liv.). "You must diligently observe and keep the practice delivered from divine tradition and apostolic observance, which is also maintained among us and almost throughout the provinces; that for the proper celebration of ordinations all the bishops of the same province should assemble with that congregation for which a prelate is ordained; and the bishop should be chosen in the presence of the people, who have most fully known the life of each one and have looked into the doings of each one as respects his habitual conduct. And this also, we see, was done by you in the ordination of our colleague Sabinus; so that by the suffrage of the whole brotherhood, and by the sentence of the bishops who had assembled in their presence, and who had written letters to you concerning him, the episcopate was conferred upon him," *Epist.* lxvii. 5 (lxvii.). "Cornelius was made bishop by the judgment of God and of His Christ, by the testimony of almost all the clergy, by the suffrage of the people who were there present, and by the assembly of ancient priests and good men," *Epist.* lv. 8 (li.); see also lix. 5 (liv.); lxvii. 4 (lxvii.). Compare Hatch, art. *Ordination* in the *Dictionary of Christian Antiquities*, p. 1518b. The mode of appointing the bishop or pastor in the third century as described in Cyprian's letters was essentially the same as the mode of appointing the pastor or bishop in Presbyterian Churches at the present time.

THE AUTHORITY OF BISHOPS

while it was the bishops who made the subordinate office-bearers.[1] His reason for his strong and reiterated assertions that bishops were made by God appears to have been that the appointment of a bishop, who is, "for the time, judge in Christ's stead," is such an important thing, that God who cares even for sparrows, must control the selection of bishops.[2]

Once appointed, the bishop possessed the "sublime power of governing the Church," and was responsible to God alone for his deeds.[3] He was the autocrat within his own Church, and every act and office culminated in his person, just as the emperor absorbed in one man all the legal powers which under the earlier republican government had been distributed among several officials.

The bishop had entire charge of the discipline of the congregation. It was his care to see that the brethren kept the divine precepts. It was his duty to instruct the people about what the discipline of the Church required, and to promote their growth in holiness.[4] To this end God might vouchsafe to grant him visions which he was bound to communicate to his people for their edification.[5] In all this the elders and deacons might assist, but always under the control of the bishop.[6] To him and to him alone belonged the right of "binding and loosing"—a right which had been given, he maintained, to St. Peter, and then to the other apostles, and which now belonged to the bishops who were for each generation what the apostles had been for

---

[1] *Epist.* iii. 3 (lxiv.); xlviii. 4 (xliv.); lv. 8 (li.); lix. 4, 5 (liv.); lxvi. 1, 9 (lxviii.).

[2] "'Are not two sparrows sold for a farthing? and one of them does not fall to the ground without the will of your Father.' When He says that not even the least things are done without God's will, does anyone think that the highest and greatest things are done in God's Church without God's knowledge or permission, and that priests—that is, His stewards—are not ordained by His decree?" *Epist.* lix. 5 (liv.); lxvi. 1 (lxviii.).

[3] *Epist.* lix. 2 (liv.); lv. (li.).

[4] *Epist.* iv. 2 (lxi.); xiv. 2 (v.); cf. xv. 2 (x.); xvi. 3 (ix.).

[5] *Epist.* xi. 3-7 (vii.).

[6] *Epist.* xv. 1 (x.); xvii. 2 (xi).; xviii. (xii.); xix. (xiii.), etc.

the first.[1] No restoration of sinners was possible until the bishop had heard their confessions, until he had approved of their signs of sorrow, or until he, along with the presbyters and deacons, had placed his hands on their head in token of forgiveness.[2] He could institute new laws of discipline, but always in accordance with the Scriptural rules, and more suitably after consultation with other bishops.[3] To him belonged the power to prescribe the signs of sorrow, and to say what were sufficient in the way of prayers and of good works such as almsgiving.[4]

He was also the head of the whole religious administration (*diligentia*). He was the almoner of the poor and the paymaster of the subordinate clergy.[5] For Cyprian seems to have been the first to make payments to the clergy, a first charge on the tenths and free-will offerings of the congregation.[6] He could give or withhold the monthly payments; and this of itself, when the elders and deacons were dependent on the Church for their livelihood, sufficed to make the bishop an autocrat over the clergy.

The bishop was, therefore, according to Cyprian, the overseer of the brotherhood, the provost of the people, the pastor of the flock and the governor of the Church, and all these terms expressed the relations in which he, as supreme ruler, stood towards

---

[1] *Epist.* lxxiii. 7 (lxxii.).

[2] *Epist.* xvi. 2 (ix.); xviii. (xiii.); xx. 3 (xiv.); lvii. 1 (liii.).

[3] *Epist.* xx. 3 (xiv.):—disponere singula vel *reformare*. Cf. lxiii. 10, 11 (lxii.):—" ab evangelicis autem praeceptis omnino recedendum esse . . . cum ergo neque ipse apostolus neque angelus de caelo adnuntiare possit aliter aut docere praeterquam quod semel Christus docuit et apostoli ejus adnuntiaverunt."

[4] *Epist.* xvi. 2 (ix.):—" They who truly repenting might satisfy God : . . with their prayers and *works*." *Epist.* lv. 22 (li.) mentions almsgiving and fasting. *De Opere et Eleemosynis*, 1:—"ut sordes postmodum quascumque contrahimus *eleemosynis abluamus.*"

[5] *Epist.* vii. (xxxv.); xiv. 2 (v.); lxii. (lix.); xli. 2 (xxxvii):—"ut cum ecclesia matre remanerent et *stipendia ejus episcopo dispensante perciperent*"; xxxiv. 4 (xxvii. 3):—"interea se *a divisione mensurna tantum contineant* non quasi a ministerio ecclesiastico privati esse videantur."

[6] Compare Achelis, *Die Canones Hippolyti* (*Texte und Untersuchungen*; VI. iv. 193 n.).

them. But he was more. He was also the representative of Christ and the priest of God.[1]

According to Cyprian the bishop was the representative (*antistes*) of Christ in the community over which he ruled, and therefore he had the authority over that single congregation or church which our Lord possessed over the universal Church. He was the lord or viceroy over that portion of God's heritage. But Christ had this position of authority over His people because He represented His people in the presence of God; because He was their High Priest; because He had offered for them His own Body and Blood. The bishop, therefore, as the representative of Christ, is the priest of God,[2] who in the Eucharist offers to God the "Lord's Passion," and "truly discharges the office of Christ" when he imitates that which Christ did. "He offers a true and perfect sacrifice in the Church to God the Father, when he proceeds to offer it according to what he sees Christ

---

[1] *Epist.* lxvi. 5 (lxviii.): "Ecce jam sex annis nec *fraternitas* habuerit *episcopum*, nec *plebs praepositum*, nec *grex pastorem*, nec *ecclesia gubernatorem*, nec *Christus antistitem*, nec *Deus sacerdotem.*" Praepositus generally signified a military commander in the later times of the Republic; it was afterwards used of a magistrate; the military association of command was probably in Cyprian's mind. It is the word from which comes the French *prévôt* and the Scotch *provost*. In early mediaeval Latin it means the chief magistrate of a town—burg-graf, *comes urbis*.

[2] Cyprian's views about the bishop as priest of God and about the sacrifice in the Eucharist are most clearly expressed in *Epistle* lxiii. (lxii.). He says that in the Eucharist the bishop does "that which Jesus Christ, our Lord and God, the founder and teacher of this *sacrifice* did and taught" (1); he calls the Holy Supper the sacrament of the sacrifice of the Lord; (4), and "the sacrifice of God the Father and of Christ" (9); he says that in the Eucharist we ought to "do in remembrance of the Lord the same thing which the Lord also did" (10); "that priest truly discharges the office of Christ, who imitates what Christ did, and he offers a true and full sacrifice in the Church of God the Father when he proceeds to offer it according to what he sees Christ Himself offered" (14); "the Lord's passion is the sacrifice which we offer" (17). The Eucharist is the *dominica hostia* (*De Unitate Ecclesiae*, 17). Cyprian's ideas about Christian priests and sacrifices, occupying as they do the borderland between the purer and more primitive ideas and the conceptions of the fourth and fifth centuries which were corrupted by so many pagan associations, deserve a much more elaborate treatment than can be given here.

Himself to have offered." The bishop brings the people into actual communion with Christ in the Eucharist, and they are united to Him in drinking the wine which is His Blood; whilst to God the Father is again presented the offering once made to Him by Christ. The bishop was also the representative of Christ because he received those who were introduced into the Church by baptism.[1] He was believed to bestow the Holy Spirit upon them in baptism and in the laying-on-of-hands. "They who are baptized in the Church," says Cyprian, "are brought to the *praepositi* of the Church, and by our prayers and by the imposition of hands obtain the Holy Spirit."[2] Thus the Church is built up around him. He creates it in baptism; he brings the members into continual contact with their Lord in the Eucharist, now become a sacrifice in which the communicants, as in pagan rites, were united to the deity by partaking of the flesh of the victim and drinking the wine of the libation. So that, to quote Cyprian: "they are the Church who are a people united to the priest and the flock which adheres to their pastor . . . the bishop is in the Church, and the Church is in the bishop."[3] Above all, the bishop is the representative of Christ because he is the judge to whom belongs the power of punishing or remitting sins. This idea is continually before Cyprian. "They only who are set over the Church . . . can remit sins."[4] He quotes again and again Deut. xvii. 12: "The man that doeth presumptuously in not hearkening unto the priest that standeth to minister there before the Lord thy God, or to the judge, that man shall die."[5] He discourses on the sin of Israel in

---

[1] Tertullian tells us that it was the bishop who baptized in his *De Baptismo*, 17:—"The *summus sacerdos*, who is the bishop, has the right of giving it (baptism); and in the next place, the elders and deacons, yet not without the bishop's authority on account of the honour of the Church." This is also Cyprian's idea; compare *Epistles*, lxxiii. 7 (lxxii.); lxxv. 7 (lxxiv.).

[2] *Epist.* lxxiii. 9 (lxxii.). [3] *Epist.* lxvi. 8 (lxviii.).

[4] *Epist.* lxxiii. 7 (lxxii.).

[5] *Epist.* iii. 1 (lxiv.); iv. 4 (lxi.); xliii. 7 (xxxix.); lix. 4 (liv.); lxvi. 3 (lxii.).

refusing obedience to the *Priest* Samuel.[1] It is the *authority* of the priest that he has always in view.

But while the thought of implicit obedience to the bishop is foremost in his mind, the sacerdotal conception was not absent. He conceived that the bishops were a special priesthood and had a special sacrifice to offer. This was a new thought in the Church of Christ. It was really introduced by Cyprian, and it requires a little explanation.

In Christianity we find from the beginning the thoughts of priest and of sacrifice. The two conceptions always go together, and whatever meaning is attached to the one determines that of the other. The idea of a sacrifice offered in the Christian congregation was continually present, and from the beginning it was intimately connected with the Eucharist. But the thoughts suggested by the words were always evangelical. It was believed that all Christians were priests before God, and that all had to do the priestly work of sacrificing. The sacrifices of the Church, the bloodless sacrifices predicted by the prophet Malachi,[2] were the prayers, the praises, and the worship of the believers. The Holy Supper, which was the supreme part of the Christian worship, was a sacrifice because it was an act of worship, and because it combined, as no other act did, the prayers of *all* the worshippers and the gifts or oblations of bread and wine which were given by the worshippers and were used partly in the Holy Supper and partly to distribute among the poor. The idea of the priesthood of all believers was firmly rooted in the thoughts of the early Christians, even although the constant use of the Old Testament naturally led them from a very early period to draw some comparisons between the leaders of their public devotions and the priests and Levites of the Jewish Church.[3] When they began to explain to themselves and to others what the sacraments of baptism and the

---

[1] *Epist.* iii. 1 (lxiv.), where the rebellion of Korah, Dathan and Abiram is also quoted to point the same moral.
[2] Malachi i. 11; iii. 3, 4. [3] Clement, 1 *Ep.* xl. 5; *Didache*, xiii. 3.

Holy Supper were, it was almost inevitable that thoughts connected with those portions of pagan worship most nearly related to sacraments should come into their minds. Hence the pagan mysteries formed the outline of the picture which presented itself to their imaginations when they tried to describe what the sacraments meant.[1] This inevitable habit could not fail to bring many superstitious conceptions round the sacraments, and many such did connect themselves with them. Notwithstanding this, the evangelical thought that the sacrifices of the New Covenant are the worship of the people, and that the priesthood is the whole worshipping congregation was always the ruling idea. The sacrifice in the Holy Supper was a sacrifice of prayer and thanksgiving, and the sacrificial act was the prayers and the thanksgivings of the worshippers. Apologists[2] defended the lack of material sacrifices in the Christian religion, and Justin Martyr could say that "prayers and giving of thanks

[1] This is seen earlier than Tertullian but it appears most clearly in his writings. In *De Baptismo*, 5 he says:—"Well, but nations who are strangers to all understanding of spiritual powers ascribe to their idols the imbuing of waters with the self-same efficacy; but they cheat themselves with waters which are widowed. For washing is the channel through which they are initiated into some sacred rites of some notorious Isis or Mithras; the gods themselves they likewise honour by washings. Moreover by carrying water around, and sprinkling it, they everywhere ceremonially purify country-houses, habitations, temples and whole cities. They are certainly baptized at the Apollinarian and at the Eleusinian games; and they presume that regeneration and the remission of penalties due for their perjuries is the effect of that. Among the ancients, whoever had defiled himself with murder, was accustomed to go in search of purifying waters." In the *De Praescriptione Haereticorum*, 40, he says:—"The devil . . . by the mystic rites of his idols vies even with the essential things of the sacrament of God. He, too, baptizes some, even his own believers and faithful followers; he promises the putting away (expositionem) of sins by a laver; and if I do not forget, Mithras there sets his marks on the foreheads of his soldiers, celebrates the oblation of bread, introduces an image of the resurrection, and under the sword wreathes the crown. What shall we say to insisting on the chief priest being the husband of one wife; and he (the devil) has virgins who live under the profession of chastity."

[2] Compare Athenagoras, *Apology* (*Plea*). 13; Minucius Felix, *Apology*, 22.

(*eucharistia*), when offered by worthy men, are the only perfect and well-pleasing sacrifices to God." [1]

But if the whole people were the priests, and if the main thought in priesthood was authority and supremacy in judging in all matters of rule and discipline, then the people, the congregation, were the rulers in the last resort. But this primitive conception did not suit the ideas which Cyprian, the Roman lawyer, had about the special omnipotence of the bishop, the representative of Christ in Heaven, as the local governor was of the Emperor in Rome. His thought was that the bishop was *the* priest, and that the people were not priests but those whom the priest introduced into the presence of God. The whole conception of Christian thought began to change, and the change dates from Cyprian and his influence.

The changes made by Cyprian in the early Christian ideas of sacrifice and priest can be best seen by comparing his language with that of Tertullian, his "master" in theology. In Tertullian we have the old ideas that the prayers of the Christian, public and private, are his sacrifices, and that all Christians are priests because they can offer sacrifices of prayer and thanksgiving well-pleasing to God. He calls the Holy Supper a sacrifice —which it is, a sacrifice of prayer and thanksgiving—but he never thinks of it as a sacrifice of *a distinct and special kind* to be carefully discriminated from the prayers of the people. On the other hand, Cyprian is very careful to distinguish between prayer and the Holy Supper in the sense that he never calls the one a sacrifice, while he invariably gives that name to the other. He never thinks of all the worshippers sacrificing; on the contrary, he is careful to distinguish between what the people and what the priests do in the sacrament—the people offer oblations, but the priest offers a sacrifice. There is, according to his idea, a specific sacrifice offered by a specific (not simply a ministering) priesthood in the Holy Supper. The

---

[1] Justin, *Dialogue*, 117; compare *Apology*, i. 13, 65-7; *Dialogue*, 28, 29, 116-8.

sacrifice which is offered, is, as we have seen, the "Passion of the Lord, the Blood of Christ," the "Divine Victim." He was the first to suggest, for his language goes no further than suggestion, that the Holy Supper is a repetition of the agony and death of our Lord on the Cross—a thought never present to the mind of an earlier generation. The ministry has become, in his eyes, or is becoming, a mediating priesthood with power to offer for the people the great sacrifice of Jesus Christ.

His thought of priesthood also leads him to externalize, if the expression may be allowed, the whole thought of sorrow and repentance. In early times if Christians fell into sin, they were required to confess their sins publicly and to exhibit manifest signs of sorrow. These signs were not always stereotyped:—prayers accompanied by tears and groanings, fasting and giving the food thus saved to the poor, setting free a slave or slaves, abundant almsgiving. The penitents were required to perform some open act of self-denial to show that their sorrow was a real thing. Of course the tendency was to connect these *signs* of sorrow directly with the pardon which followed, and even Tertullian was accustomed to speak of such signs of sorrow as something well-pleasing to God, in the sense that God accepted them as meritorious and forgave on their account. Cyprian was the first to lay hold on this familiar practice of penitence, and use it as a means to establish the power of the bishop. His thought seems to have been that some special "good works" were needed to secure the pardon of God for sins committed after baptism,[1] and that the good works must commend themselves to the bishop, who was the "priest of God" and the "repre-

---

[1] In his *De Opere et Eleemosynis*, Cyprian declares that sins will come after baptism and that God has provided a remedy for us "so that by almsgiving we may wash away whatever foulness we subsequently contract" (1); "The remedies for propitiating God are given in the words of God Himself. . . . He shows that our prayers and fastings are of less avail unless they are aided by almsgiving" (5); he quotes the case of the raising of Tabitha to show how "effectual were the *merits* of mercy" (6). The same ideas occur in the *De Lapsis*, and are to be found throughout the *Epistles*.

sentative of our Lord "—for with Cyprian priest and bishop are synonymous terms.

Thus the earlier idea of a Christian ministry was changed into the conception of a mediating priesthood. Behind the change of thought was the new conception of the authority of the clergy over the laity and of the bishop over all. In respect of their historical origin the ideas of the omnipotence of the bishop, of a succession from the apostles, and of a special and mediating priesthood, all hang together, and what made for the one made for the others. No sooner had they found entrance into the Christian Church than they were followed by a large influx of other allied ideas taken over from the paganism which lay around them.

This thought of apostolic succession which is to be found in Cyprian was very different from what is seen both in Irenaeus and in Tertullian. It was not a succession from the apostles but a succession of apostles. The historical matter-of-fact succession disappeared, and the conception became a creation of dogmatic imagination. The thought of succession from the apostles, in a line of office-bearers creating a vital connexion between the generations as they passed, was scarcely in Cyprian's mind. Unless memory fails me, Cyprian only once alludes to it: "All chief rulers who by vicarious ordination succeed to the apostles."[1] For Cyprian's thought is that the bishops do

[1] *Epist.* lxvi. 4 (lxviii.). Firmilian of Caesarea in Cappadocia uses a similar phrase:—" Therefore the power of remitting sins was given to the apostles, and to the Churches which, they, sent by Christ, established, and to the bishops who succeeded them by vicarious ordination," *Epist.* lxxv. 16 (lxxiv.). And Clarus of Mascula, in delivering his opinion at the seventh council meeting at Carthage under the presidency of Cyprian, declared that bishops "have succeeded them (the apostles), governing the Lord's Church with the same powers," *Sententiae episcoporum,* 79.

Hatch remarks that it is not necessary to take this phrase, nor the term *successio* nor the corresponding Greek which occurs in Eusebius, διαδοχή, in any other sense than the ordinary one, viz. to express the fact that one officer was appointed in another's place, as governor succeeded governor in the Roman provinces. (*The Organization of the Early Christian Church* [1881], p. 105 and note.) Dr. Benson (p. 183) in his résumé of the *De Unitate*

really represent, not the apostles, but Christ. As the apostles were the representatives of Christ to the first generation and received from Him power to forgive sins, so each succeeding generation possesses representatives of Christ, who have the same power to forgive sins. Hence the thought on which he lays so much stress, that bishops are directly appointed by God and not by man; the want of any deeper idea of ordination than a mere installation or orderly appointment to office; the belief that the gifts which bishops possess of government and power to forgive sins are more personal than official—all combine to make his conception that bishops are apostles endued with the very same powers that the twelve possessed directly from Jesus, something very different from what is commonly meant by apostolic succession in modern Christendom. He founds the divine appointment of bishops on the argument that since God cares even for sparrows much more must He directly control a matter of such importance as the appointments of bishops![1] He holds that bishops who are guilty of any heinous sin are *ipso facto* bishops no longer, and that their congregations ought to separate themselves from them and acknowledge neither their office nor their authority.[2] The bishops in North Africa

(§ 10) makes Cyprian say that the essential characteristic of the episcopal prerogative is that it is a *given*, that is a transmitted power. Cyprian undoubtedly held that it was a power *given*; but to say that given means *transmitted* is a very palpable case of begging the question. A comparison of passages plainly shows that Cyprian believed that the power was given *directly* and not by *transmission*; of course Cyprian presupposes regular ordination (*ordinationis lex*), but he also presupposes the *plebis suffragium*, which may be a means of transmission as secure as the imposition of hands. The power with Cyprian is always a *direct* gift.

[1] This statement is not a mere pious reflection; it is repeated twice, with all solemnity, when vindicating the bishop's power to forgive sins and to condemn, and when insisting on the dignity of the episcopal office; compare *Epistles* lix. 5 (liv.); lxvi. 1 (lxviii.).

[2] Compare the letters about the Spanish bishops Basilides and Martial (*Epistle* lxvii. (lxvii.); and about Fortunatianus, bishop of Assurae in Africa, who had lapsed as a *sacrificatus* (*Epistle* lxv. (lxiii.). Cyprian says: "A people obedient to God's precepts, and fearing God, ought to separate themselves from a sinful *praepositus*, and not to associate themselves with

arrived at their decisions in the case of the lapsed "by the suggestion of the Holy Spirit and the admonition of the Lord, conveyed by *many and manifest visions* "—an inspiration which was personal and not official.[1] All these things give a certain uniqueness to Cyprian's theory of apostolic succession which is often forgotten. But whatever his theory was, his conviction remained, that the bishop was the autocrat over his congregation, and that where he was, there was the Church.

The real statesmanship of Cyprian was shown, not so much in his conception, theoretical and practical, of the episcopal office, as in his making use of the opportunity of the widespread crisis provoked by the question of the lapsed to sketch a polity which would give the thought of one universal Church of Christ a visible and tangible shape. His idea was not a new one. The conceptions of statesmen seldom are novelties. Councils had been held on ecclesiastical matters before Cyprian's days. They were first held in Asia Minor in the times of the early Montanist movement, and had become somewhat common in Greece as early as the days of Tertullian.[2] They were called to deliberate and settle not only the deeper questions of faith, but the ecclesiastical usages to be observed by the churches represented. The habit of holding these deliberative assemblies which did in some measure represent the churches of a district or province was widespread, and enabled churches lying within convenient distance from each other to become a confederation, having the same ecclesiastical usages and rules of Christian life.

What Cyprian did was to seize upon what he believed to be

the sacrifices of a sacrilegious priest, especially *since they themselves have the power either of choosing worthy priests or of rejecting unworthy ones,*" lxvii. 3.

[1] *Epistle* lvii. 5 (liii.). Cyprian frequently had visions and believed them to be communications by the Holy Spirit; compare *Epistles* lxvi, 10 (lxviii.); xi. 3, 4 (vii.); he was a prophet in the old sense of the word. He also recognized the prophetic gift in others as well as bishops; compare *Epistle* xvi. 4 (ix.); xxxix. 1 (xxxiii.), but only in those subordinate to the bishop.

[2] Eusebius, *Hist. Eccles.* V. xvi. 10; Tertullian, *On Fasting*, 13.

the principles underlying this practice and formulate them in such a way as to make visible and tangible the unity of the Catholic Church which was universally held to exist. The *thought* of the visible unity of the Church of Christ was as old as Christianity. St. Paul had dwelt on it in his epistles to the Ephesians and to the Colossians. Cyprian repeated it in his famous passage, felicitously rendered by Dr. Benson: "There is one Church which outspreads itself into a multitude (of churches), wider and wider in ever increasing fruitfulness, just as the sun has many rays but only one light, and a tree many branches yet only one heart, based in the clinging root; and, while many rills flow from one fountain-head, although a multiplicity of waters is seen streaming away in diverse directions from the bounty of its abundant overflow, yet unity is preserved in the head-spring."[1] That was the old old thought. Cyprian's statesmanship was seen in the method he formulated for making this ideal unity something which could take visible shape in a polity which would produce an harmonious activity throughout all the parts. His practical thought was, that as each bishop sums up in himself the church over which he presides, the whole Church of Christ practically exists in the whole of the bishops, and the harmonious action of the whole Church can be expressed through the common action and agreement of all the bishops. This did not mean to him that every bishop was to think in the same way, or to pursue the same policy, or that there might not be very grave differences on very important, almost fundamental, matters; but it did mean that if they differed they were to agree to differ, and perhaps this last thought was the most important one practically. It is easy to be in accord when there are no differences to separate. Cyprian's thought was that there could be and ought to be agreement amidst differences. He preserved intact the independence of every bishop. The man who stood forth as the eloquent spokesman of the unity of the one Church of Christ was the champion of the independence

[1] Cyprian, *De Unitate Ecclesiae*, 5; compare Benson, *Cyprian*, p. 182.

of the most insignificant bishop whose congregation might be the church of a hamlet. He was as magnanimous in his own conduct as in his thought. In the two great controversies in which he was engaged he showed himself able to subordinate his own feelings and cherished opinions to the wishes of others. The African bishops did not adopt Cyprian's scheme for receiving back the repentant lapsed; they were much more lenient than he would have been if his opinion had prevailed.[1] He felt strongly and spoke warmly on the question of the baptism of heretics, and carried his African colleagues with him; but when the majority of the Church was plainly against him he respected the decision, however he might dislike it. The case of Therapius shows how far he was prepared to go in respecting the independence of a colleague.[2] He insisted again and again that one bishop cannot judge another, and that no one can judge a bishop but God, so strongly does he vindicate the independence of bishops and by implication of the churches over which they rule.[3] The unanimity which he pleaded for among bishops was not one to be produced by force but by brotherly persuasion, it being always understood that Holy Scripture and the apostolic tradition were their guides.[4]

If we may judge from some scattered allusions it is possible to see how Cyprian conceived that his scheme might work so as to produce a harmony not merely of bishops but of the whole Christian community throughout the world. If anything

---

[1] Compare Benson, *Cyprian*, pp. 156, 157.

[2] *Epistle* lxiv. 1 (lviii.); Therapius had admitted to communion a presbyter who had lapsed on much more lenient terms than the council of African bishops had agreed upon.

[3] *Sententiae Episcoporum*, preface:—"Every bishop has his own right of judgment according to the allowance of his liberty and power, and can be no more judged by another than he himself can judge another. But let us all wait for the judgment of our Lord Jesus Christ, who is the only one that has the power both of preferring us in the government of his Church and of judging us in our conduct there." Compare *Epistles* lv. 2, 4 (li.); lix. 14, 17 (liv.); lxxiii. 26 (lxxii.); lvii. 5 (liii.); lxxii. 3 (lxxi.); lxix. 17 (lxxv.).

[4] *Epistle* lv. 6 (li.); lxxiv. 10 (lxxiii.).

requiring deliberation arose, the first care of the bishop was to consult his elders and deacons, the deacons being the "eyes and ears of the bishop," to let him know what the people thought. If there was any doubt about the opinion of the people then the question might be referred to a congregational meeting [1] and deliberated upon by bishop, elders, deacons and people.[2] Cyprian always shows the strongest desire to carry the people along with him.[3] It is not certain whether their opinions were taken in any formal way at the councils held under the presidency of Cyprian at Carthage, but the Christian people of Carthage were always present at the councils.[4] These meetings can hardly be called "representative," as Dr. Benson calls them. An autocrat may do his best to consult the people and to carry them along with him. Yet he can scarcely be called their representative.

In fact Cyprian's conception of the bishop as the direct representative, not of his congregation, but of Christ, endued with powers coming directly from God and in no sense from the Christian people, was precisely the reason why his conception of a polity to embody the whole Church has never proved a workable theory; and soon after Cyprian's time it fell before another and very different conception with which Cyprian had no sympathy, and yet to which his own led when his thought of the autocracy of the bishop was applied to a wider field. We can see how his theory failed himself at his sorest need. He

---

[1] *Epistle* xiv 4 (v.). [2] *Epistle* xv. 1 (x.).

[3] Albrecht Ritschl thinks that Cyprian, like many another autocrat, destroyed the aristocracy of the elders and deacons by persuading the people that the monarch's interests and theirs were identical; *Entstehung der altkatholischen Kirche* (1857), p. 558.

[4] Dr. Benson calls Cyprian's councils "representative" assemblies, and is of opinion that they included "a not silent laity"; compare *Cyprian*, pp. 191 430 ff. The presence of the laity at the councils which discussed the question of the lapsed is shown in *Epistles* xvi. 4 (ix.); xvii. 1 (xi.); xix. 2 (xiii); xxx. 5 (xxx.); xxxi. 6 (xxv.); xliii. 7 (xxxix.); lv. 6 (li.); lix. 15 (liv.); lxiv. 1 (lviii.). On the other hand the most natural construction of the following passages gives the idea that none but bishops deliberated and voted:—xliv. (xl.); xlv. 2, 4 (xli.); lix. 13 (liv.); lxiv. 1 (lviii.); lxx. 1 (lxix.); lxvii. 1; lxxiii. 1 (lxxii.); lxxii. 1 (lxxi.).

desired to carry his office-bearers with him. His first idea was to consult with the office-bearers, as was evidently the custom. When he began to doubt whether they would support him he turned to the laity. When he began to doubt whether the laity did not support the presbyters rather than himself, he not obscurely threatened them with the decisions of the neighbouring bishops;[1] and in the end the consultation was not with his elders and deacons, and not with his people, but with the neighbouring bishops, in what was called the first council of Carthage, where the people of Carthage were undoubtedly present, though probably only as overawed assistants.

Another conception of how the universal and visible Church could make its ideal universality apparent to the eyes of men had been introduced before Cyprian's days; it confronted himself during the second great controversy which he had to wage, and it triumphed in the West after his death. More than one bishop of Rome had put forward the idea that the unity of the Christian Church could only be made truly visible when all the Christian churches grouped themselves round the bishop who sat, it was said, in the chair of St. Peter, and whose congregation had its abode in the capital of the civilized world.[2] They justified this claim ecclesiastically by quoting our Lord's words to St. Peter, recorded in Matt. xvi., but its practical strength lay in the fact that they presided over the church in the city of Rome. So strong was Cyprian's influence in the centuries after his death that Roman Catholic canonists felt the need of quoting him as the supporter of their claims for the primacy of the Roman See, and accordingly they have interpolated his *De Unitate Ecclesiae*

[1] *Epistles* xv. 1 (x.); xliii. 7 (xxxix.).

[2] Victor did so in the days of the Easter controversy and was denounced for so doing by Irenaeus (Eusebius, *Hist. Eccles.* V. xxiii., xxiv.); Calixtus evidently made the same claims and was attacked with bitter sarcasm by Tertullian in his *De Pudicitia*; Stephen did so in the controversy about the baptism by heretics, and the assumption of the bishop of Rome to force his opinion on the rest of the Church is no doubt alluded to by the phrases *Episcopus episcoporum* and *tyrannico terrore* found in the preface to the opinions of the African bishops.

in a manner almost beyond belief.¹ Cyprian was the determined opponent of this theory of a primacy in Rome, and constituted himself, as has been said, the champion of the ecclesiastical parity of all bishops, however insignificant their positions might be, nor would he allow any distinction to be drawn between churches founded by actual apostles and those which had come into being in later times.² He did concede a certain pre-eminence to Rome, partly on ecclesiastical grounds, and partly because of the greatness of the city.³ But he held that all bishops had equal ecclesiastical rights, and that the unity of the Church found expression in a united episcopate and not in the primacy of an episcopus episcoporum.

At the same time it was almost inevitable that Cyprian's idea that the local church was constituted in the local bishop to such an extent that without obedience to him men could not belong to the Church at all, should lead to the conception that a united episcopate could only be truly united if all the bishops owed obedience to one bishop of bishops. A one-man theory of the local church could hardly fail to suggest or to support a one-man

---

[1] The extraordinary history of the interpolations is told by Dr. Benson on pp. 200-21 in his *Cyprian, his Life, his Times, his Work*; and in Hartel, *S. Thasci Caecili Cypriani Opera Omnia*, pp. lii. ff.

[2] Compare *Epistle* lxxi. 3, where the reference to *novellis et posteris* indicates that Stephen had claimed a primacy over *ecclesias novellas et posteras*. Dr. Benson has given a very full analysis of the passages in which Cyprian refers to the Roman See; compare his *Cyprian*, pp. 193-99. It is worth noticing that Firmilian of Cesarea in Cappadocia concedes less to Rome than Cyprian does. He scoffs at Stephen's claim to hold the *Successio Petri* (*Epistle* lxxv. 17 (lxxiv.); but then he holds that the power to forgive sins was given to *churches* as well as to bishops, which is not Cyprian's position (lxxv. 16 [lxxiv.]); "Therefore the power of remitting sins was given to the apostles, and to the *churches* which they, sent by Christ, established and to bishops who succeeded them by vicarious ordination." Otto Ritschl has carefully analysed Cyprian's letters in the dispute with Stephen of Rome in which a good deal of strong language was exchanged between the two bishops; compare *Cyprian von Karthago*, pp. 110-41.

[3] *Epistle* lii. 2 (xlviii.):—pro magnitudine sua debeat Carthaginem Roma praecedere.

theory of the Church universal. The theory that the bishop owed his power, not to the influence of the Spirit of God working in and through the Christian community, but to something either given by God directly or transmitted in such a way as to be independent of the spiritual life of the membership and above it, could scarcely fail to suggest a transmission of unique prerogatives to the bishop who was supposed to occupy the chair of St. Peter. Men who insist on an episcopal gift of grace, "specific, exclusive, efficient," coming from a source higher than the Holy Spirit working in and through the membership of the Church, may protest against the thought that their theories lead to the conception of a "bishop of bishops," but the unsparing logic of history sweeps their protests aside.

CHAPTER VIII

THE ROMAN STATE RELIGION AND ITS EFFECTS ON THE ORGANIZATION OF THE CHURCH

THE Decian persecution, instead of stamping out Christianity, strengthened it. When it was over the Christian churches, pruned of their weaker members, felt stronger than ever, and pressed forward more earnestly in the path of organization and consolidation. The grouping of churches round definite centres became more conspicuous, the gradations of rank among bishops began to assume a more distinct form, a large number of bishops began to be more than simple pastors of congregations, and the lower classes of office-bearers were multiplied. The " great " Church, in short, assumed more than before the appearance of an organized whole.

The apostle Paul had taught his mission churches the secret of mutual support which might come from building up groups of churches arranged according to the provinces of the Roman Empire ; and two churches, in the two chief centres of the Empire, Rome and Alexandria, early manifested a genius for attracting within their respective spheres of influence the weaker churches around them. Both were eminently fitted to be the protectors and guides of their fellow Christian communities. They both occupied commanding positions; they were wealthy and could assist poorer churches ; and they were generally models of Christian generosity to their weaker brethren. The early pre-eminence of Alexandria and of Rome can be accounted for in the most natural ways. When the local church came to be almost identified with the personality of its chief pastor, the preeminence of the church was merged in the wide influence—almost rule—of its bishop. Perhaps the chief pastor of the Church in Alexandria was the first to stand forth as the undoubted leader of the great majority of Christians and of all the confederated churches of the vast and wealthy province of Egypt and the surrounding lands. In the fourth century and in the beginning of the fifth Athanasius and his successors wielded a personal power and were called Popes, long before the bishop of Rome had attained equal influence in the West. But if the growth of the influence of Rome was slower everything combined to make it surer, more lasting, and of much wider extent. The Church in Rome belonged to the capital of the civilized world. The Roman Empire, down to the time of Diocletian, was, in legal fiction at any rate, the rule of a town-council over the world, and this naturally suggested the commanding influence of a single kirk-session over all the other churches. This suggestion, never wholly realized, loomed before the Roman Church from a very early time; but its partial realization was much later than our period. What presents itself from the middle of the third century onwards to the time of Constantine is the increasing tendency in the churches to form groups more or less compact round central churches occupying commanding positions in the Empire, and the churches of Rome and Alexandria are distinguished examples of such great centres of groups of churches.

The instrument in effecting this grouping was the council or synod. Nothing could be more natural than that the leaders of Christian churches should meet to talk over the affairs of the communities under their charge, and the earliest known instance of this was the journey of Polycarp to visit Anicetus at Rome in 154 A.D.[1] This, however, could scarcely be called the beginning of councils. They, i.e., the councils, are frequently traced back to the meeting at Jerusalem, when the apostles,

[1] Eusebius, *Hist. Eccles.* V. xxiv. 16.

the elders, and the whole Church assembled to consider the question of receiving into "fellowship" the uncircumcised Gentile converts of Paul and Barnabas. But since, so far as we know, more than one hundred years elapsed without the example of the Church in Jerusalem being imitated, it can scarcely be urged that this meeting was regarded as the precedent which was followed. Most historians see the real beginnings of the councils in meetings "of the faithful," held frequently and in many places in Asia Minor, when the difficulties created by the Montanist movement (160-180 A.D.) demanded consultation; and the anticipations of councils may be found in that frequent intercourse by means of letters and special messengers which was such a marked feature of the early life of the Christian communities.

It is not easy to know what these earliest councils were like or who formed their members. They were most probably informal meetings of the pastors, elders, deacons and people, and it is likely that all present were permitted to take part in the conference and have a voice in its decisions. The prevailing troubles were talked over and the best way of meeting them. Whatever resolutions were come to had no legal force, but they naturally led to common action within the communities represented. Eusebius gives a graphic account of these earliest gatherings. An elder who had strong views on the Montanist movement found himself in Ancyra where Montanist sympathizers abounded, and where some active partisans had exerted considerable influence on the people. He and a fellow-elder had conferences with the people in the church, which lasted for days. The whole question was debated with earnestness in presence of the people, who were intensely interested in the matter. At length, after long discussions, the Montanist champions were driven away and their sympathizers silenced. The elders of Ancyra begged the visitor to write down his arguments for their use in case the question should be brought up again. It is added that the faithful in many places had frequent conferences which doubtless resembled those at Ancyra.[1] The technical words used, "brotherhood," "faithful," imply that all Christians, lay and clerical, took part in the discussion and settlement of the matter discussed. Such were these earliest synods.

We next hear of them in the Easter controversy (about 190 A.D.). Eusebius, writing more than a hundred years later, calls them "Synods and Conferences of bishops," but when he quotes contemporary evidence, such as that of Irenaeus, the technical terms used mean that the opinion of the whole Christian "brotherhood" was expressed. Letters were written in the name of the παροικίαι and of the brethren of Gaul;[2] and "brethren" or the "brotherhood" is the word which even in Cyprian denoted the laity,[3] while παροικία in these early days "was neither a parish nor a diocese, but the community of Christians living within a city or a district, regarded in relation to the non-Christian population which surrounded it."[4]

Tertullian, writing about 210 A.D., speaks as if it were a common practice to hold councils regularly throughout Greece, and praises the double advantage that accrued from such meetings—the handling of the deeper questions of Christian life for the common benefit and the bringing vividly before the minds of the people the fact of the universality of Christianity.[5] Afterwards synods were held in Africa, the earliest recorded being about 220 A.D.,[6] and gradually they spread over the Christian world.

[1] Compare Eusebius, *Hist. Eccles.* V. xvi. 4, 10; xix. 2.
[2] Eusebius, *Hist. Eccles.* V. xxiii. 2; xix. 2.
[3] Cyprian, *Epistles,* xvi. 2 (ix.); xviii. 1, 2 (xii.); xx. 2 (xiv.); xlvi. 2 (xliii.).
[4] Hatch, *The Organization of the Early Christian Churches* (1881), p. 190.
[5] Tertullian, *De Jejunio,* 13 :—" Aguntur praeterea per Graecias illa certis in locis concilia ex universis ecclesiis per quae et *altiora quaeque in commune* tractantur, *et ipsa repraesentatio totius nominis christiani magna veneratione* celebratur."
[6] The synod at which Agrippinus presided and which declared that baptism administered by heretics was void; compare Cyprian, *Epistles,* lxxi. 4 (lxx.); lxxiii. 3 (lxxii.).

These synods or councils were the means whereby the grouping of local churches, great and small, around great centres, was effected. They formed such a very important part of the organization of the Church in the third and fourth centuries that it is important to understand what they were and what they became. Dr. Rudolf Sohm,[1] whose life-work has been the study of ecclesiastical law and whose acquaintance with its manifestations in the early centuries is excelled by none, has collected and pieced together all the information that can be gathered from the allusions of earliest Christian literature to this subject, and has worked out something like the following theory of the origin and primitive meaning of the synod. Briefly stated, it is that a synod, in the second and third centuries, was, to begin with, a means whereby a congregation or local church received in any time of perplexity or anxiety the aid of the Church universal represented by esteemed Christians not belonging to the congregation. He combines, and rightly combines, the accounts of such synods as are mentioned above with the accounts transmitted about the way in which the pastors or bishops were chosen and appointed to their congregations or local churches, for it is plain that one of the uses of a synod in the third century was seen in the choice and appointment of the bishop over his flock.

So far as ecclesiastical regulations go, the need which a small and weak congregation had for assistance from without was first recognized when it was made a regulation that a Christian community of less than twelve families, which was required to organize itself under a bishop, was to seek the help of the nearest " well-established " churches. The weak congregation was ordered to ask for the assistance of three selected men, and with them, as assessors, the choice and appointment of the bishop was to be made. These three men associated with the congregation formed a synod of the earliest and simplest

[1] Sohm, *Kirchenrecht*, i. 247–343.

type. The regulation dates from the middle of the second century.[1]

When this central thought has once been grasped illustrations are abundant. In the conference at Jerusalem about the admission of uncircumcised converts into the Christian Church, a conference in which delegates from Antioch sought the advice of a "well-established" Church, the congregational meeting of the Jerusalem Church appointed delegates to carry down its advice to the congregation or local church at Antioch and to assist the brethren there in coming to a proper decision upon so important a matter. The real synod was held at Antioch,[2] and its members were the delegates from Jerusalem and the community at Antioch. At the close of the first century disturbances arose in the Church at Corinth, and the Roman Church, a well-established Church, which may or may not have been appealed to, sent a letter of advice and along with it *three* men selected because of their age, repute and experience.[3] These, with the congregation at Corinth, formed a synod at Corinth of the primitive type, and no doubt helped the community there out of their difficulties. So with the early synods in Asia Minor. In the perplexity caused by the Montanist movement the congregation at Ancyra sought the aid of Zoticus Otrenus and others; they, together with the members of the congregation at Ancyra, formed the council there and doubtless aided in the other councils which they wrote about to Avircius Marcellus. Judas and Silas, the deputies from Jerusalem to Antioch, were prophets;[5] the Roman deputies who went to Corinth, Claudius Ephebus, Valerius Bito and Fortunatus, do not seem to have been office-bearers; Zoticus Otrenus and his fellows were elders. There is no mention of bishops with regard to any of these earliest councils, but it is easily conceivable

---

[1] *Texte und Untersuchungen*, II. v. 7. 8; found in English in *The Sources of the Apostolic Canons* (1895), p. 8.
[2] Acts xv. 27, 30-34.   [3] Clement, 1 *Epistle*, lxv. 1.
[4] Eusebius, *Hist. Eccles.* V. xvi.   [5] Acts xv. 32.

that when "well-established" churches were asked to send delegates, "select men," to advise and assist, no men could be more suitable than were the bishops of the churches appealed to, and that bishops always formed a portion, if not the whole, of the advising deputies or assessors. The point to be observed however is that in the earliest councils or synods, whether assembled for the purpose of the appointment of a pastor or bishop or for the purpose of giving counsel in times of trouble or anxiety, the main part of the synod is the congregational meeting of the church to which the delegates come. It is also pre-supposed in the earliest times that "well-established" congregations did not need the assistance of a synod in the appointment of their chief pastor, and that everything from selection to ordination could be done within the congregation.

When the third century was reached it soon became the custom, though we do not find any ecclesiastical regulation on the subject until much later,[1] that the choice and ordination of the chief pastor was performed through a synod in *all* local churches, whether "well-established" or not, and that the neighbouring bishops were called in to be assessors to assist the congregational meeting. The desire to make the unity of the whole Church visibly manifest doubtless inspired the demand that a synod, i.e., at least three bishops or pastors from the neighbouring churches should assist at the selection of the chief pastor in a vacant congregation and confirm the choice of the people by their ordination. Still through the whole of the third century the primitive idea prevailed that the congregational meeting

---

[1] The earliest appearance of this usage as a fixed ecclesiastical law is to be found in the twentieth canon of the council of Arles (314 A.D.):—
"De his qui usurpant sibi, quod soli debeant episcopos ordinare, placuit ut nullus hoc sibi praesumat nisi assumptis secum aliis *septem* episcopis. Si tamen non potuerit septem, infra tres non audeat ordinare." This twentieth canon of Arles reappeared in the fourth canon of Nicea (325 A.D.), then almost continually (Council of Laodicea, canon 13; Council of Antioch, canon 19; Council of Toledo [4th] canon 19) until the regulation became incorporated in canon law. It appears in the *Apostolic Constitutions*, iii. 20.

was an integral part of the synod. In the case of a vacant pastorate the new pastor was chosen both by the neighbouring bishops and by the Christian people with the elders at their head, and, even when the selection came to be mainly in the hands of the assembled bishops, the assent of the people was always necessary. The ordination, which, in the course of the third century, was placed exclusively in the hands of the assembled bishops, was the sign of the visible unity of the Church, extending far beyond the bounds of the local church, and made the ordained pastor not only the minister of the Church over which he was ordained, but also a minister of the Church universal.[1]

[1] It is impossible to avoid seeing how the mode of appointment and ordination of the chief pastor now practised in the great Presbyterian Church in its many branches corresponds both in essentials and even in some unessentials with the mode in use in the third century as that is described in the letters of Cyprian and in the canons of Hippolytus. It is to be premised that the bishop of the third century was in ninety-nine cases out of a hundred the chief pastor of a single congregation and in the hundredth was at the head of a collegiate Church such as we see in the Dutch and in some German branches of the Presbyterian Church; and that bishop and pastor are interchangeable terms (Cyprian, *Epist.* lxvi. 5; compare also Eusebius, *Hist. Eccl.* VII. xxviii. 1, where certain bishops are called " pastors of the communities in Pontus "). We have the following picture common to both. When the office of chief pastor becomes vacant there is a natural anxiety among the people and especially among the elders to secure a good successor. They correspond with neighbouring ministers (Cyprian, *Epist.* lxvii. 5; lv. 8) and receive testimonies in favour of one or of another. When they are ready for an appointment, the ministers of the bounds (the bishops of the province) meet formally in the presence of the elders and of the people of the church (the brotherhood, Cyprian calls them, lxvii. 5); an examination is made of the state of feeling in the congregation, of the unanimity of choice (" the suffrage of the whole brotherhood," Cyprian, lxvii. 5; lix. 6), and objections are called for, if there be any, against the life or doctrine of the person nominated (Cyprian, lxvii. 5); then follows the solemn ordination in presence of the assembled congregation. He who has been chosen kneels before the president or moderator who places his hands on his head; all the ministers present join with the president in laying their hands on the head of the bishop or pastor-elect; the president prays over him the prayer of consecration in which God, Who gave the Holy Spirit in the early times to His apostles, prophets, pastors and teachers, is asked to bestow the same Spirit on the

Synods assembled for other purposes than the selection and ordination of chief pastors exhibit the same fact that the congregational meeting was an integral part of the synod. Thus in Carthage, Cyprian insisted that the neighbouring bishops were to be asked to assist at the determination of what was to be done in the case of the lapsed, because it was a matter which concerned "not a few, nor of one church," or it could have been decided in the congregational meeting, "nor of one province, but of the whole world."[1] It had to be settled by the presence of the African bishops at Carthage and by correspondence with Rome. But in any case the presence of the congregation of Carthage was presupposed, and the African bishops were an addition for the time being to the ordinary meeting of the elders and the brotherhood.[2]

The same thought is seen working at Rome. The Roman elders (there being no bishop) dealing with the same question of the lapsed, called to their aid some of the bishops who were near them and within reach, and some whom, placed afar off, the heat of persecution had driven from their congregations.[3] When the conduct of Novatian was causing great anxiety, Cornelius, the bishop, called together his elders and *invited five bishops* to assist them in their deliberations. When they had settled what was to be done they called together a great meeting of the congregation, and there the decisive resolution was brought forward and accepted.[4] So with other Roman synods on the

---

pastor-elect, who is named in the prayer (*Directory for the Ordination of Ministers*, sec. 8; *Canons of Hippolytus*, iii. 11-19). In both cases the presence of the ministers of the bounds (bishops of the province) implies that the act done within the individual congregation is an act of the Catholic Church and that the chief pastor in the local church is also a minister of the universal Church of Christ.

[1] Cyprian, *Epistle* xix. 2 (xiii.).

[2] Compare the phrases—"*secundum arbitrium vestrum et omnium nostrum commune consilium,*" *Epist.* xliii. 7 (xxxix.); "Cum episcopis, presbyteris, diaconis, confessoribus pariter ac *stantibus laicis,*" *Epist.* lv. 5 (li.); and so on in many passages. But compare above, p. 316 n.

[3] Cyprian, *Epistle* xxx. 8 (xxx.).   [4] Cyprian, *Epistle* xlix. 2 (xlv.).

same questions; the elders, deacons and the congregation at Rome were always present, and the whole meeting was one of the Roman congregation with several (once sixty) bishops added to assist them in their deliberations.[1] The same conception of the synod existed in the East. The celebrated synod held at Bostra in Arabia (244 A.D.) at which a large number of bishops were present, and where Origen held a distinguished place is a case in point. The question was the orthodoxy of the pastor of Bostra, Beryllus by name. The discussions, in the course of which Beryllus renounced his errors, took place ἐπὶ τῆς παροικίας,[2] from which we may conclude that the synod included the congregational meeting, for *paroichia* always means in early ecclesiastical usage the brotherhood or congregation, and not parish or diocese in the modern sense of these terms. Indications of the same usage are to be found in the account of the celebrated synods held at Antioch about Paul of Samosata, the pastor of the church there. A great number of bishops, elders and deacons were present, and took part in the discussions which must have included the congregational meeting, as the bishop was deposed, and Domnus was ordained in his place at the last Synod. Here we have the interesting fact that the chief discussion was between Malchion, one of the elders of the Church at Antioch, and his bishop, and that the assembled bishops who came from a distance took the side of the elder against his pastor. The whole aspect of the matter presents the appearance of a congregational meeting enlarged by the presence of a number of bishops from without; the theological differences between the pastor and the elder, which had no doubt been frequently discussed before a smaller audience, were brought before the assembled bishops and congregation. Malchion, who led the charge against his pastor, signed the decisions of the synod along with others.[3]

---

[1] Eusebius, *Hist. Eccles.* VI. xliii. 2.   [2] *Ibid.* VI. xxxiii. 3.

[3] The Synods held about Paul of Samosata are described in Eusebius *Hist. Eccles.* VII. xxvii.-xxx.). The case is a curious one. Complaints

Dr. Sohm completes his theory by these additional suggestions. He holds that the power of a synod was always proportional to the power of the local meeting it incorporated. If the bishops came to the assistance of the body of elders in a church, their decision had only the force of a regulation issued by a session of elders. It had to be submitted to the congregational meeting before it became authoritative. If, on the other hand, the meeting of bishops incorporated a congregational meeting, then its decisions were authoritative at once, for the final decision always lay with the congregational meeting.[1] He also believes that any synod, even if only the minimum of three bishops was present with the congregation, was believed to represent and ideally was the whole Catholic Church of Christ,[2] taking into its embrace the congregation or local church which required aid, and that in

---

against his orthodoxy, and many other things, seem to have been brought forward by members of his congregation, or at least by a section of them headed by Malchion, one of the elders and the head of a high school in Antioch. It was an instance of an orthodox elder and a portion of the congregation accusing their pastor of heresy. These men called to their aid a number of bishops. These bishops assembled at Antioch, apparently in Paul's church, and Paul presided at the meetings. At the first synod no conclusion was come to; so at the second; at the third, Paul was deposed and Domnus was ordained in his place (probably in 268 A.D.). At this third synod the chief discussion was between Paul and his elder, Malchion; their speeches were taken down in shorthand, and copies were in existence in the sixth century. The result of the decision of the synod was a division in the congregation at Antioch, the larger portion evidently siding with their pastor Paul, who retained possession of the Church buildings and of all the property. It is more than likely that political feeling lay behind this prosecution. The Romans, under the Emperor Aurelian, wished to gain posession of Antioch, which then belonged to Queen Zenobia. There was a Roman party in Antioch; and Paul was a resolute partizan of Zenobia. Six years later, when the queen was conquered by Aurelian, and Antioch came within the Roman Empire, the Church property was taken from Paul and given to the portion of the congregation which had opposed him. As all Christians were still outlaws in the eyes of Roman law, it is scarcely probable that this decision followed from the supposed heresy of Paul. It is more easy to believe that it was meant to be a punishment dealt to the anti-Roman faction. Compare Harnack, *History of Dogma*, Eng. Trans., iii. 38 f.

[1] Cyprian, *Epistle* xlix. 2 (xlv).   [2] Tertullian, *De Jejunio*, 13.

consequence its decisions were believed to express the utterances of the Spirit of God promised to the Church of Christ.

We may accept or reject Dr. Sohm's interesting theory. It appears to me to be too ideal to be an exact representation of all the facts of the case. But it seems to be made plain from the evidence he marshals, that there was a close connexion between the congregational meeting and the synods which played such an important part in the federation of the churches in the third and following centuries. The congregational meeting was the primitive type of the later synod. These congregational meetings had taken an important place in the churches from the beginning.[1] We have seen how they formed the centre and source of authority in the apostolic period; how they had the supreme power in their hands in the churches to which Ignatius sent his letters, and how even Cyprian deferred to them.[2] They were the authority in the churches in their primitive democratic stage.

If left to itself the democratic genius of Christianity might have evolved an organization which, starting from the unit of the congregational meeting, and rising through a series of synods with widening areas of jurisdiction, might have culminated in a really representative oecumenical council or synod which would have given a visible unity of organization to the whole Christian Church, and at the same time would have preserved its primitive democratic organization.

Cyprian's unscriptural and non-primitive conception of the pastor or bishop as an autocrat, claiming a personal obedience so entire that any act of disobedience was to be punished by spiritual death or expulsion from the Church, contradicted the democratic ideal which the congregational meeting embodied. His principle that the bishop was an autocrat deriving his power from God directly by a species of divine right which owed nothing to the power of the Spirit working in and through the Christian people, might be based on a misapplication of Old Testament

[1] Compare above, p. 54 ff.   [2] Compare above, p. 200 f.

texts and on an intrusion of the Old Testament priesthood into the New Testament Church, but in reality it was the introduction into the Christian Church of the Roman ideas of authority and imperial rule. These early centuries were times of imperial government, and democratic rule, save within limited areas and subject to autocratic checks, was a thing unknown. It is true that the Roman method of government admitted a great deal of local self-government of various kinds, but these popular assemblies had strictly limited spheres of action and had no control over the imperial officers who practically ruled the provinces in the name of the emperor or of the senate.[1] Cyprian's conception of the autocracy of the bishop accorded so well with the atmosphere of imperialist rule in which the Church of the third century lived that it could scarcely avoid being largely adopted. In spite of Cyprian's own limitation of the autocratic idea to the office of bishop it suggested another form of organization beginning with the bishop, rising through metropolitans, etc., to an episcopus episcoporum, who in that age could be none other than the bishop of the Church in the capital of the empire. No sooner had Cyprian's conception of the autocracy of the bishop of the local church been accepted than the path was clearly marked for an ascending scale of autocrats up to the bishop of Rome, and the appellation of Pontifex Maximus sarcastically employed by Tertullian became the legitimate title of the head of the Church in the capital city.

Thus there were two ideals of organization within the Christian churches. On the one hand, an autocratic organization which starting with the bishop as the autocrat of the individual Christian community ascended through metropolitans to the Pope; and, on the other, that which, starting from the congregational

[1] Marquardt, *Roemische Staatsverwaltung*, i. pp. 503-16, gives the details known about the provincial assemblies under the Imperial Government; their powers (507-9); the provinces where they existed (509-16) and the powers of the imperial officials (517 ff.). A good deal of information on the subject is also to be found in Mommsen, *The Provinces of the Roman Empire*.

meeting, ascended through provincial councils of varying importance to an oecumenical council of the whole Church. These two ideals, mutually antagonistic as they were, subsisted side by side within the Christian Church in the end of the third and continued to do so in the succeeding six or seven centuries. Neither was powerful enough to overcome the other. The imperialist conception proved the stronger in the West, as was natural, and the other was the more powerful in the East, but neither in the East nor in the West was the one able to vanquish the other.

In the end of the third century and onwards councils or synods became a regular part of the organization of the whole Church, and they became more and more meetings of bishops only, at which presbyters and deacons with the people of the church of the town where the council met were present but almost entirely as spectators. It was natural that these councils should meet in the provincial capitals, for the roads and the imperial postal system by which travellers could journey all converged towards those towns which were the seats of the Roman provincial administration. Conferences require chairmen, and various usages obtained with reference to the natural chairman. Frequently the oldest bishop was made the president of the assembly, and this continued to be the practice for a long time in many parts of the empire. But gradually it became the custom to place in the chair the head of the Christian community of the town in which the council met. The bishops of these towns then began to be called *metropolitans*, but the title was for a long time merely one of courtesy only, and did not carry with it any ecclesiastical rank with specific authority attached to it. In the fourth century these *metropolitans* were entrusted with the right to call the provincial councils and even with some superintendence over the election and ordination of the bishops of the province. Of course the man made the office, and metropolitans who had great personal gifts and force of character insensibly gave their churches and their successors an influence which lasted. In this growth of the metropolitan organization we can detect a disposition to be guided by the civil organization of the empire.[1]

The second third of the third century also witnessed changes in the organization of the individual local churches. The tendency was for the bishop to become more than the pastor of a single congregation. It worked both in country districts and in towns. Perhaps one of the chief causes of this was that it had become the custom to require from the chief pastors the devotion of their whole time to their ecclesiastical duties, and this implied that the Church had to provide the means of livelihood at least for the bishops.

We have already seen that whenever a small group of Christians found themselves together, even when they were fewer than twelve families, they were ordered to constitute themselves into a Christian Church with an organization of bishop, elders, deacons, reader and "widows."[2] The smallest Christian community was in this way an independent church. But this was possible only so long as the bishop did not depend for his living on a stipend coming from the congregation. A paid pastorate altered matters. The alteration took two forms, both of which can be seen working among churches in the mission field.

A very common modern form is to appoint one man the pastor of several village churches among which he itinerates, while one or more elders and deacons are stationed in the little Christian village communities to watch over the spiritual interests of the people. Inscriptions seem to prove that this form existed in the uplands of Batanea among the small and scattered villages there, and it probably existed in other places.[3]

When a small group of villagers had been won to Christianity through the evangelizing work of a congregation in the neigh-

---

[1] Compare Hatch, *The Organization of the Early Christian Churches* (1881), pp. 169, 170; also articles on *Metropolitan, Primate,* and *Patriarchate* in the *Dictionary of Christian Antiquities.*

[2] *Texte und Untersuchungen*, II. v. pp. 7–24; *The Sources of the Apostolic Canons*, pp. 7–27.

[3] Hatch, *Organization of the Early Christian Churches*, 194.

bouring town, there was often a great unwillingness to sever the connexion between them and the mother Church. We learn from Justin Martyr [1] that the Christians came in from the country to attend the services of the town congregation. It was always held that a bishop could delegate his special function pertaining to public worship to his elders or even to his deacons. This principle could easily be applied to the outlying mission districts of a congregation, and the little mission congregations became *filials* or daughters of the town congregation, and were served by the subordinate office-bearers of the mother Church. Thus the bishop became the pastor in several congregations and multiplied himself through his elders who became his delegates in the pastoral office. In doing this the Church followed civil procedure, for rural authorities under Roman rule were frequently placed under the nearest municipality. But we have abundant evidence that for many a century multitudes of the small rural congregations remained independent churches, under bishops who were often enough uneducated peasants.[2]

The same principle worked in towns also, and perhaps more strongly there. The bishop was held to be the head of the Christian community in one place, whatever its size might be. He was the pastor ; he baptized ; he presided at the Holy Supper ; he admitted catechumens to the full communion of the brotherhood. By the middle of the third century the work, in most large towns, was more than one man could overtake. Take the case of Rome. We have no record of the number of the Christian community, but we know that at the close of the Decian persecution, i.e., a little after the middle of the third century, the number of widows, sick and poor cared for by the Church was more than fifteen hundred, and that the bishop had to assist him forty-six elders, fourteen deacons and sub-deacons, with ninety-two men in what are called minor orders—acolytes,

---

[1] Justin Martyr, *Apology*, i. 67 :—" On the day called Sunday, all who live in the cities or in the country gather together to one place."
[2] Eusebius, *Hist Eccles.* VI. xliii. 8.

exorcists, readers, and door-keepers.[1] At the close of the century and during the Diocletian persecution there were over forty Christian basilicas, or separate Christian congregations in Rome itself.[2] In Alexandria the number of Christians could not have been much fewer. It is evident that one man could not fulfil the pastoral duties for such a multitude. At first the idea of the unity of the pastorate was strictly preserved. For example, it was for long the custom in Rome that the bishop consecrated the communion elements in one church, and that the consecrated elements were carried to the other congregations whether they met in churches or in private houses, to be distributed to the communicants by the elders there in charge.[3] The bishop was the one pastor in every congregation; the elders and the deacons belonged to the whole local Christian community; they served all the congregations and were not attached to any one; the organization was collegiate as we see it existing at present in the Dutch Presbyterian Church. All communities, however, were not so conservative as that of Rome. In Alexandria, for example, while the Christians who lived in the outlying suburbs were at first reckoned to be members of the bishop's congregation and had no separate constitution for the churches in which they met, this was found to be inconvenient. Special presbyters were set over the outlying congregations, and thus something like a parish system under the bishop was begun. But the original pastoral status of the bishop was always preserved by one portion of the pastoral duties being invariably retained in his hands—the admission of the catechumens to the full communion of the Church. This is still

[1] Compare the letter of Cornelius, bishop of Rome, to Fabius, bishop of Antioch, in Eusebius, *Hist. Eccles.* VI. xliii. 11.

[2] Optatus of Milevis, *De Schismate Donatistarum*, ii. 4 (Vienna ed. [1893], p. 39).

[3] This custom existed in the time of Innocent the First (450 A.D.) and is described by him in a letter he wrote to Decentius, bishop of Eugubium in Umbria; compare the fifth section. The custom preserved the conjunction of ideas strongly insisted upon by Cyprian between the one sacrament and the one bishop.

retained in the modern episcopal system, and the fact that the bishops alone are entitled to receive the young communicants at confirmation—for confirmation is simply the reception of young communicants—remains to witness to the original simple pastoral functions of the primitive bishops.

The middle of the third century also was the time when the ministry became much more complicated so far as its subordinate officials were concerned. Sub-deacons, exorcists, readers, acolytes, doorkeepers, and even grave-diggers, were added to that body of men who were called the clergy.

Before the close of the third century the associated churches, grouped now around recognized centres, had developed a somewhat elaborate organization both in their relations to each other and in the arrangement of the ministry within the individual local churches. Ecclesiastical archaeologists are disposed to recognize the influence of the political organization of the Roman Empire in much of this elaboration.[1] This is a perfectly natural explanation and there is abundant evidence to confirm it. Yet it may be that there was something more specific on which the leaders of the Christian churches had their eyes fixed. If it should ever become possible for the associated churches to come to terms with the empire, as was done in the fourth century, there was an organization which the Christian Church would necessarily displace. This was the great provincial organization for providing for the due exercise of the official religion of the empire. No account of the Church and its ministry during the early centuries can avoid some reference to that great Pagan State Church (if the term may be used), as it existed towards the close of the third century when the associated Christian churches were rapidly approaching the

---

[1] This has been done with great erudition and much original investigation by the late Dr. Hatch. The results of his work are to be found in his Bampton Lectures, *The Organization of the Early Christian Churches* (1881), and in many of his articles in the *Dictionary of Christian Antiquities* on *Orders, Ordination, Primate, Patriarchate.*

attainment of their end, and were about to give their religion to the Roman Empire.

The subject is a difficult one. Information has to be sought for in inscriptions on tombs, on public buildings, on coins and in fast fading frescoes on the walls of houses in Pompeii. It is full of details which are only partially known, and yet enough has been preserved to enable us to learn something about it as a whole.[1]

It is the universal testimony of historians that religion had lost most of its power during the later years of the Republic. The temples were in ruins and the practices of religion were

[1] Among the more important books and articles on the subject of the imperial cult the following may be named. They all discuss the subject as a whole or describe some important parts. G. Boissier, *La Religion Romaine d'Auguste aux Antonins* (1878), 2 vols.; Otto Hirschfeld, *Zur Geschichte des römischen Kaisercultus* in the *Sitzungsberichte d. k. pr. Akademie d. Wissensch.*, Berlin (1888), pp. 833 ff.; also his *I Sacerdozi municipali nell' Africa* in the *Annali dell' Instituto di correspondenza archaeologica* for 1866, pp. 22-77; V. Dury, *Formation d'une Religion officielle dans l'Empire Romaine* in the *Comptes rendus* of the *Académie des sciences morales et politiques*, vol. xiv. (1880), pp. 328 ff.; E. Desjardins, *Le Culte des Divi et le Culte de Rome et d'Auguste* in the *Revue de Philologie*, vol. iii. (1879). pp. 33 ff. R. Mowat, *La Domus divina et les Divi* in the *Bull. epigr. de la Gaule*, vol. v. (1885), pp. 221 ff., 308 ff., and vi. (1886), pp. 31 ff., 137 ff., 272 ff.; P. Giraud, *Les Assemblées provinciales sous l'Empire Romaine* (1890); Lebegue, *L'Inscription de l'ara Narbonensis* in the *Revue Archéologique* (1892), vol. xliii. new series, pp. 76-86, 176-84; M. Krascheninnikoff, in the *Philologus* (1894), vol. liii. (new series, vol. vii.), pp. 147 ff.; E. Beurlier, *Le Culte Impériale, son histoire et son organisation depuis Auguste jusqu'à Justinien* (1891) (by far the most complete treatise on the subject). *Handbuch der roemischen Alterthümer* by Mommsen and Marquardt; *Roemische Staatsverwaltung* by Marquardt, 2nd ed. i. 197 f.; iii. 71 ff., 463 ff.; *Roemisches Staatsrecht* by Mommsen, ii. 752 ff.; G. Wissowa, *Religion und Kultus der Roemer* (1902), pp. 71 ff., 82 f., 284 ff., 488 ff. (this gives the most succinct account); Beaudouin, *Le Culte des Empereurs* (1891). A very full account of the literature on the subject will be found in Roscher's *Lexikon*, ii. 901 ff. by Drexler. I have quoted only the books known to me personally. A number of references to the cult of the emperors will be found in Ramsay's *The Church in the Roman Empire* (1893), pp. 133, 191, 250, 275, 249, 304, 323 n., 324, 333, 336 n., 354, 373, 396, 398, 465 f., and in Mau's *Pompeii, its Life and Art* (1899), pp. 14, 61, 89 f., 98, 100, 103 f., 106 f., 111 f., 122 ff., 264 ff.

generally neglected. When the wars which followed the death of Julius Caesar had given the young Octavius the heritage of his mighty uncle, and that master of statecraft set himself to the task of restoring an empire exhausted by long years of civil war, he recognized that a people without a religious faith is in a state of hopeless decadence. One of his earliest tasks was to attempt to revive the ancient religious rites of the Roman people, and contemporary records tell what patience and wealth he lavished on the work. His political needs mingled largely in this successful attempt to revive the religious instincts of his subjects. He felt the need for some common sentiment to bind together the provinces and peoples of his unwieldy Empire. A state which acknowledged no limits of race and of nationality required something more than the will of the emperor and the dread of his legions to unite it into a harmonious whole. He saw that religion might be the moral cement he sought, but the religion needed to be as universal as the empire. To select one of the myriad cults which a manifold paganism presented would have availed him nothing. He turned instinctively to that outburst of popular devotion which had proclaimed his uncle a god in his lifetime, and which, after his death, had demanded that the mighty Julius should be proclaimed as a god with temples reared in his honour, sacrifices offered, and a special priesthood instituted to the new divinity.[1] Out of this popular deification of Julius Caesar there came, fostered by the guiding hand of Octavius, now called Augustus, a universal worship of the Emperor of Rome which took a three-fold shape. In almost every part of the empire, Rome alone excepted, the Emperor Augustus was worshipped as a god during his life-

[1] Julius Caesar was added to the gods of Rome by a decree of the senate and people in 42 B.C.:—Genio Deivi Juli, parentis patriae, quem senatus populusque Romanus in deorum numerum rettulit; cf. Mommsen, *Staatsrecht*, ii. 733. His temple or *aedes Divi Julii in Foro* was consecrated in 29 B.C., and a special *flamen* was appointed for the service of the new divinity. But Julius Caesar was never reckoned as the first of the *Divi Imperatores*; they began with Augustus.

ON THE ORGANIZATION OF THE CHURCH 343

time; there was the institution of the *Divi*, where the dead emperors and some near relations of the imperial house, wives, fathers, uncles and brothers were, by solemn decree of the senate, elevated to the rank of gods of the state and were voted temples, priests, and sacrifices; lastly there was the worship of *Rome and Augustus*, and Augustus in this instance was not so much the name of a particular man as the title of the supreme ruler —a title which itself implied that the prince was something more than man.[1]

The worship of the emperor during his lifetime was never part of the state religion of the Roman Empire, but it was a cult largely practised. Private persons, societies, even communities without sanction from the government built temples, consecrated chapels and instituted priesthoods in honour of Augustus while he was alive.[2] This was not always done openly; it was some time veiled by affecting to recognize the living emperor as embodied in one of the ancient gods. Thus the *ministri Mercurii Maiae* in Pompeii became first the *ministri Augusti Mercurii Maiae*, and then simply the *ministri Augusti*, and Livia was honoured as Ceres, Vesta and Rhea. But this worship of the living rulers was never part of the state religion.

The state religion was, to begin with, the worship of the *Divus Julius* along with that of *Jupiter Optimus Maximus*, *Apollo*, *Vesta* and *Mars Ultor*, in Rome; the worship of *Rome and Divus Julius* for Roman citizens in the provinces, and the worship of *Rome and Augustus* for provincials.

The beginning of this new state religion for the provinces

---

[1] "Imperator cum Augusti nomen accepit, tanquam praesenti et corporali Deo, fidelis est praestanda devotio."

Mommsen says that the word *augustus*, like the Greek σεβαστὸς, had always a religious colouring (worshipful); that it implied power so great as to be revered; that the title was not shared by any one during the lifetime of the Emperor; that Tiberius refused at first to accept it; and that it was at last imposed upon him by a special decree of the senate (*Staatsrecht*, ii. 812).

[2] "Cultores Augusti, qui per omnes domos in modum collegiorum habebantur." Tacitus, *Annals*, i. 73.

was perhaps the decree of Augustus of date 29 B.C., when, in reply to memorials from the communities of Bithynia and of Asia, he issued an order that the provincials were to worship *Rome and Augustus*, and the Roman inhabitants of these provinces *Rome and the Divus Julius*.[1] The new cult of *Rome and Augustus* in Spain dates from 26 B.C.; this worship became the state religion in Roman Gaul from 12 B.C., and it was organized in Roman Africa on the same lines as in Gaul. Thus for the earlier portion of the reign of the first emperor the state religion in the provinces for all but Roman citizens was the worship of *Rome and Augustus*.[2]

It is a question whether this worship of *Rome and Augustus* did not remain the permanent legal form which the imperial cult took in the provinces. Authorities differ and the evidence is not clear enough to admit of a decided answer.[3] Upon the whole the balance of evidence seems to be that even during the lifetime of the first emperor the official religion became the

---

[1] Compare *Dio Cassius*, li. 20; Tacitus, *Annals*, iv. 37; Suetonius, *Augustus*, 52.

[2] *Roma* was never a goddess for the Roman people. The beginnings of the deification of the city of Rome came from the East and were originally symbolic of the trust placed in the Roman State by cities and provinces in the East which had entered into treaties with the great western power and had experienced its protection. The earliest instance known is that of Smyrna, which in 195 B.C. built a temple to *Roma* the protecting deity of the city; the cult spread rapidly; even in Athens there was a temple to *Dea Roma*. In the East it was also the custom to associate as a divinity along with the city great Roman generals whose successes in arms had benefited the towns which created them objects of worship. Augustus had such precedents for *Rome and Augustus* as the earlier *Rome and Flaminius*. (Plutarch, *Flaminus*, 16.)

[3] Beaudouin (*Le Culte des Empereurs*) insists that from first to last the official religion, recognized in legal documents as the State religion in the provinces, was not that of the *Divi Imperatores* but always that of *Rome and Augustus*. This is scarcely probable; still before coming to an accurate conclusion the inscriptions found in every province would need to be gone over and analysed province by province; this has been done so far as I know for two provinces only—that of Narbonne by M. Beaudouin himself and that of Africa by Prof. Otto Hirschfeld.

ON THE ORGANIZATION OF THE CHURCH 345

worship of *Augustus* simply (*Rome* being left out) and *Augustus*[1] being taken to mean, not the person of the emperor but the symbol of the deification of the Roman state personified in its ruler. After the death of the first emperor a new development took place. Augustus, who during his lifetime had never allowed himself to be called *Divus*, but only *Filius Divi Julii*, was by solemn decree of the senate on September, 17, 14 A.D. (he had died at Nola on the 19th of August preceding) awarded divine honours, and took rank among the superior gods of Rome.[2] He was the first of a long line of *Divi Imperatores*, and the state religion assumed the form it continued to maintain in strict legal conception till the time of Diocletian and practically till the conversion of Constantine and the changes which followed that important event.

So far as Rome itself was concerned these *Divi Imperatores*, i.e., the series of emperors who were consecrated after death[3] by decree of the senate, along with the *Genius*[4] of the reigning

---

[1] Suetonius says distinctly:—"Templa quamvis sciret etiam proconsulibus decerni solere; in nulla tamen provincia nisi communi suo Romaeque nomine recepit" (*Augustus*, 52). Yet the evidence from inscriptions would leave us to infer that the cult of Augustus was instituted in many provinces without any mention of Roma.

[2] "D.XV. (Kal. Oct.) nefastus prior ludi in circo feriae ex senatus-consulto quod eo die divo Augusto honores caelestes a senatu decreti; Sex. Appuleio, Sex. Pompeio cos."

[3] Some emperors were never consecrated *Divi*; of the eleven emperors from Augustus to Nerva only four—Augustus, Claudius, Vespasian and Titus—were deified, but after Nerva the consecration of the emperor after death became the rule which had very few exceptions. On the other hand as the years passed the consecration of members of the imperial family, which was common in the early years of the empire, almost ceased. Livia was made *Augusta* on the death of her husband Augustus and *Diva* after her own death. Neither Caligula nor Nero was deified, but Drusilla, the sister of Caligula, and Claudia and Poppea the daughter and wife of Nero became *Divae*. The daughter of Titus, the father, sister, wife of Trajan, the wife and mother-in-law of Hadrian and the wives of Antoninus Pius and Marcus Aurelius were consecrated.

[4] To worship the genius of the emperor was not to worship the living man; the genius of a man was his spiritual and divine part; the genius of anything was its ideal reality which lasted while the external form

emperor, took their place among the greater gods of Rome, equal if not superior to them. They formed a compact group of new divinities. Their names appeared in the official oath. In republican days officials had been sworn in by a solemn oath to Jupiter Optimus Maximus and to the Penates of Rome; the oath was now changed (to take an example from the time of Domitian) to *Per Jovem et divom Augustum et divom Claudium et divom Vespasianum Augustum et divom Titum Augustum et genium imperatoris caesaris Domitiani Augusti deosque Penates*. Their names appeared among those of the deities to whom the great sin-offering made by the Arval Brethren was offered. At the installation of Nero the Arvales offered to Jupiter Optimus Maximus, to Juno, to Minerva, to Felicitas and " genio ipsius (Nero), Divo Augusto, Divae Augustae (Livia), Divo Claudio."

In the provinces, where the gods of the people were not the Roman deities, these *Divi Imperatores* were the gods of the state and, along with the Genius of the reigning emperor, were the divinities which were everywhere worshipped. In the eastern provinces, where the people had been habituated to the worship of the reigning sovereign, the cult of the *Divi* seems to have been inextricably mixed with the worship of the reigning emperor; but in the west the two seem to have been clearly distinguishable, and the worship of the Divi was looked upon as the state religion (as it was *legally* everywhere), and it was left to private persons and to cities to worship the emperor while yet living.

Christianity has so impregnated European thought that most modern historians, until within recent years, were inclined to regard all this worship of the rulers of the Roman Empire as merely a form of slavish adulation. We forget that when polytheism is the religious atmosphere in which thought lives, there is no such gulf between man and God as Christianity has

---

changed. When the Republic became a monarchy the *genius* of the emperor naturally took the place of the *genius* of the Roman people

made us know. If this worship of the *Divi Imperatores* be tested by any standard that can be applied to a polytheistic religion, it will be found to be as real a religion ' , any one of the multitudinous cults that paganism has produced. The household shrines of Pompeii attest how deeply it entered into the private life of the Italian people. There gathered round it the worship of the old heroes of the fatherland, the all-pervading ancestor-worship, the feelings of awe, reverence and thanksgiving which came from the contemplation of a mighty and for the most part beneficent power.

It had long been the custom in the East to worship the head of the state, and this worship had been adopted by the Greeks as soon as they became an Asiatic power. Long before Augustus laid the foundation of his new state religion it had been foreshadowed in Greece and in Asia Minor.[1] The worship of the genius of Rome personified in the *Divi Imperatores* and in the *Genius* of the reigning emperor, took root almost at once and spread amazingly. The worship of the personal reigning sovereign needed to be restrained rather than encouraged. Everywhere we find that the desire of the people to adopt the new cult went in advance of the attempts to spread and sustain it. All over the empire from centre to remote circumference this imperial cult was received with enthusiasm. It did not displace the ordinary religions in which the peoples had been brought up. There was no need for that in polytheism. It was added to the religions with which they were familiar, and this everywhere. Thus it became the one *universal* religion

---

[1] Otto Hirschfeld, founding on this, declares that the Imperial cult was neither a development of Roman customs and institutions nor an original creation in the new world of imperialism; it was appropriated entirely from the oriental Greeks. This it seems to me is only partially true. The worship of the ancient kings, Picus, Faunus, etc., was thoroughly Roman; and there was but a step between it and the worship of the *Divi Imperatores*. The worship of ancestors was thoroughly Roman; and it was a stepping stone to the worship of the deceased *pater patriae*. In India at present many a government official whose rule has been beneficial in a remarkable degree is worshipped as a god.

for the whole empire and took its place as the ruling cult, the religion of the great Roman state. Subjects were free to practise any religion which wa national; but no one, without being liable to charge of treason, might neglect to pay religious homage to the *Genius* of the emperor and to the *Divi Imperatores*.

Only Jews and Christians refused to bend before the new divinities. It was this imperial state religion which confronted Christian confessors everywhere; refusal to sacrifice to the emperor (either the living ruler in the East, or the *Divi* and the *Genius* in the West) was the supreme test to which Christians were subjected, and which produced martyrdoms; Pergamos, the centre of the imperial cult for its district, is called in the Apocalypse the place " where Satan's throne is."

This imperial cult required priests to preside over the worship rendered to the imperial divinities. Its great officials were curiously interwoven with many of the ancient priestly colleges at Rome. It gave rise to special colleges of sacred men who belonged exclusively to the new cult, and it had priests of its own all over the empire. The priests of the imperial cult in Rome would demand a special description applying only to themselves, but for our immediate purpose the organization in the capital may be neglected. What concerns our present enquiry is the position and rank of the priests of the cult in the provinces. It should also be remembered that the organization of this special priesthood differed somewhat in the East from what it was in the West; and this difference may be very generally described by saying that in the West the worship of the *Divi Imperatores* was such a new thing that it required a new priesthood, while in the East the new imperial cult seems to have been largely engrafted upon the worship of the local divinities, which necessarily implied a great variety of organization which space does not permit us to describe.

These explanations premised, it may be said that a network of imperial priesthoods was spread over the whole Roman Empire throughout all its provinces and in all its chief municipalities,

ON THE ORGANIZATION OF THE CHURCH

and that amidst the myriad cults which the paganism of the times produced, there was this one great pagan state religion in which all shared and to which all gave honour, and whose priesthood stood conspicuously forward as the guardians of the worship of the imperial divinities.

This priesthood was of two kinds—the priests who were the representatives of the state religion for a whole province, and the priests who were at the head of the religious administration for the municipalities. The priests of the imperial cult for the provinces were great personages. They were directly responsible to the emperor alone who, as Pontifex Maximus, was the supreme religious as well as the supreme civil head of the empire. It is difficult to say whether they occupied an hierarchical position of authority over the priests at the head of the imperial cult in the municipalities during the first two and a half centuries. The probability seems to be that they may have done so in the West from the beginning, but not in the East. From the last quarter of the third century, however, when a great reorganization was introduced, the priests who superintended the imperial worship in every province were made the overseers of all the priests of the cult within the province, and not only so, but they had the oversight of the priests of every pagan cult whatsoever who were within the province. There was thus from the beginning a pagan hierarchy with its Pontifex Maximus in Rome, its metropolitans at the head of every province, and the municipal flamens at the head of the organization in the municipalities; and from the last quarter of the third century these pagan metropolitans had the strict supervision everywhere of the whole religious administration within their provinces.

These pagan priests of the imperial cult who presided over the provinces were functionaries of very high rank. They were chosen from among the wealthiest and most illustrious of the provincials, and were men who for the most part had held high office in the civil sphere. Great privileges were accorded to them. They presided over the provincial assemblies which the imperial government had created in every province. They had the right of audience of the emperors when they went to Rome on the business of the province. They wore a distinctive dress—a robe with a band of purple; they were preceded by lictors; they had special seats at all public spectacles. They claimed to rank next in precedence to the civil head of the province, who directly represented the emperor.

The cult in the municipalities was more varied, but the priest at its head had a very honourable position. He was a man who had usually filled the highest municipal offices, and he was *ex officio* a member of the municipal council. Everywhere in province and in municipality the office carried with it high civil rank and rights of precedence.

This was the religion and these were the priests that the Christian Church, or rather the associated churches, had to supplant ere it could come to terms with the state and become the acknowledged religion of the empire. Christianity could not become the religion of the empire until this great state religion had been overthrown and its priests abolished or their offices secularized. The question arises—Did the churches seek to adapt themselves to the form and organization of this great imperial religious system in such a way that when the hour of Christian triumph came the Christian leaders could at once step into the position of those who held the leading places in it and who formed that great pagan hierarchy?

The answer seems to be that in two marked particulars at least the Christian churches did copy the great pagan hierarchy. They did so in the distinction introduced into the ranks of bishops by the institution of metropolitans and grades of bishops, and they did so also in the multiplication of the lower orders of clergy on the model of the organization of the state temple service.

M. Desjardins, the learned author of the *Geographie Historique et Administrative de la Gaule Romaine*,[1] has investigated carefully

[1] Desjardins, *Geographie Historique et Administrative de la Gaule Romaine*, iii. 417, 418.

the geographical organization of the imperial cult for ancient France, and has compared it with the Christian ecclesiastical administration which succeeded it after the conversion of Constantine. The result he has come to is, that the pagan organization was everywhere the forerunner of the Christian. His conclusion is that, almost without exception, every city which had a *flamen* to superintend the worship of *Rome and Augustus* or of the *Genius* of the reigning emperor and of the *Divi Imperatores*, became the seat of a Christian bishopric when diocesan episcopacy emerged—and the diocesan system began in Gaul—and every city which had a provincial priest of the imperial cult became the seat of a metropolitan archbishop. The Christian hierarchy, modelled on the earlier pagan hierarchy, stepped into its place. When the Bishop of Rome claimed to be the *Pontifex Maximus* and to rule the Christian metropolitans, and when the metropolitans claimed rights over the bishops of their provinces, and when these claims were largely acceded to, then the pagan hierarchy of the imperial pagan worship was christened and became the framework of the visible unity of the Church of Christ.

The same result appears when the other principle of association—that of councils—is investigated. M. Paul Monceaux, in his thesis *De Communi Asiae Provinciae*,[1] has shown how the councils of the Church established themselves in the cities where the old assemblies of pagan times had met under the presidency of the provincial priests of the imperial cult, and how these Christian councils had frequently the same number of members as attended the pagan assemblies. The organization of the imperial cult or the Roman pagan state religion was copied, to be supplanted, by the Christian churches.

The investigations which have led to these results have not been prosecuted with regard to every province of the empire and there is still room for a great deal of archaeological research but where the subject has been examined the results show the

[1] Monceaux, *De Communi Asiae Provinciae*, pp. 117 ff.

close resemblance between the pagan and the succeeding Christian organization. The Abbé Beurlier, whose monograph *Le Culte Impérial* is the most detailed account of the subject yet published, appreciates the force of the arguments of MM. Desjardins and Monceaux, but explains that this close correspondence did not necessarily imply that the Christian Church copied the organization of the state religion of pagan Rome. He thinks that the leaders of the Christian churches followed so closely in the footsteps of the pagan religious administration because the Christian Church found it necessary to cover the same ground, and took advantage of the same imperial administration and its land divisions.[1] He admits that the organization of the imperial state religion did not exactly follow the civil administration; that some provinces had no provincial priest, and that others had more than one; and that the organization of the Christian Church followed these deviations. But he is of opinion that all this can be explained by natural causes common to the needs of both organizations. "The geographical reasons which had grouped together cities to render a common worship to *Augustus*, and which had led them to establish the centre of the cult sometimes in the capital of the province, sometimes at a point where several provinces met, or, as in Asia, in a certain number of cities rivalling each other in size, acted in the same way in grouping together the bishops of the small towns of the province, and consequently in gradually increasing the jurisdiction of the bishop in the principal centres."

There are, however, coincidences which the distribution of population and the geographical utility of centres will not fully account for. The Christian bishops—the metropolitans and their urban bishops—had assigned to them under the Christian emperors who followed Constantine the same powers to investigate contraventions of religious arrangements which in the pagan days belonged to the provincial and municipal priests of the imperial cult. Nor will it explain how Christian bishops

[1] Beurlier, *Le Culte Impérial*, pp. 304-307.

of important centres demanded and obtained from Christian
emperors the same places of civil precedence which belonged to
the provincial priests of the *Divi Imperatores*. The fact that the
chief ecclesiastic in England has to this day precedence of every
one save princes of the blood comes down through long generations, a legacy from the state paganism of the old Roman empire.
"The conquering Christian Church," as Mommsen says, "took
its hierarchic weapons from the arsenal of the enemy."[1]

The modelling of the Church on the organization of the imperial
cult grew more intimate as the decades passed, and the resemblance between them stronger when the recognition of the
Christian religion by the state gave the leaders of the Church
more opportunities. The pagan title of *Pontifex Maximus*,
applied in scorn by Tertullian[2] in the beginning of the third
century to an overweening Bishop of Rome, was appropriated
by the Christian bishop of the capital and still remains, and with
it the implied claim to be the ruler over the whole religious
administration of the empire. The vestments of the clergy,
unknown in these early centuries—dalmatic, chasuble, stole
and maniple—were all taken over by the Christian clergy from
the Roman magistracy;[3] the word *Bull*, to denote a papal
rescript, was borrowed from the old imperial administration—
but these things take us far beyond our period.

The imitation of the pagan priesthood was also seen within our
period in the multiplication of subordinate ecclesiastical offices.
The second half of the third and the fourth century witnessed
an increase in the lower orders of the clergy, both in the East and
in the West. The organizing genius of the Roman Church
led the way. The institution of these minor orders, as they were
called, can almost be dated. They began about the year

---

[1] Mommsen, *The Provinces of the Roman Empire* (1886), i. 349.
[2] Tertullian, *De Pudicitia*, 1.
[3] Bock, *Geschichte der Liturgischen Gewänder des Mittelalters* (1859);
Marriott, *Vestiarium Christianum* (1868); also, but not so exact, Stanley's
Christian Institutions (1881), pp. 148 ff.

236 A.D. So far as the West is concerned, the minor orders seem to have reached their completion by the beginning of the fourth century, if not a little earlier.[1] We find included in the *clergy*, besides the bishops, elders and deacons, subdeacons, readers, exorcists, acolytes, door-keepers and grave-diggers. The subdeacons are evidently developed from the deacons. The readers and the exorcists represent the old *prophetic ministry*.[2] The acolytes and the door-keepers were added to the *clergy* in imitation of the officials in the state temples during the days of paganism.

The service of priests in the state temples was so arranged that there was a higher and a lower priesthood, and that the members of the latter were looked upon as the personal attendants of the former. The one was set apart for the performance of the sacrifices and other holy mysteries, the others were their servants who performed the menial parts of the services. At first they were slaves; afterwards they were usually freed-men; these servant priests could never rise to be priests of the higher class. They had different names, all of which conveyed their menial position; they were the body-servants, the messengers, the robe-keepers, etc., of the higher priests. Besides these

---

[1] The final form which the new organization of the congregation took, says Harnack, "was characterized by four moments:— (1) by the quality of the sacrificing priesthood, who now took the position of higher clergy, and were settled in it by a solemn consecration; (2) by a comprehensive adoption of the complicated forms of the heathen worship, of the temple service, and of the priesthood, as well as by the development of the idea of a magical power and real efficacy of sacred actions; (3) by the strict and perfect carrying out of the clerical organization in the sense that everything, however old, of dignities, claims and rights should be excluded, or at any rate made over and subordinated to this organization; and (4) by the dying out, that is by the extermination, of the last remains of the *charismata*, which under the new ideas were dangerous, seldom appearing, and often compromising and discrediting as far as they rose above the ranks of harmless." *Sources of the Apostolic Canons* (1895, Eng. Trans.), p. 83.

[2] Compare Harnack's masterly constructive bit of historical criticism, his essay on *The Origin of the Readership and of the other Minor Orders*, appended to *Sources of the Apostolic Canons*, pp. 54 ff.

servants of the sacred persons, there were servants of the holy places or temples. There was always a keeper (*aedituus*), and he had various servants under him, whose duty it was to open, shut and clean the sacred place ; to show strangers its curiosities ; to allow those persons who had permission to offer prayers and present offerings according to the rules of the temple, and to refuse admission to all others. All these attendants of the lower class—whether servants of the higher priests or servants of the sacred place—were included in the temple ministry, and had in consequence their definite share in the temple offerings.[1]

The acolytes and the door-keepers (*ostiarii*, πυλωροὶ) correspond to these two classes of the lower priesthood in the pagan state temples. The *acolyte* (ἀκόλουθος) was originally an attendant, a scholar, a follower, or more definitely the boy or man-servant who followed his master when the latter went out of his house. They were the servants of the Christian priests doing all manner of services for them, carrying their messages or letters,[2] and in general acting like the *calatores* of the state temples. The door-keepers or *ostiarii* had the same duties in the Christian churches that the *aeditui* had in the state temples. " He had to look after the opening and the shutting of the doors to watch over the coming in and out of the faithful, to refuse entrance to suspicious persons, and, from the date of the more strict separation between the *missa catechumenorum* and the *missa fidelium*, to close the doors, after the dismissal of the catechumens, against those doing penance and against unbelievers. He first became necessary when there were special

---

[1] Compare what Marquardt says about the state temples and their attendants and about the state priests in his *Staatsverwaltung*, Pt. ii. (*Handbuch der Römischen Alterthümer*, Mommsen and Marquardt, VI.).

[2] Acolytes are mentioned as carrying letters in Cyprian's *Epistles* frequently :—xlv. 4 (xli.) ; xlix. 3 (xlv.) ; lii. 1 (xlvi.) ; lix. 1, 9 (liv.) ; lxxviii. 1 (lxxviii.) ; lxxix. The point is, of course, not that Christian bishops should have persons to carry their letters, but that these acolytes acting as the servants of the bishops should be reckoned among the *clergy*.

church buildings, and when they, like temples, together with the ceremonial of divine service, had come to be considered as holy, that is since about 225 A.D."[1] The significant thing is not that the Christian churches should have given servants to their bishops and elders or attendants to their buildings for public worship, but that these officials should be classed among the clergy. It is this that was taken over from the pagan state religion.

The Church, however, did not copy its pagan models slavishly. It broke the pagan rule that the higher ministry was to be reserved for men of a certain rank, and that there was a social gulf between the acting and the serving priesthood. It made those lower orders the recruiting ground for the higher, and in this way constructed a ladder by which deserving men could climb from the lowest to the highest ranks of service within the Church of Christ.

Thus the ministry of the Church of the fourth century had become so closely fashioned after the organization of the imperial state religion that when the time of the Church's triumph came, which it did early in the century, very little change of previous state arrangements was needed to instal the new religion in the place of the old. The influences of religion on the state, and the support given by the state to religious rulers and teachers, acted through an administration which, so far as external organization was concerned, was surprisingly like the one that had gone before—only now the cisterns stored and the conduits distributed a wholesome water. The gradations in the hierarchy, the times and places of its synods, the additions to its lower ministry, were all borrowed from the methods of the old imperial paganism.

This need not be a matter of reproach. The Church and its leaders had a lofty aim before them in all these changes; and the evangelical life could be and was sustained under this com-

[1] Harnack, *Sources of the Apostolic Canons*, p. 88.

plicated ministry. The Church acquired an external polity which gave it not merely such a *sense* of unity as it had not previously possessed, but also endowed it with the power of acting as one great organization in its work of Christianizing the Roman Empire and the cultivated paganism which died hard. The Church undoubtedly lost its old democratic ideals; the laity counted for little and the clergy for much; but the times were becoming less and less democratic, and the principles of democratic government were scarcely understood unless when applied within very small areas. In the centuries which came long afterwards it can be seen how this centralized government helped to preserve the Church in the dissolution of the empire in the West in those times which are called "The Wandering of the Nations." On the other hand, there were evils. The spirit of compromise with paganism, which this imitation even of the externals of a pagan religious administration could scarcely fail to produce, did lead to much corruption both in the beliefs and in the life of the Christian Church. These need not be here dwelt upon. The evangelical life in the Church was strong enough to enable her to conquer for the Christian faith, not merely persecuting Rome, but the barbarian nations which overthrew the western portion of the empire. That only need be remembered now.

It is enough to say that the chief seeds of evil which lay in this new organization of the Church which had assumed a definite form by the beginning of the fourth century, were the two pagan ideas introduced mainly by Cyprian of Carthage: (1) that of a special priesthood, in the sense that a man (the bishop) could, by reason of the power ascribed to him of forgiving sin, and, flowing from that, the right claimed for him of exacting implicit obedience, stand practically in the place of God towards his fellow-men; and (2) that of a sacrifice in the Eucharist, unique in kind, propitiatory, differing essentially from all other acts of worship that imply self-surrender to God and from all services of self-denying love, and possessing an efficacy independent of the faith and the piety of the worshippers. It was these thoughts, not the organization which enclosed them, which were to breed evil more abundantly as the centuries passed.

A study at first hand of the contemporary evidence belonging to the first three centuries—and this has been accumulating wonderfully during the last quarter of a century—reveals the important fact that changes were being continually made. Almost every ancient document as it unexpectedly appears, rescued from nooks in eastern convent libraries, dug out of Egyptian sands, unrolled from bundles of forgotten parchments, tells us something new about the organization of the early churches. The unvarying lesson they teach is, that there was anything but a monotonous uniformity in the ecclesiastical organization of the churches of the early centuries. They all speak of changes, experiments, inventions in administration made by men who were alive to the needs of their times and who were unfettered by the notion that there is only one form of government possible to the Church of Christ and essential to its very existence as a Church. The changes made from half-century to half-century, and in different parts of the Church contemporaneously, are all multiplied proofs that it belongs to the Church to create, to modify, to change its ministry from age to age in order to make it as effective an instrument as possible for evangelising the world. They teach, in short, that it is the Church that makes the ministry and not the ministry that makes the Church.

The close of the third century is the limit of our period; it saw the last stage in the growth of the Church before it became absorbed within the administration of the Roman empire.

But the use of the word *Church* is very misleading. There was no one all-embracing institution, visible to the eye, which could be called *the* Church of Christ. What did exist was thousands of churches, more or less independent, associated in groups according to the divisions of the empire. The real bond of association was the willingness of the leaders of the individual Christian communities to consent to federation, for the terms of communion were never exactly settled. The federation was constantly liable to be dissolved. When the party in Rome which favoured a stricter dealing with the lapsed formed a second and rival congregation and placed Novatian at the head of it as bishop, he and not Cornelius was in communion with many of the Eastern bishops and their churches. It was only the magnanimity of Cyprian which prevented the breaking up of the federation on the question of the re-baptism of heretics. Hundreds of the associated churches broke away from the confederation in what was commonly called the Donatist schism. *Church* is therefore scarcely the word to use; *associated churches* is the really accurate phrase.

It should also be remembered that according to the view of Cyprian every bishop occupied a thoroughly independent position, and could accept or reject the conditions of federation and decline to be bound by the action of the associated churches. Examples of such bishops are to be met with very late.[1] But besides such sporadic cases, there were rival associations of churches outside what historians misleadingly call the Catholic Church of Christ. In some parts of the empire they were more numerous than the Catholics, and everywhere they were, to say the least of it, as sincere and as whole-hearted Christians. Marcionites, Montanists, and many others, lived, worked and taught, following the precepts of Jesus in the way they understood them, and suffered for Christ in times of persecution as faithfully as those who called them heretics and schismatics. The state of matters was much liker what exists in a modern divided Christendom than many would have us believe.

It is very doubtful whether the great body of associated churches would of itself have been able to overcome these nonconformists of the early centuries and stand forward as the one

---

[1] Compare article *Autocephaloi* in the *Dictionary of Christian Antiquities*, and Hatch, *The Organization of the Early Christian Churches* (1881), p. 180.

Christian Church, including all or all but a very few Christian communities. That this state of things did actually come to pass was due to the constraints and persecutions of the imperial government, which never tolerated these Christians, and whose persecution was almost continuous after the Council of Nicea till the dissolution of the empire. It was the State which first gave a thoroughly visible unity to the associated churches. The imperial unity was the forerunner of the Papal. The State supported the associated churches by all the means in its power. It recognized the decisions of their councils and enforced them with civil pains and penalties; it also recognized the sentences of deposition and excommunication passed on members of the clergy or laity belonging to any one of the associated churches and followed them with civil disabilities.[1] It did its best to destroy all Christianity outside of the associated churches, and largely succeeded. The rigour of the state persecution directed against Christian nonconformists in the fourth and fifth centuries has not received the attention due to it. The State confiscated their churches and ecclesiastical property (sometimes their private property also); it prohibited under penalty of proscription and death their meeting for public worship; it took from these nonconformist Christians the right to inherit or bequeath property by will; it banished their clergy; finally, it made raids upon them by its soldiery and sometimes butchered whole communities, as was the case with the Montanists in Phrygia and with the Donatists in Africa.[2] And this glaringly un-Christian mode of creating and vindicating the visible unity of the Catholic Church of Christ was vigorously encouraged by the leaders of the associated churches who had the recognition and support of the State.[3]

---

[1] Compare the evidence collected from the imperial codes by Dr. Hatch in his *Organization of the Early Christian Churches*, p. 176 n.

[2] Procopius, *Historia Arcana*, 11.

[3] Compare letter of Ambrose written to the Emperor Theodosius, in the name of the Council of Aquileia demanding the suppression by force of

Safe within the fold of the State, they could speak of themselves as the one Catholic Church of Christ outside of which there was no salvation; they could apply to their own circle of churches all the metaphors and promises of Old Testament prophecy and all the sublime descriptions of the Epistle to the Ephesians, while their fellow-Christians who were outside state protection were being exterminated. Such strange methods do men think it right to use when they try in their haste to make clear to the coarser human vision the wondrous divine thought of the visible unity of the Church of Christ!

non-conformist ordinations and meetings for public worship: Ambrose, *Opera*, Epist I. x. (Migne's *Patr. Lat.* xvi. p. 940).

APPENDIX

SKETCH OF THE HISTORY OF MODERN CONTROVERSY ABOUT THE OFFICE-BEARERS IN THE PRIMITIVE CHRISTIAN CHURCHES

THE history of modern discussions about the nature of the government and the office-bearers in the earliest Christian Churches begins with Dr. Lightfoot's *Essay on the Christian Ministry*, published in 1868, in his *Commentary on the Epistle to the Philippians*. This essay has been recently republished, but unfortunately the valuable dissertation on the terms *bishop* and *presbyter* has not been appended to the republished essay.

In his dissertation on the words *bishop* and *presbyter*, Dr. Lightfoot begins by examining the previous history of the words.

Episcopus in classical Greek was used to denote the Athenian commissioners appointed to take over and regulate a new territorial acquisition, the inspectors appointed by Indian kings, the commissioner appointed by Mithridates to settle the affairs of Ephesus, magistrates who regulated the sales of provisions, certain officers in Rhodes whose occupation is unknown, and perhaps the officials of a club or confraternity. In the Septuagint the word was used to mean inspectors or taskmasters, captains or presidents, the commissioners appointed by king Antiochus when he resolved to destroy the Jewish religion. From this survey Dr. Lightfoot argued that the primary meaning in the word was *inspection*, and that it contained two subsidiary thoughts, *responsibility to a superior power*, and *the introduction of a new order of things*.

Presbyter or *elder*, both name and office, was distinctly Jewish, Dr. Lightfoot thought. It was a common practice certainly to call the governing body *the aged* (senate, gerousia, aldermen), but all through Jewish history there are *elders*; these *elders* were mainly civil officials, but the synagogues of the Dispersion had religious *elders* belonging to them. It was not unnatural, therefore, that when the Christian synagogue took its place by the side of the Jewish, a similar organization should be carried over from the old dispensation into the new.

These two names, *episcopus*, with its Greek, and *elder*, with its Jewish history, mean in the primitive Christian Church absolutely the same thing; this can be proved from Scriptural and patristic evidence. The " elders " of Ephesus were also " bishops " (Acts xx. 17, 28), and the identity of the names is shown in 1 Peter v. 1, 2; in 1 Tim. iii. 1-7 and v. 17-19; and in Tit. i. 5-7. The same identity is observed in the First Epistle of Clement (42, 44). With the beginning of the second century a new phraseology began and the words took their modern significations; by the close of that century the original meanings seem to have been forgotten. But in the fourth century, when the fathers of the Church began to examine the records of the primitive times, they perceived the original meanings, and Jerome, Chrysostom, Pelagius, Theodore of Mopsuestia and Theodoret all recognized the original identity of *episcopus* and *presbyter*.

The question then arises, how it came to pass that in the end of the second century everywhere the original college of presbyters or bishops had given place to a different organization, in which we find ONE president called generally the *bishop*, and frequently the *pastor*, and under him a college of *elders* or *presbyters* and a band of deacons ? This is the question which Dr. Lightfoot set himself to answer in his essay on the Christian Ministry. He first collects his facts, which are these. That the change from a Church government where the rulers were a college of presbyter-bishops to the type in which there is one president with a college of presbyters under him is first apparent in Asia Minor. We get the information from Ignatius, who was himself at the head of the Church in Antioch, and who gives us the name of two other presidents in that region—Polycarp at Smyrna and Onesimus at Ephesus. The change came later in Macedonia and Greece ; for the Church at Philippi was ruled by a college of presbyter-bishops during the time of Polycarp. Corinth had the new constitution before 170, and from some various considerations we may fix the date of the introduction of the new organization into Greece about the time of Hadrian. The same date may be assigned to the new organization of the churches in Crete. The early history of a single presidency in the Roman Church presents a perplexing problem. Neither Clement nor Ignatius allow us to see the presidency of one man in the early Roman Church, and the evidence to be gathered from Hermas is too uncertain to be relied upon. There are lists of so-called bishops of Rome from St. Peter and Linus, but these belong at the earliest to the end of the second century, and the names they give may only be those of men known to strangers to be prominent in the Church of the Capital. We know absolutely nothing of the Church in Africa before the time of Tertullian, but the institution of the single ruler was established in strength in his time. In Alexandria there is evidence to show that up to the middle of the third century the *bishop* was not only nominated but apparently ordained by the twelve presbyters out of their own number. In Gaul the earliest *bishop* recorded was Pothinus, the immediate predecessor of Irenaeus. It is to be observed, however, that it is scarcely reasonable to suppose that the three-fold ministry only began to exist when we can prove that a "bishop" is actually mentioned, for there are many things which witness that the three-fold ministry was not regarded as a novelty at the close of the second century.

Having stated his facts, Dr. Lightfoot proceeded to construct a theory of the origin of this three-fold ministry, or, to put it otherwise, to give an explanation how the two-fold ministry of the primitive Church became a three-fold ministry in the third century.

He notes the gradual and uneven development of the three-fold order. He accepts the statements of Jerome, "that one presbyter was elected that he might be placed over the rest as a remedy against schism, and that each man might not, draw to himself and thus break up the Church of Christ." The dissensions between Jew and Gentile, the disputes occasioned by the Gnostic teachers, the necessity for preserving a united front in times of trial and persecution, were the causes for the gradual change which gave a single and permanent head to the college of presbyter-bishops which had ruled the Christian communities in the earliest times.

This statement, facts and theory, was generally accepted by all save certain Anglicans, who were too much in love with a theory to care to look closely at historical facts. It may be said to have represented the ideas of competent scholars in England and in Germany until the late Dr. Hatch published his celebrated Bampton Lectures in 1881.

Dr. Hatch was one of the most original and erudite students of early Church History that England has produced. These lectures and his articles in the *Dictionary of Christian Antiquities*, were the result of extensive reading, with the view of constructing a scientific history of the beginnings of Canon law—a work which the author's premature death prevented him from accomplishing.

Dr. Hatch set himself to investigate the origins of ecclesiastical organization from a comparative review of the political, social and religious assemblies and confraternities in society contemporary with the beginnings of Christianity. He was not the first to do this. Renan had directed attention to the confraternities of pagan times and instituted a parallel between them and the organization of the early Christian societies. Heinrici had carried on the same kind of investigation in two learned articles published in the *Zeitschrift für wissenschaftliche Theologie*, in 1876-7, and in his *Commentary on the First Epistle to the Corinthians*, published in 1879. But Dr. Hatch brought to the work a wealth of material more abundant than had been collected by any of his predecessors, and grouped it in a much more skilful way. His idea was that the term *episcopus* came into the Christian Church from the heathen confraternities, and was used for the leaders in the Gentile, as the term presbyter was used in the Jewish, Christian societies. If the Gentile Christian churches are to be alone considered, Dr. Hatch thought that the *presbyters* whom we find in them had an origin quite spontaneous and independent of the example of the Jewish communities. He derived the Christian *presbyters* from the common practice of a council of elderly men which superintended most of the confraternities which abounded in the early centuries of our era.

Dr. Hatch seems to have thought that the office as well as the name *episcopus* was distinct from that of *presbyter* from the beginning, but he did not make this opinion very emphatic. His idea was that the *episcopus* filled an administrative and financial office, and its duties in both respects came from the position of the *episcopus* as the leader of the worship, and therefore the receiver of the "gifts" of the people, who gave them after the service to the officiating minister, by whom they were distributed to those to whom they were due. Dr. Hatch thus disputed the identity of *presbyter* and *episcopus*, at least in Gentile Christian societies. He agreed with Dr. Lightfoot, however, in declaring that all the Christian churches were originally governed by a plurality of office-bearers, none of whom had a pre-eminence over his fellows. In attempting to account for the fact that in course of time we find this government by a plurality of office-bearers of equal rank superseded by a three-fold ministry, in which the local Church was governed by one *episcopus*, a college of *presbyters* and several deacons, Dr. Hatch followed Dr. Lightfoot's argument. He adduced the general tendency in all societies to have a president at their head, and the natural tendency when once a single president had been appointed for power to grow in his hands; the specific tendency in the Christian societies of the second century to believe that the coming of the Lord was at hand, and the consequent endeavour to represent each society as having at its head one who would represent the Lord until

He came; and lastly the need felt in times of danger, whether from persecution or from speculation, to have one head who could be obeyed by all. He declared that his explanation of the change was exactly that made by Jerome.

Dr. Hatch's Lectures, at once original and erudite, attracted a great deal of attention both in this country and abroad. They were the object of some grossly unfair and almost virulent attacks on the part of High Church Anglicans, and these attacks continue. In Germany the Lectures made a very great impression, all the more so that the distinguished Church historian, Dr. Adolf Harnack, then a professor at Giessen, now at Berlin, was so struck with the book that he translated it into German and published it with elaborate notes of his own. With this translation modern German critical research into the organization of the primitive Church may be said to have begun.

While Dr. Hatch had denied Dr. Lightfoot's starting point, the identity of *episcopi* and *presbyters*, he had done so mainly by insisting on a difference in origin and perhaps in work; but he had not made very clear the real relation between the *episcopus* and the *presbyter*, nor had he explained why it was that when the three-fold ministry emerged the superior officer was called *episcopus* and not *presbyter*. Dr. Harnack, in his "analecta" to his translation set himself to supply these defects. He insisted in a much more thoroughgoing way than Dr. Hatch that the two offices of *episcopus* and *presbyter* were distinct in their origin, and represented two distinct types of organization which could never throughout their whole history be completely identified. The former, along with the *deacons*, were administrative officers, and had mainly to do with the distribution and reception of the offerings of the worshippers, and through these with the worship of the congregation, while the *presbyters* were from the first and always men who had charge of the discipline and morals of their fellow Christians. In his "analecta," Dr. Harnack attempts to trace this clear distinction down through sub-apostolic literature. This translation was published in 1883. In the same year appeared the *Didache*, issued by Bishop Bryennios—a venerable relic from primitive times, which shed a light on many things hitherto obscure in primitive Christianity. The appearance of the *Didache* was the occasion of a very thoroughgoing resifting of the earliest literature bearing on the organization and worship of the primitive Church. As a result of this we have now the completed hypothesis of Dr. Harnack about the beginnings and growth of the Christian organization, which is as follows. While we have traces of at least four separate roots of organization in the primitive Church, which may be called the "religious," the "patriarchal," the "administrative" and the "aristocratic," it may be said that a completely organized congregation possessed at the end of the apostolic age : (1) "prophets and teachers," who were awakened and taught by the Spirit, and who spoke the "Word of God"; (2) a circle of "presbyters" or "elders," select old men, but perhaps not yet elected "old men," who in all emergencies which affected the congregation could guide them, and whose special duty it was to watch over the life and behaviour of the members of the community, and who therefore comforted, admonished and punished; they also formed the court of arbiters before whom all cases of dispute between members of the Christian society were brought and judged ; (3) the administrative officers—"episcopi" and deacons—who possessed the "gifts" of government and public service, and who had to act especially in public worship and in the care of the poor ; the "episcopi" were also members of the circle of "presbyters." But besides these there were also in the congregations many varied "gifts" (1 Cor. xii.) ; and each individual "gift" or talent which was useful to edify, in the widest sense of the word, the members of the society, was considered a "gift" of the Spirit; but only those who possessed in peculiar measure the "gift" of speaking the "Word of God," the apostles, prophets and teachers, held a special *rank* in the congregation. That was the first stage in the organization.

The second stage arose during the second century, when the basis of organization was thoroughly altered and the alteration was mainly due to the gradual dying out of the "charismatic" element. It shows three elements. (1) The "prophets and teachers" either gradually died out or probably the calling led to so many abuses that these men lost their original pre-eminence, and their places were taken by the "episcopi." (2) The worship and other things made it more and more necessary for one man to be at the head of the administration—the "episcopi" coalesced into one "episcopus" or "pastor." (3) The college of "presbyters" lost much of its earlier standing and became more an advising college supporting the "episcopus" or "pastor." Thus the organization became a three-fold order of ministry—"episcopus" or "pastor," presbyters or "elders," and deacons—and these officials formed a consecrated body of men set over the laity. This change came with varying degrees of rapidity in the various parts of the empire, and we find transitional forms. One of the most important parts of the change was that the duty of edifying the people by sermon and hortatory address passed for the most part to the "episcopus" or "pastor," and in a lesser degree to the "elders"; but on into the third century there were, surrounding the "pastor," laymen who not merely edified the congregation by exhortations, but who instructed it in the faith. Such gifted individuals, along with members who bore eminent testimony to the faith in peculiar holiness of life or in suffering, such as the confessors, virgins and widows, held a place of special honour within the congregation alongside of the clergy.

The first half of the third century saw the final form of organization adopted, and it is characterized by attributing a sacerdotal character to the clergy, who had this character fixed upon them by a solemn service, by a comprehensive adoption of the complicated forms of heathen worship, of the temple service, and of the priesthood, with a corresponding idea of the magical power of priestly actions, by strictly and thoroughly including within the clerical order everything of ancient dignity and rule, and by the complete extinction of the old "charismatic" gifts of edification, or their relegation to a very subordinate place.

These views of Dr. Harnack will be found stated at length with his proofs in his second volume of the *Didache*, in his *Sources of the Apostolic Canons* (*Texte und Untersuchungen*, II. i. ii. v.), and in an article contributed to the *Expositor*, 1887, January-June, p. 321. In the same number, on pp. 1 and 97, will be found two articles by Dr. Sanday summarizing and criticising Dr. Harnack's positions.

Dr. Harnack's theory was at once adopted by many distinguished students of early Church History in Germany, such as Weizsäcker and Sohm, and has been assented to by many Americans, such as Dr. Allen in his *Christian Institutions* (1898); but it has also met with a good deal of opposition. The hypothesis is marked by all Dr. Harnack's originality of view, and is illustrated by a wealth of references which perhaps he alone could give. It fascinated me at first, and it was only after reading and re-reading the evidence that I was obliged to come to the conclusion that it was untenable. Its leading opponents are Seyerlen (*Zeitschrift für praktische Theologie*, 1887, pp. 97 ff. 201 ff., 297 ff.), Loening, Loofs and lastly Schmiedel.

Dr. Loening (*Die Gemeindeverfassung des Urchristenthums*, 1889) is Professor of Law in the University of Halle, and the author of a valuable work on Church Law. He has a lawyer's demand for exact evidence and a lawyer's love of precedents. He holds that there was little or no organization in the Christian communities during strictly apostolic times.[1] What we find are little societies of Chris-

---

[1] Dr. Loening belongs to that school of New Testament critics who are

tians meeting and worshipping together in house churches; we see no traces of office-bearers in the proper sense of the word; we have various terms applied to men because of the work they do, but no word of office. In the last genuine Epistle of St. Paul, that written to the Philippians, we meet for the first time with real office-bearers who are called "bishops and deacons." This epistle and these names must be the starting point of investigation into the origins of primitive Christian organization. After a rapid criticism of the statements of Dr. Hatch and Professor Harnack, he comes to the conclusion that no real proof has been brought forward to enable us to explain these names from the titles of the officials of heathen confraternities; as little have they any connexion with the organization of the synagogue. We can learn nothing about "bishops and deacons" save from the ordinary uses of the Greek words and their special use in Christian literature. It would almost seem, thinks Dr. Loening, that the Apostle Paul used these special words to show that the organization of the Christian societies founded by him had no connection with Judaism on the one hand, nor with heathenism on the other. When we examine patristic and sub-apostolic literature there is a much closer connexion between the function of teaching and these office-bearers than Harnack allows; indeed, Dr. Loening is inclined to question Dr. Harnack's opinion that the "bishops and deacons" of the *Didache* were the officials who had specially to do with the worship as distinct from the instruction. He finds that the *Poimenes* of the Epistle to the Ephesians, the *Hegoumenoi* of the Epistle to the Hebrews, and the *Episcopi* of the *Didache*, meant the same kind of officials, and that there was a

furthest removed from the traditional ideas about the date and authorship of the New Testament writings. He does not believe that we can accept the account given in the Acts of the Apostles as trustworthy history for apostolic times. Therefore while he accepts the account of the election and setting apart of the Seven, he refuses to admit that Paul and Barnabas saw "presbyters" appointed in the Churches founded during their first mission journey, and to accept the fact of the existence of "presbyters" in the primitive Christian Church in Jerusalem. He holds that Rom. xvi. 3–15 is not part of the Epistle to the Romans, but a letter to the Church at Ephesus, and to be taken as evidence for the organization of the Churches in further Asia and in Greece. He does not believe in the Pauline origin of the Epistle to the Ephesians or of the Pastoral Epistles. He dates the former at 70–90 A.D. and the latter at sometime during the first quarter of the second century; while he relegates the date of the Acts of the Apostles to the beginning of the second century. He makes up for this incredulity by accepting with unquestioning faith the gossip of Hegesippus and such writers.

close union between teaching and oversight in the last quarter of the first century. But what of the "presbyters"? Dr. Loening asserts strongly that the "presbyters" in the Gentile Christian communities had no connexion whatever with officials in Greek city life, social or political. The name comes from Judaism; but the Christian presbyters have nothing in common with the Jewish presbyters but the name. Although he does not accept the Acts of the Apostles as a testimony for the organization of the churches in the earliest days of Christianity, yet it is a trustworthy witness for the organization which prevailed in the beginning of the second century. That book, the First Epistle of St. Peter, and the Apocalypse, all show that there were "presbyters" in the Gentile Christian communities in Palestine, in Syria, and in Asia Minor, and that that office had been established in these parts for some time. Where did it come from? From Judaism, says Dr. Loening; and his proof is that it, he thinks, brought with it "ordination," which was a distinctly Jewish institution. He finds this in the Pastoral Epistles, and further declares that in these epistles we see the Jewish term "presbyter" and the Gentile term "bishop" applied to one and the same set of office-bearers. Thus Dr. Loening arrives at the conclusion of the identity of "presbyter" and "episcopus," with which Dr. Lightfoot started. But he has a difficulty to encounter from his rejection of the authority of the Acts of the Apostles, and from his placing the Pastoral Epistles at such a late date. Dr. Harnack had said, standing on the same critical ground as Dr. Loening, that if the Gentile Christian organization had taken elders from the Jewish, these officials would surely have appeared earlier than the last years of the first century, which is the earliest date which the critical theories about certain New Testament writings permit. Dr. Loening gets round this objection by supposing, on the authority, or at least on what he calls the authority, of Hegesippus, that there was no organization at all in Jewish Christian communities until after the death of James, and that the Jewish Christian Church was first thoroughly detached from Judaism and furnished with an organization of its own when Symeon became its head. His refusal to accept the trustworthiness of the Acts of the Apostles, and his full credence of all the gossip of Hegesippus, justifies Loofs' sarcasm that Loening is an ideal "modern critic," because the only sources of information that are not to be accepted uncritically are the canonical Scriptures. Coming to the question of how the single president of a Church emerged from the college of "presbyter-bishops," Dr. Loening has a theory which is all his own. The thick veil which covers the change from the two-fold to the three-fold order of the ministry can be lifted, he thinks, by the aid of the Epistles of Ignatius. With these to guide us we can gather that while in Rome and Macedonia there was still a collegiate constitution, there was in Antioch and Asia Minor a three-fold ministry; but the "bishop" was not considered a successor of the apostles but a representative of Jesus Christ and of God. The change did not come from the colleges of "presbyter-bishops" taking to themselves a permanent president, for there is no evidence of any such movement, nor did it follow any analogy of heathen gilds or civic constitutions, for no such analogies present themselves. It came from an imitation of the position of Symeon at the head of the Jewish-Christian community at Pella. Symeon, of the natural family line of our Lord, was the representative of Jesus; and Ignatius got the "ecclesiastical precedent" required there, and that is why he considers the "bishop" or permanent president of the college of "presbyter-bishops" the successor of the Lord. Ignatius seized on this idea, and his enthusiastic support of it made the conception widely known. Besides, it was useful in the circumstances of the second century, and so the practice spread throughout the Church. Only the main thought of Ignatius—that the permanent president represented Christ—was departed from, and the "bishop" was looked upon as the successor of the apostles. Then came Cyprian with his sacerdotal ideas, and the simple president changed into the hierarchical bishop through the idea of an ordination which gave a "charismatic" character to an office held for life.

The theory of Professor Loofs of Halle is given in an elaborate article published in the *Studien und Kritiken* for 1890 (pp. 619-658). Professor Loofs is the most distinguished of the younger Church historians of Germany, and is an eminently sane and scientific worker and thinker.

Professor Loofs agrees with all our authorities that there was in apostolic and in sub-apostolic times a "charismatic ministry" of "apostles, prophets and teachers," and that they were in no sense the office-bearers in local Churches; but he thinks that some authorities have drawn too hard and fast a line between the two classes of ministry. As to the office-bearers in local Churches, the controversy concerns these points: Whence comes the name "episcopus," and what were the original functions of the men so called? What was the origin of the "presbyteri," and what was their relation to the "episcopi"? At what time did the guidance of the community fall into the hands of ONE episcopus, and how did it come about? These questions exhaust the points in dispute.

He has not much belief in the relation of the name "episcopus" to the officials of heathen confraternities or to civil officials; the references given by Dr. Hatch and Dr. Harnack do not prove their contention. He does not think that the word is a direct term of distinct office in the New Testament writings any more than *poimen* (pastor) or *hegoumenos*; in the address to the Epistle to the Philippians *episcopi* are merely those members of the brethren who take an active oversight, and *diakoni* are those who render active assistance. When we get beyond the New Testament writings and come to the *Didache*, the *episcopi* are undoubtedly the officials of the congregation who preside over the public worship, but the question is whether they did this and nothing else, and whether this was their original work. He thinks that they were more than merely the presiding officers at public worship and what that included, for they are continually called *poimenes*, and "to shepherd" surely means more than to preside at worship and distribute the offerings. And he is of opinion that originally they were simply *prohistamenoi*, and gradually became the presidents of the public worship. It is difficult to say whether they taught, but 1 Thess. v. 12 seems to imply that teaching was from the first associated with leading the congregation.

Then as to the "presbyters"—excluding for the sake of argument the Acts of the Apostles, the Apocalypse and the Epistle of James—the first fairly debatable places where they are mentioned are in the First Epistle of St. Peter and the First Epistle of Clement. The *presbyters* or *elders* mentioned in these epistles are undoubtedly office-bearers; and it is impossible to prove that the "presbyters" in the Gentile Christian Churches were not the same as in, and taken from, the Jewish Christian Churches, unless it can be shown that the office they held in the one was different from what they held in the other, or that there was a period when there were no "presbyters" in the Gentile Churches, and to prove this more is needed than the argument of silence from St. Paul's epistles. If "presbyters" were in Gentile Christian Churches then they were exactly the same as "episcopi"; and "presbyter" is the name of the office, while "episcopus" tells us that this official exercised the function of "oversight." This can be proved without reference to the presence of the word "presbyter" in writings disputed on critical grounds. The testimony of Jerome is not to be set aside lightly; it is unquestionable that Clement calls "episcopi" "presbyters"; even if the word "episkopountes" be rejected in 1 Peter v. 2, "presbyters" are called "pastors" in that epistle, and "pastor" is a common equivalent for "episcopus"; the "presbyters" of Ephesus are called "episcopi" (Acts xx. 17, 28), and this evidence is quite independent of the date or historicity of the book; and there is finally the witness of Tertullian (Apol. 39) and of Irenaeus. All this is much stronger evidence for the identity of the words than anything that Hatch or Harnack has brought forward against the conception. But this does not settle the question whether the "presbyter" and the "episcopus" were identical from the first, or when the term "presbyter" came into the Christian organization. All the probabilities are that it came from the Jewish Church; Christianity came out of Judaism, and that gives an antecedent probability. This does not mean that they got the word from Palestine; Jewish synagogues abounded all throughout the Roman Empire, and converts must have come from them into the Christian Churches. But there is no need to suppose that all Christian congregations got hold of the word in the same way; some may have got it from others, and some may have taken the idea and the function from the civil and social organizations around them; we need not suppose any monotonous uniformity of derivation. At all events, the word and the function were within the Christian congregations, and if St. Paul says nothing about "presbyters," he recognizes "prohistamenoi," who were much the same. But of course it is quite unnecessary to suppose that the organization of Christian congregations took from the very first the form it afterwards assumed in apostolic and post-apostolic times. There is a growth which takes time. It is much more credible to believe that the terms "presbyteri," "prohistamenoi" and "episcopi" all mean the same thing than to accept any of the more recent reconstructions. Thus it will be seen that Professor Loofs reaches exactly the same position as Dr. Lightfoot. In all that has been said, it is presupposed that there was at the head of each local Church a number of "presbyter-bishops," and the next question is, How did the three-fold ministry arise? Dr. Loofs answers that we really do not know. We are in absolute ignorance about two things which might give us light on the question if we could learn something about them—the relation of the "House Churches" to the body of Christians in the town to which they belonged, and what provision was made for the instruction of candidates for baptism, and by whom this instruction was given. But while we can give no certain answer to the question, something can be said both negatively and positively. We can say negatively that the change from the one to the other did not come by any sudden alteration which gave rise to contentions; there is no word of such contention in the whole round of primitive Christian literature; the change came naturally, so naturally as to make it seem that there was no change. We can say positively that there is great likelihood that the channel of the change was the relation of the officials to the conduct of public worship, and more especially in their relation to the Eucharist. What happened there while a college of "presbyter-bishops" was at the head of the congregation we do not know; but it is manifest that there could not be a collegiate superintendence of the Lord's Supper. Did the "presbyter-bishops" take it in turn to officiate, or was one of their number appointed to undertake this service usually? We do not know. But it did become the duty of one man to superintend the administration of the Eucharist; we see this in Justin Martyr; and the man whom Justin calls the προεστώς is plainly the forerunner of the single *episcopus*. This, however, is not all that is needed to account for the change which did come about; and probably something has yet to be done in the line of following up Harnack's idea that the single president was supposed to inherit the spiritual gifts of the *charismatic ministry*. Once, however, the single bishop became the rule, the growth and the importance of the higher order can easily be traced.

The theory of Professor Schmiedel on the origin and growth of the ministry in the primitive Christian congregations is to be found in the article on *Ministry* in the *Encyclopaedia Biblica*. It is easily accessible. I have recently described and criticised it in an article contributed to the first number of the *Hibbert Journal*. It may be sufficient to say that the whole of the recent discussions in Germany on the origin of the Christian Ministry are condensed in the article.

The article *Church*, contributed by the Rev. S. C. Gayford to *Hastings' Bible Dictionary*, is one of exceptional interest. It is a very exhaustive account of the Churches of the New Testament, based on a searching analysis of the documents of the New Testament. Unfortunately the author confines himself almost exclusively to the canonical writings. The article is marked by two things which are treated in a fresh clear way—a description of the gradual growth of organization to be seen within the Churches during apostolic times, and a clear account of the prophetic ministry. The article is in every way worthy of attention and of study.

INDEX OF REFERENCES[1]
To Contemporary Authorities Canonical and Non-canonical

Josephus:
  Antiquitates IV. viii. 14, 38 ..117
  „   XIV. x. 8   ..132
  „   XV. x. 3   .. 3
  Bell. Jud. I. xxi. 3   .. 3
  „   „   II. xx. 5   ..117

1 THESSALONIANS (circa 48-52 A.D.)

I.: 1. 10, 11, 80 ; 6. 80.
II.: 6. 88 ; 14. 10, 11.
III.: 2. 62, 143
IV.: 1. 87 ; 9-11. 21 ; 10. 22
V.: 12. 60, 72, 123, 150, 216 ; 13. 60, 123 ; 14. 60, 96, 150 ; 20. 91, 93 ; 21. 71, 100.

2 THESSALONIANS (circa 48-52 A.D.)

I.: 1. 10 ; 4. 10
II.: 15. 104

1 CORINTHIANS (circa 53-55 A.D.)
I.: 1. 84 ; 2. 7, 10 ; 11. 50 ; 12. 12 ; 13. 12 ; 14. 50 ; 26. 50
II.: 6. 104 ; 7. 46 ; 14. 71 ; 15. 69
III.: 1. 69 ; 3-9. 113 ; 5. 62 ;
IV.: 9. 50, 80 ; 13-21. 89 ; 14. 89 ; 16. 87, 89 ; 17. 10, 12, 87 ; 21. 89
V.: 1-8. 55, 96 ; 1-13. 89 ; 3. 87 ; 3-5. 33

VI.: 1. 56 ; 4. 10 ; 5. 46, 57, 176 ; 9. 12, 50, 80 ; 16. 46
VII.: 1. 55 ; 6. 88, 104 ; 7. 63 ; 10. 87, 88, 89, 104 ; 12. 87 ; 17. 10, 12 ; 25. 87, 88, 104 ; 31. 50 ; 40. 87. 88
VIII.: 10. 50
IX.: 1. 80, 82, 84 ; 2. 82, 83, 88 ; 5. 79, 81, 98 ; 6. 79 ; 8-13. 46 ; 13. 73 ; 14. 73, 98 ; 24-27. 50
X.: 1-4. 55 ; 14-22. 64 ; 15. 71, 100 ; 32. 10, 18, 22
XI.: 1. 89 ; 2. 12, 84 ; 5. 98 ; 13. 71, 100 ; 16. 10, 48 ; 18. 10, 55 ; 20. 51 ; 21. 51 ; 22. 18, 51 ; 23. 12, 16, 104 ; 23-27. 16 ; 30-32. 51
XII.: 8, 58 ; 1-4. 71, 100 ; 3. 44, 94, 102 ; 4. 49 ; 4-11. 63 ; 5. 62 ; 8. 46 ; 10. 47, 71, 100 ; 13. 22 ; 27. 14 ; 28-31. 63 ; 28. 18, 60, 61, 74, 93, 103, 149, 165.
XIII.: Whole Chapter, 58 ; 2. 104
XIV.: 1. 93 ; 2. 47, 104 ; 4. 10, 47 ; 5. 66, 93 ; 6. 94 ; 7. 47 ; 8. 47 ; 10. 47 ; 11. 47 ; 12. 10 ; 13. 47 ; 14. 47 ; 15. 48 ; 16. 44 ; 19. 10, 55 ; 21. 46 ; 23. 10 ; 25. 47, 95 ; 26. 45, 48, 94, 104, 110 ; 27. 47 ; 28. 47 ; 29-33. 48, 93 ; 30. 46, 94 ; 31. 46 ; 32. 91, 94 ; 33.

---

[1] Arabic numerals followed by a full stop (21.) denote the verses or small sections of the books quoted ; all other Arabic numerals denote the pages on which they are quoted.

10, 48 ; 34. 10, 55, 146 ; 36. 91 ;
37. 87, 91, 188 ; 39. 48, 93 ; 40.
48.
XV. : 1-3. 104 ; 2. 104 ; 5-8. 31 ;
7. 81 ; 8. 84 ; 9. 10, 118 ; 10. 75,
122 ; 32. 50 ; 51. 104
XVI. : 1. 10, 12, 22 ; 1-2. 55 ; 10.
43 ; 15. 42, 62, 125 ; 16. 123 ;
19. 10, 21, 22, 123

2 CORINTHIANS (circa 53-56 A.D.)

I. : 1. 10, 22, 80, 84 ; 24. 87
II. : 5. 87 ; 5-8. 96 ; 6. 33, 55 ; 6-9. 55 ; 9. 89
III. : 1. 55, 81, 173 ; 1-3. 83, 88 ;
2. 55 ; 3. 62 ; 6. 62 ; 7. 62 ; 8.
62 ; 12. 83
IV. : 1. 62
V. : 16. 82 ; 18. 62
VI. : 3. 62, 87 ; 4. 62 ; 16. 46 ; 18.
46
VII. : 5. 83 ; 11. 87
VIII. : 1. 10 ; 4. 62 ; 9. 104 ; 15.
46 ; 19. 10, 55, 60, 62 ; 20. 62 ;
23. 10, 79 ; 24. 10
IX. : 1. 62 ; 9. 46 ; 12. 62 ; 13. 62
X. : 1. 82, 83, 104 ; 5. 46
XI. : 5. 81 ; 6. 46 ; 8. 10, 73 ; 9.
73 ; 13. 81 ; 21. 83 ; 22. 10, 82 ;
23. 82 ; 28. 10
XII. : 1. 82 ; 1-4. 78 ; 1-5. 9, 94 ;
10. 83 ; 11. 81 ; 12. 82, 83 ; 13.
10 ; 18. 142 ; 28. 10
XIII. : 2. 89 ; 3. 89 ; 5. 100 ; 6.
100

GALATIANS (circa 53-55 A.D.)

I. : 1. 84 ; 2. 10, 21 ; 7. 80 ; 8. 80 ;
13. 3, 10, 118 ; 15-17. 78 ; 19.
81, 119 ; 22. 10, 118
II. : 1. 32 ; 3. 142 ; 6. 80 ; 7. 75 ;
7-9. 84 ; 8. 75 ; 9. 20, 75, 79,
119 ; 12. 119
III. : 3-5. 91 ; 26-28. 58 ; 27. 16 ;
28. 12
IV. : 6. 44 ; 11. 122 ; 13. 89 ; 14.
95 ; 19. 89

VI. : 1. 33, 69, 96 ; 6. 73, 98, 104 ;
16. 5

ROMANS (circa 54-57 A.D.)

I. : 7. 72
III. : 29. 22
VI. : 3-6. 16 ; 17. 105
VIII. : 15. 44
XI. : 13. 62 ; 27. 12
XII. : 1. 34 ; 3-16. 8 ; 6. 71, 91,
93, 150 ; 6-8. 60, 63 ; 7. 62, 70,
91 ; 8. 61, 123
XIII. : 4. 62
XV. : 8. 62 ; 16. 34 ; 20. 75 ; 25.
62 ; 31. 62
XVI. : 1. 10 ; 1. 62 ; 1-3. 123 ; 2.
123 ; 3-5. 42 ; 3-15. 59 ; 4. 10 ;
5. 10, 123 ; 6. 122 ; 7. 79 ; 10.
42, 123 ; 11. 42, 123 ; 12. 122 ;
14. 42, 123 ; 15. 42, 123 ; 16. 10,
21 ; 21-23. 21 ; 23. 10, 42, 50

EPHESIANS (circa 58 A.D.)

I. : 1. 7 ; 22. 10
II. : 20. 74
III. : 7. 62 ; 10. 10 ; 21. 10
IV. : 4-6. 14 ; 4-13. 8 ; 7-12. 63 ;
11. 74-80 ; 12. 62 ; 15. 105 ; 16.
49, 105
V. : 23. 10, 25 ; 24. 10 ; 25. 10 ;
27. 10 ; 29. 10 ; 32. 10
VI. : 21. 62

COLOSSIANS (circa 56-58 A.D.)

I. : 1. 80 ; 2. 7 ; 7. 62 ; 18. 10, 25 ;
23. 62 ; 24. 10 ; 25. 62
III. : 14. 14
IV. : 1. 21 ; 2. 21 ; 7. 62 ; 15. 10,
42, 123 ; 16. 10, 21 ; 17. 62

PHILIPPIANS (circa 56-58 A.D.)

I. : 1. 7, 62, 80
II. : 17. 34 ; 25. 81
III. : 6. 10 ; 17. 89
IV. : 10. 73 ; 15. 10 ; 18. 34 ; 21.
21 ; 22. 21

INDEX

PHILEMON (circa 56–58 A.D.)

2. 10, 42, 123 ; 13. 62

1 TIMOTHY (circa 64 A.D.)

I. : 12. 62 ; 18. 143
II. : 7. 74 ; 11. 146 ; 12. 146
III. : 1. 87, 146 ; 1–7. 163 ; 1–9. 60 ; 2–7. 146 ; 5. 10, 146 ; 7. 146 ; 8. 146 ; 8–10. 147 ; 8–13. 62, 163 ; 9. 146 ; 10. 146 ; 12. 146, 147 ; 13. 146, 147 ; 15. 10
IV. : 6. 62 ; 14. 143
V. : 9. 202 ; 16. 10 ; 17. 70, 73, 163, 202 ; 18. 202 ; 17–20. 147 ; 19. 187, 188 ; 20. 87

2 TIMOTHY (circa 64 A.D.)

I. : 6. 143 ; 11. 74 ; 18. 62
II. : 2. 146 ; 4–7. 202
IV. : 5. 62, 80

TITUS (circa 64 A.D.)

I. : 4. 142 ; 5. 87 ; 5–7. 163 ; 7. 165 ; 7–9. 158.
III. : 10. 87

ACTS (circa 80 A.D.)

I. : 17. 62 ; 21. 82 ; 21–23. 82 ; 22. 80 ; 23. 32 ; 23–26. 82 ; 25. 77
II. : 16. 91 ; 46. 41. 53
V. : 11. 10
VI. : 1. 54, 62 ; 2. 54, 60, 62, 65, 115 ; 3. 65, 87, 115, 117 ; 4. 62 ; 5. 32
VIII. : 1. 10 ; 3. 10 ; 5, 66 ; 14–27. 24 ; 40. 66
IX. : 2. 113 ; 10. 77 ; 31. 10
X. : 46. 47
XI. : 1–4. 32 ; 22. 10, 24, 32 ; 23. 24 ; 26. 10 ; 27. 91 ; 28. 91, 98 ; 29. 62 ; 30. 21, 153, 163
XII. : 1. 10 ; 5. 10 ; 12. 41 ; 17. 42, 119 ; 25. 21, 62
XIII. : 1. 10, 91, 92, 95 ; 1–3. 74 ; 2. 79, 82, 95 ; 3. 79 ; 6. 233

XIV. : 4. 79 ; 14. 79 ; 23. 10, 118, 137, 154, 158, 163 ; 27. 10
XV. : 3. 10 ; 4. 10, 163 ; 6. 163 ; 12. 32 ; 13. 119 ; 16. 5 ; 22. 10, 92, 163 ; 22–29. 32 , 27. 328 ; 30–34. 328 ; 32. 91, 110, 328 ; 41. 10
XVI. : 1–4. 143 ; 4. 163 ; 5. 10
XVIII. : 2. 123 ; 8. 50 ; 22. 10 ; 26. 123
XIX. : 6. 47 ; 9. 41, 126, 134 ; 10. 22, 41 ; 22. 62 ; 23. 134 ; 41. 4
XX. 7. 22 ; 17. 10, 158, 162, 163 24. 62 ; 28. 5, 10
XXI. : 8. 80, 117 ; 9. 91 ; 10. 91; 98 ; 18. 42, 119 ; 19. 62
XXII. : 4. 113 ; 21. 92
XXIV. : 14. 113 ; 17. 34
XXVI. : 27. 92
XXVIII. : 33–35. 53

REVELATION

I. : 4. 10 ; 11. 10 ; 20. 10
II. : 10 ; 1. 10 ; 2. 100, 233 ; 7. 10 ; 11. 10 ; 14. 100, 233 ; 15. 100, 233 ; 17. 10 ; 19. 62 ; 20. 92, 100, 233 ; 29. 10
III. : 6. 10 ; 7. 27 ; 13. 10 ; 20. 53 ; 22. 10
IV. : 4. 163 ; 10. 163
V. : 46 ; 5. 163 ; 6. 163 ; 8. 163 ; 9–13. 45
VI. : 46
XI. : 17. 45 ; 18. 92
XV. : 3. 45
XVI. : 6. 92
XVIII. : 20. 74
XXI. : 9. 10
XXII. : 9. 95 ; 16. 10

HEBREWS

I. : 14. 62 ;
VI. : 10. 62
XIII. : 7. 72, 73, 92 ; 15. 34 ; 16. 34

1 Peter

I.: 1. 163; 12. 62
II.: 5. 34; 9. 10; 12. 165; 17. 10, 21; 25. 167
IV.: 9–11. 63; 10. 30, 62; 11. 62
V.: 1. 155, 158

2 Peter

II.: 1. 233

James

II.: 2. 113
III.: 1. 105
V.: 14. 10

1 John

IV.: 1. 102; 1-3. 71, 100, 233; 20. 115

3 John

6. 10; 9. 10; 10. 10

Clement of Rome. 1 Epistle (circa 96 A.D.)

I.: 3. 159
III.: 3. 159, 161
V.: 139; 6. 269
IX.: 3. 165
XXI.: 6. 159, 161
XXXVI.: 1. 123
XXXVII.: 194
XL.: 5. 307
XLII.: 80; 1-2. 75; 4. 123, 159; 5. 159, 161
XLIII.: 4. 152
XLIV.: 1. 152, 160; 4. 160; 4-6. 160; 5. 159, 160
XLVII.: 6. 159, 160, 161
XLVIII.: 80; 5. 216
LIV.: 2. 159, 160, 161, 176
LVII.: 1. 159, 160, 161
LXI.: 3. 123
LXIII.: 1. 178
LXIV.: 123
LXV.: 1. 328

Pliny (111–113 A.D.)
Epistles to Trajan

96 (97). 45, 128, 135
VIII: 16. 124

Ignatius (circa 116 A.D.)
Epistle to the Ephesians

1. 186, 200; 2. 197, 198, 200; 3. 191, 193; 4. 188, 191, 197, 198; 5. 191; 6. 189, 197, 193; 7. 188, 189, 200; 9. 188, 194; 13. 191; 14. 188; 15. 194; 19. 188; 20. 191, 197, 198; 31. 200

Epistle to the Magnesians

1. 189, 191, 192; 2. 171, 196, 197; 198, 200; 3. 192, 193, 197; 4. 197; 6. 171, 190, 191, 196, 197, 200; 7. 190, 191, 197; 8. 171; 10-11. 194; 11. 200; 13. 191; 196, 197, 198; 15. 190

Epistle to the Trallians

1. 200; 2. 171, 190, 193, 196, 197, 198; 3. 190, 191, 197, 198, 199; 5. 192; 6–11. 194; 7. 171, 196, 198; 12. 197; 13. 197, 198

Epistle to the Romans

Preface, 269; 4. 188; 5. 186

Epistle to the Philadelphians

1. 188; 3. 193; preface 4. 171; 196, 198; 5. 198; 6. 194, 200; 7. 66, 171, 189, 193, 196, 197, 198, 236, 241; 8. 195, 196, 197; 9. 196; 10. 171, 196, 200

Epistle to the Smyrneans

1. 190; 4. 200; 5–7. 194; 8. 14, 50, 171, 190, 194, 196, 197; 9. 193, 197; 11. 200; 12. 171, 196; 14. 36; 16. 66

Epistle to Polycarp

1. 188; 2. 188, 189, 200; 3. 199, 200; 4. 197, 199; 5. 198, 199, 200; 6. 171, 196, 197; 7. 200

INDEX

POLYCARP
Epistle to the Philippians
36; 3. 199; 4. 115, 183; 6. 115; 6-12. 199

EPISTLE OF BARNABAS (circa 130)
IV.: 9. 105; VIII.: 3. 80; XI.: 221

THE DIDACHE (circa 135 A.D.)
I.-VI.: 174
IV.: 1. 70, 72, 90, 95
VII.: 174
VIII.: 44
X.: 52, 53; 1. 50; 7. 95, 99, 174
XI: 175; 1. 100, 234; 2. 100, 234; 3. 74; 4. 82; 5. 82; 6. 82; 7. 213; 8. 103, 234; 9-12. 103; 10. 92; 11. 100
XII.: 173
XIII.: 98; 1. 74, 100, 202; 1-3. 73; 2. 74, 105; 3. 174, 307; 3-7. 174; 12. 175
XIV.: 54; 1. 52; 1-2. 175
XV.: 1. 175, 176; 2. 70, 105, 175, 176
XVI.: 2. 74

SOURCES OF APOSTOLIC CANONS (140-180 A.D.)
I.: 4. 178; 10-15. 178; 15-23. 178; 22. 178
II.: 180; 15. 178, 185; 18. 178; 19. 178, 180; 23. 180
IV.: 181
V.: 181; 13-15. 203

VICTOR OF ROME (circa 190)
De Aleatoribus
1. 15, 21

PASTOR OF HERMAS (circa 140)
Visiones
II.: 4. 123, 207
III.: 5. 74; 7. 95, 268; 9. 165
Mandata
IV.: 295; 3. 97, 268
XI: 234

Similitudines
IX.: 15. 74

JUSTIN MARTYR (circa 150 A.D.)
1 *Apology*
229; 13. 113, 309; 65. 123, 255; 65-67. 309; 67. 50, 123, 173, 201, 208, 252, 253, 255, 256, 338

Dialogue with Trypho
28. 309; 29. 309; 39. 240; 82. 234, 240; 116-118. 309; 117. 36, 309

TATIAN (circa 172 A.D.)
Address to the Greeks
§ 28. 231; § 29. 231; § 42. 231

ATHENAGORAS (circa 177-180 A.D.)
Plea for the Christians
§ 3. 230; § 7. 242; § 9. 242; § 13. 308; § 37. 230

IRENAEUS (circa 180-202)
Contra Haereses
I.: x. 1. 223; x. 2. 223; xiii. 234; xiii. 4. 227, 241
II.: xxxii. 4. 227, 240; xxxii. 5. 240; xxxiii. 3. 227
III.: i. 269; ii. 1. 223; ii. 2. 225; iii. 269; iii. 1. 225; iii. 2. 228; iii. 3. 225; iv. 1. 223, 224; iv. 2. 223, 224; xi. 3. 222; xi. 9. 213, 227, 234; xxiv. 1. 223, 227
IV.: xxvi. 2. 213, 225, 227; xxvi. 4. 225; xxvi. 5. 225, 227; xxvii. 1. 223, 225; xxxii. 1. 225; xxxiii. 8. 225
V.: vi. 1. 96, 227; vi. 47

CLEMENT OF ALEXANDRIA (circa 190-202)
Stromata
VI: 13. 282
VII.: 6. 36; 5. 43

TERTULLIAN (200-217 A.D.)

Apology
§ 1. 230; §5. 232; § 21. 134; § 39. 21, 172, 202; §42. 232

De praescriptione Haereticorum
§ 4. 80; § 19. 221; § 20. 21, 156, 172, 268, 271; § 24. 269; § 32. 225, 226, 271; § 36. 225, 226, 271; § 37. 75; § 39, 221; § 40. 308; § 41. 208; § 42. 222

De fuga in persecutione
§ 14. 15

De pudicitia
§ 1. 275, 276, 281; § 7 275; §13. 21, 297; § 21. 15, 97, 268, 270, 272, 274, 295, § 22. 227, 274, 296, 317

De pœnitentia
§ 10. 15; § 7. 274

De exhortatione castitatis
§ 7. 15, 245

Ad uxorem
I.: 7. 36, 115

Ad martyras
I.: 1. 296

Adversus Marcionem
I.: 1. 222
IV.: 5. 269; 9. 267

De anima
§ 9. 240

Adversus Praxean
§ 1. 243

Scorpiace
§ 5. 269

De jejunio
§ 13. 313, 326, 333

De baptismo
§ 5. 308; § 17. 306

CANONS OF HIPPOLYTUS (circa 230-250 A.D.)
I.: 250
II.: 246, 250; 7-9. 71
III.: 246, 253, 255; 11-19. 331
IV.: 249
V.: 249, 255; 14. 248; 15. 248
VI.: 248
VIII.: 248
IX.: 183, 246, 256
XI.-XVI.: 250
XII.: 253
XIV.: 232
XVII.: 251, 257, 258
XIX.: 249, 250, 251, 253, 254, 257, 258
XXI.: 251
XXII.: 251
XXIV.: 254, 257, 258
XXVII.: 251, 252
XXIX.: 254, 257, 258
XXXII.: 202, 255, 256, 257
XXXIV.: 258
XXXV.: 256
XXXVI.: 254, 257
XXXVII.: 253

HIPPOLYTUS (235-258 A.D.)

Refutation of all Heresies
I.: 281
VII.: 26. 222
IX.: 6. 274, 281; 7. 135, 274, 276, 281

CYPRIAN (250-258 A.D.)

Epistles
III.: 1. 265, 302, 306; 3. 303
IV.: 2. 303; 4. 265, 306
V.: 1. 292
VII.: 304
XI.: 3. 4. 300, 303, 313; 7. 303; 8. 297
XIII.: 5. 300
XIV.: 2. 292, 303, 304; 4. 292, 297, 316.
XV.: 1. 292, 297, 303, 316, 317; 2. 303, 304
XVI.: 4. 297, 313, 316; 3. 293, 303; 2. 326
XVII.: 1. 316; 2. 293, 303; 3. 298, 293

INDEX

XVIII.: 293, 306, 303; 304, 1. 2. 326
XIX.: 1. 2. 290, 293, 303, 316, 331
XX.: 1. 292, 293; 2. 294, 326; 3. 300, 304
XXI.: 289
XXV.: 294
XXVI.: 294
XXX.: 5. 8. 294, 316, 331
XXXI.: 3. 289; 6. 7. 298, 316
XXXIII.: 299
XXXIV.: 4. 304
XXXIX.: 1. 313
XL.: 294, 301
XLI.: 301, 304
XLII.: 294
XLIII.: 301; 1. 288; 3. 294; 7. 266, 306, 316, 317, 331
XLIV.: 316
XLV.: 316
XLV.: 316; 4. 355
XLVI.: 2. 326
XLVIII.: 4. 303
XLIX.: 2. 331, 333; 3. 355
LII.: 1. 355; 2. 318
LV.: 2. 4. 303, 315; 5. 331; 6. 315, 316; 8. 302, 303, 330; 21. 275; 22. 304
LVII.: 5. 66, 227, 313, 315; 1. 300, 304
LIX.: 1. 9. 355; 4. 265, 303, 306; 5. 302, 303, 312; 6. 302, 330; 13. 316; 14. 17. 315; 15. 316
LXII.: 305
LXIII.: 10. 11. 304
LXIV.: 1. 316, 315
LXV.: 312
LXVI.: 1. 9. 303, 312, 316; 4. 311; 5. 305, 330; 8. 306; 10. 66, 313; 3. 265
LXVII.: 1. 316; 3. 212, 4. 302 5. 302, 330; 6. 127
LXVIII.: 302
LXIX.: 302
LXX.: 1. 316
LXXI.: 1. 303, 317; 4. 326
LXXII.: 1. 316; 3. 315
LXXIII.: 1. 316; 3. 326; 7. 304, 306; 9. 306; 26. 315
LXXIV.: 10. 315
LXXV.: 7. 306; 16. 311, 318; 17. 318
LXXVIII.: 1. 355

De Lapsis

§ 6. 203, 310; § 8. 288

Ad Donatum

§ 15. 285

Testimonia

III.: 28. 297

De Ecclesiae Unitate

§ 17. 305; § 5. 314; § 20. 300

De Opere et Eleemosynis

§ 1. 304, 310; §§ 5. 6. 310

INDEX OF NAMES AND SUBJECTS

"Above, from," 25 n, 121, 235
Achaia, Churches of, 22
Achelis, Dr. Hans, 245 n, 252 n, 256, 304 n
"Activities (ἐνεργήματα) become offices, 64 n, 149, 150
Acolytes, 355
ἀδελφότης (the church), 21, 182
" (the laity), 326
Agabus, 91, 98
Agape. See Love-feasts
Alcibiades, 95 n
Alexandria, 49, 106, 129, 323 f, 339
Almoner of the Church, 185, 304
"Altar" (the poor), 115 n, 183; 208, 257. See θυσιαστήριον.
Ambrose of Milan, 360 n
"Amen" in public worship, 44
Amentia. See Ecstasy
Ammia, prophetess, 236
ἀναλογία τῆς πίστεως, 71 n
"Anamneseis," 257 n
Anicetus of Rome, 324
Antioch, Church in, 24, 32, 74, 83, 90 f, 98, 186, 328, 332
Ancyra, 325 f, 328
Antiphonal singing, 45 n
Antistes Christi, a bishop is the, 305
Apelles' creed (Gnostic), 222 n
Aphrodite, 49
Apollos, an apostle, 80
Apologists, The, 230 f
Apostles, the word, 76 n, 85; marks of, 75, 82 ff; others besides the Twelve, 31, 76 ff, 79 ff; increased in number, 82; differed in call and preparation, 76; and evangelists, 80 n; of the Churches, 78; false, 80 n, 81; "pre-eminent," 81; their twofold action, 86; succession of, 311; 8, 31, 73, 74 ff
ἀποστολή, 77
"Apostolic Canons," 177 n. See Sources of the Apostolic Canons
Apostolic Churches, 225, 271
"Apostolic Constitutions," 56 n, 5 183n, 184, 281, 282 n
"Apostolic men," 225, 279
"Apostolic Succession," 224 ff; a legal fiction, 278 ff; a creation of the Roman Church, 278, 280; historical basis, 223 ff, 279 ff; growth of idea, 280; "gnostically perfect" men, 282; Neo-Platonic succession, 283 n; succession of Apostles, 311; not in Ignatius, 197, 198; nor in Apostolic Constitutions, 281; and Judaising Christians, 19 n
Apprentice mission of the Twelve, 31, 77
"Approaching God," 84
Aquila, 42 n
Arena, The, 50
Arian idea in thought of priesthood, 25 n
Aristides, the Apologist, 36 n, 230
Arles, Synod of, 179 n, 329 n
ἀρχισυνάγωγος, 130, 131 n, 153 n
ἄρχοντες in Synagogues, 130, 153 n
Asceticism, 220, 233
Assembly of the Church. See Congregational Meeting

INDEX

Assimilative power in Oriental religions, 101, 140 n
Astarte, 49
Athenagoras, 230 n, 242, 308 n.
Attalus, 95 n, 236
Audience Halls, 42, 124, 286
Augsburg, Confession of, 72 n
Augustus, the word, 343 n; worshipped as a god, 3, 342 f; protected the Jews, 129; restored Roman religion, 342; instituted the Imperial cult, 342
Aurelian, 333 n
Authority in the Church, 24, 25 n, 26, 28, 32, 298 ff

Bannerman, D.D.; 11 n, 26 n
Baptism, 3 n, 16, 136, 174, 198, 249 f, 306
Barnabas, 22, 24, 32, 91, 95, 98, 116, 118, 143 n; Epistle of, 65, 177 n, 221
Basilica. *See* Audience Hall
Batanea, 337
Beatitudes, The, 172
Beaudouin, 341 n, 344 n
"Benediction," The, 44
Benson, Archbishop, 284 n, 285 n, 291 n, 292 n, 300 n, 314, 318 n
Beryllus, 332
Beurlier, Abbé, 341 n, 352
Bible-woman, 181
"Bind and loose," 26
Bishops, heads of local churches, 178; pastors, 178 n, 323, 327, 330 n; qualifications and duties, 179 n, 182, 199, 301 f; appointment of, described, 246, 302, 330; elected by the people, 175, 246; ordained by elders, 246; by three bishops (Synods), 179 n, 327, 329 f; unlettered, 182; worked at trades, 203; elders and deacons an inseparable unity, 171 n, 196; limited powers, 179, 196, 200, 277; centre of congregational life, 198, 304 ff, 338, 246 f, 253; presided over discipline, 199, 300, 303; distributed offerings, 180, 185, 209, 255; paymaster of the clergy, 304; supremacy of, 195, 298, 301 f, 304, 314, 334; representative of Christ, 305 f, 197; have *charismatic* gifts, 227, 313; judges of teaching, 223 ff; have power to pardon sins, 276 n, 300, 303, 306; power comes from God directly, 301 f, 312 n; represent God, 282 n, 301; priests in a unique sense, 305 ff, 357; took the places of the priests of the Imperial Cult, 352 f; Imperial ideas influenced later conceptions of, 335; cease to be bishops when guilty of grievous sins, 65, 128 n, 152, 176, 312
Bithynia, 128 n
Bleek, 47 n
"Body of Christ," 14 n, 136
Boehmer, 116 n
Boissier, Gaston, 101 n, 127 n, 341 n
Boxing match, 50
"Brotherhood," The Church, 10 n; 20, 21, 52, 54, 181, 182; the laity, 326
"Brethren," Christians called the, 11, 114 n; the laity, 326; members of *confraternities*, 125
Bruston, Edouard, 187 n
Bryennios, Philotheos, 171 n, 172 n
Burial Clubs, 126, 133; the Roman Church, 129 n, 135 n
Burial Usages, 135, 257 n

Caesarea, Church in, 91, 98
Caesarea Philippi, 3
Calixtus of Rome, on penitence, 274, 276 n, 297, 299, 317 n; on Apostolic Succession, 280
"Call" of an Apostle, 76, 84
Calvin, John, 72 n
Canon (Scripture) of Marcion, 220; of Gnostics, 222

Canons of Basil, 203 n, 267 n
Canons of Hippolytus, 50 n, 53 n 54 n, 71 n, 183 n, 202, 205, 245 ff 331 n
Cassius. *See* Dio Cassius
Catechetical School of Alexandria, 106 n
Catechumens, 52, 104, 251, 267
Celsus caricature of prophets, 109 n
Cenchrea, 49, 124 n
Character, the qualification for office, 145 f, 178 f, 247
Charisma Veritatis, 227 f, 280
Charismata, 15, 63, 71, etc. *See* " Gifts "
Charismatic Ministry, 70
Charity, 22; its place in the Primitive Church, 115 f. *See* Almoner, Bishop, Offerings, Poor
Chloe, 50
Christ. *See* Jesus Christ
" Christ-trafficker," 173
Church, the word; used by Jesus, 3 n; by Paul, 5; uses in N.T., 10 n, 14, 55. *See* Ecclesia
Church, The, crystallizes round Christ, 190, 192; a fellowship, 6 ff, 20, 271; an organism, 8, 15 n; a unity, 10 ff; a visible unity, 16 ff, 156, 182, 268 ff; historical continuity, 223 ff, 19, 24; Household of God, 23, 145 f, 189; a theocratic democracy, 4, 25, 33, 177; has authority, 24 ff, 309; a sacerdotal society, 33 ff, 307; what makes it, 9, 18; 266, 268 ff
Church, The Local, what makes it; 69, 266; of less than twelve families, 178, 337; must elect office-bearers, 175, 178; self-governing, 20, 32, 49, 121; intercommunication, 21 f, 73, 173, 178, 199, 271, 290 ff (*see* Synod), power of discipline, 27, 32, 55 ff 199 f (*see* Bishop, Elder); ruled by a senate, 155 f, 170; by bishop and council, 180 ff, 197 f; merged in the bishop, 306; external likeness to Jewish synagogue; 134; to pagan confraternity; 128 n, 135
Chrysostom, 64 n, 79 n
Cilicia, 118
Clarus of Mascula, 311 n
Clement of Alexandria, 15, 36 n, 43 n, 171 n, 282
Clement of Rome, 65, 76 n, 80 n, 123 n, 141 n, 151, 152 n, 176, 183, 193, 216 n
Clergy, unsalaried, 202 ff; worked at trades, 203; 245, 246, 276. *See* Pastor, Bishop, Elder, Deacon, Minor Orders, Orders
Cohn, 127 n
Collection, The Great, 22 f, 34 n; in *kind*, 254
Collegia. *See* Confraternities
Collegia tenuiorum, 133
Collegiate Churches, 260, 330n, 339
Colossae, 22, 42 n, 59
Commands of Jesus, 88 n, 104
Commission, a, superseding the office-bearers, 294, 301
" Commissioners of Sacrifices," The, 288
Communicatio Pacis, 156, 270
Conciliar system of Church Government, 170 n
Confession, The Augsburg, 72 n; The Westminster, 72 n
Confession, The, of St. Peter, 6, 25 ff
Confession, in Public Worship, 44
Confessor, 289 n, 290; made Elders, 247
" Confirmation," 340
Confraternities, pagan, to practise religions, 50, 54 n, organization, 125 f; illicit, 133, 135; not models for Christian organization, 128 f

INDEX

Congregational Meetings; for exhortation, 44 f, 251 ; for the Eucharist, 50 f, 252 ; for business, 54 ff, 60, 66, 173, 175, 199 n, 200, 250, 316 ; passed judgment on Apostles, 32 f
Congregationalism and Primitive Organization, 259
Constantine, 134
Converts, The first, earliest officebearers, 60, 122 f, 152, 154
Cornelius, 24
Corinth, Church at, 7, 12, 14, 17; 33 n, 49 f, 56, 59 ff, 74, 83, 91 f, 101, 160 f, 299 n
Corycus, Inscriptions at, 203
Cramer, 120 n
Creeds, Gnostic, 222 ; a common creed, 222, 270
Cureton, 187 n
Cybele, 49
Cyprian of Carthage, dates, 286 n ; relations to his elders, 291 ff, 294, 331 ; to the Roman Elders, 291, 293 ; the Lapsed, 294 ff ; authority, 298 ff ; independence of bishops, 315 ; sacerdotalism, 305 ff ; his visions, 66, 95 n, 97 n, 284 n, 313 ; use of Synods, 313 f ; his character, 284 n ; pagan ideas, 357
Cyrene, Jews in, 129

Damascus, 77, 114 n
Dates of N.T. writings, 121 n, 137; 138 n, 139 and n, 159 n
Deacons, 62 n, 65, 152, 180, 249 ff, 251, 316
Dead, memorial feasts for the, 135, 257
Decian Persecution, 287 f, 296, 338
Decuriones, 125
Deissmann, 119 n, 154 n
Delegates from Churches, 23 f, 55, 200
Democracy, The Church at, 4, 25, 177, 334, 357

Demons, Fear of, 258 n
Derbe, 118, 142, 154
De Rossi, 124, 135 n
Desjardins, 341 n, 350
διαδοχή, 311 n
διακονία, 8 n, 60 n, 62 f n, 70 n
διάκρισις, 64 n, 99 f
διδάχη, 46, 105 n
Didache, The, 65, 74, 82, 170, 171 ff, 183, 213, etc.
Diligentia, 292
Dio Cassius, 4 n, 133 n, 344 n
Dionysius of Corinth, 299 n
Directory for Ordination of Ministers, 331 n
Discernment, The Gift of, 64 n, 70, 71 n, 149, 175
" Disciple Company," 190
Disciples, 9, 25, 27, 30, 113 n
Dispensatores Dei, 301
" Dispersion," The, 116 n, 129, 153
Divi Imperatores, 345 f, 351, 353
Dobschütz, 17 n
Döllinger, 274 n
Domnus of Antioch, 332
Double element in things, 18 ; in missionary work, 86 f
Doxology, The, in worship, 47
Dress of the clergy, 253, 353
Dury, V., 341 n
Dutch Presbyterian Church, 260 n, 339

Eastern Religions within the Empire, 100 f, 140 n, 218
Ecclesia, the history of the word, 4 and n
Ecstasy, in Prophecy, 94, 241
Egyptian priests called Elders, 154 n ;
" Election by show of hands," 118 ;
" Eleven," The, 30, 84 f
ἐκλεκτοὶ τρεῖς ἄνδρες, 179 n
Elders, common name for rulers, 154 ; among the Jews, 130 n ; in Churches in Palestine, 116, 118 ; in the Acts, 137, 142 ; in Pastoral Epistles, 142, 150 ;

elsewhere, 180, 196, 250, etc.;
applied to first converts, 154;
qualifications, 145, 180, 247 *f*;
ordination of, 248; theoretically
same rank as bishops, 164 *n*, 205,
250, 259; received money for
the poor, 116, 180; superintended the bishop 180; a council
round the bishop, 196; could
ordain a bishop, 246; successors of the Apostles, 197, 225,
282 *n*; have a *charisma veritatis*,
227

Eliakim, 26

ἐνεργήματα, 64 *n*

Ephesus, Church at, 59, 74, 100 *f*;
114 *n*; Epistle, 10, 12, 74

Epiphanius, 114 *n*, 153 *n*, 237 *n*

ἐπιταγή, 88 *n*

Esculapius, 217

Etecusa, 289

Eucharist, prophets presided at the,
99 *n*, offerings, 209; in the third
century, 252 *ff*; a unique sacrifice, 257, 305 *ff*; 3 *n*, 31 *n*, 35 *f*,
43, 50 *f*, 172

"Evangelists," 80 *n*; *Readers* to
take the place of, 182

Exhortation, the meeting for, 44 *f*,
250 *f*

External Unity of the Church,
exhibited in fruits of the Spirit,
20; by Synods, 334; by harmony of bishops, 314; by
Roman supremacy, 335, 353

Fabian of Rome, 290

False Prophets, 91, 100 *f*, 109, 234 *n*

Family Council assist at election,
120

Fechtrup, 284 *n*

Felicissimus of Carthage, 299

Fellowship, the Church a, 6 *ff*,
191; 20 *ff*, 55, 181, 268, 271

Firmilian of Caesarea, 311 *n*, 318 *n*

"Firstfruits," 98, 147, 174 *f*, 202,
254, 282 *n*, 304

"Five," The, 117

Flesh, Sins of the; to be pardoned,
275

Forum of Rome, ancient Church
in the, 42

Foucart, P., 54 *n*, 127 *n*

Francis of Assisi, St., 82

Fraternitatis Appellatio, 156. *See*
Brotherhood

Freewill offerings, 147, 201, 304

Fruits of the Spirit, 20, 24

Fundanus, Minucius, 229

Funk, F. X., 172 *n*, 245 *n*

Gaius of Corinth, 42, 50; of Didda,
295

Galatia, Churches of, 22, 91

Gayford, S. C., 90 *n*, 149 *n*, 377

Gérard, 127 *n*

γερουσία, γερουσιάρχης, 130

"Gifts," use of the term, 63 *n*, 70;
two great classes, 214; manifest the presence of Christ, 8, 33,
113; create a Church, 121; of
speaking the Word, 8, 70, 75,
214; of healing, 64 *n*, 248; of
leadership and service, 64, 113,
151, 214; of discernment and
judging, 64 *n*, 71 *n*, 99, 149; all
service a, 8 *n*, 16, 60, 69, 71,
86

"Gilds" of soothsayers, 100; 50,
54 *n*. *See* Confraternities

Gladness in the Eucharistic Service, 53 *n*

γνώμη, 88 *n*

Gnostics, 65, 141 *n*, 218 *f*, 221; a
Gnostic creed, 222 *n*; Gnostic
idea in mediating priesthood, 25 *n*

Gore, Bishop, 6 *n*, 89 *n*, 171 *n*

"Great" Church, The, 243, 259,
323

Greek worship of rulers, 347

Gregory the Great, 203 *n*, 284

Groups of Churches, 21 *f*, 323 *f*;
of congregations, 337

Gwatkin, H. M., 75 *n*, 89 *n*, 116 *n*

INDEX

Hadrian, Emperor, 229
Hands, Laying on of, a Jewish benediction, 143 n; in ordination, 246; in restoration to Church communion, 147, 304
Harnack, Adolf, 65 n, 70 n, 74 n, 75 n, 80 n, 90 n, 97 n, 114 n, 121 n, 130 n, 139 n, 150 f, 171 n, 176 n, 177 n, 230 n, 238 n, 240 n. 274 n, 281 n, 291 n, 333 n, 354 n; relation of bishops and elders, 157 ff; on organization, 369 ff
Hartel, 283 n, 318 n
Hatch, Edwin, 4 n, 116 n, 127 n, 128 n, 202, 219 n, 302 n, 311 n; on organization, 369 ff
Hegesippus, 119 f, 141 n
ἡγούμενοι, οἱ, 73, 92
Heinrici, C. F. G., 9 n, 47 n, 57 n, 81 n, 90 n, 127 n, 128
Hermas of Rome, 65, 74, 95, 97 n, 123, 169 n, 176 n, 207 n, 234, 241
Hierapolis, 22, 236
Hierarchy, none in Early Church, 32 f; of the Imperial Cult, 348 f; copied in the Church, 350 ff
Hinduism, 140 n, 218
Hirschfeld, Otto, 341 n, 347 n
"Honoured," The, 70 n, 73, 105, 176 n
Hort, 4 n, 6 n, 9 n, 11 n, 13 n, 31 n, 60 n, 75 n, 77 n, 89, 147 n
Hospitality, 21, 173, 256
House Churches, 41 f, 59, 286

Iconium, 118, 142, 154 n
Ideal Reality, The Church is an, 16; the Ideal Israel, 33, 5
Idol Feasts, 50, 54 n
Idolatry, a deadly sin, 295
Ignatius, of Antioch, a prophet, 66, 189 n, 192, 209, 236; 14, 50 n, 186 ff, 233; his epistles, 186 n; prophetic chants in, 189 n, 192
Inner circle of disciples, 30, 84

Innocent I. of Rome, 339 n
Inscriptions, 114 n, 203
Intercourse between Churches, 21, 55, 153, 156
Interpolation of Cyprian's writings, 317
Invocation of Jesus in worship, 44
Irenaeus, on a succession from the Apostles, 225 f; on a *charisma veritatis*, 227; on Prophecy, 240 f; 47 n, 65, 213, 221, 223
Isis, 49

James, pre-eminence in Jerusalem, 119 f; 5, 22, 42, 81
Jerome, 164 n, 205
Jerusalem, 11, 21 ff, 91; its poverty, 116 n; Church, 20, 28, 53 n; 83, 98, 114 n, 117, 118
Jesus Christ, promise of the Church, 3 f; fellowship with, 9, 190; manifests His Presence in His "Gifts," 7, 32, 113; commands of, 88 n, 104; sayings of, 46, 63, 104; Head of the Church, 14, 25, 32, 190
Jewish Synagogues, organization, 129; resemblance to confraternities, 125, 131; had patrons, 124 n, 130 n; resemblance to Churches, 131, 153; Churches, 91, 153; religion, protected, 129, 133
Jezebel, a prophetess, 92 n
Josephus, 3 n, 117 n, 132 n
Judge, power to, spiritual "gifts," 70, 71 n, 99 ff, 175
Julius Caesar, protected the Jews, 129; worshipped as a god, 342 f
Justin Martyr, 36, 50 n, 65, 105, 114 n, 123, 173 n, 201 f, 234, 252, 308
Justinian's persecutions, 243, 359

Kataphrygian Church, The, 243
Keating, 44 n
Keys, Power of the, 26 f

Kiss of Peace, 47
κοινωνία, 9, 20, 271
κοπιῶντες, οἱ, 61 n, 122
Krascheninnikoff, 341 n
κυβερνήσεις, 8, 60, 64 n, 70 n, 136, 149, 214.
Kühl, 9 n

Lagarde, P. de, 245 n
λαλοῦντες τὸν λόγον, οἱ, 72
Lange, 116 n
Laodicea, 21 n, 42 n, 59
"Lapsed," The, 290 ff, 295 f; Roman Elders on the, 290; Martyrs and pardon, 295
Law, Christians not to go to, 56
Leaders, Leadership, in the kinsfolk of Jesus, 119 f; related to service and gifts, 63 f, 113, 151; 23, 60 f, 73, 92
Lebanon, 43 n
Lebegue, 341 n
Lechaeum, 49
"Letters of Commendation," 55, 81, 83, 172
Libellatici, 289
Libellus, from magistrates, 288 f; specimens of, 289 n; from martyrs, 290
Licentious cults, 3, 17
Liebenam, W., 54 n, 124 n, 127 n, 134 n, 135 n
Lightfoot, Bishop, 35, 74 n, 76 n, 79 n, 80 n, 81 n, 82 n, 92 n, 116 n, 152 n, 188 n, 187 n, 193 n, 195 n, 197 n, 198 n, 229 n; on organization, 365
Littledale, 43 n
Liturgy of St. Clement, 43 n
"Living sacrifices," 34
Loening, Edgar, 75 n, 87 n, 88, 90 n, 127 n, 151, 152 n, 172 n; on organization, 371
λόγος σοφίας, 46 n, 64 n
Loofs, Fr., 152 n, 166; on organization, 374
Lord's Day, 52, 172, 252

Lord's Prayer, in worship, 44 n
Lord's Supper, 31 n, 36, 43, 50 f, 52, 172, 174, 208, 305. *See* Eucharist
Lordship, excluded from Christian ministry, 31; introduced, 305 f, 276 n, 282 n, 300, 301
Love-feast, 17, 44, 50, 54 n, 198, 255 f
Lucian, 17, 129 n, 153, 173, 188 n
Lucius of Cyrene, 91
Lüders, Otto, 127 n
Luther, 35, 275 n
Lycaonia, 98
Lycus Valley, 22
Lyons, The Martyrs of, 95 n, 296
Lystra, 118, 142, 143 n, 154 n

Macedonia, Churches of, 22
Major-Domo, 26
Majority of votes decides, 33, 55
Malchion, Elder at Antioch, 332 f
Manaen, prophet, 91
Marathi schoolmaster, 106 n
Marcion, 219 f; Marcionite Church, its organization, 208 n; persecuted by Christian Emperors, 243; 65, 114 n, 219 f
Marks of an Apostle, 82 n, 83
Marquhardt, J., 335 n, 341 n
Martyr, Justin. *See* Justin
"Martyrs," 290; their power to absolve, 97, 293, 295; made Elders, 247
Martyrs of Lyons, 95 n, 296
Mary, mother of John Mark, 41
Massebieau, 172 n
Mater Synagogae, 131 n
μαθηταί, 9, 113 n
Matthias, 32, 77
Mau, Auguste, 341 n
Meals, Common, 51, 53 n, 255 f
Meetings of whole Church. *See* Congregational Meeting
Membership of the Church, the seat of authority, 32, 121, 309
Messiahship without suffering, 6 n

"Metropolitans," 336, 350, 352
Milton, 154 n
Ministry, use of word, 62 n ; based on "gifts," 63 f, 70 f, 75, 85, 99, 113, 151, 235, 248 ; two different kinds of, 63 n, 65 f, 149, 228, 272 ; the local ministry created by the Churches, 113–166 ; changed in second century, 169 f, 205 ff; became a lordship in the third century, 266 ff, 276 ff, 303 ff; modelled on pagan hierarchy, 356 ; "from above," 25 f, 121, 235 ; not a plastic medium between God and His people 25 n; included from the first oversight and subordinate service, 154, 169 ; of women, 181, 249. See Bishop, Elder, Deacon, Minor Orders, γυβερνήσεις, Priesthood, Prophetic Ministry
Minor Orders, 246, 340 ; modelled on pagan priesthood, 354 f; absorbed remains of prophetic ministry, 354 n
Missa catechumenorum, *Missa fidelium*, 355
Missionary analogies in organization, 41, 106 n, 117, 121, 140 n, 144, 162 n, 254 n, 256 n, 258, 337
Mommsen, Theod., 127 n, 229 n, 335 n, 343 n, 353
Monceaux, P., 351
Montanus, 236 f; Montanism, wider and narrower, 236 ff; Phrygian, had new elements, 237 ; movement conservative, 235 ff; divided the Church, 271 ; Montanist Prophecy, 239, 271 f; persecuted by Christian Emperors, 243, 360
Monthly payments to the clergy, 304 ; in confraternities, 125, 202
Moses' seat, 27
Mosheim, J. L., 90 n, 162 n
Mother Church (of Jerusalem), 20, 118, 153 ; 337

Mowat, R., 341 n
Municipal Priests, 349 f
Muratorian Fragment, 140
"Mysteries," 104 ; Pagan Mysteries, 308

Names given to Christians, 113 n f
Naturalist Religions, 100
Nazareth, 75 n
Neale, J. M., 43 n
Nestorians, 85 n
Nicopolis, 142
νουθετοῦντες, οἱ, 61 n
Novatian, 331, 359
Nurses in Christian communities, 181, 249 f
Nymphas, 42 n

Obedience to ecclesiastical authority, 24 f, 60, 69, 193, 197, 265 f, 277 ; by believers to each other, 191
Oblations. See Offerings
Octavius. See Augustus
Offences and offenders within the Church, 27, 175
Offerings, 34, 174, 181, 201, 209, 254 ff, 277, 309
Office-bearers were frequently prophets, 66, 209, 217 ; taught from the first, 155 n, 216 ; obedience due to them, 60, etc ; earliest, were the first converts, 60, 122 f, 152 ; existed in the Pauline Churches, 60 ff. See Ministry
Old Testament Scriptures, 46 ; prophecy, 100 ; priesthood, 196, 307, 334
Orders, 25 n, 32
Ordo et Plebs, 245 n
Ordination, 246 ff; of bishops, 246, 302 n, 330 ; of elders, 248 ; of presbyterian ministers, 330 n ; the entrance to ecclesiastical office, 302
Organization, of confraternities, 125 f; of Synagogues, 129 f; of

the Pagan State Religion, 348;
copied by the Church, 350, 355 *f*;
of the Churches, 113 *ff*; several
roots, 115 *ff*; followed a course
of its own, 128; in Pauline
Churches, 136 *ff*; in Pastoral
Epistles, 144 *f*; passed through
several stages, 149 *f*, 155 *f*, 169 *ff*,
183, 350 *f*; two ideals in, 335 *f*;
social, dreaded by Roman Emperors, 132 *f*

Organism, the Church an, 8, 15, 51

Origen, on Celsus' account of Christian prophets, 109 *n*; 15, 79 *n*

Ostiarii, 355

Paganism, intellectual, 217 *f*

Palestine, the home of prophecy, 91; Churches in, 118

Pamphylia, 98

Paraphrases, Scotch, 45 *f*

Pardon may not be granted for some sins, 96 *f*, 213, 267, 272, 295, 297 *n*; but may if prophet or Martyr demands it, 97, 268, 272, 295; if bishop remitted the sin, 265, 272 *f*, 276 *n*, 300, 303, 306; 28, 29 *n*

Parish system, beginning of, 339

Paroichia, 326, 332

Pastoral Epistles, 139 *ff*, 139 *n*, 202 *n*, 216; and sources of Apostolic Canons, 146 *n*

Pastors, 8, 65, 152; synonymous with Bishops, 178, 330 *n*

Patron and Client, 123 *f*, 124 *n*; in Confraternities and Synagogues, 124 *n*, 126, 131 *n*

"Pattern of Teaching," 105

Paul, St., use of the word Church; 3 *n*, 5, 10, 18; fellowship, 7 *ff*, 20 *ff*, 271; grouped his Churches, 21 *ff*; method of making the unity of the Church visible, 22 *ff*; call and preparation, 77; the typical Apostle, 88; attacked in the Pseudo-Clementines, 78; apostolic career began at Antioch, 92 *n*; what makes a Church, 49, 69, 121, 149; cultivated the sense of responsibility in his Churches, 48 *f*, 56 *ff*, 148; thought highly of prophecy, 61; 31 *n*, 32 *f*, 41 *n*, 44 *n*, 46 *n*, 58 *f*, 70, 77 *ff*, 87 *n*, 88, 93 *f*, 96, 102, 113, 118, 141 *n*, 143 *n*, 154 *n*, 172 *n*, 214, etc.

Paul of Samosata, 332 *f*

Pearson, John, 284 *n*

Peloponnesus, 85 *n*

Penitence, alteration in conditions of, 273 *ff*; how to be shown, 297, 310 *f*

Pergamos, a centre for the Imperial Cult, 348; Church in, 22

Peter, St., the Rock-man, 6 *n*; his confession, 6, 25 *ff*; at the head of the Church in Jerusalem, 119

Peter, Epistle of, 10 *n*, 137

Phanar, The, 171 *n*

Pharisees, 27

Philadelphia, The Church at, 22, 27, 236; Ignatius had the prophetic afflatus in, 189 *n*

Philemon, 42 *n*

Philip, one of the "Seven," 24, 117

Philip, daughters of, prophetesses, 91, 236

Philip of Sidé, 120 *n*

Philippi, The Church at, 36 *n*, 136, 194

Phoebe of Cenchrea, a "patroness," 124 *n*

Pisidia, 98

πίστις, 46 *n*, 71 *n*

Pistis Sophia, The, 222 *n*

Plebs et Ordo, 245 *n*

"Plastic Medium," A special priesthood a, 25 *n*, 35

Platonic exegesis, 221

Pliny's Letters to Trajan, 45, 50 *n*, 124 *n*, 128 *n*, 135 *n*

Plumptre, E. H., 107 *n*

Plutarch, 123 *n*

πνευματικοί, οἱ, 69

INDEX

ποίμνιον, 36, 115, 155 n, 183
Polycarp, a prophet, 66, 194, 199, 236
Pontifex Maximus, the official head of the Pagan State Religion, 349; the Bishop of the Roman Church, 335, 351
Pontius, 286 n, 287
Poor, care of the, 21, 115 *f*, 148, 255 *f*; Church poor-roll, 148
Poverty in Roman Empire, 116 n
Praise in Public Worship, 44, 251; a sacrifice, 34, 307
Prayer in Public Worship, 44, 52 and n; the Lord's Prayer, 44 n; ejaculatory prayers, 47 *f*; liturgic prayers, 52 n, 174, 246; Prayer of consecration at Eucharist spontaneous, 201, 253 n; prayers of prophets, spontaneous, 95
Preaching Ministry of Apostolic Church, 72
Preparation of Apostles, 76, 84
Presbyters. *See* Elders
πρεσβύτερα, 131 n
πρεσβύτεροι, 118, 159, 161 *ff*
Presbyterian system of Church government, has the threefold ministry, 170 n; close resemblance to what is found in Ignatius, 198, 205; where it differs from early organization, 259; 330 n
Presbyterium, 196, 198 n
President (προεστώς), 173 n; 208; 52
Prisca, 42 n
Priests, N.T., 34 *f*, 307, 309; limited to bishops, 305, 309; of Roman State paganism, 349 *ff*, 354; of provinces, 349, 351; of towns, 350; Christian imitation, 355 *f*
Proclamation about sins of the Flesh, 274, 276 n
προϊστάμενοι, προεστώς, προστάτις, προστάτης, 61 n, 72 n, 123, 150, 155 n, 192 n

Promise of the Church, 25; of authority, 28 *f*, 274, 303, 317
προνοεῖσθαι, 185, 180 n
Prophecy, N.T., 61, 90 *ff*; ecstatic and non-ecstatic, 94, 241; compared with O.T., 107; despisers of, debarred from the Eucharist, 233; in Asia, 236; Montanist, 94, 239 *f*
Prophetic Ministry, 69 *ff*; Threefold division in, 73; passed away, 109, 213 *ff*, 244, 272; in the *Didache*, 172 *f*; its duties undertaken by local ministry 215, 229; *Charisma* of, supposed to belong to office-bearers, 228; deterioration of, 108, 233; was "from above," 235; maintained by the Montanists, 271
Prophet, Christian, uses of the word, 92; was the messenger of God, 95; influence, 96 *f*; 61, 71*f*, 192, 241
Prophets, Christian, 46, 65, 73; presence universal, 90 *f*; names of, 91, 189 n, 236, 313 n, 328; were teachers, 93; wandering, 98; received the firstfruits, 99, 175 *f*; not office-bearers, but might be, 66, 96; controlled by the "gift of discernment," 92, 102, 175; controlled by office-bearers, 216 n, 235, 238, 298; false, 100, 174, 234; tests of, 102, 213, 272; could pardon sins, 97, 268, 272, 295; active in great cities, 101; caricatured by Celsus, 109 n
Prophetesses, 91, 236, 240
Punchayat, Hindu, 117

Quadratus, 236
Qualifications of office-bearers, 145 *f*, 178 *ff*, 247 *f*
Quarrels among the Brethren, 56, 175 *f*
Rackham, R. B., 203 n

INDEX

Ramsay, W. M., 12 n, 23 n, 92 n, 134 n, 204 n, 207, 229 n, 341 n
"Readers," read the scriptures and preached, 182 f, 253; 46
Reformation, The, 72, 205
Religio licita, 125, 129 f, 133
Religions losing their power, 92
Renan, E., 127 n, 128, 239 n
Representative principle in Christian organization, 23, 115, 118, 146, 150 f, 175, 178, 305, 316, 334
Responsibility imposed by the Apostles, 33, 89, 118, 148
Rethberg, 283 n
Revivals and Prophecy, 72
Réville, J., 127 n, 141 n, 195 n, 196 n
Riedel, W., 203 n, 245 n, 256 n
Ritschl, Alb., 94 n, 116 n, 169, 239, 283 n
Ritschl, Otto, 283 n, 291 n, 292 n, 318 n
Roads, Imperial, 22, 100, 336
Robinson, Dean A., 75 n, 85 n, 90 n
Roma, the goddess, 343 f, 344 n
Rome, the Church in, early pre-eminence, 318, 323; size in third century, 338; the sins of the flesh, 275; Apostolic succession, 280; Jews in, 129; 7, 23, 42, 59, 89, 93, 101, 123, 228, 335, 351
Roman, Africans, 285; lists of bishops, 281 n; law and Christian thought, 278; Lawyers, 278, 298, 301, 309; State Religion, 343 ff; Captivity of St. Paul, 10, 12, 23, 150; Elders and the Lapsed, 291 f
Rossi, Com. de, *See* De Rossi
Ruinart, 187 n

Sacerdotalism, 33 ff, 37 n, 196, 307 f, 357
Sacrificati, 288, 289 n, 312 n

Sacrifice, Christian, 34, 307 f
Saints, 114 n
Salmon, George, 238, 240 n
Sanday, W., 14 n, 139 n, 152 n, 176 n, 177 n, 204 n, 215 n, 260 n
Schmiedel, P. W., 3 n, 75 n, 81 n, 89 n, 117 n, 127 n, 128 n, 135 n, 150 n, 152 n
Schola, 126; 41
Schoolmasters in pagan lands, 106 n
Scotch paraphrases, 45 and n
Schultze, 135 n
Schürer, E., 4 n; 117 n; 124 n; 130 n, 132 n
σεβόμενοι, οἱ, 123 n
"Secret Doctrine," 222
Secularize the Church, movement to, 238, 273
Self-government in the Churches, 32 f, 55, 58, 99, 156
Selwyn, 90 n
"Sent Ones," 5, 75 n
Service, gifts and rule, 64, 113, 151; of Tables, 115
Services necessary for a community, 122; crystallize into office, 149
Seufert, 75 n, 76 n
'Seven,' The, 115 f, 139 n
"Signs of an Apostle," 83
Silas, 79, 80, 91, 143 n, 328
Sins not to be pardoned, 213, 267; 272 n, 273 f
Smith, G. A., 4 n
Smyrna, The Church at, 22, 100
Socrates (historian), 203 n
Sohm, Rudolf, 4 n, 70 n, 71 n, 75 n, 80 n, 87 n, 97 n, 208 n, 296 n; Theory of Synods, 327 ff
Soldiers and the Church, 232
Soter (Esculapius), 217
Sozomen, 203 n, 243
"Speaking the Word of God," 65, 72
"Specialized Gifts," 70
Spence, Canon, 172 n

INDEX

Spirit of Christ, 8. *See* Fruits of the Spirit
Spiritual sacrifices, 34, 307; men 69, 272 n
Stephen of Rome, 317 n, 318 n
Succession, historical, in manifestation of the fruits of the Spirit, 19 *f*; in the continuance of circumcision, 18; in rulers of the kinsmen of Jesus, 119 *f*; in generations of office-bearers, 225, 227; of bishops succeeding by vicarious ordination, 226, 270, 311 *ff*
Suetonius, 132 n, 133 n, 344 n, 345 n
συγγνώμη, 88 n
Summus sacerdos, 306 n
Supper, The Lord's. *See* Eucharist
Symeon Niger, a prophet, 91; son of Clopas, 120
Synagogue, use of word, 4 n; Christian Church, 114. *See* Jewish Synagogue
Synod, grouped Churches, 324 *f*, 328; ordination of bishop, 327 *f*; and congregational meetings, 328, 333, 334; met in Provincial capitals, 336, 353; Sohm's theory, 327 *f*; Synods in Africa, 326; Ancyra, 325, 328; Arles, 329 n; Antioch, 328, 332; Carthage, 286, 316; Corinth, 328; Bostra, 332; Greece, 326; Rome, 331; Nice, 329 n; the laity at Synods, 316 n, 331

"Table of the Body and Blood of the Lord," 257
"Tables," service of, 60 n, 115
Talmud, 117 n
Tatian, 105, 230 *f*
Teachers, 8, 73, 92, 103 *ff*; office-bearers were, 216; 113 n
Temples for the worship of the Imperial Cult, 3, 342 *f*; priests in State, 354
Temptation, The, 7

τέρμα τῆς δύσεως 141 n
Tertullian, 15, 36 n, 47 n, 65, 76 n, 80 n, 97, 106 n, 115 n, 129 n, 134 n, 172, 201, 208 n, 221, 225, 227 n, 228 n, 230, 238, 240, 245 n, 267 n, 268 n, 274, 297, 298 n, 300 n, 308 *f*
Testamentum Jesu Christi, 233
Testing the Prophetic Ministry, 70, 71 n, 99 *ff*, 175, 213
τετιμημένοι, 70 n, 105
Timothy, 74, 79, 143
Thanksgiving. *See* Eucharist
Theocracy, the Church is a, 4, 25, 33, 177
Thessalonica, The Church at, 11, 22, 60, 61, 63, 91, 93, 101, 123
θίασος, θιασάρχης, 129 n
Thomas Aquinas, 205
Threefold ministry, not Episcopacy, 170 *f*; how it arose, 207; earliest in Asia, 236; 195, 259
"Three Men," 28, 179 n, 327
Thurificati, 288
Θυσιαστήριον Θεοῦ, of the poor, 115 n; 208
Thyatira, 22, 100
"Tongue, speaking in a," 47 n
Town Council ruled the world, a, 324

ὑπηρέτης, 131
"Unified Church," 12 n
Uniformity of organization, not necessary, 24, 60
Union with Christ, 7, 189, 190 *ff*
Unity of the Church, 10 *ff*, 24; manifested in the gifts of the Spirit, 20 *f*; by fraternal intercourse, 55, 156; made visible by councils, 313 *f*; by papal supremacy, 317 *f*; dogmatic, 229
Universal Church visible, 16, 19 *f*, 58, 172, 182; the Prophetic Church belonged to, the 73; shown in ordination, 329, 331 n never expressed in a polity, 359 *f*

Ussher, Archbishop, 187 n

Vestments. *See* Dress
Victor of Rome, 15, 317 n
Villages, Mission to the, 31; Christians in, 106 n, 289 n
"Virgins," 249
Visible Church, 16 ff, 57, 172, 182, 191, 313 f, 329, 335 n
Visions, 77; and Prophecy, 92, 94, 143 n; in the Apocalypse, 94; in Hermas, 95; Cyprian's, 95 n, 284 n, 313 n
Vitringa, 131 n
Voigt, 239 n
Voss, 187 n
Voting at Congregational meetings, 33, 55

Wandering preachers, 73; prophets, 98; teachers, 105
Wansleben, 256 n
"Way, those of the," 114 n
Weinel, 90 n, 100 n
Weingarten, 127 n, 128

Weizsäcker, 5 n, 9 n, 23 n, 44 n, 47 n, 57 n, 75 n, 81 n, 83 n, 89 n, 114 n
Westcott, Bishop, 29 n
"Widows," to pray for the Brotherhood, 183, 249; Suppers for, 256; 181 f
"Wise Men," 57, 176, 182
Wissowa, 4 n, 101 n, 341 n
"Witness of the spirit," 72. *See* Discernment, "Gifts"
Women prophesied, 44, 91, 182, 236, 240; ministry of, 147, 181 f, 249
Worship, Christian, 44 ff, 250 ff; of the Emperors, in Palestine, 3; in Rome and in the Provinces, 342 ff; popularity of, 347

Zahn, 172 n, 187 n, 198 n
Zenobia, Queen, 333 n
Zephyrinus of Rome, 129 n, 135 n, 274 n
Ziebarth, 127 n, 129 n
Zoker and James, 120
Zoticus Otrenus, 328